'Phil Scraton's research over two decades has been conducted with tireless determination to uncover the truth; a unique example, accumulating evidence and grounding analysis in so masterly a fashion, reactivating better informed public debate and making a compelling case to release a mass of undisclosed police and official documents'

Emeritus Professor David Downes, London School of Economics

HILLSBOROUGH – THE TRUTH

'This book is dynamite. A brilliant achievement . . . I couldn't put it down. Passionate and committed, yet meticulously researched and fiercely intelligent'

– Jimmy McGovern

'A disturbing new book . . . reveals the whole truth in brutal detail. It cannot fail to make everyone who reads it feel shocked and furious'

– Sunday Mirror

'Disturbing and emotionally charged . . . puts all the bitterness and grieving about Hillsborough into context . . . puts into perspective the profound despair still tangible among the bereaved families'

– Daily Post

'Chronicles [the disaster] through eye-witness accounts and the legal aftermath . . . an invaluable summary of the available evidence . . . the bare facts are so extraordinary and appalling'

– When Saturday Comes

'A book that should leave anyone with a heart not just sad but angry too'

– Philosophy Football

'Well written . . . readable . . . excellent . . . at one and the same time an informative, compelling and accurate historical account of the disaster and its aftermath . . . An extremely valuable addition to the continuing quest for justice'

– Sports Law Bulletin

'Phil Scraton has done an invaluable service, for those who lost their lives and for the bereaved, in this book . . . meticulously researched . . . passionately written . . . will leave you angry and committed to fight for justice for those who lost their lives'

– Bookmarks

Phil Scraton PhD is Professor of Criminology in the Institute of Criminology and Criminal Justice, School of Law, Queen's University, Belfast, and Director of the Childhood, Transition and Social Justice Initiative. Formerly Director of the Centre for Studies in Crime and Social Justice at Edge Hill University, his books include: *Causes for Concern: Criminal Justice on Trial*; *The State of the Police*; *In the Arms of the Law: Coroners' Inquests and Deaths in Custody*; *Law, Order and the Authoritarian State*; *Prisons Under Protest*; *'Childhood' in 'Crisis'?*; *Beyond September 11: An Anthology of Dissent*; *Power, Conflict and Criminalisation*; *The Violence of Incarceration*; *The Incarceration of Women: Punishing Bodies, Breaking Spirits*. His recently published research reports include: *Childhood in Transition: Experiencing Marginalisation and Conflict in Northern Ireland*; *The Hurt Inside: The Imprisonment of Women and Girls in Northern Ireland*; *The Prison Within*; *Children's Rights in Northern Ireland*.

His work on Hillsborough includes two substantial reports: *Hillsborough and After: The Liverpool Disaster* (1990) and *No Last Rights: The Promotion of Myth and the Denial of Justice in the Aftermath of the Hillsborough Disaster* (1995). *Hillsborough: The Truth* was first published in 1999, the second revised edition in 2000 and the third revised edition in 2009. In 2010 he was appointed by the Home Secretary to the Hillsborough Independent Panel to lead the panel's research team, based at Queen's University, and he is primary author of *Hillsborough: The Report of the Hillsborough Independent Panel* (2012). He was seconded to the Hillsborough families' legal teams throughout the new inquests, 2014–16. He was research consultant for Dan Gordon's Emmy-nominated BBC/ESPN film *Hillsborough*.

In 2016 he was awarded the Freedom of the City of Liverpool. He lives in Belfast with his partner Deena Haydon and has two sons, Paul and Sean.

HILLSBOROUGH
THE TRUTH

PHIL SCRATON

MAINSTREAM
PUBLISHING

EDINBURGH AND LONDON

TRANSWORLD PUBLISHERS
61–63 Uxbridge Road, London W5 5SA
www.penguin.co.uk

Transworld is part of the Penguin Random House group of companies whose
addresses can be found at global.penguinrandomhouse.com

Penguin
Random House
UK

First published in Great Britain in 1999 by Mainstream Publishing Company
an imprint of Transworld Publishers
Mainstream edition revised and reprinted 2000, 2006, 2009, 2012, 2014
This Mainstream paperback revised edition published 2016

A CIP catalogue record tor this book is available from the British Library.

ISBN
9781910948019

Typeset in 10.5/13pt Adobe Garamond by Falcon Oast Graphic Art Ltd.
Printed and bound in Great Britain by Clays Ltd, Bungay, Suffolk.

Penguin Random House is committed to a sustainable future for our business,
our readers and our planet. This book is made from Forest Stewardship
Council® certified paper.

MIX
Paper from
responsible sources
FSC® C018179

1 3 5 7 9 10 8 6 4 2

Dedicated to the memory of

John Alfred Anderson

Colin Mark Ashcroft

James Gary Aspinall

Kester Roger Marcus
   Ball

Gerard Bernard Patrick
   Baron

Simon Bell

Barry Sidney Bennett

David John Benson

David William Birtle

Tony Bland

Paul David Brady

Andrew Mark Brookes

Carl Brown

David Steven Brown

Henry Thomas Burke

Peter Andrew Burkett

Paul William Carlile

Raymond Thomas
   Chapman

Gary Christopher
   Church

Joseph Clark

Paul Clark

Gary Collins

Stephen Paul Copoc

Tracey Elizabeth Cox

James Philip Delaney

Christopher Barry
   Devonside

Christopher Edwards

Vincent Michael
   Fitzsimmons

Thomas Steven Fox

Jon-Paul Gilhooley

Barry Glover

Ian Thomas Glover

Derrick George
   Godwin

Roy Harry Hamilton

Philip Hammond

Eric Hankin

Gary Harrison

Stephen Francis
   Harrison

Peter Andrew Harrison

David Hawley

James Robert
   Hennessey

Paul Anthony
   Hewitson

Carl Darren Hewitt

Nicholas Michael
   Hewitt

Sarah Louise Hicks

Victoria Jane Hicks

Gordon Rodney Horn

Arthur Horrocks

Thomas Howard

Thomas Anthony
   Howard

Eric George Hughes

Alan Johnston

Christine Ann Jones

Gary Philip Jones

Richard Jones

Nicholas Peter Joynes

Anthony Peter Kelly

Michael David Kelly

Carl David Lewis

David William Mather

Brian Christopher
   Matthews

Francis Joseph
   McAllister

John McBrien

Marian Hazel McCabe

Joseph Daniel
   McCarthy

Peter McDonnell

Alan McGlone

Keith McGrath

Paul Brian Murray

Lee Nicol

Stephen Francis
   O'Neill

Jonathon Owens

William Roy
   Pemberton

Carl William Rimmer

David George Rimmer

Graham John Roberts

Steven Joseph
   Robinson

Henry Charles Rogers

Andrew Sefton

Inger Shah

Paula Ann Smith

Adam Edward Spearritt

Philip John Steele

David Leonard
   Thomas

Patrick John
   Thompson

Peter Reuben Thompson

Stuart Paul William Thompson

Peter Francis Tootle

Christopher James Traynor

Martin Kevin Traynor

Kevin Tyrell

Colin Wafer

Ian David Whelan

Martin Kenneth Wild

Kevin Daniel Williams

Graham John Wright

and to

The bereaved, the survivors, the rescuers
The Hillsborough disaster
15 April 1989

HILLSBOROUGH

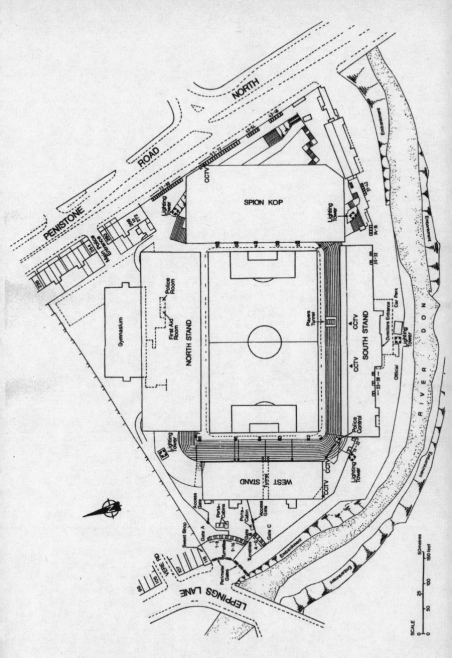

Map of Hillsborough Stadium and Approaches, April 1989,
from Lord Justice Taylor's Interim Report

CONTENTS

ACKNOWLEDGEMENTS

So many people have contributed to this work and it is impossible to name everyone individually. I owe immense gratitude to those who worked together on the initial Hillsborough Project, Sheila Coleman, Ann Jemphrey and, in the early days, Paula Skidmore. The Project provided a level of analysis previously not attempted, let alone realised, in post-disaster research. The team's first report, *Hillsborough and After* (1990), and its second, *No Last Rights* (1995), were major contributions to the literature, their findings and recommendations resonating well beyond Hillsborough, to propose a new agenda in dealing with the context and aftermath of disasters.

During the 1990s I received exceptional support from my co-workers at the Centre for Studies in Crime and Social Justice, Edge Hill University, particularly Eileen Berrington, Howard Davis, Hazel Hartley, Ann Jemphrey, Margaret Malloch and Lizzy Stanley, who listened, discussed and commented on the work. Margaret McAdam's personal empathy and sensitivity in carrying out some of the interviews with families was remarkable. My close friend and long-time academic collaborator Kathryn Chadwick never ceased to provide strength and support when most needed and has contributed as a research consultant to the most recent phase of the research. Throughout the early stages, and leading to publication of the first edition of this book, the support of the uniquely talented Jimmy McGovern was important to me but also to the families. His award-winning drama-documentary, *Hillsborough*, written and produced with the indefatigable Katy Jones, presented the pain of injustice to an international audience. Thanks to Mainstream, great publishers and fine people, particularly Bill Campbell, for committing to a project without knowing whether or not the 'academic' could 'write accessibly'. To all at Penguin Random House, particularly Brenda Kimber, who have brought this edition so speedily to production. Special thanks to Ailsa Bathgate, who has been a patient and sharp-eyed editor throughout.

In January 2012 I was appointed by the Home Secretary to the Hillsborough Independent Panel to head its research into the disclosed documents and to take the lead in writing its report. It is important to acknowledge the work of Merseyside MPs and politicians in the region whose interventions led to the panel: Andy Burnham, Maria Eagle, Steve Rotheram and Derek Twigg. The collective endeavour of the panel, chaired by the Right Reverend James Jones, then Bishop of Liverpool, integrated the broad range of skills necessary to meet the challenge of such complex work. Personal thanks to James and to others on the panel: Raju Bhatt, Christine Gifford, Bill Kirkup, Paul Leighton, Peter Sissons, Sarah Tyacke; to the panel's secretariat and technical support staff, particularly Matt Lewsey's research contribution; and to the research team with me at Queen's University: Janet Clark, Jo Doody, Shaun McDaid and Gemma Ní Chaoimh. Working to a tight schedule, it was daunting to meet the demands associated with accessing so many documents from such a diversity of sources. Katy Jones, who died suddenly in 2015, was a key member of the panel. An outstanding researcher with a sharp intellect, she was also a dear friend.

Throughout the years I have benefited greatly from the insights of, and reflective discussions with, numerous co-workers and friends: Hilary Arnott, Lilly Artz, Sara Boyce, Flair Campbell, Bree Carlton, Pat Craddock, Sheri Chamberlain, Louise Christian,

David Conn, Jonathan Corke, Anna Eggert, Niall Enright, Barry Goldson, Dan Gordon, Faith Gordon, Penny Green, Ian Herbert, Paddy Hillyard, Barbara Hudson, Sue and Chris Hughes, Janet Johnstone, Karen Lee, Mark Lusby, Feargal Mac Ionnrachtaigh, Deirdre Mahon, Chelsea Marshall, Peter Marshall, Anne-Marie McAlinden, Siobhán McAlister, Jude McCulloch, Laurence McKeown, Linda Moore, Alan Morris, John Muncie, Mick North, Mahesh Patel, Tony Platt, Denise and Paul Prescott, Edel Quinn, Sue Roberts, Bill Rolston, Sheila Scraton, Neil Shanahan, Patrick Shanahan, Ann Singleton, Tony Souza, Pete Strange, Marilyn and Tony Taylor, Adrian Tempany, Mike Tomlinson, Margaret Ward, Frances Webber, Juliet Wells, Leah Wing, Ian and Margaret Wright, Tony Bunyan and Trevor Hemmings at Statewatch, Debbie Coles and Helen Shaw at Inquest, Harmit Athwal, Jenny Bourne, Liz Fekete, Hazel Waters and our great mentor, A. Sivanandan, at the Institute of Race Relations. And to Madeline Heneghan, Mike Morris and Stuart Borthwick at Merseyside Writing on the Wall. I am also grateful to colleagues at Queen's University, particularly in the School of Law, who have supported the research.

Many thanks to Dan Gordon, Helen Spedding, Andy Worboys and all at VeryMuchSo Productions for the remarkable Emmy-nominated BBC/ESPN documentary *Hillsborough*. And much respect to all members of the legal teams who represented bereaved families throughout the 2014–16 inquests for their dedication in securing a just verdict.

My sons, Paul and Sean, lived with Hillsborough through much of their childhoods. Their support, understanding and insights have been and remain a significant part of my work. Thanks also to Paul's partner, Katrin, and our granddaughter, Lotte. To Sean's partner, Ailis, and our grandson, Cillian. The book could not have been written, completed and updated without the critical reviewing, attention to detail, love and compassion of my partner, Deena Haydon. Her knowledge and understanding of Hillsborough has been invaluable, as has her selfless support to many of the bereaved.

I thank, with utmost respect, the bereaved families and survivors with whom I have formed strong bonds. As a consequence of Hillsborough, my family and I have developed friendships that we will always treasure. The collective contribution of the bereaved and survivors of Hillsborough has been central to the completion of the book. Your resilience and dignity in sharing personal stories, reliving the traumatic experiences of the disaster and its immediate aftermath, provided the foundation on which the unswerving campaign for justice has been built. Following the 20th anniversary of the disaster it was your determination that persuaded the Government to appoint the Hillsborough Independent Panel and facilitate the disclosure of all documents held by all relevant organisations involved. It is to you – the bereaved and survivors – and your continuing struggle for justice in the face of adversity and desolation, and to the memories of those who died, that this book is dedicated.

Phil Scraton
Belfast and Liverpool
May 2016

PREFACE

15 April 1989. When families and friends parted on the beautiful early spring morning, the last thing on their minds, heading to Hillsborough, Sheffield, for the FA Cup semi-final between Liverpool and Nottingham Forest, was tragedy. Over 50,000 fans witnessed a crush so severe that it claimed the lives of 96 men, women and children. For thousands of Liverpool fans who entered two pens down a steep tunnel onto a decrepit and inherently unsafe terrace, the trauma of injury and survival would leave an indelible mark on their lives. All who died or survived were victims of the organisational complacency and compromised safety deeply institutionalised in the management, regulation and policing of large crowds at many sports and leisure events. The warnings of previous disasters and other close calls – even at Hillsborough – had passed unheeded as those entrusted with the safe passage of paying customers failed in their duty of care.

As it unfolded, the disaster was filmed, photographed and reported by an international media. Soccer is the country's national sport and this was one of the three most significant club fixtures of the year. On BBC television the afternoon sports coverage was interrupted to broadcast live scenes of attempts to rescue dying fans from the pens as the match was abandoned and players left the field. Watching from the safety of home, the realisation was profound. There had been many occasions at football matches when I had experienced the compression of overcrowded terraces. A Liverpool fan who had followed the team since childhood, I knew I could have been there. With that knowledge my first instinct was to view the crowd density in the two central pens behind the goal, and the sparse numbers in the pens to each side, as immediate evidence of a catastrophic failure in managing and directing a crowd entering an unfamiliar stadium.

* * *

On 15 April each year the families and friends of the 96 men, women and children killed at Hillsborough gather on the Kop at Anfield, home of Liverpool Football Club. The annual remembrance service brings together the bereaved families, survivors and others who will never forget that dreadful afternoon in Sheffield. At 3.06 p.m. the thousands who attend fall silent. This is the moment that the match, just six minutes of which had been played, was halted by the referee. It remains the symbolic moment of death. A silence to remember loved ones, to share the pain.

Given that Hillsborough was a disaster of such magnitude it is a salutary reminder of organisations' built-in aversion to liability, prioritising corporate interests over the public interest, that it took until 1998 for the bereaved to access the details and evidence concerning the circumstances in which their loved ones died. Nearly a decade of legal wrangling and campaigning finally brought the release to families of body files on each of the deceased. These files contained the evidence gathered in each case, the medical and witness statements. It was information that, by any definition of 'natural justice', should have been theirs in the first place.

To make matters worse, the entire documentation, including body files, produced by the various investigations into the disaster, was held at the headquarters of the South Yorkshire Police – the police force responsible for managing the crowd on the day. Legally, the documents and material gathered in the course of the investigations, including those into the criminal and civil liability of the police, revert to the force under investigation as the

22

'property' of its Chief Constable. Yet this was the force whose senior officers' testimonies had been condemned by a judicial inquiry, the force whose lack of control and failure to manage the crowd effectively at Hillsborough was considered by that inquiry to be the 'main reason' for the disaster.

Also in 1998, hundreds of South Yorkshire Police officers' statements, already made available to the previous investigation and inquiries, were relocated by Jack Straw, the Home Secretary, to the House of Commons Library. These, however, were no ordinary statements. Prior to their submission to the various inquiries, including the judicial inquiry, many had been transformed through a process of review and alteration, approved and part-managed by the force's solicitors. I had uncovered this process a year earlier when gathering material in preparation for submission to a 'judicial scrutiny', a discretionary procedure without the statutory powers of a public inquiry, set up by the Home Secretary to consider 'new evidence' relating to the disaster.

My revelations exposed the extraordinary, anomalous and unprecedented procedures adopted in the aftermath of the disaster. At the time of making my submissions to the judicial scrutiny I had researched and written about Hillsborough for eight years. Although my involvement began in the days after the disaster, my relationship with Liverpool Football Club went back to my early childhood. In my teens I followed the team home and away, to European finals, to league and cup matches. By the mid 1980s I had grown weary of the often appalling treatment meted out to committed fans whose hard-earned money supported their clubs. Those entrusted with the stewardship of the game, and those managing and policing the crowds, were indifferent to the fans' experiences. Undoubtedly soccer-related violence, dubbed 'hooliganism' by journalists, academic commentators, the police and politicians, was an issue. Yet, the authoritarian, universally applied 'solution' to a complex problem was the 'corralling' and 'penning' of fans. I was not only disillusioned with being aggressively herded and policed, I loathed the racism, sexism and homophobia that prevailed on the terraces and the reluctance by club owners and the game's administrators to intervene.

I remained passionate about the game and identified with a club I had supported when Liverpool were in the Second Division and a mild-mannered Scot, Billy Liddell, was my hero. A week after Hillsborough I stood with my family in the 'mile of scarves' across Stanley Park, linking the Liverpool and Everton grounds. It was at that profoundly moving and personal moment I decided, as someone who had researched deaths in controversial circum-stances and coroners' inquests, that the disaster itself and the impending investigations should be independently scrutinised. I was angered, as were so many others, by the shameful lies about Liverpool supporters that had emerged in the press throughout the week following the tragedy.

While thousands struggled to come to terms with the enormity of their loss and trauma, Kelvin MacKenzie, editor of *The Sun*, published outrageous front-page allegations against those who survived the disaster under the banner headline 'THE TRUTH'. Demonstrating that the depths of tabloid journalism could always be plumbed deeper, this deceit caused enormous suffering, exchanging compassion for vilification. Ironically, just four days after the disaster, MacKenzie had shown that 'truth' was not only open to interpretation, it could be the victim of fabrication. While MacKenzie took the allegations at face value, publishing them without reservation, *The Sun* was not alone in carrying the story. Tabloids and broadsheets joined together in a near universal chorus of condemnation of Liverpool fans. Soon, public denigration extended beyond the fans to include the city and its people. It was always my position, however, that the negative media coverage did not originate in the minds of journalists and editors. Willing conduits, maybe, but its roots lay elsewhere.

I expected the already convened judicial inquiry under Lord Justice Taylor, and the West Midlands Police investigation, to become battlegrounds for vested interests. I expected the criminal investigations would not result in corporate or individual prosecutions. I expected, as a consequence, the coroner's inquest, despite being a court unable to address issues of liability, would be fiercely adversarial and would frustrate bereaved families determined to hold individuals and organisations to account. It was anticipation based on a decade's research into deaths in contested circumstances, particularly involving the police. Through researching these cases I had witnessed the systemic denial of rights to bereaved families.

In September 1989 the Hillsborough Project gained funding from Liverpool City Council to research, publish and make recommendations concerning all aspects of the disaster's aftermath. In 1990 the research team – Sheila Coleman, Ann Jemphrey, Paula Skidmore and myself – published an initial report, *Hillsborough and After: The Liverpool Experience*. This work provided a critique of the judicial inquiry and the media coverage, exposing for the first time the unacceptable treatment of the bereaved and survivors in the immediate aftermath. The Hillsborough Project continued its research throughout the early 1990s, culminating in publication of the book *No Last Rights: The Denial of Justice and the Promotion of Myth in the Aftermath of the Hillsborough Disaster*, co-authored by myself, Ann Jemphrey and Sheila Coleman.

No Last Rights was an exhaustive, in-depth investigation into the legal processes, particularly the inquests and their judicial review, together with a thorough critique of the role and excesses of local, national and international media. Making over 80 recommendations, the report concluded that the official responses to Hillsborough – the failure to prosecute or to discipline police officers, the conduct and outcome of the inquests, and attempts to pervert the course of justice – together amounted to a major 'miscarriage of justice'. No Last Rights laid bare the inadequacies of the legal processes, particularly the inquests, in handling controversial deaths.

* * *

'Truth' is a small word, but a daunting concept. While supposedly investigating the 'truth', *The Sun* and other newspapers contributed to its degradation. Its use in the title of this book is a form of reclamation. I have studied and compared thousands of witness statements and relevant documents to ensure consistency and accuracy. Over the years, I attended inquiries, court cases and read transcripts in their entirety. I interviewed many of the bereaved, survivors and others directly involved in the disaster. First published in 1999, this book was written to pull together the full range of issues to have emerged from the legal processes, political debates, media coverage and – most significantly – the families' and survivors' experiences of the disaster and its aftermath. For the first time it revealed the process through which police statements had been subject to review and alteration, its prevalence and its impact.

In the original preface I wrote that much of the evidence held by the authorities, if not destroyed, had been buried in archives – probably for all time. It was clear from the limited available documentation that important statements and files were missing or beyond reach. Documents, including many witness statements, remained restricted, covered by legal privilege. While instructive in their review and alteration, the many hundreds of police statements I had accessed were just one element of a much deeper process to deflect blame and escape accountability. At the time I was party to representations attempting to negotiate access to missing material and was well aware that, in the days and months after the disaster, the many crucial conversations and informal meetings held behind closed doors, on corridors of influence, would not have been recorded. This was not naïve conspiracy theory. My research already had revealed just how systematic and institutionalised were the questionable procedures adopted by the senior management of the South Yorkshire Police in preparing for the inquiries and investigations.

'Truth' also has another dimension. My research was intended not only to establish truth in terms of context and culpability, I was also committed to discovering the truth of people's experiences: their 'truth'. Much of the early part of this book provides contrasting experiences of those directly involved in the disaster and its aftermath. I edited some of the most desperate accounts for obvious reasons but what is presented here leaves little to the imagination. Throughout, I retained the integrity of the statements and interviews by not quoting out of context or misrepresenting particular comments. First published in 1999, these chapters remain in their original form. Nothing has happened subsequently to challenge their veracity.

In the immediate aftermath of the 2000 private prosecution of David Duckenfield and Bernard Murray, the senior South Yorkshire Police officers responsible for managing the crowd at Hillsborough, I added a further chapter to the first edition. At this stage it appeared that, other than for individual cases – most notably Anne Williams' relentless campaign, taken to the European Court, to uncover the facts relating to the disputed circumstances in which her son, Kevin, died – the private prosecution had closed legal avenues. Nine years later, prior to the 20th anniversary it was suggested that I should update the text in acknowledgement of the sustained campaign for truth and justice. I was hesitant. What more could I add?

At that time it was almost two decades since Hillsborough, an avoidable disaster that cost the lives of 96 men, women and children and blighted the lives of thousands – the bereaved, the survivors, the witnesses, their families and their friends. The book already had established that the tragedy was rooted in institutionalised complacency, authoritarianism and negligence in an industry that had exploited the passion and loyalty of fans with stadiums not fit for purpose, potentially lethal pens on broken terraces, poorly trained stewards and policing that aggressively prioritised crowd control above crowd safety. As the Heysel and Bradford disasters had demonstrated four years earlier, in very different circumstances, grounds from bygone eras were not only unsuitable, they were death-traps. Yet the authorities – owners, hirers, licence-givers and the police – appeared oblivious to the warnings. Disaster followed. What more could be said?

Hillsborough exposed the inadequacies of crowd safety in dangerous environments but it also revealed grave flaws in on-site medical facilities and emergency planning and response, as well as a lack of preparedness in dealing with the immediate aftermath of incidents involving mass fatalities. The treatment of survivors and the bereaved in the immediate aftermath, the insensitive handling of those searching for lost loved ones and the inhumane process of identifying the dead exacerbated their suffering. While Taylor's judicial inquiry and the inquests had considered the circumstances in which people died on the terraces, there had been no investigation into the immediate aftermath. *Hillsborough: The Truth* had examined all aspects of the disaster and its consequences up to and including the private prosecution in 2000.

Yet there was more to be added, more to be said. In the 2009 edition I included a further, reflective, chapter and a new preface. In the latter I wrote that it was important to consider the issues, controversies and campaigns that had kept the disaster at the forefront of the public's collective mind. The growth of communications technology, particularly the Internet and the consolidation of websites, had given many people the opportunity to share their personal accounts of survival and loss. Exchanges of information on dedicated Hillsborough forums provided a vast resource of considered opinion, personal experience and, occasionally, invective – the latter directed towards insensitive and opportunistic statements from those ignorant of the facts. Mobile phones had revolutionised instant communication and information exchange.

Had it been available at the time, how such technology would have impacted on Hillsborough and the immediate aftermath can only be surmised but, as more recent events have shown, it would have provided an extensive evidential record.

I stated that the campaign for justice had been unrelenting. Following its success in bringing a private prosecution of Duckenfield and Murray, the Hillsborough Family Support Group had continued its support to bereaved families, organising the annual memorial service at Anfield and pursuing local and national government at every opportunity. The Hillsborough Justice Campaign (HJC) had mobilised a wide network of support based on its strong representation of survivors. Each had developed a website and provided a significant information resource. Anne Williams' campaign led to 'Hope for Hillsborough'. Fan-based websites with dedicated Hillsborough forums developed, most notably including redandwhitekop. A significant online resource, Hillsborough for Dummies (HFD), was published in 2008 as a direct response to misinformation about Hillsborough broadcast by the BBC. HFD provided an impersonal account focusing on the circumstances of the disaster and detailing all key events that followed. It exposed how myths regarding the causes were conceived and disseminated, and how they affected subsequent legal proceedings.

The 2009 edition's final chapter raised issues not covered previously. It revealed the 'endless pressure' suffered by the bereaved and survivors, and generated by the myths of hooliganism that evolved and consolidated following the initial media coverage, particularly in *The Sun*. Those myths endured and, as the new chapter showed, were repeated in and reinforced by a wide range of media and academic accounts. It was a myth that connected to a sustained attack on Liverpool as a city and Merseyside as a region whose people were demonised as attracting, even celebrating, misfortune. The chapter also reflected on the status of the 'apology' initially given by the then editor of *The Sun*, Kelvin

MacKenzie, only to be retracted. It also considered the significance of the case taken to the European Court of Human Rights by Anne Williams. Finally, I interviewed again bereaved families whose experiences were, and remain, central to the analysis. With great dignity they portrayed how the bereaved and survivors, their families and friends, were failed, deeply hurt and further victimised by the inadequacies of the investigations and the courts.

I concluded the 2009 Preface as follows:

Twenty years on, *Hillsborough: The Truth* remains dedicated to the bereaved, survivors and rescuers, and also to those who have suffered physical illness, mental ill-health and premature death. We will never know the full extent of the damaging legacy of 15 April 1989 and the institutionalised injustices that followed. What is certain is that it does not diminish over time. Nor should it.

My pessimism was short-lived.

* * *

This is the fourth and final edition of *Hillsborough: The Truth*. Following the September 2012 publication of the Hillsborough Independent Panel report, of which I was the primary author, I believed its content should be the final word. Its exhaustive research, extensive findings and detailed conclusions derived entirely from the disclosed documents were so powerful and revelatory that it seemed nothing further could be added. Yet it was the very impact of the report and all that followed that led to this edition. From the moment of Prime Minister David Cameron's immediate response in Parliament, when he acknowledged the 'double injustice' suffered by bereaved families and survivors, the sequence of events that followed could not have been anticipated: a full investigation into all organisations and individuals against whom there could be criminal prosecutions;

the largest ever investigation by the Independent Police Complaints Commission into approximately 2,000 officers from 30-plus police forces; the quashing of all 96 inquest verdicts and the ordering of new inquests; reviews of all health organisations' arrangements for responding to and handling disasters and medical pathology; and an assessment of the potential of 'independent panels' in truth recovery and dispute resolution.

Adding three new chapters, this edition addresses the background to the panel's appointment, including my own as the panel member with lead responsibility for the research, analysis and report writing. The first of these new chapters discusses the panel's terms of reference, the principles of 'families first' and confidentiality, the methods used to analyse disclosed documents and the issues that arose during the panel's work. The penultimate chapter reviews the launch of the panel's report in September 2012, its reception and its impact. The chapter extracts the key issues from the report's 12 detailed chapters and its 153-point summary, demonstrating what its findings add to public understanding. Picking up on the previous chapter, it shows how the media received the report and how those entrusted with progressing the new investigations and inquests have grounded their work.

On 11 February 2014, the coroner for the new inquests, Lord Justice Goldring, issued a statement affirming that the jury's verdict would be reached 'solely on the evidence they hear in court'. While the media could report 'accurately and in a balanced way' the evidence heard in court, other commentaries or publications would 'run the risk of prejudicing the outcome of proceedings' and therefore could not be published or broadcast. Any breach of this direction would be in contempt of court. Throughout the inquests I worked closely with the families' lawyers. The final chapter contextualises the new inquests, focusing on the evidence presented to the court between March 2014 and January 2016, the coroner's marathon summing-up and the jury's verdict – beyond reasonable doubt – that the 96 had been unlawfully killed. It presents the jury's complex narrative verdict that unequivocally exonerated Liverpool fans, while delivering severe institutional criticisms of the South Yorkshire Police, Sheffield Wednesday Football Club, the club's safety engineers, the then South Yorkshire Ambulance Service and Sheffield City Council.

From the initial research, begun in autumn 1989, to the delivery of the panel's report in autumn 2012 and the inquest verdicts in spring 2016, it has been my commitment to research and tell the story of Hillsborough with thoroughness, rigour and authority. It is a story contextualising the inevitability of the disaster within institutional complacency. It is a story of how those in authority sought to cover their tracks to avoid blame and responsibility. It is a story of how the 'law' fails to provide appropriate means of discovery and redress for those who suffer through organisational neglect and personal negligence. It is a story of how ordinary people can be subjected to the insensitivity and hostility of agencies that place their professional priorities ahead of the personal needs and collective rights of the bereaved and survivors. It is also a story of how, in the face of extreme adversity and prolonged suffering, the bereaved and survivors remained resilient, their resistance and their determination to honour those who died challenging powerful institutions, changing history and serving a wider public interest.

Chapter One

COURTING DISASTER

At the back of every police officer's mind is the nagging worry that the next incident, however apparently insignificant, could mean injury, even death. The risk of police work is the ever-present fear of being on the receiving end of a violent attack. Statistics show that the killing of British police officers in the line of duty is rare, that the actual risk is minimal. Death is so rare, in fact, that the names of those who die remain forever inscribed in the consciousness of fellow officers. Yet these are random deaths, their very unpredictability feeding the fear: any time, any place, any officer.

In early October 1988, a 24-year-old South Yorkshire Police probationer came face to face with the reality. Alone, cut off from his fellow officers, he was subjected to a ferocious attack in the night-darkened grounds of a convent in the Ranmoor district of Sheffield. Two armed men in military fatigues, faces hidden by balaclavas, dragged him to waste ground. They forced him face down in the mud, hands cuffed behind his back, a gun to his head. His trousers were pulled down. He feared the worst. Shaking uncontrollably, expecting to die, he heard the click, saw the flash; not a gun, but a camera.

Prostrate and terrified on the ground, the young officer turned his head to see the armed men removing their balaclavas. They were laughing. Laughing policemen. He was in shock, throwing up as he tried to dress himself and regain some semblance of composure. The humiliating and degrading assault, not uncommon in military regiments, was some kind of initiation, later described as a 'prank'. It involved a group of officers and all were based at Sheffield's Hammerton Road police station.

As the victim of the attack underwent stress counselling, five of his colleagues, including an inspector, were suspended from duty. A damage-limitation statement from the South Yorkshire Police confirmed that no members of the public had been involved. Hillsborough MP, Martin Flannery, was unimpressed, arguing that officers were members of the public and the assault had taken place in the public domain. Further reports suggested that initiations at Hammerton Road were institutionalised and a woman officer claimed that she had been forced out by a group of officers who 'made life hell for new recruits'.

Flannery was unhesitating in demanding that the officers face prosecution. Following an investigating officer's report, however, the Crown Prosecution Service decided that criminal proceedings were 'inappropriate'. Consultation between the South Yorkshire force and the Police Complaints Authority led to internal disciplinary actions against the officers. Four officers, including the inspector and two sergeants, were forced to resign. Two other sergeants were demoted and two constables reprimanded and fined.

Although the officers, in effect, had been dismissed, resigning meant their opportunities for alternative employment and their police pensions were protected. Martin Flannery, together with Conservative MP Irving Patnick, demanded publication of the police investigation's findings. It was refused. Soon after the resignations, in early March 1989, the head of Hammerton Road, Chief Superintendent Brian Mole, was moved to Barnsley. The announcement stated that the move was 'part of changes in the rank structure'. No reference was made to the Ranmoor incident, the disciplining of officers or the broader concern about behaviour at Hammerton Road.

Not only was the timing of Chief Superintendent Mole's transfer coincidental, it was unfortunate. Writing in the *Sheffield Star*, reporter Bob Westerdale noted that the experienced officer had 'been repeatedly praised for his crowd control at big matches at Sheffield Wednesday's ground'. Indeed, it was under his jurisdiction that the Hillsborough stadium had been reinstated as an FA Cup semi-final venue following its suspension over problems with crowd management and ground safety in 1981. The 1987 semi-final returned Hillsborough to its former status and Chief Superintendent Mole had established the Operational Order for policing the event. He carried this through, with some modification, to the 1988 Liverpool v Nottingham Forest semi-final. That was to be his last semi-final as match commander.

Without disclosure of the documentation relating to either the disciplinary proceedings or Mole's transfer, a direct and incontestable connection cannot be made between them. What is certain is that relieving him from his Hammerton Road duties just 21 days before Hillsborough's 1989 semi-final denied the event the services of the most experienced match commander in the force. It also meant that his replacement, Chief Superintendent Duckenfield, took command of one of Britain's foremost sports events with minimal appropriate professional experience. Virtually all the weight of responsibility would fall on the shoulders of the senior officers he had inherited from Mole. With the exception of names and allocation of duties, the Operational Order for the day remained unchanged. The force had given the job, at the eleventh hour, to a rookie at managing football crowds. And it had happened in the most controversial of circumstances. If Mole had offered, his services were refused, because on 15 April 1989 he was on duty elsewhere.

* * *

At about 2.15 p.m. on an early spring afternoon at one of England's premier football grounds the crowd massed excitedly at the turnstiles. It was a big crowd for a major cup match between a team from the Midlands and one from the North-West. The pressure built quickly around the turnstiles and fans were crushed against walls. On the terraces, close to the turnstiles, the terraces were packed. So packed that some young boys were passed over the heads of the crowd to the front.

As the turnstiles continued to supply a regular flow on to the back of the terraces, those near the front began to feel the pressure. Some fans attempted to escape the tight crush but by 2.35 p.m. it was impossible to move in any direction. Twenty-five minutes before the game was due to start the enclosure was full. There was confusion between police and ground staff over closing the turnstiles.

Outside the ground five minutes later the crowd was as tightly packed as it was on the terraces. Communication between the two areas was virtually impossible. Within minutes the position inside became serious as people in obvious distress tried to escape the awful crush. Some fell to the ground to be trodden underfoot by fellow fans unable to avoid stepping on their bodies.

With ten minutes to go to kick-off an exit gate behind the terraces was opened. Instantly the crush at the turnstiles was relieved. Through the gate, and by other means, over 2,000 people poured into the stadium, adding to the already unbearable pressure on the terraces. Some fans who squeezed in at the back found themselves squeezed out at the front of the terrace without any control over their own movements.

At 2.55 p.m. the teams ran out to a massive reception. The crowd swayed and those on the terraces stretched to catch a glimpse of their heroes. Strategically placed crush barriers prevented the swaying crowd from compressing all the way down the terrace. The metal barriers broke up the crowd. But there was one funnel where no barriers had been installed until near the bottom steps. The compression here was immense, bearing the full weight of fans up to the back of the terrace. Under the strain two barriers collapsed and the crowd went down over buckled steel.

Bodies were piled three or four deep, with those compressed against the pile unable to push back up the steps. Realisation dawned among the police, St John's Ambulance officers and other fans that a serious disaster was taking place. Twelve minutes later the referee stopped the game and took the players from the pitch. English football's worst crowd disaster had happened. But this was not Hillsborough 1989, it was Burnden Park on 9 March 1946.

Forty-three years and one month before Hillsborough, 33 people died and over 500 were injured at an FA Cup tie between Bolton Wanderers and Stoke City. A much bigger crowd than expected had turned up: 50,000 were anticipated but an estimated 85,000 arrived. The exit gate opened because a man trying to leave the ground with his young son picked the lock.

The Home Office inquiry, chaired by Moelwyn Hughes, criticised the police and ground officials for not realising the significance of the build-up outside the ground given the packing on the terraces inside. While witnesses to the official inquiry talked about the enclosure's 'capacity', it had never been properly assessed: 'What they mean by capacity is the greatest number that has been safely accommodated there on a previous occasion,' stated the report.

It was estimated that the terraces were full at 2.35 p.m. but the turnstiles went on admitting fans for a further ten minutes thus projecting another 2,000 fans into already full enclosures. With these additional 2,000 fans gaining entry just before kick-off the terraces were well over capacity. The authorities were roundly criticised for their lack of strategy, slow reactions and lack of organisation.

The report 'regretted that there was no simple exit for those who, for any reason, wanted to leave the ground, and that it was so lamentably easy to open the exit gate'. While the 'barrierless path' from top to bottom was not identified as a principal cause, the weight on the collapsed barriers had been immense. One of the barriers was 'heavily rusted'.

Moelwyn Hughes made many recommendations to prevent such a disaster happening again. His suggestions focused on expert examination of terraces; the siting, strength and type of barriers; the situation and condition of the entrances; adequate facilities for exit during play; and the means for uninterrupted movement within each enclosure in the ground. He also recommended the scientific calculation of the maximum number of people admitted to each enclosure. But, the report argued, 'fixing a maximum is of no value unless there is a method of knowing when the figure is reached or . . . when more want to get in than can be got in . . .' It recommended 'mechanical means' to establish precisely the figures for each enclosure which could be then transmitted to a central point. As each enclosure filled to capacity the turnstiles feeding into it could be closed. Central co-ordination would be achieved, by a 'responsible ground official' and a 'responsible police officer' working together and using telephones to close areas and have them adequately policed and managed.

The report noted that the FA official who gave evidence 'feared that the disaster at Bolton might easily be repeated at 20 or 30 other grounds'. 'How simple,' it concluded, 'and how easy it is for a dangerous situation to arise in a crowded enclosure. It happens again and again without fatal or even injurious consequences.' One or two additional influences were all that was needed to translate 'danger' into 'death and injuries'.

In 1958, Bolton Wanderers enjoyed their FA Cup final success over the tragedy-stricken Manchester United after the Munich disaster. Controversy raged over whether Nat Lofthouse fouled Harry Gregg, United's courageous goalkeeper, as he dispatched player and ball into the back of the net. It is indicative of football's priorities that the debate over that single incident has remained vivid for generations, while the death of 33 people at Burnden Park, just a decade earlier, passed silently into history.

Outside Bolton, one of the most significant lessons in football's history was laid to rest alongside those who died.

* * *

The 'Beautiful Game' . . . the 'Glory Game' . . . the 'People's Game'; professional football has always captured the imagination. Well before players could negotiate massive shares of their exorbitant transfer fees or be paid half- decent wages, their names were widely known, their feats were enduring. Few fans could hope to play even semi-professionally but all could watch and dream. Post-war football remained predominantly a male spectator sport but its impact was felt throughout entire communities. Factory owners and business managers continually told of productivity waxing and waning along with the fortunes of the local team.

While players struggled for recognition as entertainers in a mass observation sport, the cost of the game was carried on the terraces. The cloth-cap image of the 'people's game' dominated thinking, provision and investment. As the rich and locally famous took their seats in the directors' boxes, and those who could afford advance payment bought season tickets for the seated stands, the mass of punters stood in all weathers, often without cover, on concreted mounds of earth.

The conditions, considering regular attendance was not cheap, were dreadful. For all the 'golden age' romanticism of hot Bovril, tepid tea and meat pies, watching football was hardly spectator friendly. Yet, incredibly, the thrill of the game, the bright green turf of floodlit night matches and the roar of the crowd over-shadowed the realities. Realities of decrepit grounds, filthy toilets and blocked views; of being ripped off.

The warning signs were there for all to see. Especially from the Paddock beneath Liverpool's Main Stand, right in front of the directors' box from where men in suits and camel coats, women in furs, looked out over 50,000 in the packed ground. To the right, thousands were banked high in Anfield's famous Kop.

How everyone admired the Koppites as they sang, swayed and surged; waves of bodies breaking down the steps like a rolling sea on a beach. Back up the steps, a brief calm, and the next wave. Every now and then a limp body passed over the heads to St John's Ambulance officers on the perimeter track. How they whistled if it was a woman.

Passing out on the Kop was all part of the game. Pale-faced bodies would be stretchered along the touch-line to the players' tunnel and off to recovery. In 1960s Liverpool it was difficult not to be caught up in the passion of the game. Under Bill Shankly the team was promoted from the Second Division, won the FA Cup for the first time in its history and became First Division champions. Soon Europe came to Anfield and with it the first of many memorable nights. Tickets for derby games against Everton, the self-proclaimed 'School of Science', were like gold-dust.

Shankly, a conservative moralist with a maverick socialism rooted in Scotland's pit towns and villages, was sharp-tongued and quick-witted. Football, he said, was not a matter of life and death, it was more important than that. Of course these words were never meant to be taken literally although they now haunt his memory. He was merely mirroring the incredible passion generated on the packed terraces. 'What would you do if Jesus Christ came to Liverpool?' read the hoarding outside a church on Everton Brow. 'Move St John to outside-right' was the response scrawled below. Ian St John was one of Shankly's most successful signings.

In 1966, just weeks before England's success in the World Cup, the team reached the semi-final of the European Cup-winners' Cup. The tie, over two legs, was a further omen of things to come. It was against the hugely talented Celtic. At 4 a.m. on the morning that tickets went on sale at Anfield the queue stretched out of the gates right around Stanley Park almost reaching Everton's ground, Goodison Park.

Many had waited through the night. Football was ill-prepared for the new market-place. The club's attitude was that if fans were prepared to queue through the night it was their business, not the club's responsibility. As people realised that they might miss out on tickets, mini-stampedes occurred. Crowd control was minimal, crowd safety non-existent.

On the night of the Celtic match the Kop was as electrifying as it was terrifying. An injured Geoff Strong scored a glorious winner into the Kop goal. Few Koppites saw the ball enter the net as the tidal wave went down the steps. At the other end, the Anfield Road end, Celtic fans were stunned. Then it happened. Bottles rained down the terrace into Tommy Lawrence's goal-mouth. He ran from the penalty area to escape the wrath of his countrymen – Scotland's goalkeeper in a Liverpool shirt. At the front a young Liverpool boy was hit by a bottle destined for Lawrence. He was left in a coma. According to Bob Paisley, a later Liverpool manager, over 4,000 bottles were collected from the pitch.

A few weeks later, by coincidence, Liverpool played the final in Glasgow at Hampden Park against Borussia Dortmund. Celtic supporters opened their arms to the Liverpool travelling thousands. It was an attempt at reconciliation for what came to be remembered as Anfield's most violent episode. The bond forged in Glasgow has lived on; Liverpool–Celtic scarves are still worn by Liverpool fans.

It was a miserable night in May. Tens of thousands made the journey, mainly by coach, up the seemingly never-ending A74 to Glasgow. It rained incessantly and Liverpool lost to a spectacular fluke late in extra time. A man called Libuda hit a possible shot, possible centre from just inside the Liverpool half, striking both the crossbar and Liverpool's towering centre-half Ronnie Yeats, the ball and the giant both ending up in the net.

Drenched and demoralised, the fans trudged back to the coaches and the long haul home, their European dream over. Windows steamed up as soaking wet clothes dried on chilled bodies. This was the reality of football's legacy. Loyal fans who had queued through the night, missed work, and taken more time off to go to Glasgow, were dumped unceremoniously at 5 a.m. in the middle of Merseyside's towns to walk home damp, miserable, exhausted and broke.

No one batted an eyelid. It was par for the course, part of the weekly exploitation of pride and passion. That thousands of fans would stand for hours on dangerous terraces, exposed to the elements, was accepted as part of the 'people's game'. Looking back at those few weeks in 1966 the twin towers of football's growing malaise were on view. The danger of watching football in volatile, over-packed crowds on crumbling terraces was matched by the emerging danger of football-related violence. Whose responsibility was it to read and respond to the writing on the wall?

* * *

Ten years on from that wet May night in Glasgow, Liverpool travelled to yet another memorable evening match. It was 4 May 1976 at Molineux, home of the once-great Wolverhampton Wanderers. This was Liverpool's next generation of stars, a winning team at home and in Europe. Success against Wolves, and the Reds would be champions again.

While many clubs were supposed to be in the grip of 'football hooliganism', Liverpool's travelling support did not attract organised violence. The fans were consistently praised for their good humour and fair-mindedness. On the M6 that pleasant May evening it seemed that every Merseyside home had sent a representative; nose-to-tail, red-and-white banners poured into the heart of the Midlands.

Many took the afternoon off work and the congestion approaching Wolverhampton was well beyond normal match days. Molineux, like so many other big grounds, was surrounded by a rabbit warren of terraced houses. Soon the narrow streets filled to bursting as tens of thousands converged on slow turnstiles. As it was a non-ticket game, paying took extra time.

It was obvious that the crowd outstripped the stadium's capacity and as the 7.30 p.m. kick-off drew close those outside knew that not everyone would get in. Queues disintegrated into a solid mass of people compressed against walls, exit gates and turnstiles. Crowd control had long been lost. On the terraces, where most of the Liverpool fans were packed, there was little elbow room.

The terrace behind the goal stretched the width of the pitch and fans moved sideways, forwards and backwards to find a half-decent 'spec'. As the pre-match buzz of excitement grew, talk was of a lock-out and the chaos outside the ground. Fans inside were reassured that once the terrace reached capacity the turnstiles would close automatically and the lucky ones inside could settle down.

Without warning there was an almighty crash. The huge wooden exit gates immediately behind the terrace collapsed under the sheer weight of the crowd outside. Hundreds spilled on to the back of the terrace. Police and stewards struggled to prevent more fans getting in. For those already on the terrace, the crush immediately became desperate as elbows were compressed into ribcages. People struggled for breath.

At the front it was serious. As if synchronised, fans pulled themselves over the perimeter wall to the safety of the track and the pitch. Police and St John's Ambulance officers helped them scramble to safety, dragging people over the wall. There was no way those on the terrace could push back. Hundreds were on the pitch. Fortunately the teams were still in the dressing rooms and the police began to sort out the crowd.

They escorted fans to different parts of the ground. Some sat on the track in front of the walls. It was a pulsating match. Liverpool won 3–1 with goals from Keegan, Toshack and Kennedy. The championship was theirs, won in style. Thousands were locked out but hung around to share in the celebrations. For those caught up in the near tragedy it was just one of those things soon to be forgotten. They had been minutes from death but probably never realised it.

* * *

Bradford City v Lincoln City: not usually a game to capture the imagination. But 11 May 1985 was a special day for Bradford. They had won the Third Division Championship and the trophy was presented and paraded before the game. A regular gate of 6,000 was nearly doubled as the town turned out to celebrate promotion. Bradford City, in receivership and liquidation only two years earlier, were tasting the success of a remarkable recovery. So often the case when the party is in full swing, the game was boring, an anti-climax. Just before half-time all hell broke loose.

Two photographs, just minutes apart, tell the horrific story. The first shows fans standing on wooden floors among primitive, backless wooden seats. Beneath their feet, through gaps in the cigarette-strewn flooring, flames can be seen. Smoke is rising through the cracks. People seem reluctant to move: it's a small fire, and someone has gone off to find a fire extinguisher. The second photograph shows the entire stand ablaze; an inferno from top to bottom. It took hold 'as fast as a man could run'. Fifty-six people died and many more were seriously injured.

Bradford's main stand was built when the club was founded in 1908. The rear section, running the full length of the pitch, comprised wooden benches on a timber floor. At the front were plastic seats on a concrete base. The close-boarded roof was covered by roofing felt, sealed with asphalt. Beneath the wooden floor decades of rubbish had accumulated, falling through the gaps in the boards. It was estimated that in its original unburnt state the rubbish would have been a foot deep.

Much of the debris underneath the wooden stand had been there for years. A newspaper dating back to 1968 was found in the charred remains along with wrappers bearing pre-decimalisation prices. Cigarette packets, polystyrene cups, matchboxes and paper extended the full length of the stand. It was a tinder box, set like so many domestic fires. Beneath the dried timber was a mixture of compressed paper and other combustible materials, with a superstructure of wood and highly flammable asphalt above. It only needed one carelessly discarded match or cigarette to ignite the paper and the fire would draw, like a chimney. Someone obliged and the shape of the stand's roof drew the flames.

An expert witness to the subsequent public inquiry reckoned that a 'substantial rubbish fire' beneath the stand 'may have developed in 90 seconds' and this was 'capable of igniting adjacent timbers within about 30 seconds'. The ceiling of the stand drew the flames up to five times their normal height, which 'gave the witnesses the impression of a moving ball of fire coming towards them'. Ahead of the flames was dense smoke, overwhelming fans as they tried to escape at the rear of the stand.

There was chaos and confusion as fans rushed to leave by the way they came in. There were no fire extinguishers and several exits were locked, obstructed or difficult to locate. Even in normal circumstances it took up to ten minutes to clear the stand and certainly it could not be evacuated in under the recommended two and a half minutes. As the inquiry concluded, 'the available exits were insufficient to enable spectators safely to escape the devastating effects of the rapidly spreading fire'.

One lasting image of the Bradford fire is of a police officer running for his life from the blazing stand, his clothes igniting in the intense heat. Many people made good their escape on to the pitch. The inquiry concluded it was 'undoubtedly true' that 'if there had been closed perimeter fences . . . the casualties would have been on a substantially higher scale'. It noted that 'emergency evacuation' could be necessary in a range of circumstances and this would be achieved only if 'sufficient and adequate means of exit, including exits through the perimeter fence itself' were guaranteed.

The Bradford fire could and should have been avoided. The

1976 Green Guide to safety at sports grounds, drawn up after the Ibrox disaster, noted that 'voids' beneath the floor were a 'common feature' in stands vulnerable to fire. They became a 'resting place for paper, cartons and other combustible materials which can be ignited, unnoticed, by a carelessly discarded cigarette end'. The Guide recommended inspections before and after every event to clear rubbish. Nine years after the Guide was published, Bradford's main stand was ignited by rubbish accumulated over three decades.

The inquiry also considered the relationship between football clubs and the police, particularly responsibility for crowd safety within the ground. It concluded that, while the club was responsible for physical safety and maintenance of the stadium, the police have a '*de facto* responsibility for organising the crowd, with all that entails, during the game'. What concerned the inquiry was that police forces provided no training or briefing 'in the question of evacuation'. Although officers had shown 'commendable efficiency' at Bradford, the inquiry recommended that 'evacuation procedure should be a matter of police training and form part of the briefing by police officers before a football match'.

* * *

Within three weeks of the Bradford fire, 38 people died and approximately 400 were injured on the terraces of the Heysel Stadium, Brussels. If one single event brought together soccer-related violence, poor crowd management and unsafe grounds this was it. 'Heysel', as it became known, was the inevitable outcome of football's neglect: a malaise so serious that only fundamental changes to the structure, organisation and management of the game – nationally and internationally – could overcome it. It brought home the tragic reality of the risks that corporate interests, as well as violent individuals, were prepared to run in the name of competitive sport.

Liverpool, the defending European champions, against

Juventus, one of Europe's great clubs. It was one of the matches of the year carried live by television across continents. The stage was set for an exhilarating exhibition of football supported by two of Europe's most passionate groups of fans. Liverpool's followers were conspicuously absent from much of the violence of the previous two decades, winning widespread praise for their loyalty and fairness. No trouble was anticipated from their travelling fans although there were reliable rumours that a number of known English 'hooligans', some with ultra-right political affiliations, were making the trip to Brussels.

Throughout the warm summer's day there were skirmishes in the city centre. While the police reported incidents of violent behaviour, many civilian witnesses claimed that it was little more than groups of boisterous, noisy and, in some cases, drunken fans. There was some concern that the police over-reacted, going in hard and without provocation. Certainly they were in no mood to tolerate any hint of violence.

There was a legacy of antagonism between some of the rival fans. A year earlier Liverpool had played Roma FC in the European final in Rome. Over 40 Liverpool fans were seriously injured in knife attacks and many, who had camped on approved sites close to the city centre, had been under sustained siege by local gangs throughout their stay. At the time the authorities failed to take these incidents seriously. Yet they had raised serious doubts over the choice of Rome for the final and the role of UEFA in protecting the well-being of visiting fans. While Juventus is a Turin team, resentment smouldered among some Liverpool fans towards the Italians.

There was considerable debate over whether the 1985 final should have been held at Heysel at all. Certainly the Liverpool club was unhappy with the venue, particularly the state of the stadium. It was nearly 60 years old, its terracing at both ends of the ground in an appalling condition. The steps were little more than concrete edging on packed earth. Much of the concrete had disintegrated and crumbled and the crush barriers were in a poor condition.

The eventual Belgian Parliamentary Commission of Inquiry called the stadium 'dilapidated' with 'columns, crush-barriers and steps' structurally deteriorated. The terracing in particular was 'neglected', with 'normal maintenance work' not carried out. Lack of exits at the front of the terrace posed a fatally dangerous problem for evacuation.

Lateral fencing, separating three enclosures – X, Y and Z – was flimsy, made from wire net meshing like those surrounding park tennis courts. Some of the walls appeared to be free-standing, neither bedded in mortar nor fixed to adjacent concrete walls. The flank wall in enclosure Z, where most died, and the perimeter fencing were structurally weak, not strong enough to support a sustained crush.

The enclosures were divided top to bottom by three 'corridors' to aid policing of the curved terrace. But there was no means of monitoring access to each enclosure once fans had gone through the turnstiles. There were only three gates in the perimeter fence, one for each enclosure, and they could be opened only from the pitch side. Access and egress from the terraces was dangerously inadequate and the ground certainly would not have been granted a safety certificate in the UK.

Enclosures X and Y were allocated to Liverpool fans, Z was intended for 'neutral' supporters with tickets sold in Brussels. But this was a European Cup final and tickets were at a premium. It was obvious that the touts and other dealers would be desperate for the enclosure Z tickets. And so it proved. Despite reassurances that ticket sales would be controlled, arrangements disintegrated. At least 2,000 fell into the hands of travel organisations and touts. One agent had 60 tickets which he sold at 100 times face value. With many of the 'neutral' tickets going to Juventus fans, the plans for segregation went out of the window.

The sale of these tickets contravened UEFA directives as well as the pre-match agreement. 'It is clear,' stated the Commission of Inquiry, 'that natural animosity developed into altercations, fights and charges; the third of these had tragic consequences and could no doubt have been avoided had there not been so many Italian supporters in section Z . . . the ticket sales organised by the RBFA [Belgian Football Union] were a decisive element in this and they are to blame in this respect'.

Enclosures X, Y and Z were policed by the national Belgian gendarmerie. At the pre-match briefings between the RBFA and other authorities it was agreed that gendarmes would be stationed on each step of the corridor separating enclosures Y and Z. Incredibly, the gendarmerie match commander did not attend the briefings and was unaware of the agreement. His organisation was criticised by the Commission for its deficient command structure, ambiguity in the orders issued, poor communication and lack of adaptability. There were too few officers to carry out the 'onerous task' of segregating the enclosures.

One of the sad ironies of Heysel was that the crowd trouble throughout the late afternoon and early evening occurred at the Juventus end of the ground with pitched battles between Italian fans and the police. Fences were cut, temporary barriers destroyed, weapons confiscated and the police inside subjected to a constant hail of concrete and metal. Twenty-seven officers were injured in the near riot on the Juventus terraces and a pitch invasion was only narrowly averted.

At the other end, in keeping with pre-match intelligence, Liverpool fans had been calm. As enclosure Z began to fill with Italian fans, some stones and a few flares were thrown. Liverpool fans in Z tried to escape into Y. By 7 p.m. enclosures X and Y were packed, holding approximately 15,000 fans, while the crowd in Z was less dense, about 5,000. As tension mounted, fans in Y tried to break the mesh fencing through to Z. With so few police officers around, and the corridor virtually unpoliced, some fans made it through. A third charge by a small group of violent

English men caused wholesale panic in Z. In the rush to escape the charge those at the front were trampled underfoot; there was no way through the perimeter fence and the weak flank wall collapsed. With bodies piled on bodies and the pressure from behind unrelenting, 38 people died. Hundreds were injured.

Even as the enormity of the disaster unfolded it was decided that the match would go ahead. Unreality took over as both teams emerged on to the pitch. In front of a capacity crowd, and world-wide television audience, Juventus beat Liverpool, the European Champions, 1–0. The disaster led to a long-term European ban on all British clubs from European competition. It stood longer on Liverpool than on other clubs and it destroyed their status as one of Europe's premier teams. While anger raged against the small handful of English fans who had caused the panic on the terraces, the crucial debate over ground safety, crowd management and effective policing was lost. Once again the spectre of hooliganism overshadowed the reality of inadequate, dangerous terraces, ineffective policing and flawed crowd management.

* * *

What is shocking about these accounts is how much was known, understood and recommended but to no avail. Politicians, journalists and academic researchers seemed caught in the head-lights of hooliganism, their gaze transfixed on crowd control. Crowd safety and the ever-present danger of unsafe grounds were virtually ignored. With crowd control and policing viewed through the lens of hooliganism, important issues of corporate responsibility and duty of care rarely featured. Yet, a major disaster was always on the cards. As Moelwyn Hughes stated in his prophetic Burnden Park report, only a few ingredients needed adding to the regular sequence of events and tragedy would follow.

It wasn't as if the warning signs were absent or appropriate advice lacking. Football's reality, like many other sports, was that its venues were falling apart. Hastily built stadiums dating back to the turn of the century relied heavily on wood in their construction. Terraces were often timber-based, their entrances and exits wholly inadequate. Concrete terraces were regularly laid on nothing more substantial than compressed slag heaps. In the 1960s it was still possible to visit grounds with terraces no more substantial than compressed clinker and earth, the backs of which were overgrown and patterned with channels carved by the rain.

Football suffered from over-exploitation of gate receipts by club owners and under-investment in bricks and mortar. Alterations tended to be 'add-ons', rather than much-needed reconstruction. Some grounds, including Hillsborough, underwent modification for the 1966 World Cup, but even these retained much of the original fabric. Most top clubs renewed crush barriers, gates and fences but it was piecemeal. By the late 1980s terraces, such as Hillsborough's Leppings Lane, were a mixture of old and new barriers, bits removed and bits added.

It was policing, segregation and containment that brought the most significant changes. Soccer-related violence, or football hooliganism, was not on the political agenda until the late 1960s. As the bottles rained down on Tommy Lawrence's goal at Anfield in 1966, the 'increasing tendency' of fans to run on to the pitch at the end of games was delicately noted in the House of Commons. But within three years 'hooliganism' was a regular feature in political debates, fanned by media coverage of unruly behaviour, violence and vandalism on trains, coaches and around grounds.

The 1968 Harrington Report into 'hooliganism' noted the 'ease with which a dangerous situation' could 'occur in crowded enclosures'. It continued, 'some club managements do not feel obliged to put their grounds into a state . . . necessary for [safe] crowd control'. The report, mindful of Burnden Park, called on the 'appropriate authorities' to act 'before another disaster occurs'. Harrington, despite his focus on 'hooliganism', warned that the proliferation of perimeter fences to keep fans off the pitch 'could be dangerous in the event of massive crowd disturbances as safety exits to the field would be blocked'. He concluded that gangways or tunnels to and from terraces created bottlenecks, rendering them 'useless' for evacuation.

The 1970s became the decade of the 'football hooligan'. To the exclusion of all other considerations, attention was focused on violence and its control. Virtually every parliamentary exchange or media feature on soccer was dominated by 'hooliganism' and its policing. In 1971 a disaster at Ibrox Park towards the end of a Rangers–Celtic match cost the lives of 66 fans in a dreadful crush on an exit gangway leading from the terraces. This led to the Wheatley Report on crowd safety at sports grounds, a centralised licensing system for designated grounds and supporting guide-lines known as the 'Green Guide'. Wheatley warned club owners that crowd safety was 'primary consideration'. New conditions had to be implemented even if some clubs were forced 'out of business'. Lord Wheatley's Report was delivered in1972 to a cool, if not silent, reception.

The headline-writers were much more interested in 'hooligans' and 'mindless morons'. Political and media-led public opinion powerfully combined in demanding effective policing, rigorous control and harsh punishments. In a wide debate about lawless male youth, mods, rockers, skinheads, punks and hooligans had to be brought into line. In football this led directly to the strategy of policing by containment. The idea was that if fans, particularly away fans, could be 'contained' from the moment they left their home town to the moment they returned then the potential for violence, disorder or damage could be minimised.

Keeping rival fans apart became central to police strategies of containment. Its ultimate logic was to ban away fans from grounds; and some clubs, in consultation with their local police force, went down that road. Segregation, however, became the most favoured strategy. Fans were segregated on transport with heavily policed 'football specials' and coaches travelling in convoy.

Police then escorted fans to the ground where they were accommodated in specifically allocated sections.

After the match, away fans were held inside the ground, often up to an hour, and then escorted back to their transport and out of the town. It soon became apparent that many of those who committed the most violent acts were highly organised and would not entertain travelling on organised transport. They travelled by car and met their rivals well away from the ground. Often they were anything but the stereotype of unemployed, working-class hooligans.

The 1977 McElhone Report into football crowd behaviour recommended lateral fences within terraces to prevent sideways movement. Such 'improvements designed to prevent crowd movement should include the provision of suitable access points'. Perimeter fencing should be 'not less than 1.8 metres in height', yet 'access points' were vital 'to allow the pitch to be used if necessary for the evacuation of spectators in an emergency'. Unwittingly, with all the influential authority of government reports, the trap was laid.

Not only were terraces altered to segregate rival fans, but also they were divided into pens. There could be as many as six pens behind the goal, separated by lateral fences and what became known as 'sterile areas' occupied by the police. At the front were perimeter fences, high and overhanging, designed to make access to the pitch impossible. It was difficult to reconcile perimeter fencing, designed to stop pitch invasions, with the use of the pitch for emergency evacuation. The bottom line being that at Burnden Park, Molineux and Bradford the death toll would have been considerably greater had there been perimeter fences.

Pens, just like cattle pens, restricted access from the rear and prevented movement sideways or on to the pitch. Narrow gates in perimeter fences were locked and policed. Fans in pens, hooligans caged. It was no longer possible to keep a check on overcrowding. The checking systems at the turnstiles simply gave the numbers for the entire terrace. With fans left to distribute themselves, some pens, particularly those behind the goal, were regularly packed while others remained under-populated. The unswerving commitment to penning introduced a potentially lethal strategy of containment by segregation.

Then, in March 1985, at the height of the coal dispute, a televised pitch-battle between Millwall and Luton fans at the latter's ground dominated the news. Apparently the Prime Minister, Margaret Thatcher, saw the scenes on television and was outraged. A bullish Government anticipating a 'law and order' victory over the miners had another target at which to direct its authoritarian crusade. Leon Brittan, then Home Secretary, did not disappoint. Two months later, introducing the draconian white paper on public order, he thundered: 'People have the right to protection against being bullied, hurt, intimidated or obstructed, whatever the motive of those responsible may be, whether they are violent demonstrators, rioters, intimidatory mass pickets or soccer hooligans.'

The following day the *Daily Express* warmed to Brittan's theme, adding 'race riots, animal rights demos, Greenham, the miners' strike, and the Libyan Embassy siege' to 'soccer violence'. As Thatcher railed against the 'enemy within', she and her ministers fed the voracious appetite of a violence-obsessed media. Together they created a litany of lawlessness, and 'football hooliganism' was central to their political intentions. But how accurate was this portrayal? How extensive was the violence that seemingly instilled fear into the heart of the nation?

The 1984–85 season, the focus of the Thatcher Government's zealotry over football violence, had an arrest rate of 0.34 per 1,000 attending matches, with a joint arrest/ejection rate of 0.72 per 1,000. Over the following season, while 'hooliganism' was catching the headlines and hyping political imaginations, the arrest and ejection figures dropped by 51 per cent and 33 per cent respectively. The figures remained consistent over the next few seasons, leading the newly formed Football Supporters' Association to conclude that 'many fans' considered the problem of hooliganism to be 'overstated . . . the average football stadium does not become a battleground on Saturday afternoons'.

'Hooligan' hysteria, however, continued unabated. After the 1985 Heysel tragedy, earlier calls for a return of the stocks, public flogging and spraying with dye were resumed on a wave of righteous indignation. This 'moral panic' seriously inhibited a necessary broader debate around crowd management, public safety and civil liberties.

While violent fans were policed and arrested for fighting and wrecking property, such instances were projected as mass civil disorder at all football matches. Over-policing of supporters led to the erosion of their right to move freely on match days, assumed 'guilty' until proving their 'innocence'. There was no parallel in British society: herded on to trains and coaches; body searched; placed under constant surveillance; stopped at motorway services and searched again; herded from trains and coaches; and marched through towns.

Comparisons with controlling animals extended to the very terms used by the police in developing strategies of containment. Meeting and escorting fans from stations, coach parks or other arrival points was termed 'corralling'. Once there, fans were routinely searched and segregated, then herded into pens on decrepit terraces.

Policing by containment delivered control at the expense of care, security at the cost of safety. With the stakes upped by a rigid authoritarianism, and fans corralled and penned, the violence of control generated the behaviour it intended to quell. These military-style operations using special powers led to anger, frustration and confrontation. In making arrests, sometimes for the most innocuous reasons, the police often meted out arbitrary and violent punishments. If a 'football hooligan' took a beating, who cared?

With the benefit of hindsight it is always possible to argue that disasters or other tragedies 'wait to happen'. Inevitably, their origins can be shown in bad habits, flawed custom and practice and institutionalised complacency. Others argue that disasters are the outcomes of a set of unfortunate circumstances, both unpredictable and random. While match crowds at many grounds are vulnerable and consistently at risk, there are always circumstances specific to the moment.

As the Molineux crush showed, near-misses occurred and went virtually unrecorded. Yet the authorities, as Harrington noted, seemed unwilling to take initiatives to ensure the safety of paying customers. There was also universal complacency over the management of the crowd at turnstiles. In the half-hour before kick-off turnstiles were always at their busiest. A simple mathematical exercise could have established the length of time necessary to move a capacity crowd through the turnstiles. This was rarely done. Unless crowds arrived evenly over two hours prior to kick-off, it was impossible to have a smooth operation without congestion.

The potential danger of thousands outside the ground minutes before kick-off had been identified time and again. McElhone had commented that grounds were particularly vulnerable when larger crowds than usual were expected. He was concerned that the 'build-up of crowds at turnstiles, especially in the half-hour before kick-off ' could 'lead to a feeling of frustration among spectators' resulting in 'trouble both outside the ground and inside'. What had to be avoided was a late influx of fans 'on to terraces when the game is under way'. Yet it had become all too easy to neglect the broader context of institutionalised practices, material circumstances and professional priorities.

So whose responsibility was it to foresee potential tragedy and plan accordingly? What were the relative responsibilities of the club owners, the hirers of the ground and the local authority safety officers? How were the crowd-management responsibilities of the police and club stewards defined, apportioned and translated into practice? Again, the Bradford inquiry, like those before it, emphasised the pivotal role and responsibilities of the police both outside and inside the ground. It stressed the necessity for adequate and appropriate training in crowd safety and evacuation procedures. This included thorough briefings for each game, noting that crowd safety was absent from training and briefings within police forces.

Instead the emphasis, in line with police priorities but also reflecting political direction and public concern, was on harderline policing by containment. Training and briefing prioritised regulation and control from escorting coaches, trains and cars to corralling fans and penning them in cages without adequate access or escape. It was a policy of intolerance, of 'going in hard' – a macho response to a macho condition. To appreciate the balance of priorities between crowd control and crowd safety little more was needed than to read the police operational orders for policing major games.

* * *

After all that had happened over the previous decade, particularly a near-fatal crush on Hillsborough's Leppings Lane terraces at the 1981 semi-final, crowd safety should have been a priority in the South Yorkshire Police Operational Order for the 1989 match. It hardly featured. Between 1981 and 1987 no semi-finals were played at Hillsborough and the terraces underwent some modification. The 1987 game, Leeds against Coventry, was a noon kick-off. Chief Superintendent Mole wrote the Operational Order, was match commander and took the decision just 15 to 20 minutes before kick-off to delay the start. Both sets of fans were held up travelling to Sheffield.

Despite this, the 1988 semi-final, Liverpool against Nottingham Forest, made no reference to possible delays or appropriate action. Nottingham fans were on the doorstep, but most Liverpool fans travelled across the Pennines, a journey of over two hours. Overall, the 1988 match went off without incident. Two events left a lasting impression. On approaching the ground, fans recalled being asked to show tickets by police officers. It was a kind of 'filter', slowing the crowd's approach. Many others, including police officers on duty, remembered being crushed in the central pens, 3 and 4, immediately behind the goal. Access to these pens was beneath the West Stand, down a 1-in-6 gradient tunnel, the entrance to which was directly opposite the turnstiles. In 1988 officers restricted access to the tunnel once these pens were full, redirecting fans to the side pens.

There is no adequate explanation as to why the police did not incorporate the lessons from the 1988 match into the 1989 Operational Order. When, on 20 March, Liverpool were again drawn to play Forest, the previous year's Order was taken down, dusted and, with a few minor alterations, reissued; complete with uncorrected spelling mistakes. The Operational Order for the 15 April 1989 match consisted of a 12-page general overview, signed by the match commander, followed by a detailed account of the responsibility of every serial of officers on duty on the day. Each serial – usually ten police constables under the command of one sergeant – was named.

It was the stated intention to 'allow this match to take place' ensuring public order and safety both inside and outside the football ground' and to 'segregate and control opposing fans' preventing 'unnecessary obstruction of the highway and damage to property'. Whatever the disputes that followed, there was an implicit acceptance within the Order that the police took responsibility for managing the safety of the crowd within the stadium.

Yet nowhere in the Order, or in the appended list of duties, was there any discussion of what this responsibility entailed. A reference to 'emergency and evacuation procedures' was confined to a bomb call or fire response. It simply informed senior officers that to initiate evacuation a coded message would be broadcast over the public address system. No reference was made to emergency procedures concerning overcrowding, congestion or problems on the terraces.

Twenty-one officers were given responsibility for policing the perimeter track. They would stand facing the crowd before the kick-off, at half-time and full-time or if there was 'crowd unrest'. They were instructed to pay 'particular attention . . . to prevent any person climbing the fence to gain access to the ground'. The perimeter fence gates were to 'remain bolted at all times' with 'no one . . . allowed access to the track from the terraces without the consent of a senior officer'. The latter statement was in capitals and underlined.

Inside the ground, two serials, each comprising ten officers and a sergeant, were responsible for policing the rear enclosures – one north, one south – of the Leppings Lane terrace. They were instructed simply to enforce ground rules concerning banners, weapons, missiles and alcohol. No mention was made of crowd management or safety, their instructions being concerned only with control. In the event of evacuation the officers were to assist fans in leaving safely through the exit gates. Four serials were stationed at the Leppings Lane turnstiles, their duties consisting entirely of enforcing ground rules.

The Operational Order showed the extent to which police planning for football matches had become a full military-style operation. Liverpool fans travelled by train, coach, minibus and in private cars. From the moment they arrived in South Yorkshire they were to be tracked, directed, randomly stopped and searched, disembarked and 'supervised' to the ground. Those arriving by rail, depending on which station, were to be bussed or 'walked . . . under police supervision' to the Leppings Lane end of the ground.

Coaches and minibuses were to be randomly stopped by 'search squads' to ensure that passengers had tickets, were not under the influence of drink or carrying alcohol. Officers had to be satisfied that fans were 'fit to attend this event'. Following a thorough search, the vehicles allowed to continue their journey would be given a label of approval. Obviously this applied only to those coaches and minibuses stopped but many would be delayed by the searches.

Coaches, minibuses and 'transit vans' were to be directed to designated parking areas, their passengers checked and briefed by reception officers and then walked to the ground under police supervision. As far as possible the same restrictions were placed on private vehicles. The Order stated that after the game no vehicle could leave until authorisation was given by Ground Control, and then only by designated routes.

As fans walked to the ground their freedom of movement would be limited by the closure of streets and the access road alongside the stadium. Police serials would be stationed at barriers around the ground in order to maintain segregation of fans. Forest fans would experience the same regulation and restrictions at the other end of the ground. For those trying to meet friends beyond the barriers, access would be denied.

According to the Order, the 'great majority' of pubs had agreed to close from lunchtime through to early evening. Those that remained open would 'operate a "selective door" whereby football supporters [were] not admitted'. The responsibility for policing these arrangements was given to serials outside the ground identifying 'those premises which remain open' and monitoring 'the behaviour of persons resorting thereto'.

The Operational Order prioritised alcohol as a major problem. Much of the policing outside the ground, from the random coach searches through to the monitoring of pubs, was supposed to be directed against drinking. From the Order's instructions and the sheer numbers of officers on duty, it should not have been possible for those drunk or carrying cans of beer to have reached the ground.

What the Operational Order failed to address was as striking as its priorities. Despite the warning signs, the 'Green Guide', police guidelines and official reports, there were no contingencies for the inevitable build-up outside the ground immediately before kick-off. There was nothing in the Order about the bottleneck at the Leppings Lane turnstiles and the obvious danger of congestion in the turnstile area. Both problems were well known to the police and there had been serious congestion in 1988. There were no contingency plans for delaying the kick-off, for opening exit gates, for coping with over-full pens or for closing the tunnel leading into the central pens.

It was an Operational Order written in good faith from past experience. Yet it carried the infection of complacency. It failed to incorporate the experiences of 1987 and 1988 and it assumed an air of confidence that the South Yorkshire Police had got it right in its custom and practice. In its omissions it was flawed. Hung up on a dedication to containment and regulation, it neglected the well-being and safety of the fans. In its stated intention it ensured public order and safety; in its written instructions the latter was lost to the former.

* * *

This was Duckenfield's inheritance from Mole as the two men met on 22 March, just five days before Mole's transfer out of Hammerton Road. According to Mole it was an 'urgent' meeting involving his planning team and other interested parties. It seems that the adoption of the previous year's Operational Order was agreed in principle. No mention was made of the problems of packing in the central pens or the decision to close off the tunnel and redirect the crowd to the end pens. Duckenfield felt that he was being handed a tried and tested procedure operating under the guidance of a first-rate, experienced team of senior officers. He had no reason, nor did he have the specialist experience, to think otherwise. If no serious problems had arisen previously then the policing priorities and strategies must have been effective.

On 29 March, Duckenfield met the planning team again, this

time without the departed Mole. Only minor modifications were made to the Operational Order. Duckenfield's trust in his inheritance was evident from his decision to adopt the existing Order without even a brief visit to Hillsborough. In fact, his first visit came a few days later when Sheffield Wednesday played Millwall. Although technically in charge, he left the management of the game to his assistants and spent time walking around the ground 'familiarising' himself with the operation.

It was hardly an appropriate comparison. Millwall probably had a maximum of 2,000 travelling fans and the ground was well below capacity. It all looked so straightforward; no build-up, no congestion, no overcrowding and no emergencies. The police operation ticked over like clockwork, nothing to alert the senses to impending disaster.

Whatever Duckenfield was hoping to achieve from his familiarisation, no warning bells sounded. Although he visited the Leppings Lane turnstiles, inner concourse and the central tunnel he saw no potential problems, not even the absence of signs directing fans to the end pens. He remained ignorant of the layout of the Leppings Lane terrace, particularly the arrangements concerning the gates in the lateral and perimeter fencing. He had no grasp of the club's crowd-management responsibilities as they had been agreed with Mole. It was Duckenfield's mistaken view that the primary responsibility for crowd management in the ground lay with the club and that club stewards would be on duty at the rear of the pens and at the tunnel entrance.

Possibly because of the onerous demands in taking over at Hammerton Road, Duckenfield rested assured over the semifinal. He did not read most of the background papers and guidelines relating to policing football. He assumed that his senior officers were well versed and could handle all eventualities. Neither did he make any enquiries about the serious crush in 1981 or the delayed kick-off in 1987. Nor did he brief his officers on the potential danger of crushing in the pens, although he later claimed to have recognised it as a possibility. In a typical example of wisdom after the event he maintained that crushing in the pens should have been monitored by police officers on duty above the pens in the West Stand. He was adamant about this. So why was this important duty not written into the Operational Order?

As match day approached, Duckenfield held further briefings, including a press conference. The decision to move Mole sideways just weeks before the semi-final caused eyebrows to be raised among senior and junior officers alike. For all his professional experience, his brief encounter with policing football a decade earlier hardly prepared Duckenfield for succession at Hillsborough. He was way out of his depth and the job of keeping his head above water fell to the senior officers around him.

It is not difficult to imagine how news of the change in command rippled around the South Yorkshire force, given the controversy over events at Hammerton Road and the subsequent resignations of officers. Those loyal to Mole saw him as the can-carrier for pranks that got out of hand. Whatever the conflicting views of those events, most officers considered his transfer untimely, given the semi-final. He had written and operation-alised the two previous Orders and was set to take charge of the 1989 semi-final. Yet he went.

Undoubtedly the newly promoted Duckenfield had close friends in the force. He met with them often outside work. As they met regularly at the golf club, the group of senior officers became known within the canteen culture as the 'T-set'. While there is no evidence of unprofessional conduct, their close association was seen by other officers as influential, referred to as a 'force within the Force'.

It is impossible to gauge the significance of divided loyalties and the impact of seemingly inexplicable organisational decisions on the morale of those on the shop floor. Like all other complex organisations, police forces have a powerful canteen culture with a voracious appetite for rumour and innuendo. What is clear is that on 15 April 1989 when Duckenfield walked out to brief the massed ranks of junior officers he possessed little credibility in their eyes. Who was he? What did he know? What could he tell them? Yet the most important question raised by this shameful tale is how it could be considered appropriate to entrust the command of an FA Cup semi-final to a minimally experienced officer just days before the event. Whatever Duckenfield's abilities, he was set to fail.

All the ingredients for disaster were now in place. On the day all it would need was an unfortunate coincidence of circumstances and tragedy would follow. Yes, some fans would be the worse for drink and a small minority would be abusive and belligerent. Yes, some fans would travel to Hillsborough, as others would to Wimbledon, Lord's or a rock concert, without tickets. That's why touts make a living. And, yes, most fans would arrive at the ground, not late, but in the 30 minutes before kick-off. After all, the instruction printed on their tickets required them to be in the ground just 15 minutes before kick-off. None of this was news. It was to be expected: part of the routine. It was all perfectly foreseeable. But who was looking?

Chapter Two

15 APRIL 1989

Within 24 hours of the Heysel disaster Joe Fagan, a long-term servant of Liverpool, stood down as manager. His retirement had been planned and was not linked to the tragedy. Kenny Dalglish was named as player–manager and the following season, the European ban in place, Liverpool were almost invincible. In May 1986 a Dalglish goal at Chelsea clinched the Championship. A week later the team outclassed Everton to win the FA Cup. Nearing the end of a glittering playing career, Dalglish had won the double in his first season as manager.

The following season Liverpool lost in the League Cup final, finishing second to Everton in the League. Merseyside was buoyant, although European competition was sorely missed. In 1988, following a convincing semi-final victory over Nottingham Forest at Hillsborough, Liverpool were on for another double. After an opening run of 29 unbeaten First Division games they took their seventeenth championship in emphatic style. At Wembley, in one of the decade's great upsets, lowly placed Wimbledon won 1–0. The defeat rocked the champions.

Despite this set-back, the late 1980s Liverpool squad was exceptional. It boasted a tremendous record, impressively remaining at the top while undergoing transition. Throughout the 1988–89 season yet another double was on the cards. They looked favourites to recapture the League Championship and were through to the semi-final. Four teams remained, including Everton. Incredibly, the draw put Liverpool against Nottingham Forest again and Everton against Norwich. The Everton fans would travel to Villa Park, Birmingham, and the Reds were back at Hillsborough. An all-Merseyside final was possible for a second time in three years. Throughout the region the anticipation was infectious.

On 15 April families and friendships divided as Liverpool fans went off to Sheffield, the Evertonians to Birmingham. Their shared hope was that the next journey down the M6 would have Wembley's twin towers at its end. Football seems to bring out the oddest characteristics in the most conventional of people. Many, like their football heroes, stick religiously to a set routine on match days. The same shirt, jacket or 'lucky' shoes are worn to every match. Scarves or banners remain unwashed often for a whole season in case a winning run of matches is disrupted; thousands of fans with all kinds of superstitions.

Habit often structures the day: same pubs, same streets, same mates, same food. Although the game is only 90 minutes long, hundreds of thousands of supporters live for the day. A big match, a cup match, particularly a semi-final, dominates the week leading up to the game. Shop fronts and houses are decorated as the estates and streets prepare for the mass exodus.

Like any other big event, tickets are scarce, with fans booking seats on football specials and coaches or arranging to share cars. Talk is of little else: who will be in the team, what formation will be played and, inevitably, the opposition. Forest was always a big game for Liverpool, the two teams meeting regularly in the later stages of both cups. And the outspoken Brian Clough was their manager. That morning, as the lucky ticket-holders met at the pick-up points, the excitement was tangible. For every one of the 50,000 Merseysiders off to Sheffield and Birmingham hundreds would listen on Radio Merseyside or Radio City.

As the fans departed and the motorways east and south filled up, the last thing on anyone's mind was danger; a beautiful early spring morning, a glorious drive over the Pennines. As a bereaved mother said later, 'You don't expect to go to a football match and die.' The assumption being that a Football Association showpiece at a premier stadium, policed by one of Britain's main forces, was a safe place to be.

The road journey, like the train, through the Peak District to Sheffield is particularly beautiful. In early April the bleakness of winter gives way to the first flowers of spring, the last traces of late snow quickly receding from the tops. The two most picturesque roads, over the Woodhead and Snake Passes, run alongside rivers and reservoirs, the sun glinting on the slightest movement of water. They are two of England's finest inter-city routes, matched by the rail journey. To get to these roads from Merseyside involves a loop south of Manchester or, alternatively, across the city via the Mancunian Way. It is normally a straightforward two-hour journey with delays usual around Glossop.

Hillsborough is west of Sheffield's city centre, so the Woodhead and Snake were obvious choices. Others, however, remembered the hold-ups of 1988 and opted for the considerably longer M62/M1 route expecting it to be free of delay. Coaches and hired mini-buses mainly complied with the police directions in using this route thus coming into Sheffield from the east and crossing the city to Hillsborough. Always unpredictable were the persistent and ever-changing roadworks on the M62.

Big matches on neutral grounds have a unique atmosphere. As the game approaches, the media hype and endless permutations of how it will be played, debated on *Grandstand* and street corners alike, seem to take place in a world of their own, detached from the mundane and the routine. Travelling is part of the 'rush', a graphic illustration of the passion. Convoys of coaches, transits and cars bedecked in banners, flags, ribbons and scarves; horns sounding in apparent recognition of people who have never before set eyes on each other. All they want to do is get there, park, have a bite to eat, a drink and find the ground.

Whichever route, the South Yorkshire Police received, monitored and directed the football traffic as it flooded into Sheffield. Random checks on coaches and minibuses delayed many, as did congestion around two sets of roadworks on the motorways. The checks included spot searches for alcohol as well as requests for fans to show their tickets.

Despite this, and occasional overbearing officers intent on throwing their weight about, the fans took all in their stride. Sharp-tongued sarcasm and quick-fire routines, rehearsed and honed over years of following the team, soon took the heat out of any jobsworth officiousness: a quick laugh and on with the journey. No one wants their big day spoiled. While Heysel was still at the back of people's minds, Liverpool's reputation for well-behaved support was widely recognised. The police were not expecting any problems from either set of fans and neither were the fans themselves.

Some coaches and cars stopped on the way. A Liverpool-based university lecturer was having lunch at a pub en route when a coach-load of fans arrived. They were 'boisterous but well behaved and there was good humour between them and the local people who were eating in the dining area'.

'Having a quick pint and a bite to eat is part of the trip,' said a fan who travelled on an official coach, 'no one's interested in anything but having a laugh and a couple of bevvies with [their] mates.'

As the coaches, minibuses and cars reached their final destination, they were guided to designated parking by traffic-control police and greeted by officers checking for alcohol and tickets. Those previously stopped and checked in the outskirts of the city disembarked after a few words from the police. Otherwise it was a quick search and briefing. On leaving their transport, fans walked the police-supervised route to the ground. Trains to

Sheffield Midland were met and fans transported to the ground on double-decker buses. Special trains coming in to the local Wadsley Bridge Station were met and fans walked under police escort.

Approaching the ground there was a carnival atmosphere. The policing was neither heavy nor intrusive. There were plenty of police about but fans were left to walk freely, laughing and singing. Any attempt to leave the designated route was prevented, especially close to the ground. The terraced streets surrounding Hillsborough were closed off by barriers and were patrolled by police. While the policing was easygoing, there was a determination that Liverpool fans would stay on the agreed route and, at all costs, be kept away from Forest supporters.

As always in these situations there was some anxiety. Most fans were unfamiliar with the area and the layout of the ground. Tickets had been hard to come by, spoken for by shareholders, season-ticket holders and those who had collected match vouchers throughout the season. The allocation, given Liverpool's regular support, was nowhere near adequate. In the scramble for tickets during the days before the game, families and friends ended up with tickets for different parts of the ground, some at the Forest end. As they approached the ground they split up, hastily making arrangements to meet outside shops, on street corners or back at the car parks at the end of the match.

* * *

By any standards, policing Hillsborough was a massive and complex operation. Two sets of fans totalling 54,000 arrived in an already busy city over a two- to three-hour period on a Saturday afternoon. Most of the fans were unfamiliar with the roads, the approaches to the ground and the ground itself. There were 1,122 officers on duty, approximately 38 per cent of the entire South Yorkshire force. While senior officers were prepared in advance, many of those on duty on the day were volunteers: well paid, but volunteers all the same.

Senior officers, inspectors and above, were briefed at the ground the day before the match. Duckenfield, as match commander, read from a prepared brief. Superintendent Murray followed as the officer 'in charge of the control post'. After this general briefing those with overall responsibilities briefed their teams. Superintendent Marshall, who in 1988 had taken charge inside the stadium, had swapped duties and was responsible for Liverpool supporters outside the ground. He briefed his team in an area 'off the main stand', ensuring that they were familiar with the Operational Order and their management responsibilities. Then he took officers unfamiliar with the area on a quick 'guided tour'.

The following morning, match day, most officers reported for duty around 8 a.m. Many commented on the fine weather, relieved that they would not have to stand around in the cold and rain. There was a buzz of excitement: 'it was like a party really . . . a happy atmosphere . . . probably a lot of them would have worked it for nothing.' Everyone assembled at 10 a.m. in the North Stand for the main briefing. First up was Duckenfield to 'set the scene'. Murray gave 'the order of the day and what [was] required'. Two other officers gave short briefings on 'intelligence' and arrangements for relief and meals. Then inspectors in charge of serials discussed the specifics of duties with their officers.

The initial briefing was over by 10.18 a.m. Comments were passed between officers about Duckenfield. Most did not know him and had expected to see Mole. For those who did, a number were doubtful that he could tell them anything about policing Hillsborough. It is not unusual for lower-ranked experienced officers to feel patronised or undervalued by their bosses. But this was worse, Duckenfield seemed to have been appointed at the last minute.

Soon they were on duty, the turnstiles opening just before noon. A 'steady stream of Liverpool fans' began to arrive 'in good spirits and well behaved'. An inspector commented that there were 'no problems, not a lot of fans about' and those at the ground were 'all in good spirits'. The overall mood, according to another officer, was 'happy with many of the fans joking with us': a 'good humoured' atmosphere, 'without problems'.

Inside the ground, officers waited to check fans as they came through the turnstiles. They had been searched outside but, 'We were instructed . . . to search the same individuals a second time.' The instruction was issued 'even if we could see that they had been searched outside', and some fans 'were searched two or three times'. Despite this, in the officers' opinions, the fans remained 'very good natured' with 'much good humour about the searching'. 'All this time,' stated another officer, 'all the fans appeared to be quite amicable . . . jokes were passed between police and supporters in light-hearted banter.' A chief inspector was 'a little surprised that at 1 p.m. there were so few cars and pedestrians in the area'.

With the first arrivals 'generally good-humoured' there were few problems. At Sheffield Midland railway station the special trains started to arrive at 11 a.m. through until 2 p.m. Fans were bussed to the ground without incident. Other trains arrived at Wadsley Bridge Station and fans were escorted to Hillsborough on foot. A train arrived just after 2 p.m. and a 'party of some 500 Liverpool fans' were led to the ground by mounted officers. A mounted officer not involved with the escort thought that the numbers doubled as the escort passed through the streets, arriving at the turnstiles at about 2.20 p.m. She estimated a further 1,000 fans were arriving over the Leppings Lane Bridge at the same time.

A Merseyside mounted officer noticed that, after 2 p.m., as people began to arrive in greater numbers, entry to the ground was slow. This was 'part due to the fact that supporters were being searched prior to entering . . .' As the crowd swelled and became packed around the turnstiles in what was an enclosed area the mood 'was one of high spirits, what may be described as a carnival atmosphere prevailed, with many people singing and chanting, but all good-humouredly'.

While the crowd was building at the turnstiles, it was clear to officers at the designated parking areas that many fans were only just arriving in Sheffield. At 2.30 p.m., about a mile from the ground, 'coaches were arriving now one after the other almost'. Each was directed to park up and then the fans were briefed by the police before being allowed to disembark. 'It was apparent,' stated an officer, 'that the mood of the bus occupants was more excited but this was probably due to the kick-off being only 30 minutes away.'

Ten minutes later the same officer 'could see right down Halifax Road' where several coaches were 'unloading . . .. about a quarter of a mile away'. It was around this time that a senior ambulance officer was on Halifax Road where he 'noticed that there were a large number of Liverpool supporters trying to park'. With train escorts arriving just before 2.30 p.m., coaches backed up along main roads and cars searching for parking, it was clear that the steady stream of supporters arriving at Leppings Lane prior to 2.15 p.m. would become a torrent as fans, delayed on motorways and the bottlenecks around the ground, reached the turnstiles in the last half-hour before kick-off.

Yet still there was little trouble as far as the police were concerned. This is evident from the radio logs which kept track of incidents throughout the morning and early afternoon. They make informative reading. At 12.15 p.m. the ground control log noted that at two public houses, the Horse and Jockey and the Freemasons, there were 'drinking supporters'. Fifteen minutes later it recorded that the Royal Hotel was, 'Full – possible problems later'. A couple of coaches were turned around, presumably sent back, shoplifters escaped at a newsagents and a vehicle carrying six passengers was stopped on suspicion of 'stolen sweets'.

At 1.30 p.m. special constables radioed for assistance at an unidentified pub in Neepsend and both the Victoria and Royal were 'full and very boisterous'. The Royal was closed at 1.37 p.m. At 2.03 p.m. the extended incident log recorded supporters urinating in a private garden and at 2.28 p.m. 'approximately ten youths on waste ground, appear to arming [*sic*] themselves with wooden sticks'. There was nothing to connect this last incident with the match. Apart from one or two reports of vehicles being driven at speed or erratically these incidents are the sum total of those logged. Given the number of people in the area and the hype around football 'hooliganism' it was hardly the stuff of headlines.

From their 'intelligence' reports, the South Yorkshire Police did not expect any significant crowd violence before, during or after the match. Neither set of fans had a reputation for street or terrace fighting. They did expect, and plan for, drunken behaviour. It was covered in the Operational Order and officers were instructed by the Order to keep a tight rein on drinking, whether in pubs or on the street. If drink-related problems developed, particularly around pubs, the Order made it clear with whom the responsibility for monitoring and sorting it lay: the police.

An inspector responsible for overseeing Liverpool fans from coach reception and supervision through to the turnstiles, briefed his officers 'to expect a high incidence of people to be drunk'. Incredibly, however, he went on, 'although it is not our policy to allow this, on this particular day we would have to relax the rules a little and only arrest people who were extremely drunk or couldn't look after themselves or were causing trouble'. In other words drunkenness, unless associated with disorderly behaviour, was to be tolerated.

At the ground the last half-hour point, 2.30 p.m., had come and gone. The build-up at the turnstiles was sudden and intense. Any semblance of queuing had disappeared as more and more people arrived and the bottleneck started to take its toll. The simple equation was that more people were arriving at the back of the enclosed area than were passing through the turnstiles at the front. Those just arriving from coaches, trains and cars knew that thousands more were still to come. As one officer observed: 'The crowd . . . were getting very heated as time was getting on towards three o'clock and movement through the turnstiles appeared to be very slow.' A mounted officer felt the change all around: 'What had a few minutes earlier seemed to be a carnival kind of atmosphere was rapidly becoming electric and very hostile . . .'

* * *

Modern stadiums, like the versatile arenas of the last decade, are purpose-built. They are located in city regeneration areas or out-of-town developments with close attention paid to access roads, extensive car-parking, public transport and efficient crowd movement. Inside they are designed more like small villages than old-style venues, offering a range of food and drink outlets, amusements, modern seating and planned stewarding. They have adequate basic amenities, a far cry from many of the remodelled football grounds.

While there has been an attempt to improve facilities at grounds, with stands demolished, replaced and all-seater stadiums statutorily introduced, most remain prisoners of their history. Football grounds, built and developed at the turn of the century, often squat uneasily among the compact terraces of working-class communities. Pick up any A to Z of Britain's towns and cities and the pattern is consistent. These formerly vast, previously uncovered grounds were constructed when few people travelled by car.

Today, most top Premier clubs are embattled with the communities in which they exist. Height restrictions on new stands, problems over established road networks and inconvenience on match days are the stock-in-trade of most big clubs' public relations officers. Car-parking remains a real bugbear, with drivers leaving cars on side roads anywhere within a two-mile radius of grounds.

In 1989 Hillsborough was typical of so many First Division

grounds. It was built 90 years earlier, two miles out of Sheffield's city centre, alongside the River Don. The South Stand, partly uncovered, ran the full length of the pitch, separated by a private access road from the river. The South Stand complex accommodated the directors' entrance and reception areas, the players' changing rooms and all of the usual VIP facilities. It was from beneath this stand that the players emerged on to the pitch.

The East End, substantially redeveloped in 1986, was the impressive Spion Kop, accommodating 21,000 spectators on a modern, roofed terrace. This was the 'home' end, where most of Sheffield Wednesday's standing supporters gathered. It was tightly fitted into an area between the pitch and Penistone Road. The North Stand, which backed on to a network of terraced houses, ran the full length of the pitch seating 9,700 spectators. A first aid room and police room were located in this complex and a gymnasium backed on to it. There was a small parking area at the entrance to the gymnasium and the main police access to the ground was off this area between shops and houses. A gap between the North Stand and the Spion Kop, just behind the corner flag, gave access to the pitch.

The west end of the pitch behind the goal was known as the Leppings Lane end. In 1965, in preparation for the World Cup, the West Stand was built at the back of the Leppings Lane terrace. It was a covered stand for approximately 4,500 spectators. The uncovered terracing in front and to the sides of the West Stand held 10,100. Leppings Lane was the designated area for 'away' fans.

Leppings Lane itself runs roughly north to south bending in towards the ground just as it passes over the River Don. At this slight bend in the road between a corner shop and the river fence were six sets of wrought-iron double gates, like those around school playgrounds or local parks. The three gates to the left opened into a small area feeding 16 turnstiles, those to the right accessed a smaller area feeding 7 turnstiles. Alongside the turnstiles were large exit gates, A and B, and around the corner from the smaller area was exit gate C. These 23 turnstiles processed all spectators entering the Leppings Lane terrace, the West Stand and the North Stand: 24,447 spectators. The rest of the ground, numbering 29,800 spectators, was fed by 60 turnstiles.

The 10,000 fans with tickets for the Leppings Lane terrace walked through the three outer gates into the confined area to queue at the seven turnstiles. Fans in the North or West Stands entered via the other three outer gates, heading for one of 16 turnstiles. This tightly confined area had to cope with nearly 25,000 people. It was a potential bottleneck and a significant danger. In fact, just three years earlier, on 11 June 1986, a police inspector with considerable experience of policing the ground wrote to the Chief Superintendent of 'F' Division warning of the serious problem of 'access to the ground, particularly at the Leppings Lane end'. He stated that the 'redesigned turnstiles do not give anything like the access to the ground . . . needed by away fans'. Supporters had become 'justifiably irate because of the inefficiency of the system, which was turned on the police and could have resulted in public disorder'. This was his assessment for ordinary club matches; a semi-final guaranteed a full house.

Once through the seven turnstiles fans found themselves on an inner concourse. Directly opposite was a tunnel dropping down a 1-in-6 gradient on to the terrace. The word 'standing' was posted over the tunnel alongside the letter 'B'. This matched the letter on all terrace tickets. Fans automatically went down the tunnel assuming that this was the only terrace entrance. In fact the steep tunnel led only to the central pens, 3 and 4.

Ironically, the first lateral fences were installed in 1981 after crushing occurred on the terrace because of overcrowding. Tragedy had been narrowly averted by opening the gates in the trackside perimeter fencing. Further, because at the time it was an unrestricted terrace, fans escaped sideways, although this was not straightforward as the entire terrace was over-full. Two radial fences were introduced in 1981, two more in 1985, giving five 'pens' on the terrace.

The crush barriers were reviewed in 1979, leaving a mixture of relatively new and old. Some modifications to the barriers were made in 1985 and 1986. Consequently, the distribution of barriers in pens 3 and 4 was quite different. In pen 3 there was a gap between barriers that stretched from the front barrier almost to the back of the terrace. A crush down this channel would clearly place the front barrier under considerable pressure. Pens 3 and 4 each had narrow, shoulder-width gates up steps on to the perimeter track. These were locked.

Hillsborough was not easily accessed. There was minimal parking near the ground, which was enclosed between residential housing to the north and the river to the south. Liverpool fans were channelled both ways along Leppings Lane until they arrived at the bend in the road by the corner shop. Here they were faced with a bottleneck of extraordinary proportions. The end of their journey comprised two confined outer concourses, together no bigger than a small school yard, leading to old and inefficient turnstiles. They were funnelled into these enclosures without any thought of slowing or filtering their arrival. The Inspector's 1986 memorandum had gone unheeded.

* * *

In the last half-hour before kick-off fans arrived at the bottleneck from both directions and the two restricted areas through the outer gates became tightly packed. With walls, fences or gates to the sides and front, the only relief was behind but more and more fans arrived, oblivious to the potentially fatal crush at the front. Within minutes the crush became desperate, the situation critical, as men, women, children and police officers struggled for space and breath. Police and fans' accounts of what happened next differ.

Superintendent Marshall, in overall command of officers supervising the arrival and approach of Liverpool fans, had earlier patrolled the area and noted many 'mostly male' fans 'lying or sitting on the grass drinking from cans and bottles in the bright sunshine'. But 'there was no trouble' and 'despite what seemed to me to be far too much drinking going on fans were well behaved'. Marshall's statement concentrates heavily on the extent of alcohol consumption among Liverpool fans.

At Wadsley Lane he confronted two youths walking along with glasses of beer in their hands. The off-licence at the end of Marlcliffe Road was 'very busy indeed' and 'about 30 males' outside 'were drinking a variety of intoxicating liquor'. Outside the Park Hotel, 'groups of fans . . . were drinking on the pub forecourt and were chanting football slogans'. The Gateway supermarket off-licence was 'doing a roaring trade' with a queue of fans buying drink through a door. Wherever he went Marshall instructed police officers in the vicinity to keep a close watch on the drinking fans.

An inspector on duty outside the ground also noticed that fans, as expected, were arriving 'carrying cans of beer, bottles of beer and bottles of spirit'. Those approaching the ground 'carrying . . . alcohol had it taken from them and put in the large bins provided for that purpose'. He urged fans to move along and go into the ground, suspecting that some had no tickets, while others were 'stupid drunk and wouldn't listen to advice and instructions'. There was no violence.

Near the ground, a mounted officer 'noticed a general aroma of beer coming from the crowds of fans . . . It appeared to me that they were affected by alcohol consumption and becoming more hostile.' A senior officer felt that there 'was increasing evidence of drunkenness amongst the supporters who were all Liverpool fans'. At the ground, 'The crowd was at a complete standstill and it was not safe to force the "bottleneck situation".'

The police around the turnstiles 'were having a great deal of difficulty in controlling the crowd at this point . . . the turnstiles were not coping efficiently with the crowd which was swelling by the minute'. Inside, officers were trying to help people through 'antiquated' turnstiles. They were repeatedly jamming, either caught in people's clothes, one person having to be cut free, or because the ratchet mechanism was defective.

In the crush, 'tempers became frayed and evidence of drunkenness became more and more pronounced'. Another officer considered the crowd to be growing 'more and more unruly and nasty', beginning to 'swarm over the walls into the ground'. He thought the 'late arrivals were worse for drink but may not be classified as drunk'.

'The rowdy mob at the back just kept pushing forward . . . by this time there were a large number of youths and men – considerably worse for drink – many were drunk . . .'

A senior officer 'went further towards Leppings Lane roadway and could see that fans were converging on the ground in vast numbers. Many . . . were carrying alcohol and many were drunk. I was shouting at them not to push and they were taking no notice. They appeared to have one purpose and that was to get into the ground.'

Another officer agreed: 'The bulk of supporters appeared to be gripped by an urgency to get into the ground and get in now and if someone was hurt, so what . . . They appeared fanatical to gain entrance . . . although I didn't think it at the time, I now think the fans were storming the turnstiles.' As officers pushed their way through the crowd to the outer gates or retreated to safety through the turnstiles it was clear that the situation between the outer gates and the turnstiles was out of control.

On the inside, 'people coming into the ground . . . were in a very distressed condition . . . trying to catch their breath. Others who came through, either through panic, shock or drink, were very aggressive towards myself or other officers. Many had obviously been drinking heavily.' Another officer stated that they were 'hyped up and in a state of distress and anger shouting and screaming that persons would be seriously injured if the situation outside wasn't sorted out . . .'

With radio contact breaking up, the officers inside could not fully appreciate the extent of the problems outside. Some fans climbed over the wall, dropping down from the roof of the turnstiles. Officers helped them and others clambering over the turnstiles as they realised that the crush outside was so intense. Children were put on shoulders and passed through.

Outside, a senior officer instructed mounted officers to form a cordon across the outer gates, closing the gates to 'slow down the crush at the turnstiles'. The blue outer gates were closed but were soon forced open again by the 'seething mass of people'. Two of the three mounted horses withdrew beyond the gates 'because of the serious risk of injury to people in the crowd'.

The third was in the middle of the crush. Its rider 'saw young children being passed over the heads of the crowd, and other people being pulled over the side barriers . . . Despite vehement pleading . . . the crowd would not take heed and the crushing intensified. The mood had now changed to one of panic with some hostility.' A senior officer stated: 'Conditions deteriorated, missiles were thrown, a beer can with beer spilling from it striking a police officer on horseback.' There was 'another surge . . . which appeared to be a concerted attempt to unseat this same officer and the horse started dancing about in fright'.

Appeals were broadcast over the loudspeakers from the police control box inside the stadium asking people in Leppings Lane not to push towards the turnstiles. A police Land Rover with a public address system was requested to go to the outside gates to 'assist with crowd control'. The driver appealed to the crowd to pull back, to 'no effect'. According to a mounted officer the announcements could not be heard above 'the noise of the crowd'. The officer in the Land Rover 'then called ground control . . . and asked for the kick-off to be delayed to offer the crowd something to stop the crushing but I was informed that it was too late'.

For Superintendent Marshall, himself caught up in the crowds, the situation was 'unprecedented', being 'no ordinary crowd of fans but an enormous press of people determined to enter the stadium come what may'. An inspector shouted that he should order the opening of the exit gates to relieve the intense crush. Marshall was 'unhappy to agree to the request', for 'to implement it would lead to uncontrolled access to the stadium and negate all [their] efforts to prevent hooliganism inside'.

The situation outside was now impossible. A senior officer not in the crush could see his colleague in the thick of it 'beginning to look frightened and, frankly, I was not surprised'. Communications between officers inside the turnstiles, in the stadium proper and in the control box were erratic as the radio system developed a fault at precisely the time it was most needed. Marshall could see the 'look of extreme anxiety' on his inspector's face. At that point, taking account 'that this was an Inspector speaking to me . . . I made my mind up immediately that the only practical way to prevent deaths outside would be to open the gates.

'I nodded . . . and told him that I would contact ground control. He returned to his position at the steel barrier and I pushed my way back to my vantage point on the bridge parapet. The situation was unchanged and worsening by the minute. It had outgrown our capacity to manage it effectively. The situation was unprecedented in my experience . . . I radioed ground control and asked for the gates at the Leppings Lane end of the ground to be opened. There was no acknowledgement.' Thinking his radio defective he used another officer's radio, 'and repeated my request for gates to be opened at the Leppings Lane end. There was no acknowledgement.'

* * *

The fans, however, gave a considerably different account of the crush. A group of three friends arrived at the ground just after 2.30 p.m. and waited in Leppings Lane to swap a stand ticket for a terrace ticket so they could stay together for the match. Eventually they went through the outer set of blue gates where mounted police officers were 'trying to keep people out while people between the gates and the turnstiles got through, thereby releasing the pressure on the turnstiles'. At this point there was a 'huge number of people' outside, with the 'main crush . . . outside the blue gates'.

A Merseyside doctor, also arriving just after 2.30 p.m. with three of his family, had stand tickets for the West Stand: 'Outside the ground there were a large number of supporters trying to get into a small number of turnstiles . . . there was very little police presence.' He saw no stewards outside the ground and, apparently, 'no attempt to marshal supporters into lines in advance of our approaching the turnstile areas'.

Close to the turnstiles 'the crush was becoming unpleasant' and he 'heard a police officer telling the supporters that it was their own fault for coming late'. His family went on and he withdrew to the wrought-iron fence. 'After a few minutes I thought I would try again. I could not see my family and assumed that they had managed to get through to the turnstiles . . . it was now much worse and again I withdrew.' He saw an officer trying to close one of the outer gates but it was impossible given the density of the crowd.

'I noticed that there was now a police landrover in the lane just outside the [outer] gates, and experience of 30 years as a Liverpool supporter told me that things were going badly wrong.' He went to the Land Rover and told a police officer, 'You've got to get a grip of this situation, it is out of control, there is going to be a tragedy.'

Another fan arriving with his brother noticed straight away that there were no queues, 'just, like, a crowd outside the turnstiles'. They joined the crowd, 'and then a lot of fans started coming down . . . behind us. That's when we first started getting into trouble . . . We started getting crushed at the turnstiles.'

After parking their car at 2.15 p.m., five friends arrived at the ground at approximately 2.30 p.m. As they walked to the ground the crowd was 'good-humoured' and they only saw 'one or two' people drinking, certainly not 'excessive numbers'. Within the outer gates there was 'already a mass of people' and nobody 'sectioning people into queues which is the kind of arrangement I am used to when I go to football matches at Liverpool . . .'

People became distressed as the 'crush got more and more' and the 'numbers we are talking about originally, obviously were swelled by the people arriving behind us . . . everybody was being pushed'. He, and others around him, were frightened and many in the crowd were shouting not to push as fans were getting hurt. Eventually he managed to enter through a turnstile.

'Once we got through . . . everybody thought that they were out of the worst of it because it was such a bad crush outside and we were relieved to get through.' Of the four who tried to enter through the turnstiles three met up inside. 'I distinctly remember a police officer saying, "Make your way straight in. There's plenty of room on the terraces, plenty of room inside."' And they walked straight down the tunnel opposite into pen 4.

One father with his son and two friends arrived by car around 2.30 p.m. They walked together to the ground. 'It was a normal day like so many other games that I've been to. No violence or heavy drinking, nothing like that.' At the ground the two friends went to a corner shop. They were going their own way because they had stand tickets. 'When we got to the turnstiles it was chaos. There were hardly any police. It was nothing like Anfield where the police outside the ground get everyone sorted out as they arrive.'

Keeping out of the crush at the turnstiles, they stood back by the side railings. There he bumped into a friend from work and had a quick chat. 'My attitude was, "It's an all-ticket game, we've got tickets and I'd rather get in a bit late than risk the crush." It was obvious people were in trouble and I didn't want to get involved.'

One of the striking things about so many of the fans'

recollections of the build-up to the crush at the turnstiles, is how few mention alcohol as an issue. In fact, in several accounts, fans commented on how little drunken behaviour there was. The real consensus of opinion was that there was no attempt to manage the crowd, no filtering and no queuing. 'It was inevitable that the areas between the blue gates and the turnstiles would become choked with people, and it happened.' The crush took its toll, with older people, children and many of the women protected by relatives and friends who were equally frightened for their lives.

'What I couldn't work out was where the crowd control had gone. It stands to sense that if you have people trying to find their turnstiles in a narrow space which leads to three different parts of the ground you need a filtering system further back.' This older fan was trying to find the turnstiles for the West Stand but, without guidance well before the turnstile area, he ended up with everyone else in the same place.

Another fan remembered that the previous year he had been 'marshalled' on arrival at Leppings Lane. This time he was caught in the crush without warning: 'I couldn't get my arms up and while people all around me were screaming, I could hear the fans arriving behind singing and chanting. They had no idea what it was like at the front.' While the mounted officer was shouting to the crowd behind, the horse was a danger to many of the fans in the crush. 'A horse might be effective in a loose crowd but when it is a packed crowd like that it was awful. As the horse panicked, people around were screaming that they were being kicked or stood on. It just caused more panic in the crowd.'

People were compressed against the side walls and against the walls between the turnstiles, some were bent double over the railings to the right of the turnstiles. To the left, others were hard up against a concertina exit gate which was particularly painful. Fans who were able climbed the wall to escape the crush, walked along the narrow ledge and on to the roof of the turnstiles, dropping down the other side.

Caught up in the crush, a woman and two children with tickets for the North Stand became trapped: 'There was no control, no queuing, there was nothing. I just pushed the kids in front of me, trying to get in . . . it just got tighter and tighter . . . there was a pregnant woman in front of me, she was screaming. It just got worse and worse.'

The mood was a mixture of panic and anger. With breathing so difficult and movement impossible many fans thought that they would lose consciousness. Others were screaming abuse at the police for allowing the crush to develop. Everyone knew that unless they managed to get to the turnstiles they were in real danger. As a young fan was passed over the heads of the crowd it was obvious that unless relief was brought at the back those at the front would die.

The crush at the turnstiles was entirely foreseeable. From Burnden Park onwards the danger of a large crowd arriving at a bottleneck entrance within minutes of the start of a match was obvious. That so much of Hillsborough's stadium was serviced by so few turnstiles in such a confined and limited area amounted to a serious risk. Only three years earlier an experienced police officer had made this very point.

In their accounts of the build-up the police almost universally laid the blame on the fans. They had arrived late through choice. Many had been drinking for hours and the whole place reeked of alcohol. Intent on forcing their way into the ground they had rushed the turnstiles, with no consideration for their own safety or that of others. Worse still, many were ticketless and determined to get in by hook or by crook. When the police tried to intervene, through public announcements, using horses or closing the outer gates, the fans were not only unresponsive but were abusive and violent. They were unbiddable.

For those trapped in the absurdly confined areas outside the turnstiles it was a different story. They had arrived around half an hour before the kick-off, could not easily find the right turnstiles and no one was stewarding the crowd. The old turnstiles were slow and within minutes a generally uncomfortable situation was dire. Undoubtedly some were drunk, others aggressive, but it was nothing out of the ordinary. What they considered unprecedented was the lack of organisation and direction. As they struggled to breathe, and those who were fortunate got through the turnstiles, it was little wonder they vented their anger on the police. They had just escaped death.

* * *

Hillsborough's police control box was in the south-west corner of the ground, elevated above the Leppings Lane terrace, giving a commanding view of the pens, below which stretched the width of the pitch. Around 2.30 p.m. the CCTV monitors showed the sudden build-up of fans in Leppings Lane and at the turnstiles. Chief Superintendent Duckenfield saw this, simultaneously making 'an assessment from the control box of the way in which the ground was filling'. He asked his assistant, Superintendent Murray, for his opinion, bearing in mind the crowd outside and the space inside'. Murray replied 'that with half an hour to kick-off we should get them all in on time'.

Both men then had a discussion about the 'circumstances under which we would consider delaying the kick-off'. Previously they had agreed that they would delay only if there was an 'identifiable problem' such as 'a serious incident, accident on the motorway or fog on the Pennines . . .' These were justifiable 'as opposed to those who had been brought to the area within a reasonable time but had chosen not to enter the ground as soon as possible'. This suggested that crowd safety and public order at the turnstiles hinged on some arbitrary judgement of whether or not a crush had a genuine cause.

Within a few minutes the congestion at the turnstiles had worsened and, according to Duckenfield, it was 'plain we had a difficulty'. Just at that moment he was 'overcome by events', namely, the radio link with 'officers in the operational field' went

86

down. Still he did not think it appropriate to delay the kick-off even though he was 'concentrating on the very serious situation outside the ground'. Delay 'was not my best weapon'. He resorted to appeals over the public address system and the deployment of 'extra officers to calm the crowd'.

It was at this moment that Superintendent Marshall, directing police operations in the crush, was 'having to shout to make himself heard on the radio'. A senior officer overheard a colleague shouting to Marshall 'for the [exit] gates to be opened to relieve the pressure on the turnstiles'. At 2.47 p.m. Marshall's request for the gates to be opened reached the control box.

Detective Inspector McRobbie, off duty but observing the police operation in his own time, was standing at the back of the control box. He could see from the monitor what was happening at the turnstiles but 'sensed they were well in control'. When Marshall's request came in he thought, 'you can't open the gates or you will lose control over who is admitted . . . and may create a difficult public order situation for police inside the ground'.

Duckenfield was thinking along similar lines. His instinct was to refuse: 'It would have defeated the objectives of the Operational Order . . . drunken fans may get in; people who had got drink; people who had got missiles and people who were without tickets . . .' It was an instinct derived in the expectations of 'hooliganism' rather than the imperatives of safety.

Looking at the monitor, Duckenfield saw gate C 'burst open' and thought 'the gate's burst open anyway, why am I being asked?' McRobbie also saw this, and witnessed 'a surge of people rush into the ground'. He said out loud, 'The gates have been forced,' but the gate was soon closed. Gate C had not been forced but was opened to eject a fan. Outside, Marshall saw this and an inspector 'physically pulling people from the press [of the crowd] under the barrier and thrusting them bodily through the gate'.

It was tense in the control box. Duckenfield was reflecting on

Marshall's first request when he came through a second time. There was a sense of urgency in his voice, a 'demand': 'Open the gates or someone is going to be seriously injured or killed.' Duckenfield's reflection is exactly how McRobbie remembered it.

Duckenfield, the match commander with virtually no experience of policing football, in a ground with which he was unfamiliar, faced a massive dilemma. He thought: 'A man who I have known for many years, a man who I respect and admire, was demanding of me something that I would not normally give . . . I took the view that Superintendent Marshall was telling me that unless I opened the gates there would be serious injury and possible death . . .'

The man with whom the final decision rested was 'all consumed'. Superintendent Murray broke the long silence: 'Mr Duckenfield, are you going to open the gate?' In his hand was a personal radio on 'talk through', ready for all officers to hear the reply. The pause seemed to last for ever. Then, as if thinking aloud, Duckenfield muttered, 'If there's likely to be death or serious injury outside I have no option but to open the gates.' He looked at Murray and said, 'Open the gates.'

Chapter Three

'FINDING THEIR OWN LEVEL'

Most audiences arrive at theatres, cinemas, concerts and sports events in the half-hour before the main event starts, especially if they already have tickets. Often, they meet earlier with friends, go for a meal or a couple of drinks. It happens every evening in every town. Only football assumes that fans will turn up hours before the game. It is a tradition that became a necessary expectation. How else could so many fans be processed through so few turnstiles?

Major stadiums hosting sell-out matches depended on the crowd's goodwill to start filling the ground well before kick-off. Clubs did nothing to encourage this. Pre-match entertainment was rare, other than badly distorted music played over poorly maintained loudspeakers. Yet, for some fans 'getting to the ground early' was part of their routine: soaking up the atmosphere, reading the match programme cover to cover and chatting with others that they only ever saw at the game.

On the terraces, surrounded by familiar faces, fans had their own 'spec'. They were on first-name terms with those around them but knew nothing of their lives in the world beyond the turnstiles. There was a kind of intimacy of the terraces cemented by years of shared excitement, joy and despair. Yet despite the camaraderie, terraces, often open to the elements, were not pleasant places to while away the hours.

Hillsborough's Leppings Lane terrace was just such a place. 'The first thing I noticed was what a dump it was. I got in about 1.15 p.m., walked around the back of the stand – there was nothing there. The toilets were awful. We went down the tunnel and the first thing that struck me was the pens. They were really small, surrounded by fences. It was nothing like the Kop at Anfield.' These were the sentiments of so many fans seeing the Leppings Lane pens for the first time.

As more arrived the two central pens began to fill. It was a warm, dry day and many of the fans sat on the steps taking the weight off their feet. 'It was a good laugh. We were just takin' the piss, shoutin' to our mates and stuff like that. Everyone was really up for it.'

'It's like you've known people for years. You just start talkin' and others join in. You don't know them, never seen them before in your life, but you get on 'cos it's the team. It's great.'

Soon both pens began to fill quite rapidly. Even open terraces always filled from the centre outwards as many fans wanted a 'spec' right behind the goal. At Hillsborough there was another, later to prove fatal, reason. As fans with Leppings Lane tickets entered through the designated turnstiles, they emerged directly opposite the tunnel under the West Stand. There seemed to be no other way on to the terraces.

At about 1.45 p.m. three friends entered pen 3, one of the two central pens, and were settling down to wait for the game. Within 20 minutes they began to feel uncomfortable: 'the crushing behind the goal . . . was as bad as I can remember experiencing'. Still an hour to go, they decided to 'find a more comfortable position elsewhere'.

Moving sideways they were surprised to find their path blocked by fences; 'with strenuous effort we eventually forced our way back to the sole exit and our entry point of the central tunnel'. They stood in the 'open courtyard' between the tunnel and the turnstiles, 'recovering from [their] exertions and relishing the fresh air'.

Behind the West Stand they watched a 'steady stream of fans making their way down the tunnel' with 'no steward or policeman to check this flow'. Although at that time neither central pen was overcrowded each was uncomfortably full. The three friends had to push and shove to make it back to the tunnel. Yet no one was monitoring the pens. As they passed through the turnstiles, fans were searched but from there on they were left to their own devices.

The three friends eventually moved to the 'empty terracing of the left-hand pen'. Here, just a fence-width away from the packed central pens, fans were sitting on the steps, reading newspapers, basking in the sun. Over the fence the crowd was buoyant although movement was increasingly difficult. Some pushed back to find a 'better spec' or nipped out to the toilet. The tunnel was still busy as the steady flow continued.

There was no accurate way of knowing how many fans were in each pen. The two central pens had a designated combined capacity of 2,100 with 10,100 for the whole terrace. But all that was recorded at the turnstiles was the overall number; individually the pens were left vulnerable to overcrowding.

At about 12 noon Chief Inspector Creasor had asked Superintendent Murray if the Leppings Lane terrace was to be filled one pen at a time. Murray replied that all pens should be open from the outset and fans would be left to 'find their own level'. It was a chilling reminder of the complacency which had come to infect crowd management and safety at football matches.

Duckenfield was of the mistaken opinion that the police had no responsibility for ensuring there was no overcrowding. For him 'crowd management and control' was 'the responsibility of the club'. He presumed that club stewards were managing the crowd in the pens but he had not liaised with the club over distribution of responsibilities.

Photographs taken from the North Stand around 2.30 p.m. show clearly the uneven distribution of the crowd between pens.

While pens 3 and 4 were packed, solid towards the front, the pens on each side had plenty of room. Although taken from the other side of the pitch, the view on the photographs differed little from the view of those in the control box.

* * *

It was to prove a sad irony that many of those who had managed to escape the crush at the turnstiles, standing back by the fence above the river, were among the first to enter through gate C. 'We were just hanging back waiting for the crowd to thin out and the big blue gate opened. They called us through and we went. I had my ticket out but no one was interested. I thought, "Great, we're in," and walked straight down the tunnel in front of us.'

'It was incredible, one minute I was in the crowd outside the ground and couldn't move, screaming for all I was worth, then I was pulled out and found myself by the big blue gate. Then next thing it opened and the police shouted, "Go through, don't bother with your ticket, straight in." And we all did. The tunnel was opposite. I don't remember seeing any stewards or anyone. We went down the tunnel and into the area right of the fence. It was really packed.'

A young mother arrived at the ground at about 2.30 p.m. 'My friend and I decided to move away to the side to get away from the police horses. We stood and watched the crowds trying to get in, the police asking one another what to do. By now we didn't know what the time was and getting into the match seemed a low priority. Then someone opened "the gate" and because we were standing at the side we were among some of the first through.'

There was no pushing or jostling: 'We didn't fight or run through – we walked quickly so we didn't lose each other. Straight in front of us was the tunnel where we could see daylight at the end. We didn't even notice the two side entrances and there was no one there to tell us where to go.' A young woman outside had been worried; 'I said, "Don't worry . . . it won't be as bad once we get inside." How wrong I was.'

While some fans remember seeing police officers as they walked through the gate, it was clear that they played no part in directing the crowd. Within minutes, over 2,000 fans walked into the ground. Most went down the tunnel and into the back of the full pens. The pens were now holding twice their capacity. At first there was enough room to push through to the front. Moments later the pens were packed so tightly that no one could move their arms, let alone their bodies. 'I've never known anything like it. I've been in crushes where you can ease the pressure by turning or finding a bit of space. This was different, it was a real heavy pressure. Then it hit me, I couldn't breathe.'

With the teams on the pitch, the crowd was noisy, chanting and cheering the names of the players as they were announced. But in pens 3 and 4 people were screaming while others fell silent, unconscious. 'I couldn't believe what was going on. No one could move, not an inch. People around me were contorted in whatever position they'd been compressed. Heads were locked between arms and shoulders, the faces gasping in panic.

'I'd been in packed crowds before but I knew this was different. We'd all been uncomfortable for nearly half an hour but thought it would sort itself out once the ground was full, everyone in and the game under way. It didn't happen. Once the teams were out it seemed to tighten. I was bent forward, from the waist, my full weight pressing down on people in front of me. At first the pain in my back was sharp but then it was in my chest. Suddenly it hit me, I was going to die.'

In pen 3 it was bedlam. The pressure was so great that the fans at the front were squashed into the perimeter fencing, their faces distorted by the mesh. Most of these people had fallen silent, either already unconscious or unable to snatch breath. 'I suddenly realised that the guy next to me was dead, his eyes were bulging and his tongue out. It was sheer horror. People had lost control of their bodies and the smell was horrible.

'I saw a young boy go down and knew that was it for him. He

went under people's feet but no one could do anything about it. The pressure was so great. I remember loads of people shouting at the police on the track to open the gates but they just seemed transfixed. They did nothing.

'We went into pen 3, got through the crowd, took up positions to the right of the gate . . . just got pushed over a bit and then it started getting tighter where you couldn't move. You were just crushed against people . . . there was a lad in front of us who vomited on his jumper and there was another lad who fell on to the floor . . .

'We were fighting for our lives. At one point I looked across to him [his son] . . . he looked a bit pale but I thought he was okay and I was going to die . . . My wrist watch was ripped off and somebody bit a chunk out of my shoulder because they must have been in agony . . . People were shouting at him [police officer] to open the gate or do something and he was just ignoring these cries.' His son died.

'Before I got out of the gate there was a lot of shouting to the police officers . . . on the track, for help, to do something, but it was as though he [police officer at the gate of pen 3] was waiting for an order to come through before he would act.' Another fan went through the gate when it 'gave way' but the 'policeman got hold of us and pushed us back in and shut the gate.' The fans had no chance to help themselves. 'I was forced down, sort of diagonally towards the front of the pen. I think I was turned round, then facing the people, not the pitch. I couldn't breathe and I was just confined, in agony, and thought I was going to die.'

A fan who felt he had been 'propelled forward' by the steepness of the tunnel ended up in pen 3 facing back up the terrace. He tried to manoeuvre himself in front of a barrier. 'There was no way I could use my arms . . . I was on tiptoes most of the time and I made a conscious decision to concentrate on my breathing . . . Seeing the colours on the faces, one lad I know, he died stood next to me, so I gave up on watching people around me and concentrated on my breathing.' He lost consciousness.

Some fans just sank to the floor. 'I got to that stage where I couldn't get myself up then someone's hand came out of the blue and dragged me up by my hair . . . The person's hand lost grip, the hand came again and dragged me up again. This time with a bit of help from myself he managed to get me in a head-lock.' Having saved a life, both the rescuer and his brother died.

The game was under way but the sheer desperation on the terraces was fully evident from the faces of those pressed up against the fences. Then a crush barrier, just feet away from pen 3's perimeter gate, collapsed under the weight of the crowd from the back to the front of the terrace. Those behind the barrier went over the buckled metal. Those behind them were compressed downwards on to the pile of bodies. Most had no chance as they went down in a tangled mass of limbs. It was now almost a carbon copy of Burnden Park in 1946, when a corroded crush barrier collapsed under excessive weight stretching to the back of the pen.

At the rear of the pen, fans struggled to climb up into the West Stand. 'A group of lads were pulling people up to the top tier. My friend and I were pulled up but even then we didn't realise what was happening.' To the sides, fans climbed over the lateral fences and into the half-empty adjacent pens. 'The lad gave me a bunk up and I just dragged myself over. I just thought that if I got spiked at least I wouldn't die.'

The most harrowing experiences were endured by fans at the front of both pens. Initially, as some tried to climb the overhanging perimeter fence, police officers on the track pushed them back into the crowd. Trying to make it to the gates, they felt the bodies of the dying beneath their feet. It was unavoidable, the vice had tightened, forcing them over those who had already fallen.

* * *

Eddie and Adam Spearritt's day had started like so many other match days when fans travel away. They met up with Eddie's friends, Tony Curran and Derek McNiven, just before midday at Runcorn's Norton Arms. After a quick drink they left for Sheffield via the M56 and the Snake Pass. It was a beautiful journey and they arrived in Sheffield at 2 p.m., an hour before kick-off. Leaving the car about half a mile from the ground, they walked the short distance in the company of many other Liverpool fans. Everyone was in good spirits.

At the ground, about 2.30 p.m., Eddie bumped into an old friend. While they stood chatting, Tony and Derek went to a shop, before leaving to find their seats. Adam and Eddie had Leppings Lane terrace tickets and walked to the turnstile area. It was packed, so they stood back against the fence above the River Don. According to Eddie, 'there was no point in trying to get in. We had tickets, there was no hurry and it was pointless getting crushed.'

A blue exit gate, directly in front of them, opened and they were called through, 'fully expecting to go through some turnstiles and be met by stewards and police, but there were neither'. Their tickets still intact in their pockets, they 'were near enough the first through'. Eddie recalls only 'the tunnel, it was in front of you, you could see the pitch out the other end. I can't remember going down.'

Once through they went left into pen 4. Eddie has no recollection of emerging from the tunnel or moving down the packed terrace. 'All I remember is being down the front. I could almost reach the gate in the perimeter fence.' The teams were on the pitch. Eddie and Adam were 'made up' to see that Alan Hansen, the 'boss man', was playing; 'then it all happened so quickly'. Neither saw the kick-off as the crush in the pen became unbearable, the screams and the pleas of the dying caught up in the roar of the crowd.

'We didn't actually see the players coming down to the goal. The crush came, and I've heard this word several times but I don't reckon they're right, this word surge. This wasn't a surge. It was like a vice getting tighter and tighter and tighter. I turned Adam round to me. He was obviously in distress. There was a police officer just slightly to my right about five or six feet away and I started begging him to open the gate . . . I was screaming, I literally mean screaming.

'Adam at this time had fainted and my actual words were, "My lovely son is dying," and I begged him [the officer] to help and he didn't do anything. He just stood there looking at me. I realised that he wasn't going to do anything so I grabbed hold of Adam. He had a tracksuit on and I grabbed hold of his lapels and I tried to lift him over the fence, and the fence is about ten feet or thereabouts with spikes coming in. I couldn't lift him.

'So then I started punching the fence in the hope that I could punch it down . . . I wasn't successful and all I managed to do was to make my hands double in size and full of holes where I had actually punched the fence. No one opened that gate. Right at the beginning when I was begging the officer to open the gate, if he had opened it then I know I could have got Adam out. I know that because I was there and I know what the situation was.' Panic-stricken and desperate, Eddie followed Adam into unconsciousness.

* * *

While people died in pens 3 and 4, what on earth was going through the minds of the police officers around them? Photographs taken as the game kicked off, show the dense overcrowding of the central pens alongside the sparsely populated end pens. This must have been obvious. The chilling screams and desperate pleas from fans were audible from the perimeter track. Awful though it sounds, those pleas were ignored. Fans attempting to escape the fatal crush over the fence or through the gates were prevented.

It is hard to believe that the struggle for life, the reality of the central pens, was mistaken for crowd violence or a pitch invasion. There was no precedent for fans fighting among themselves and there were no signs of blows being exchanged. In fact, all the evidence was of fans trying to help each other.

Difficulties with the police radio system at the crucial moment of opening gate C meant that officers inside the ground were unaware of the problems outside. They had no means of knowing that just as the teams ran on to the pitch over 2,000 fans converged on the tunnel. Within minutes the central pens went from being packed to full compression, as bodies were squeezed against each other, the barriers and the fencing.

Outside the stadium, officers were relieved that no one had been seriously injured or killed in the crush at the turnstiles. Opening gate C had worked, instantly recovering a near-fatal situation. They were equally unaware of the consequences of opening the gate. The bottleneck was simply transferred to the tunnel and the central pens. Those who had endured the crush outside were now confronted with a more serious crush inside.

The plain, obvious truth was that in the circumstances no one who went into the central pens could escape the crush. With the exception of the energetic few, strong enough to climb over the side fences or be pulled up into the West Stand, it was a matter of chance rather than judgement as to whether they lived or died.

A police inspector in the West Stand had a 'clear aerial view' of the terracing below. At 2.30 p.m. he thought that the central pens were 'reasonably full' with room for more fans behind. There was 'plenty of standing room' in the end pens. Unlike the descriptions of the fans, many of whom had been in considerable discomfort for half an hour, he saw nothing that 'caused [him] concern as to the safety of the . . . crowd' up to the kick-off. At this point he went to the back of the stand from where he could see fans climbing on the perimeter fences. He then left the stand.

On the perimeter track an officer could see a 'lot of pushing' in the crowded central pens as the teams came on to the pitch. While the players warmed up, he 'continued to monitor the fans'. At one point the perimeter gate to pen 3 'flew open and the crowd moved back from the fence. I closed the gate immediately, no one

98

tried to get out.' There was 'no great pressure on fans at the front'. Yet the gate sprang open again, 'and I attempted to re-close it but was unable to do so from the pressure of the fans'.

Joined by other officers, they closed the gate; 'I am unaware of whether or not the gate was fully locked at this point, but the fans were again screaming and shouting, "We're squashed, open the gates, you bastards."' He stepped back and 'saw people were tight up to the fence, particularly two or three young women to my right of the gate'. Taking out his personal radio he 'tried to pass a message asking if we could open the gate to relieve pressure'. He received no reply.

'The noise was terrible and people were screaming, a different type of scream and I opened the gate fully. I saw people were being forced on to the fence and turning blue. I passed another radio message, "This is serious, people are dying in here." I attempted to pull people out of the gate but they were jammed solid. The female . . . was turning a dark colour and I gestured for the fans to get back but was spat at and someone shouted, "Fuck off, copper." I got down and returned to the gate where a number of officers had arrived.'

There was considerable disagreement over whether or not the perimeter gates were locked. The Operational Order instructed that the gates should be locked at all times, only opened in an emergency and then with the permission of a senior officer. Chief Superintendent Mole, however, stated that the gates were not locked as such but secured by a spring-loaded bolt. The view of the fans, and this was confirmed by the officer at the gate to pen 3, was that whether or not the gates were technically locked the officers on duty sought permission from a higher authority before opening them. In the circumstances it was permission not easily found.

As the gates to the track opened and fans spilled over the fences or were hauled up into the West Stand, the scale of the crowd problem began to dawn throughout the stadium, even though the match was under way. Up in the police control box, Duckenfield, Murray and their colleagues had a perfect view of the central pens. Elevated above the terrace they were only a stone's throw away from the crush, also served by a range of strategically place CCTV cameras.

At 2.45 p.m. Duckenfield noted that both central pens were 'getting on for being quite full'. As far as he was concerned the responsibility for regulating the 'inflow' into the pens lay with the club stewards, an opinion at odds with the decision taken earlier by Murray when, in consultation with another senior officer, he had considered the method of filling the pens. Also, Duckenfield thought that part of the responsibilities of officers up in the West Stand was to monitor the pens, 'and I would expect them as trained officers, and trained in crowd control, to assess the situation and if they saw a difficulty to relay that back'.

His decision to open gate C was taken in 'a very difficult situation' but he 'did not follow it up with a direct instruction' to monitor or seal off the tunnel. Confident that police officers 'were patrolling the concourse area', he presumed that through their training they would 'act on their own initiative' and 'would have hoped they would have taken some action in the tunnel'. As for the stewards, he 'hoped' that they were in the concourse area although he knew Murray had been unsuccessful in contacting the club's chief steward to let him know that gate C had been opened. Finally, he assumed that, 'if the terracing was overcrowded . . . reasonable people going down that tunnel would surely turn round and walk back'.

Once gate C was opened, Duckenfield was looking for 'movement . . . and difficulties in the crowd as a result . . . and from where I was I did not appreciate there was a density'. Even after such large numbers entered through gate C, 'I had been watching the Leppings Lane terrace and I had not seen an indication that made me think that there was anything untoward occurring . . . the terrace appeared in order.'

Having relieved the desperation outside, there was no real awareness that the site of congestion had been transferred. With so many people released from one bottleneck and encouraged to 'flow', like molten lava, they had to converge at another point. To anyone familiar with the movement of crowds and the layout of Hillsborough, the tunnel – opposite gate C – drew the flow down its slope and into the central pens. It was the only obvious route.

Watching the terrace, Duckenfield saw fans climbing out of the pens to the sides and at the front. It did not strike him that they were trying to escape a crush or that the crowd was dangerously packed because of the influx through gate C. Then he saw a perimeter gate open, apparently without authority. 'My perception is that . . . there were one or two fans coming on to the perimeter track . . . I thought individuals were taking advantage of the gate being opened to come out on to the perimeter track . . . I thought it was a pitch invasion.'

And this was the message conveyed to officers around the ground as they were instructed over their personal radios to rush to the Leppings Lane perimeter track. One officer, without a radio, was told to go to the pitch: 'I assumed the message had come to our serial sergeant . . . and was spread to us all by word of mouth . . . I was under the impression that I was going to stem a pitch invasion at the Leppings Lane end . . .' Another officer, on turnstile duty, 'at approximately 3.06 p.m. . . . was informed that there had been a pitch invasion' and went immediately to the pitch.

An officer outside the ground heard a radio instruction, 'All officers to the pitch.' He climbed through the turnstiles and, with other officers, ran towards the South Stand, 'believing there must have been some sort of crowd trouble'. At about 3.06 p.m. another officer 'was informed that there was a pitch invasion and that officers had been requested to attend on the pitch'. At the same time, an officer at the other end of the ground recalled being instructed to 'attend inside the ground at the Leppings Lane end'.

Once inside the ground he 'could see supporters milling around on the side of the playing area. I then started to run to what I thought was crowd disorder.'

Even when the fatal consequences in the pens were recognised, they were still viewed and transmitted from the control box as crowd disorder. As police officers converged on the Leppings Lane terraces they were told their objective was to stem a pitch invasion. The senior officers in the control box, like officers in the ground, did not anticipate disaster because they were looking for trouble. The mindset was hooliganism.

* * *

As the officers arrived at the perimeter fence the full realisation of what had happened hit them: '. . . it was immediately apparent that this was not a pitch invasion . . . There were a large number of dead/dying and injured persons in the crowd. People were crushed hard against the fence . . . a blob of humanity crushed behind them not moving. Some crushed against the fence were blue violet in colour, others had glazed eyes, apparently dead, others were covered in vomit.'

Another officer 'could see that people were disfigured as their faces were pinned to the wire meshing . . . it was clear that a number were dead and others were dying. Some of the people pinned to the fence were unable to move. Their skins had turned to a blue/purple colour and their eyes were lifeless.'

This was the grip of the vice which had been tightening for nearly half an hour. Fans had been 'forced up into the air by the pressure . . . in great distress their faces distorted . . . they appeared to be moving in slow motion. I could see a great disaster was happening and I felt so helpless to prevent it.' As the game was stopped, an officer arriving behind the goal was horrified by the realisation that 'the first three or four rows of supporters within my view were dead'.

'They were still in an upright position packed into each other, some beyond the first few rows were dying as the pressure from the people behind continued. All the dead were purple in colour and some had bulging eyes. There was a considerable amount of vomit. I could see that some people had attempted to protect the persons in front as their arms were wrapped around them and crushed into the chest of the person protected. Some were so small that you could only see their heads.'

Another officer described what he found as 'total chaos'. Climbing on to the perimeter fence he 'leant over the top to assist fans in climbing over to escape the crush'. In pen 2 an officer pulled fans out of pen 3 with the help of other fans. As they came over the spiked railings he dropped them into the arms of fans behind him. He tried to 'select people who were clearly in distress'. Those 'less distressed . . . behaved impeccably, without panic and ignoring their own fears for personal safety'.

At the front of pen 3 an officer saw a young boy close to the front. 'He was still alive and had his fingers on the steel mesh. He was turning purple and looking straight into my eyes. I was totally helpless and could not reach [him]. I jumped down . . . and attempted to push my hands through the metal fence to pull him clear. It was futile. I spoke to him and told him to hang on and held his hands.'

Just as the game was abandoned, at approximately 3.06 p.m., many of those who could move in pen 3 were in a state of panic, trying to climb over those dying to reach the fence and the hands of those reaching over to pull them out. It was then that the gruesome reality of the collapsed barrier became evident to those outside the pen.

By the perimeter gate in pen 3 was 'a pile of people . . . in a heap, reaching ten to twelve feet back from the fence. My immediate thought was that people had just fell [sic] and because some of the crowding had been relieved, they were all going to get up.' Another officer estimated that there were 50 people 'intertwined' in the pile, 'a large number of them were/appeared dead. They were lifeless, their eyes glazed . . . others were moaning, others trapped by their limbs were screaming for help . . . [they] appeared to be six or seven deep.'

One of the first officers into pen 3 climbed over the radial fence from pen 2. He realised that many people were dead or dying but tried to 'free people from the entangled pile'. He was 'surrounded by supporters trying to help'. But the perimeter gate 'was still closed . . . a pile of bodies under it'. He could see fellow officers pulling fans over the fence and shouted to a senior officer 'to get the gate open'. This was done and officers on the track were instructed to enter the pen.

Unavoidably, 'entry to the pen was gained only by climbing over and on to the bodies in order to get behind the spaghetti of bodies'. The officer already in the pen stated that there was 'no way to select the living from the dead in the pile' as fans were dragged from the pile and out through the gate. Another officer worked with a 'chain of officers'; he passed the bodies he recovered to the officers and 'out through the gate and on to the pitch'.

Who lived, who died was a matter of luck: 'I found a man/ youth . . . still alive, he was breathing, however he was trapped from the neck down. He was pushed hard against the concrete wall below the metal barrier fence. The youth was unconscious. I shouted at him and remember slapping his face and telling him to hold on. We removed the bodies that were around him and he was subsequently passed through the gate. I saw officers and fans pulling the perimeter fence down with their bare hands.'

These deeply distressing scenes unfolded directly in front of the police control box. They were taking place as the game was stopped at 3.06 p.m. and soon after. Yet, when the Assistant Chief Constable went to the control box to find out what was happening, Duckenfield was 'unable to give an accurate account of what the situation was other than a possible pitch invasion which had resulted in [the police] stopping the game'.

Not long after 3.15 p.m., Graham Kelly and Glen Kirton of

the Football Association, accompanied by Graham Mackrell, the Sheffield Wednesday club secretary, also arrived at the control box. Duckenfield told them that Liverpool fans had forced gate C, causing an inrush into the stadium, down the tunnel and on to the backs of those already in the central pens.

Duckenfield stated, 'The blunt truth [was] that we had been asked to open a gate. I was not being deceitful . . . we were all in a state of shock, one might say.' He continued, 'I thought it correct to collect my thoughts and to assess the situation . . . I just thought at that stage that I should not communicate fully the situation . . . I may have misled Mr Kelly.' He did. And Graham Kelly unwittingly and in good faith repeated Duckenfield's lie to the waiting media. Within minutes it was broadcast around the world: an appalling disaster was happening and Liverpool fans were blamed.

* * *

As the game stopped, the chaos and confusion behind the goal escalated. Fans, many in shock from their own survival, worked frantically alongside police officers and St John's Ambulance officers to pull the dying and injured from the pens. It was a near impossible task. The pens were packed, the force of compression stretched to the back, and the perimeter fence gates were locked. On the other side of the only perimeter gate in pen 3 was a pile of bodies. Fans tore at the fencing, equipped only with bare hands and brute force. Eventually they managed to break through. But vital minutes had been lost.

The Liverpool doctor, who earlier stood back from the crush at the turnstiles, had since entered the ground: 'I became aware of a man crying and beseeching the police: "There are kids dying in there," he said, "You've got to do something." He seemed to have come out of the terraced area. The police were unresponsive to him.' When the doctor got into the West Stand he could see the problem. Fans were being pulled up from the central pens below and were trying to climb out over the fences. 'I could see people lying on the pitch, unattended . . . the overall impression was of a large and growing number of casualties and not much response . . . supporters impatient and angry at the slowness of response to the emergencies.'

On the pitch a number of police officers stood helpless, frozen in disbelief, unable to respond to what they saw. Whatever Duckenfield's faith in police training, few were prepared for such an eventuality. In the heat of the moment photographers, at Hillsborough to record a football match, moved between rescuers and the dying, photographing the determined attempts, often in vain, to save lives. The strongest images were the faces pressed against the wire fencing. Inevitably, those with cameras were given short shrift by angry fans. Ironically, in their possession was evidence later to take on real significance.

Police officers around the tunnel pulled fans back, demanding that they move to the outer concourse area. Those in the tunnel had no way of knowing what was happening at the front of the pens. Eventually the officers, themselves in the dark, pushed their way into the pens. As fans left, there was enough room to carry people out through the tunnel to the concourse area. This led to the rumour that some fans had actually collapsed in the tunnel.

Without information, the Forest supporters on the Spion Kop, like many of the police, thought they were witnessing a pitch invasion. Inevitably, they taunted the Liverpool fans who they thought were disrupting the match with violent behaviour. Soon, however, the grim reality began to dawn around the stadium: there were serious casualties, possibly deaths. Many were dying literally before their eyes, hundreds were injured – some seriously. This was not crowd violence, but they were violent deaths.

Within minutes the area around the goalmouth, the scene of so many joyous celebrations, was like a battlefield. Bodies, dragged from the pens, were laid on the turf, most on their backs. Fans with broken limbs, bruised ribs or other injuries sat or lay, half-prone, among the seriously injured. Others ran among the growing number desperately seeking lost loved ones or friends. Around those not moving, clusters of fans and officers knelt trying to breathe life into the lifeless, to start hearts that had apparently stopped.

Few people knew what they were doing. However sophisticated British education may be, it poorly prepares its citizens for saving lives, even the administering of basic first aid. The only medical assistance officially on duty was provided by thirty St John's Ambulance officers, five of whom were young cadets. It was remarkable that at major sports and leisure events throughout Britain, attended by tens of thousands of spectators, the only medical provision came from a voluntary organisation working for a donation to their charity. A cheap price for an essential service.

Fans were beside themselves: 'I tried to remember what to do. The guy was barely alive and needed immediate, proper treatment. I pinched his nose and breathed into his mouth. He'd been sick, but I tried. He just wouldn't respond. As he got weaker someone else was pumping his chest. None of us could save him but I'm sure with oxygen and proper treatment he'd have lived.'

A police officer in one of the pens remembered fighting to save a young man who had gone down on the steps: 'I gave him mouth-to-mouth and desperately willed him to live. His face was staring back at me and I was convinced he would breathe. These flecks were showering down on me, like snow, and then I realised that they were trying to bend the fencing to get into the pens to help. It was paint cracking from the fencing. I tried so hard, but he'd gone.'

Inevitably, the shock and the frustration took its toll on fragile tempers. A young fan separated from his friends typified the emotions and reactions of many: 'I was on the pitch. I just hadn't a clue. I wanted to help but I couldn't see how . . . I was shaking, terrified. Then I saw these three coppers, just standing there. I'd seen one of them before at the fence. I lost it, pointed at them, and screamed, "You fuckin' murderin' bastards." I said it 'cos I meant it . . . I meant it 'cos I felt it. It was awful.'

As the bodies multiplied there was congestion on the pitch. Those first pulled from the pens had been put down near to the fence, blocking the way for those still being pulled out. A St John's Ambulance drove through the gap between the North Stand and the Spion Kop on to the pitch. It carried three stretchers, complementing the six held under the North Stand in the Club's first aid room. Yet stretchers for more than a hundred people were now required. Those dying had suffered asphyxiation and needed proper medical care and aid. To get them to hospital it was necessary to carry them the entire length of the pitch to the main ground access area off Penistone Road or back out through the tunnel to Leppings Lane, in the hope that ambulances were on their way.

With the majority of the dying and injured evacuated from the pens on to the pitch, carrying was the only option. Realising the urgent need for paramedical attention and hospital treatment the rescuers, mainly fans, ran to the trackside and tore down the advertising hoardings to use as makeshift stretchers. Bodies were placed on the hoardings and fans ran the length of the pitch to try and save lives. It was a tremendous, spontaneous effort but it underlined the inadequacy of medical support.

A police officer in the thick of the evacuation of pen 3 helped carry fans on to the pitch and tried to give those unconscious the 'kiss of life': 'The first came round and some other people took him away. I then helped to get another one from the gate, laid him on the pitch and again administered mouth-to-mouth resuscitation, but it became apparent that this person was not going to respond . . . I realised now that the incident was far more serious than perhaps anyone could have imagined.'

With a group of fans, the officer used a hoarding to carry one of the injured to the far end of the pitch and out between the Spion Kop and the North Stand. Not knowing where to go, they found an ambulance and put the person in, immediately returning to pen 3 where a sergeant was 'shouting at us all to work harder and faster'. The officer went into the pen and helped evacuate those being 'passed over' the lateral fence.

A young man, apparently evacuated through pen 3's perimeter gate, was found alive on the pitch by two other fans and two police officers. He needed urgent medical attention. Loading him on to a hoarding, they set off towards the other end of the pitch. Halfway across they could see he was 'going' and stopped to give mouth-to-mouth resuscitation and then heart massage.

While they were trying to keep him alive, an 'unidentified doctor' told them to continue with resuscitation. This they did but realised that the young man was dying despite their efforts. The doctor returned, quickly checking the young man. Then 'he indicated that there was nothing further we could do'. The young man was carried into the gymnasium; assumed dead on the basis of a cursory examination by an unidentified doctor.

At the Spion Kop end of the ground, a police officer saw a man 'lying on the pitch' but 'hadn't seen anyone deposit him there'. He heard someone say, 'Don't worry about him, he's dead.' A black coat covered the upper part of this man's body. Realising that he was lying in the path of an ambulance leaving the pitch the officer moved the body to one side. Then two fans shouted for help with the resuscitation of a young boy and the officer gave 'mouth-to-mouth resuscitation'. He did this for an estimated 15 minutes, registering the boy's pulse and breathing. 'I then placed this youth on an advertising board and with the assistance of a fireman I removed him from the pitch.' Eventually the officer found an ambulance and accompanied the boy to hospital, where he died in intensive care.

Meanwhile, the serious lack of communication between the police themselves, as well as with the other emergency services, continued. In the control box, as the game was stopped, Duckenfield instructed that a message be sent to headquarters requesting operational support. An officer on duty at the police driving school typified the response to this request: 'At that stage it was assumed there was fighting or a crowd invasion.' Down on the pitch, however, Murray – sent by Duckenfield to find out what was happening – radioed to the control box for a 'fleet of ambulances'.

At 3.13 p.m., a request for fire service hydraulic cutting equipment was made via police headquarters. Fans had been pressed hard up against the perimeter fencing for at least 15 minutes when this request was made. Within ten minutes the appliances arrived at the back of Leppings Lane. The police outside the ground, unaware of the crush in the pens, initially told the fire officers that they were not needed. It was only when another police officer arrived on the scene looking for resuscitators that the enormity of what was happening inside was realised.

Again, owing to confused messages, an emergency tender arrived at the Spion Kop end of the ground. Then it was unable to proceed along the private South Stand road because of its height. Reversing out and driving round to Leppings Lane added nearly ten minutes to its arrival time. By the time the cutting equipment arrived at the perimeter fencing the last of the bodies had been carried from the pens.

The South Yorkshire Metropolitan Ambulance Service (SYMAS) had a minimal and slightly ambiguous presence at Hillsborough. Two SYMAS officers, one ambulance and crew were at the ground and another ambulance was on standby. The officers, accommodated in the South Stand for club matches, were not allocated seats and stood by the ground access between the North Stand and the Spion Kop. On realising that there were problems on the Leppings Lane terrace the officers went to help.

Minutes earlier a senior police officer heard a reference over his personal radio to possible injuries at Leppings Lane. He immediately requested police headquarters to establish if ambulances were needed. The response from the control box was that no injuries had been reported but to keep 'standing by'. It was only after the game had stopped, at 3.07 p.m., that headquarters told SYMAS of the possible need for ambulances. Then came Murray's request from the perimeter track for a 'fleet of ambulances'. The first ambulances arrived at 3.13 p.m. at Leppings Lane and 3.17 p.m. at the Penistone Road yard, adjacent to the gymnasium.

Between 3.06 p.m., when the game was stopped, and 3.45 p.m., when Kenny Dalglish, Liverpool's manager, broadcast an appeal for calm, no one in the ground other than those caught up in the crush knew fully what was happening. Although a call for doctors was made over the public address system, Duckenfield decided against an information announcement to avoid a 'public order situation' due to the fans' potential 'anger' at the postponement of the game. The crowd was left in ignorance, assuming that supporters behind the goal had caused trouble. Ironically when the full announcement was made, around 4 p.m., it drew widespread approval, the Forest supporters in the Spion Kop vigorously applauding the efforts of Liverpool fans to save lives.

As the disaster unfolded, the doctor who was in the West Stand left his seat and, answering the call for medical assistance, went to the concourse area outside the tunnel. He 'tried to find somebody in charge to tell [him] who to report to', asking several police officers but to no avail. 'There were people lying everywhere in the yard area between the stand and turnstiles.' A senior officer could not tell him where to report; 'I realised that there was no organised response and I was angry.' A police officer who had carried a body from the terraces agreed: 'his [the doctor's] comments regarding casualties were partly justified. Certainly no senior officers were in attendance at this time.'

The tunnel was, according to the police officer, 'still very busy. A lot of people just stood against the walls of the tunnel and were told to get out and make room for people being carried out.' Going back into pen 3, this officer could see a large number of officers trying to free fans from the pile of bodies. With others he carried a young man to where he had previously laid another who had died. They tried mouth-to-mouth and heart massage, eventually covering the dead man with a police coat. A woman nurse arrived. 'I told her that they were both dead and she felt both men for a pulse and said they both appeared to be dead.'

A fan who lost consciousness in pen 3 was carried out through the tunnel and laid in the recovery position on the concourse in a row of others who were dead. As he came round his vision, vividly bright and colourful, and his hearing returned. He watched as a dead man had a jacket put over his face. 'The thought that kept going through my mind was, "I'm here, I'm here." I was just thankful looking at that fella . . . the pain was unbelievable . . . I couldn't feel my legs.' Left for dead, he had regained consciousness without resuscitation and was taken to hospital.

According to the doctor, 'All around were people either dead or unconscious, or seriously hurt. The supporters were fantastic . . . helping each other and trying to resuscitate people. Individual police officers were also doing what they could . . . somebody needed to take an overview of the situation . . . I became aware that some casualties were being taken out into Leppings Lane itself and I went out there. There was one ambulance.'

Police officers were then instructed to take the bodies 'to an area outside the main part of the river area that runs at the back of the Leppings Lane Stand'. An officer moving two men recalled: 'As other bodies arrived at this location constables were deputed to form a line between the bodies and supporters leaving the ground.' He continued: 'Ambulances had now been arriving in convoys and a doctor from Liverpool . . . was good, examining people and placing them in priority for ambulances.'

Realising the necessity of triage (attending the injured according to the seriousness of their condition) the doctor went between people trying to establish who needed the most urgent treatment. 'There were . . . other health workers in evidence who were assessing and doing what they could. There appeared to be no medical or emergency equipment. The dead were taken to one side and I allocated the other casualties to category one or category two. I told the police who should be despatched by ambulance and who could wait. The officers were mostly very good. They took my instructions and acted on them immediately.'

Meanwhile, in the ground, the evacuation of the pens continued; the dead, dying and injured were carried to the gymnasium. It was vital to waste no time in getting casualties first to the ambulances and then to hospital. 'We picked up this bloke. He was really heavy. I shouted to others to help and about eight of us ran down the pitch. We expected to see loads of ambulances waiting but they [the police] sent us into a sports hall [gymnasium].' It was about 3.20 p.m. and the ambulances were just arriving via Penistone Road.

One of the first ambulance crews to respond to the emergency call travelled the mile from its station to Hillsborough. Initially instructed to go to Leppings Lane the crew was redirected to the Penistone Road gymnasium entrance. The driver was asked by a 'high ranking police officer' to reverse his ambulance to the first aid room. Three St John's Ambulance women officers together with two or three cadets directed the ambulance officer to the first aid room where there were three casualties. Two others with crush injuries arrived while the ambulance officer went for his equipment.

Within minutes, 'police and supporters were running into [the] area carrying dead and injured on boards . . .' His colleague was 'with the mobile resuscitation unit tending to someone who had stopped breathing'. 'I then got my bag and mask and about a dozen airway tubes. I went from casualty to casualty checking pulses and breathing and inserting airways on unconscious patients. Shortly afterwards I saw the first of other ambulance personnel coming into this area.'

Another ambulance was directed into the yard by the police

but had to stop, 'because of the number of vehicles and people at this point'. A person carried from the pitch on a hoarding was immediately put in the ambulance and the paramedic on board examined him, deciding that he was dead. At the same time another casualty, in a poor state, was also put into the ambulance. Attempts to put a third casualty in the ambulance were resisted as this would have prevented work on the person who was alive. The ambulance set off with the dead man still on board.

Arriving at the entrance to the ground off Penistone Road, another ambulance crew was directed towards the gymnasium. There were two ambulances in front, another behind. The Assistant Chief Ambulance Officer then told the driver, who he knew quite well, to drive on to the pitch. It was now about 3.35 p.m. 'We didn't get very far. There was a line of policemen across . . . the entrance to the pitch.' A police officer approached the ambulance and said, 'You can't go on there, they're still fighting.'

The driver called his senior colleague who told them to proceed regardless of what the police officer had said. He 'reached across and put our two tone horns on . . . that's when we started to make some sort of progress through the police cordon'. As they drove on to the grass they realised the seriousness of the situation. Young fans were carrying bodies across the pitch. 'I noticed a fireman doing fairly effective resuscitation. People were banging on the side of the ambulance.'

The ambulance officer left the vehicle and its driver as they arrived at the goalmouth. It was an impossible task. Fans were relieved that an ambulance had arrived but 'in a sense we were becoming a diversion'. The plain fact was that one ambulance crew could not deal with the numbers and everyone turned to the officer for help.

Unable to locate colleagues, the ambulance officer tried to organise triage and establish quickly who most needed care and attention: 'It was more than I could cope with. If I had just seen another ambulance coming up then I would have been all right.'

With the ambulance doors open and people putting in bodies they decided to move: 'People were screaming for oxygen. "Have you got any defibrillators?" People were attempting resuscitation.' The ambulance was soon packed: three or four bodies, a father, a nurse and two police officers. 'I told my driver to get the hell out of there.'

Access to the parking area outside the gymnasium was awkward. According to a senior ambulance officer, there was room for a 'maximum of four ambulances'. With three ambulances, 'space was cramped' and an officer 'was directing ambulances to reverse in because there was no room to turn round'. As more ambulances arrived they were instructed to queue in the road.

With space so limited it was inevitable that congestion slowed the operation: 'There were still three ambulances in the yard, two of which were parked side by side with their backs towards the ramp which leads on to the pitch and the third was parked between them and the gate . . . the ambulance in front of the gate had been left by its crew without any keys and it was blocking the exit so that one of the ambulances behind it could not get out . . . It was unusual for a driver to leave his vehicle because the Major Accident Plan requires every driver to remain with his ambulance . . .'

It was not that straightforward. An ambulance officer arriving in the yard found the situation chaotic. The police were marshalling traffic and he was asked to move his ambulance to let another out. Police vehicles were 'parked adjacent to the gymnasium which I considered to be a hindrance to the casualty clearing operation . . . access and exit from the ground [was] very difficult'. As he assisted with the injured, 'many people [were] screaming for attention . . . The scene . . . was a mass of fans, many in shock and many people moving around in a confined area.' He helped to provide essential medical supplies, particularly airways, the priority being to 'clear serious casualties'. Along with another ambulance officer he boarded the ambulance, attempting to keep a young casualty alive. A police officer drove the ambulance on what was to prove a difficult journey to Sheffield's Northern General Hospital.

* * *

As it became evident that the terrible compression in the central pens was neither crowd violence nor a pitch invasion, the need for a co-ordinated, swift and appropriate response was clear. The responsibility for putting the Major Incident Plan into operation lay with Duckenfield as match commander. According to the operations manual, 'Overall control and co-ordination of the effort of all the [emergency] services involved in dealing with a major incident is a police responsibility.' Duckenfield now became 'site commander'. Yet he gave no specific instructions to prepare the gymnasium, as the designated clearing area for a major incident, or for the removal of vehicles from its vicinity. When the Deputy Chief Ambulance Officer arrived, 'I went to the agreed rendezvous point [designated in the emergency plan] but I was the only one there.'

In the early stages, everything rested on the initiative of individual police officers. A detective superintendent was by the Spion Kop when he saw a disturbance at the other end of the ground. He walked to the gymnasium where he was told that there had been injuries. Back at the pitch he discovered that about 20 people were dead in the central pens. He immediately went to the police room under the North Stand, contacting Chief Superintendent Addis, head of South Yorkshire CID, at headquarters: 'We discussed setting up an incident room and activating a casualty bureau.' Another call, initiated by the Assistant Chief Constable, was later put through to Addis from the police control box, calling him to Hillsborough.

In the gymnasium, a chief inspector shouted, 'We are going to set up a temporary mortuary in here, clear those tables.' Another senior officer who had 'assisted with getting medical care and ambulances down on to the track' realised that 'dozens' of bodies were following the first few carried across the pitch. He helped clear tables and chairs laid out earlier for officers' meals. An officer already in the gymnasium 'assisted to clear the gymnasium, not knowing why.'

The detective superintendent stated, 'The first victim to arrive was a young man . . . apparently dead and I touched one of the officers, introduced myself and explained to him that the body was his responsibility . . . under no circumstances was he to leave that body' ensuring 'that no one else had any dealings with the property or clothing or identification . . . instructions that I was to repeat dozens of times on that afternoon.'

Those injured were directed 'to the far end of the gymnasium', beyond a partition. The 'dead were arriving in such numbers that it was impossible to try to establish whether, in fact, they were dead, but I have to say that every body that I saw bore what I recognised to be classic signs of asphyxia and I am satisfied that every body that I saw and directed into the area designated as a temporary mortuary was, in fact, dead.'

It proved impossible for senior officers to always 'give instructions before the officers who had brought in bodies had departed'. According to another senior officer, 'the bodies kept being brought in fast and I was asking control for a doctor to ensure that they were dead. There was nothing to suggest that any of the bodies were alive, but I was conscious that they had not been certified as dead. The bodies were covered with the table-cloths previously laid out for the meals.'

Several officers were 'bewildered and some were crying'. Friends of those being laid out 'were hysterical', a few more were angry and aggressive towards officers. As bodies were carried in by fans, who themselves had survived the crush, some 'were distressed, weeping openly, screaming, aggressive and I saw several fights and scuffles break out in the area around, between and over the bodies that were being deposited'.

Yet, 'officers and civilians were attempting to resuscitate some of the victims and I saw two groups attempting to revive, what were obviously to me, dead bodies'. The gymnasium soon became as chaotic as had been the pitch a few moments earlier: 'The scene was one of general confusion with bodies being put down haphazardly.' Outside the gymnasium there were 'numerous bodies and injured lying on the ground'. A senior officer saw 'about six St John's personnel . . . all under 14 or 15 years of age, who were very distressed'. He detailed a police officer to 'look after them'.

An officer recalled 'moving coughing, shocked boys out of the way' as bodies were placed 'against the gymnasium and around the prison bus'. He gave 'heart massage and the kiss-of-life, all to no avail, and still the dead and injured kept coming'. Fans copied him, 'asking, "Are we doing it right?" I kept shouting "five pushes, one breath" . . . The panic and upset were unimaginable and many senior officers were in a state of shock.' The office 'deeply regretted that children had to see this carnage'.

A nurse who had been in the West Stand and had assisted with resuscitation on the pitch went with a doctor to the gymnasium. 'There were people on the floor outside the ambulances and a doctor was doing resuscitation . . . he asked me to take over . . . but the man died. I was told that there were never people outside [the gymnasium], either on stretchers or on the floor . . . but there were.'

In the gymnasium she, another nurse and a doctor examined the 'walking wounded'. She went to the end of the gymnasium to find a pair of scissors and was told that the first aid equipment was in another part of the ground. A police officer gave her his pen-knife. There was a need for oxygen because the available tanks were empty. The nurse lifted a young boy on to a stretcher, the doctor thought he might need a tracheotomy. A man, who appeared to have a broken leg, was drifting in and out of consciousness; 'He kept saying, "Don't worry, please look after my boy." ' The last person she helped was a 'young lad' with leg injuries. There were no splints available so they lifted him on to a chair: 'It was a case of tip the chair and drag.'

She asked the police if they thought they should screen off the area where the dead were laid out. Two officers were examining the bodies for any possible identification in their pockets. She started to help but, overcome by her own shock at what she had been through, she said, 'I can't do this', and left the gymnasium; 'I'd just had enough.'

At approximately 3.45 p.m. a doctor, who had been treating people on the pitch, was asked by a senior police officer to go to the gymnasium to examine bodies and certify death. On arriving in the gymnasium he found four or five rows of bodies and, with a general practitioner, they each examined a row of bodies: 'We were accompanied by a police officer who made a note of every body I examined and a police officer was allocated to each body . . . I performed a normal examination on each body and pronounced life extinct in turn.' In an estimated 25 minutes he examined and certified 20 bodies.

The failure to identify and respond to the protracted crush in the pens coupled with the lack of immediate medical aid to the dying raised serious questions over whether more lives could have been saved. That resuscitation was successful in some cases, that some placed with the dead actually recovered, left lingering doubts about the adequacy of much of the spontaneous treatment administered.

Added to this, cursory examinations, often no more than feeling for a pulse, were conducted in the heat of the moment by inexperienced, non-medical people. With certainty of death often so difficult to establish in asphyxiated victims, the deeply disturbing possibility remained: that some people were taken into the gymnasium, laid out on the floor, their faces covered by clothes and bin-liners, solely on the assumption of death. Of the 96 who eventually died, only 14 made it to hospital and of them 12 were pronounced 'dead on arrival'. It was expected, however, that when the inquests were eventually held, the precise circumstances of each death, including the attempts at resuscitation and the quality of care received, would be fully explored.

* * *

Chief Superintendent Addis arrived at Hillsborough just before 4 p.m. Initially, at the control box, he met with the Assistant Chief Constable, 'who was busy with other senior officers'. A few minutes later the detective superintendent who had phoned him earlier from the police room arrived. Together they went to the gymnasium where Addis 'supervised the necessary arrangements'. As they left the control box, Kenny Dalglish, Liverpool's manager, was making his appeal to the fans in the stadium.

At the gymnasium, Addis was introduced to the Deputy Chief Ambulance Officer. He then 'took charge and after a few minutes . . . assessing the situation he stood on a chair, and told the police what he intended to do. The gymnasium floor was littered with bodies.' And the superintendent remembered 'someone telling me . . . "Seventy-odd and more at the Northern General." Most . . . had been draped with what appeared to be white shrouds . . . they were, in fact, the paper tablecloths . . .'

At 5 p.m. Addis was informed that the coroner, Dr Stefan Popper, 'had instructed that bodies should not be moved from the temporary mortuary [gymnasium] until . . . they had been photographed in situ and their identities confirmed'. Realising that this would take some time he told an officer to organise the transportation of relatives and friends waiting outside the gymnasium to the Hammerton Road police station 'where suitable accommodation could be found for them'.

Addis set about 'instilling some discipline' and establishing some 'semblance of order'. One officer recalled that Addis twice addressed the officers in the gymnasium. The first time he informed them that 'all the bodies would remain in the gym'. Later he explained to all officers dealing with the bodies that 'each body would be photographed facially and a gallery of photographs exhibited for friends and relatives to peruse'. Once a photographic identification had been made, 'the body would be brought through for formal identification', the CID then completing the paperwork.

When the coroner arrived, at 6.45 p.m., the identification procedure was decided. Polaroid photographs of the faces of the dead were to be used as a 'first line method' of identification, followed by a viewing of the body. The photographs would be displayed on screens in the entrance area of the gymnasium into which waiting relatives and close friends would be shown. The numbers on the photographs corresponded to the numbered bodies on the gymnasium floor.

Following photographic identification, the number would be called and the body brought to the gymnasium entrance for physical identification. 'If a positive identification ensued then the police officer would accompany the person identifying the body to a nearby area where they would be joined by a detective and details of identification, medical background . . . and the details of the incident surrounding the death, if known, would be obtained on a statement form.' Once identified, bodies were to be moved to Sheffield's Medico–Legal Centre, each accompanied by an assigned officer.

The gymnasium was divided into three areas using sheets hung from nets to provide a semblance of screening. At the top end, bodies were put fully clothed into body bags and laid out in rows on the gymnasium floor. Each numbered body was assigned an officer. Each officer was given a cloth or sponge to wipe the face. Each face was photographed using a Polaroid camera. The gymnasium's middle section was an eating area for police officers. And the area closest to the door was laid out with 'interview tables'. The 'appropriate preparation . . . [was] completed by 9.15 p.m.' The coroner 'toured the area concerned and voiced his satisfaction . . .' At 9.30 p.m., six hours after the evacuation of the pens, the slow and painful process of identifying the dead began.

Chapter Four

FROM DISASTER TO TRAGEDY

Barry Devonside was up in the West Stand when the disaster happened. He watched with growing anxiety: 'There was a coldness, a fear, something I've never experienced . . . standing watching people collapse, being carried off on boards, arms flopping down, bodies lying motionless.' Barry knew that his son Christopher was down below on the terraces with ten mates. There was a good chance they were caught up in the crush.

Barry told those around him that Chris was down there but that he was a big man. 'Actually I was scared; I'd seen him and his friend in front of the tunnel, quarter of an hour before the kick-off and I could see the [centre] pens were grossly over-populated compared to the end pens.' He stood looking for Chris but there was no sign of him. Then he left, expecting to meet Chris at their pre-arranged rendezvous point. 'It was so sombre, thousands pouring out of the ground totally shell-shocked . . . the biggest funeral march I'd ever seen. People walking shoulder to shoulder, crammed tight, not saying a word . . . people were scared stiff at what had happened in front of them.'

In Leppings Lane the ambulances, police cars and fire engines were 'jammed solid' and it was difficult to get through. One man walked directly up the bonnet, over the roof and down the boot of a police car. By the roundabout were two telephone boxes:

'The queue must have been 60 yards long and 3 deep . . . all I was thinking about was seeing Chris.'

At the rendezvous Barry met his friend, his friend's son and one of Chris's mates. 'I just shouted, "Where's Chris?" and my mate turned away. I thought, "Oh Jesus, no."' Chris's friend told Barry that Chris was seriously injured: 'I said, "How d'you mean?" And in virtually the same breath he said, "You'd better expect the worst." I said, "What d'you mean, expect the worst?" I was getting aggressive with him, I didn't mean to, I was just so frightened. He said, "He's dead." I think I fell to the floor on one knee, people were sort of looking at me, and I thought, "Hang on, this is not real, it's not happening."'

Barry ran to two police officers and was taken to the gymnasium. By this time it was under siege with friends, relatives, the press and clergy. He was approached by a woman who had 'come in off the street' to offer help. She took him to the St John's Ambulance officers and he was given a cup of tea. Barry told them that he did not want tea or to talk; finding Chris was his priority. They went across to the gymnasium where he told the police inspector on the door that he had lost his son.

The inspector asked, 'What makes you think he's here?' Barry replied that he had been told that Chris was dead. 'And he said, "Can you describe him?" So I described Chris. The most distinctive thing was a Welsh international rugby shirt. I said, "I don't think anyone else in the whole ground will be wearing that today." The inspector went in. I was not allowed in. Ten minutes seemed a lifetime. He came out and very positively said, "He's not there, son. There's nobody of that description here." I said, "Are you absolutely sure? Because I've been told he was dead." He just replied, "He's not there."'

While there was a sense of relief, Barry realised that Chris could have been taken to hospital. He was hoping against hope that Chris's friend had been mistaken. First, he wanted to ring his wife at home. Barry was taken to a telephone at the back of the gymnasium but, finally connected to the operator, he was in such a state he could not remember his number. Realising that he was in the thick of the disaster the operator broke down and put her supervisor on the line. The number he was requesting was ex-directory. He said it was his home number and that it was not ex-directory: 'It is an emergency call of the worst kind.' The supervisor withheld the number. 'I said, "Hold on, you must know about the Hillsborough disaster." She said, "Yes," and apologised. I said, "But you must override rules and regulations, this is an emergency."' Barry gave the phone to a police sergeant who explained what was happening. The supervisor remained adamant; neither the number nor the connection was granted. Eventually, Barry contacted his brother-in-law through directory inquiries, and asked him to tell his wife the dreadful news.

Accompanied by the woman he had met and a St John's Ambulance officer, Barry went to the Northern General Hospital where most of the injured had been taken. They waited for a long time at casualty and no one there recognised the description of Chris or his distinctive shirt. 'I kept thinking logically: "If he's not in the gym, he must be in a hospital . . . And if he's not in a hospital he must be in the gym. He can only be in one of those places. He can't be walking around in a daze. That's not possible . . . outside the realms of reality."'

Barry was then taken to the hospital mortuary. There were ambulances and police cars outside. A mortician told him that he could not go inside. He replied that he had worked in a mortuary so they let him in. 'There were policemen and policewomen just sat all over the floor . . . like a bare, concrete floor . . . a pile of clothes dumped in the middle of the floor.' He was not allowed further, 'in case your son's in there'.

Some of the officers were in tears, all were shocked. The mortician went through the clothes and checked the bodies; no one matched the description. Barry was left, hanging about, not knowing what to do or who to turn to. A police officer directed him to a boys' club which had been opened close to Hammerton Road police station as an information and holding centre.

'There were literally hundreds of people there, inside. I've never seen so many people shell-shocked . . . a social worker asked me for my name, offered me sandwiches and tea . . . I went upstairs and people were coming up to me to ask for descriptions of Chris and I kept relating, time and again, this Welsh international rugby shirt. People were coming up to me, policewomen and social workers. They were basically trying to comfort [me].' Barry was left there until after 11 p.m. when a woman went to him and said, 'I think it's time you went to the gymnasium.' He asked her why and she replied, 'They'd just like you to look at some photographs.'

* * *

Even though many people never go to a game, have little or no interest in football, big match days are hard to escape. In homes all over Britain at the time, BBC's *Grandstand* was a regular Saturday afternoon feature. Televisions stayed on as the programme jumped between the main sports events of the day. It was like a national institution. Except for the FA Cup final, live football coverage has rarely featured on the non-satellite stations. But the BBC's cameras were at Hillsborough, as they were at Villa Park, covering both semi-finals for *Match of the Day* highlights that evening.

The cameras, coincidentally, were also in Sheffield at the Crucible Theatre, transmitting live action from the Snooker World Championships. For those keen to keep up with the football, both national and local radio were broadcasting live from Hillsborough. In many houses the snooker was on television, the sound turned down, alongside football commentary on the radio.

People shopping all over Merseyside were accompanied by the radio coverage. Market stalls in Chester, Ormskirk, Birkenhead, Liverpool City Centre and so on had the commentary blaring out, as did hundreds of small shops. Banks of televisions in windows of numerous electrical and TV rental stores showed multiple images on their screens of close-up shots of the snooker table's green baize. As the football kicked off, people hesitated to hear snippets of the action, controlling far-removed excitement as Beardsley hit the bar for Liverpool.

And then, throughout the city, the region, the country, people were stopped in their tracks. Something had happened in the central pens behind the goal. The game was halted and fans were spilling on to the pitch. Television was now broadcasting live from Hillsborough, the snooker interrupted. In homes throughout Merseyside people watched the disaster unfold, scenes all-too-reminiscent of Heysel just four years earlier. And it was happening to Liverpool fans.

Out on the street they clustered around shop radios and market stalls, pressed up against the windows of electrical stores, and collectively fell silent. It was serious. As television coverage jumped between the studio and the ground, the enormity of the tragedy began to sink in. Almost everyone watching or listening from Merseyside knew someone at the game.

For those who not only knew that their loved ones were at Hillsborough, but were certain that they had tickets for the Leppings Lane terrace, and would, more than likely, be in the area behind the goal, the tension was unbearable. As the pictures were broadcast into their living-rooms they sat close to the screen looking to catch a glimpse of something familiar: 'What was he wearing? . . . Is that her hat?'

As the minutes ticked by, and group after group of fans ran across the pitch carrying bodies on hoardings, the terrible reality dawned. No one wanted to broadcast it, but people were dying. Dying, live on television, before the eyes of millions. And somewhere in the midst of the chaos and panic were the loved ones, close friends and classmates of those watching and listening.

As Barry Devonside looked down from the West Stand and began his painful but ever-hopeful journey in search of Chris, thousands – miles from Hillsborough – became increasingly desperate for word of their relatives and friends. Like any other situation in a highly technological society where the state responds daily to the needs of its citizens, the assumption was that once the initial confusion and disorganisation subsided, a well-planned, co-ordinated and effective emergency response would take over.

People at home found reassurance in the emergency numbers flashed on their television screens. But soon the switchboards were overwhelmed and, even if they managed to get through, the information available was minimal. Many relied on their loved ones to phone home. But as phones remained silent, those waiting began to panic. 'We must go to Sheffield' was the obvious response. The death toll was mounting, hundreds were injured. It was a journey the stuff of nightmares.

* * *

Risk is ever present in most people's lives. With over 3,000 people killed each year on Britain's roads and even more in accidents at home and at work, much of daily life is dangerous. Yet risk is taken for granted. As flight passengers chew on fast-receding fingernails or tap nervously on mobile phones in their last moments before boarding, it is ironic that much else they do as a matter of course is statistically more life-threatening. Whether the risk is obvious or hidden, in private or in public, at work or at play, minds are put at ease by the reassurance that, whatever the emergency, the appropriate services will respond.

Summerland, the *Marchioness*, King's Cross, Clapham, Piper Alpha, Bradford, Lockerbie, the *Herald of Free Enterprise*, Abbeystead, Dunblane; names robbed of their original meaning or identity by appalling tragedy. Each now, probably for ever, associated with the loss of life in harrowing circumstances. Yet each happened, claiming lives, disabling and traumatising, while ordinary people were going about their ordinary business.

Disasters are regularly caused by a coincidence of predictable circumstances coming together unexpectedly.

So often, the first rescuers are survivors themselves: pulling people from wreckage, saving others from drowning, breathing life back into still bodies and returning to smoke-filled rooms. Occasionally they include people with medical or first aid training. But in the terrifying first moments, the hope and expectation is that emergency services will arrive, rescue and evacuate, save life and minimise injury, bring order from chaos.

According to the Home Office, the 'core of the initial response' should come from the emergency services with co-ordinated backup from appropriate local authority departments and voluntary bodies. Other than saving lives and containing the disaster, the emergency response focuses on managing and sealing the 'site' for investigation and providing accurate casualty information. It is the police who have the primary responsibility for controlling information, dealing with the dead and handling the bereaved.

The local coroner, in whose jurisdiction people have died, has the legal responsibility for discovering their identities and investigating the cause and circumstances of the deaths. This demands close liaison with the police, who set up arrangements for identification, removal of the dead and organisation of the mortuary. The police also activate a casualty bureau, a central contact point to process enquiries from the public about missing relatives and friends, keeping track of survivors, providing information about their well-being and location.

The organisation of the immediate aftermath is vital as survivors and those at the scene search for friends and relatives, while others ring for information or travel to the scene. People go to the site, to hospitals and to local police stations in search of loved ones. Essential to effective disaster planning or incident plans are agreed procedures for holding the dead, accommodating survivors, relatives and friends, and identifying the bodies.

In any serious incident involving death and injury hospitals need to be fully mobilised to meet the emergency. Apart from the broader context of emergency planning, each hospital has its own procedure, or major incident plan, for dealing with extraordinary demands. Inevitably the weight of treatment falls heavily on the accident and emergency department as the hospital's first port of call. With multiple casualties, each with quite different medical needs, the accident and emergency department immediately establishes a system of triage.

Part of hospital emergency planning is to use a 'cascade' telephone system to bring in appropriate off-duty staff as quickly as possible. Operating theatres are put on stand-by, intensive care prepared, casualty reception cleared of all but the most serious patients, a temporary mortuary designated and so on. It is vital, therefore, that hospitals have clear and detailed instructions from the incident site so that necessary arrangements for reception and treatment can be made.

Once casualties arrive in numbers the hospital has to deal with relatives, friends and the 'walking wounded'. People searching for their loved ones visit and ring hospitals as a first response. In Hillsborough's case many friends and relatives were already in Sheffield, adding to the pressure on the accident and emergency departments of both main hospitals, the Northern General and the Royal Hallamshire. Hillsborough's incident plan specified the Northern as the main receiving hospital with the Royal Hallamshire in reserve.

The Northern General accident and emergency department was functioning with the usual Saturday afternoon cover. There was a waiting time in casualty of about two and a half hours. At 3.20 p.m. the department received a call putting it on 'stand-by'. The charge nurse on duty had no idea of the nature of the incident, thinking that it was probably a traffic accident or something similar.

Within minutes a further call informed staff to 'expect

casualties' and SYMAS sent a message to 'expect a child with cardiac arrest'. There was 'no reference to Hillsborough or that a major incident was taking place'. Yet the agreed procedure in such circumstances was to 'telephone the hospital switchboard with the message, "Implement the major disaster plan." No such message was ever received.'

Worried over the calls, and having a sense that something serious might be unfolding, the charge nurse telephoned the senior consultant for accident and emergency, James Wardrope, at his home. Wardrope left immediately, at 3.23 p.m., arriving ten minutes later. He 'ran' into the department and confirmed that the hospital's major incident plan had been implemented.

In a later article, written with colleagues, Wardrope considered that 'Failure to implement the major incident alert earlier meant that only a few staff had to cope with a large clinical workload in addition to implementing the [hospital's] major incident plan.' In other words, the hospital was left in the dark as to what was happening and this delayed the arrival of necessary support personnel. The consultant physician on call, for example, was missed from the initial call-out, arriving at 3.55 p.m. in response to what he had seen 30 minutes earlier on the television.

* * *

Meanwhile, Hammerton Road police station, the divisional headquarters covering Hillsborough, had activated an incident-room. Detective Superintendent McKay, who had been with Addis in the gymnasium, went to Hammerton Road to assist with its setting up. He 'found the place under virtual siege' by many Liverpool fans urgently seeking information. Social workers had also arrived. They proved to be 'invaluable', providing 'a buffer between distressed fans who had lost contact with relatives and friends . . . and the police'.

The casualty bureau arrangements were already under way and McKay briefed the incident room staff on events at the ground. With the incident room and the casualty bureau operational, the next priority was finding a suitable place to 'hold' waiting relatives, friends and those arriving from Merseyside. While some remained at the hospitals, Hammerton Road was the obvious point of convergence.

A senior church official, one of the many clergy to have arrived at Hammerton Road, recalled a police request for 'anywhere immediately adjacent which could be used as a relatives reception centre'. The local vicar suggested the boys' club directly opposite the police station: 'It was one of those youth centres that have been ravaged by years of aggressive wear: one accessible telephone, poor toilets, not enough chairs or tables . . . there was no way of making the drab surroundings any more welcoming.'

The intention was that friends and relatives would wait at the boys' club before being taken to the police station to give details of those missing. They would then return to the boys' club where they would be registered as they entered and wait for further information in the company of social workers, clergy and voluntary agency staff. If descriptions that were given matched those of the bodies at the gymnasium they were to be transported there to await identification.

Addis confirmed that the boys' club was used because it was close to the police station, considering it to be as 'adequate as it could be in the circumstances'. A Roman Catholic priest described it as 'like a waiting-room for the police station'. The assumption was that the boys' club was under the organisational control of the police. Certainly they directed the course of events. While the director of social services later conceded that it was 'not ideal for receiving people', he considered that 'it was important that it was close to the police station'.

Sheffield's Medico–Legal Centre, one of the most advanced in Britain, housed the city mortuary, the pathology department and the coroner's offices and court. At the time of the disaster there was one mortuary technician on duty and one on call. Once the scale of the disaster became apparent, a further seven technicians

131

were brought in. The early indication from the police was that bodies would be transported directly to the Medico–Legal Centre prior to identification.

Initially the centre's manager had difficulty in establishing whether a temporary mortuary was going to be set up for identification purposes. Friends and relatives, told at the ground that the dead were to be sent to the Medico–Legal Centre, began arriving as early as 4 p.m. Later, the initial decision was reversed and the gymnasium was designated a temporary mortuary. Under the eventually agreed procedure, bodies were transported by ambulance to the Centre after identification at the gymnasium. The first body arrived at 10.06 p.m., the last at 6.05 a.m. on the Sunday.

While the plan was to have all bodies identified at the gymnasium before relocation to the Medico–Legal Centre, the last 15 to arrive were unidentified. Arrangements were made for subsequent identifications to take place during the Sunday. At the Centre, bodies were undressed and accommodated in the refrigerators or laid out on the floor, kept cool by newly installed chiller units. Postmortems began on the Sunday morning and were completed by Monday midday.

* * *

It was inevitable that once the ambulances, and other vehicles carrying the injured, began to arrive at the Northern General the chaos at the gymnasium – and the pitch before it – would be transferred to the hospital. The figures for the two hospitals speak for themselves: in the first hour 88 people were taken to casualty at the Northern. Of these, 11 were recorded as dead on arrival, 56 were admitted and 21 treated and discharged. At the Hallamshire, of the 71 taken to casualty, one was dead on arrival, 25 were admitted and 45 treated and discharged.

With a large number of seriously ill patients, some in cardiac arrest, others deeply unconscious, arriving in quick succession, the first attempts at triage were hampered. The priority was to save life. Eventually, triage was established. The unusual feature of the disaster was that almost all patients suffered only one form of injury: asphyxiation. Disaster planning for medical treatment usually prepares staff for a whole range of injuries, many needing operating theatres. In this case the overwhelming need was for resuscitation.

The demand for space and attention was in danger of outstripping possible provision. At one point, according to a charge nurse at the Northern, there were 'three or four patients per resuscitation bay' and insufficient equipment to meet demand. The waiting-room also became a resuscitation area. With nearly 20 people needing ventilated support and three ventilators in the accident and emergency department, equipment had to be transferred in from other parts of the hospital.

Inevitably, the casualties were in different states of consciousness. Some were deeply unconscious while others were hysterical. It was not always possible to judge the latter as being caused by trauma or as a result of oxygen deficiency. A temporary mortuary was set up and a reception staff member was asked to check the bodies. Walking through the door she was confronted by bodies on couches and on the floor.

Friends and relatives arriving at the Northern General were desperate for information. A social worker, responding to a call for help on the radio, was taken to the canteen, presented with a sticker marked 'social worker' and told to 'do your stuff'. The canteen was 'filled with people in various states of distress . . . some sitting on tables, some just standing up, some banging on the walls, others just numb'.

When Barry Devonside arrived at the hospital canteen, 'There must have been a couple of hundred . . .. all scousers, every age. People were being sick, people fainting and others just sat there gobsmacked.' About half an hour later a man walked in and stood on a table 'reading descriptions like: "We have a person in the mortuary who is six foot with a tattoo on his left arm, LFC. He's got £6.45 in his pocket and he wears so-and-so watch." And they were given descriptions like that . . . I must have been there an hour and a half and he was giving descriptions of people in casualty . . . people in the mortuary.'

The social worker confirmed that each time the administrator walked into the canteen it fell silent. Then, 'He started to reel off information . . . as he did, people were collapsing like dominoes.' Barry Devonside stated that, as some of the details were explicit people around him knew it was their loved one and broke down. 'I shouted out, above everybody, "Have you got anyone there wearing a Welsh international rugby shirt?" And he said that there was no one of that description at all.' As time wore on people became more openly anxious: 'There were kids of 10 and 11, people of 50 and 60.'

At the boys' club, those waiting in the damp, cold and pungent atmosphere were suffering similar anxieties. A priest who arrived from the gymnasium was incredulous: 'a disused boys' club with one telephone'. A senior clergyman felt that, 'Looking after those in need was in danger of becoming secondary to the task of managing the log-jam of helpers . . . Information was scarce. We had been given an inspector to act as our liaison officer with the police. He seemed to know less than we did about what was happening.'

A social worker stated: 'It didn't seem to me that it [the boys' club] was under the control of a clearly functioning management group.' This was evident in the confusion over registration: 'You had to register when you arrived, then you had to go over to the police station to make a statement, then you had to come back to the boys' club and re-register.' But re-registration depended on proof of initial registration. Worse still, 'Some people in the boys' club were kept waiting even though people in charge knew their relative or friend was dead.' Despite criticism of the use of the boys' club, Addis defended it as 'the right decision'.

This was also his opinion on the use of the gymnasium as a

temporary mortuary for identification purposes. The Deputy Chief Ambulance Officer recalled that before 6 p.m. Addis had arranged to transfer bodies to the Medico–Legal Centre: hence the decision by the centre manager to call in his colleagues. The coroner, Dr Popper, however, under whose jurisdiction the bodies were held, stated that as far as he was concerned the use of the gymnasium for identification was never in doubt.

He considered that, as the gymnasium was holding most of the dead, it was already operational as a temporary mortuary. Returning bodies from the hospitals to the gymnasium 'was my decision', he said. Popper concluded, 'We weren't going to break our procedure, we would have been in a worse mess than we were in already.' Addis stated that he 'saw it as an ideal situation, if you don't mind me saying so, to put all the eggs in one basket'.

At some point after his arrival at the gymnasium, Popper also took what was to prove a most controversial decision with lasting and painful consequences. In an unprecedented move he authorised the taking of blood-alcohol samples, and the recording of blood-alcohol levels, from all who died, including children. It was a defining moment. While he 'realised that the vast majority were in fact extremely young', once he had 'made up mind that we [sic] wanted alcohol levels done, I said we were doing them for all, irrespective of other considerations.'

At the time, Popper was not sure 'whether or not alcohol would be relevant', taking the view that 'youth . . . is no guarantee that alcohol is not ingested'. It was justifiable, he claimed, 'given where it [the disaster] happened and all the circumstances surrounding it . . . the alcohol level was something which sprang to mind as [a factor] which could possibly be relevant'.

Just how did it 'spring to mind'? What were the dynamics in the gymnasium in those first moments of discussion? There was no medical, clinical or legal justification for this unprecedented and intrusive action. Reserved only for those in positions of responsibility – train and coach drivers, pilots, and so on – no victims of previous disasters had been tested in this way.

Phrases such as 'given where it happened', 'all the circumstances surrounding it' and 'could possibly be relevant' suggested deep-seated prejudices and assumptions about football supporters, regardless of their actions or age. And, more precisely, in the gymnasium 'we wanted alcohol levels done', indicating that the first accounts Popper received from senior officers who briefed him emphasised drunkenness among the fans.

Popper's decision immediately implied that each of the deceased could have been drunk and, in some way, could have contributed to their own and others' deaths. It was a received agenda already set by Duckenfield's lie and senior officers' initial assessments. It guaranteed that allegations of drunkenness would remain centre stage. It deeply hurt the bereaved as they realised that the naming of their dead would imply the shaming of their lives.

* * *

It was after midnight when Barry Devonside finally arrived back at the gymnasium where his search had begun over eight hours earlier. There were 'hundreds of people milling around, TV crews and press'. Kept outside with his brother, 'It was like winter . . . then they asked us to go inside and said, "Be prepared, because you're going to look at a board." I think they said 81 faces were going to be on this.

'The first few I looked at, it was so hard, looking at faces and praying to God that Chris wasn't there among them. I saw injuries to faces, and they were just faces, totally unrecognisable. I kept going through about ten or fifteen and then going back because I wanted to know something but I didn't want to know the obvious. And we got past the main bulk . . . I think the serious ones were together . . . we were getting towards the end and I'm thinking, "Chris is not here." I was sort of building my hopes up . . . right to the end.'

Barry began to 'get excited, thinking, "He's not dead," but I had a feeling of guilt at the same time . . . because I was looking at 70 or 80 dead people . . . my brother-in-law just put a hand on my shoulder and said, "Hold on." We just stood back about 15 paces and it was our Chris . . . number 17.' The police led them to a doorway: 'They virtually manhandled us . . . sort of grabbed our shoulders, grabbed our arms and said, "Stay there. Don't move." I was strong in coming back without using [bad] language.'

Chris was brought to the door on a trolley, 'he was just in . . . like those sacks that you put people in, from an air disaster, with a zip right down the middle. A copper put his head around the door and I said "Yes, okay" . . . he sort of held my arms and I said, "Get off." I walked through, and they unzipped the bag and said, "Would you look down." I just said, "No, just shut your mouth for two minutes . . . I'll deal with this." And I walked round the side and knelt down and I kissed him on the head.'

As Barry held his son he could see that Chris was still wearing the distinctive Welsh international rugby shirt. He had never left the gymnasium. All that time while Barry was in doubt, in hope, Chris had been on the floor of the gymnasium. 'The police didn't want me to stay for a second longer than was necessary. A copper leaned down and put his hand on my shoulder and I shrugged him away . . . I kissed Chris again and patted him and they whisked him away.'

Stunned, silent and alone with the desolation of a parent's loss, Barry was led to a table at the near end of the gymnasium. 'I thought, "Whatever you've got to do now, Chris is dead. He's never given you one ounce of problem in life, so you've got to stay dignified." They sat me down and two CID blokes and a police-man in uniform . . . wanted a statement of identification.'

He was asked for his name, address and age and details of Christopher. Suddenly, without warning, the 'formal statement of identification' turned into something quite different. Barry was asked what time they had arrived in Sheffield and whether they had stopped for a drink. Barry asked why these questions could be considered relevant to the identification: 'We're trying to build a picture of the whole day,' came the reply.

The questioning focused on alcohol, pubs, off-licences and supermarkets, whether he had seen heavy drinking or bad behaviour. Barry continued to argue with the police and he was disgusted that, minutes after identifying Chris, and after all that he had been through, he was subjected to challenges of his account of events. He left the gymnasium at about 1 a.m.: 'Nobody tried to assess the physical or mental condition you were in. You were left to go off, that was horrendous. I was fortunate that I had a brother and brother-in-law that came and supported me completely . . .'

Barry's account is typical of the experiences endured by the bereaved at the gymnasium. From the moment they arrived to the time they left, the bereaved felt that their treatment was appalling. Addis disagreed. He stated that a chief inspector 'addressed all people on the buses [arriving from the boys' club] in terms of procedure. They were certainly put in the picture as to expectations. It was impossible to say how long it would take . . . we bent over backwards to accommodate families.'

Relatives and friends sat, some wrapped in blankets, on double-decker buses in the car park which had been the scene of chaos just hours earlier. Only one family at a time was admitted to the gymnasium and each stage of the 'procedure' had to be completed before the next in line could enter. The police were keen to hurry the process along, while some of the carers argued vehemently that the needs of the bereaved were more important than those of the procedure.

A senior ambulance officer felt that the entire operation added significantly to the suffering of the bereaved. 'One woman threw herself on the trolley and wouldn't be moved. Her screams echoed all around the gymnasium. The screams were more than a person could stand.'

The experiences of James Delaney's mother, recounted by her on Channel 4's *After Dark* programme, brought home the full impact of the procedure adopted by Popper and Addis. 'A social worker took us to the ground where our son was killed . . . they didn't give, not only our son, but the other 94 [at that time] poor people who were killed . . . any dignity. When we got to the ground, we had to look at these photographs to try and identify our son. We looked and looked, we couldn't recognise our son . . . eventually we did . . .

'So we were led into the sports hall and when we walked in our son was lying on a trolley, inside this green zipped-up bag, number 33. So his dad and I bent down to kiss and talk to James and as we stood up, there was a policeman who came from behind me and was trying to usher myself and my husband out, straight out of the hall. The total attitude was, you've identified number 33 so go!

'Unfortunately I went hysterical . . . I had to ask if I could take our son away from the public's eye. Again there were poor people, people like ourselves, being ushered into the hall and our James was there, in the public's eye, people looking down at his poor face. I had to scream at these police officers and ask them please to allow us privacy for the three of us to be together . . . thankfully the policeman pulled James over to another part of the sports hall . . .

'I started to examine my son's body, he had blood in his nostrils, blood in his teeth, his poor face was hardened with blood on the side of his cheek. His face was dirty, his hair was very dirty and dusty . . . and in the meantime my husband was ushered to a table to be asked questions, at which again I began to scream . . . I know these questions have got to be asked but there is a time and a place for everything . . .

'I thought it only right that his dad should be with him. We went together to look for our son James, and that was the time that was owed to us, because at the end of the day, when you carry a child for nine months, and you bring them into the world, it is your right to be with your child. We asked if we could possibly – we wanted to stay with James – we were told "no" we couldn't. So I asked if we could be allowed to come back to see James – we were told "no", it was for identification purposes only . . .'

* * *

A social worker who had helped the police in organising the gymnasium as a temporary mortuary concluded that the police priority was gathering information: 'They wanted to take statements. That was their primary concern.' And it appeared that Duckenfield's earlier lie was informing the line of questioning. The personal reputations of those who died were explored, particularly any associations with alcohol or violence. Collectively it seemed that the 'mind' of the police was set.

The Deputy Chief Ambulance Officer voiced his concern over 'row after row of bodies' in the gymnasium while 'all around the walls there were police officers sitting down eating chicken legs'. He felt that the police were not trained to deal with the bereaved and that a 'factory-type process' was not compatible with the necessary 'humanitarian' response: 'There was a reluctance to give out information, they were preoccupied with dotting i's and crossing t's . . .

'To have CID officers sat at tables ready to take statements seconds after identification was awful . . . We had to stand and listen to the identification of sixty-odd people. The screams and crying could be heard everywhere. It was awful and will be with me forever.' Yet Addis felt that, faced with an unprecedented set of circumstances, the 'procedures were the right procedures' and 'worked very well'.

He continued, 'By 4.30 a.m., 74 of the [then] 94 bodies had been positively identified. This was first-class . . . the remaining bodies were transferred to the Medico–Legal Centre. Further identification could take place there. By 5.30 a.m. all bodies had been transferred.' From the police perspective it had been a significant organisational and administrative achievement.

While voicing reservations over the unreasonableness of the police 'to expect grieving relatives to queue for hours in the freezing temperatures waiting to go through the dreaded blue doors', a senior clergyman co-ordinating the clergy's response endorsed Addis's view about the process: 'Clergy and social workers learned that it was not words that counted, but an embracing, supportive presence . . . we all learned quickly as we were doing the job . . . It was often the clergy who were closest when the green bag was opened to reveal the often little-marked and youthful bodies . . . we later learned how good an environment we had established in many respects for the identification process . . . There was a need for space – a space to touch, to weep and not to be hurried. The gym provided that.'

An assessment not endorsed by many of his colleagues, social workers or ambulance officers. The overwhelming rejection of the gymnasium by the bereaved can too easily be dismissed as reflecting the immediacy of grief: that whatever the physical environment their pain and suffering could not be assuaged. Not so. It was a procedure informed by pragmatism, professional convenience, which handled people during their most vulnerable moments as if objects on a conveyor belt.

From the registration process at the boys' club to the bussing and waiting at the ground. From the dreadful gallery of the numbered dead to the physical presence of loved ones in body bags. From restricted access, being told that sons, daughters, relatives and partners 'are no longer yours, they are the property of the coroner', to the accusatory statement-taking procedure. At each stage there was a denial of the rights and needs of the bereaved: an unnecessary and debilitating tragedy constructed out of a foreseeable and reckless disaster.

As the Deputy Chief Ambulance Officer concluded: 'It was totally unnecessary for people to go through that torment . . . the presentation of a body for identification and a time for the nearest and dearest to come to terms with their shock is a very important part of the grieving process . . . the body should be presented clean, washed, hair fixed, with dignity in a humanitarian way, not in a chuffin' body bag. There is no dignity in death . . . we wanted to bring dignity to those who died at Hillsborough.'

Chapter Five

THE PAIN OF DEATH

Dolores and Les Steele, their sons Philip and Brian, arrived in Sheffield just before 2 p.m. The boys, with tickets for the Leppings Lane terrace, set off at 1.55 p.m. and Dolores and Les followed five minutes later. Dolores has since returned to Hillsborough to time the walk; it took her eight minutes. 'We couldn't believe our luck that we'd managed to park so near.' On the day, the police sent them in the wrong direction and they ended up 'walking the perimeter of the ground with Forest supporters', arriving at Leppings Lane at 2.20 p.m. They entered without difficulty.

Their tickets were for the West Stand and they soon realised that something had happened in the central pens, 'heads were looking down'. Dolores was immediately worried, 'if someone has fainted, why hasn't the person been passed out through the gate?' Within seconds 'there were screams from all the crowd, "Open the gates! Open the gates!" . . . It was just so quick. You could see the police were just standing as if they weren't seeing what everyone else was seeing.'

As bodies were pulled out and 'somebody was trying to do heart massage', Dolores heard a shout, 'Leave him, that man must be dead.' Yet there was a 'slow motion reaction from the police'. Eventually the gate was opened and the police began 'to drag people out' while others were 'pulled up into the stand'. Les watched astonished as 'more and more things were happening on the pitch, you couldn't believe what you were looking at . . .'

When the ambulance drove on to the pitch people in the West Stand were incredulous, 'One ambulance! Why only one ambulance?' Dolores and Les rushed from the stand to find their boys. Brian was standing on a wall. 'We asked him where Philip was and he said that he'd lost sight of him in the pen.' Thinking that Philip might have returned to the car, Les and Brian left while Dolores waited by the tunnel.

Dolores asked the police if she could go into the pens and was told that she could not, 'because they're bringing up the injured'. A man, helping bring out his elderly father, passed a remark to a police officer and was told, 'You've done all of this yourselves. You've all come without tickets.' With that the man produced his tickets and said bitterly, 'My father nearly died in there and you did not know what you were doing.'

Les returned and, together with Dolores and Brian, went back and forth between the car and the ground three times. Still not allowed down the tunnel, Les asked, 'What's happening? What can we do to find out?' By now, deeply worried, they were sent to the gymnasium 'and [the police] weren't very helpful'. Eventually they were given the emergency and hospital numbers. But there 'were massive queues at every phone box'.

Then a woman came out of a house asking if they wanted to use her phone. Leaving Brian in the car they rang the emergency number for 20 minutes to no avail. They rang the Northern General only to be told to ring the emergency number. Les said, 'Then this lady's lad said he'd drive us to the hospital. We made a decision, in case Philip made his way back to the car, to leave Brian in the car.' The woman from the house said he would be all right.

They were dropped at the hospital and, according to Dolores, 'we went up to the canteen area. They were simply saying, "Who is it you've lost?" and you gave your name . . . a very brief description and age.' Les and Dolores sat near the back of the canteen: 'The next thing these two guys walked out and one stood on the table and said, "I've got the worst news for some people." He said there were 11 fatalities there . . . and read out the descriptions and there was nothing. The majority of it was jeans and trainers . . .'

Dolores continued, 'Then he said signet ring . . . the eye colouring was wrong, the hair colour was wrong. Nothing sounded like Philip except the signet ring. The initials he read out were PGS and Philip's ring was PJS, but it was too close for comfort. A nurse said to us, "You're not happy, are you?" I said, "No." We just wanted to go up and ask.' This they did and the man with the list said, 'If the initials aren't right, and the eye colouring's not right just go and sit down because it's nothing to do with your son.'

They returned to their seats. A social worker put her arm around Dolores and said, 'You really want to know more about this person, don't you?' Dolores replied, 'I just know it's him.'

'Right,' said the social worker, 'we're going to do something about it.' They went upstairs and spoke to a policewoman who, in turn, spoke to a police sergeant. 'No,' he said, 'that can't possibly be. Even the initials are wrong.' The policewoman asked, 'Can't you just get the things and show them, then that clears things up.' 'No,' he replied, 'It won't be right.' She said, 'Just get them . . .' He said, 'No.' The policewoman then shouted, 'For God's sake go and get them. Let these people see!' He fetched the envelope. 'And it was his, I knew.' Dolores and Les were then taken to a side-room.

They were told that if they waited they could identify Philip in the hospital mortuary. They waited, although they told staff at the hospital that their other son was expecting them back. Les said, 'They had us sitting in the morgue for about half an hour and then they came and said to us that Philip wasn't there any more, his body was gone.'

Reunited with Brian and accompanied by a social worker and a nurse, Dolores and Les, for no obvious reason, were taken to

Hammerton Road police station. Dolores said, 'Nothing is clear to me; I know from statements that one body was left at the hospital by mistake, and I think it was our Philip. I think they were delaying taking us back to Hillsborough because they didn't know where he was.'

Next they were moved across the road to the boys' club. There, Les 'lost my rag . . . I was fed up sitting around, nothing was happening . . . they were just playing for time.' Among the first to go to the ground, they arrived just after 9.30 p.m. Les went with the police while Dolores stayed with Brian. 'They had all these photographs, so you look at them all and hope you don't see the photograph, but eventually I saw a photograph which resembled Philip . . . then I seemed to wait and it was two minutes past ten when they brought a body to me and I identified Philip.'

Prevented from going back to Dolores and Brian, Les was 'taken for questioning'. He was quizzed about travelling and whether they had stopped for a drink. 'Eventually I thought they were trying to get something out of me. They were on at me for about half an hour when eventually the nurse came and said, "This man's wife is waiting there and he's in no fit state to talk to you."'

Until this point, Dolores and Les had not been able to contact their daughter at home. 'She thought we'd all died . . . the priest had been and all her friends . . . The police had phoned to go down and tell them what we were wearing – she didn't know because she'd gone to work before we'd left. Obviously she feared the worst, and until eleven o'clock, when we got through, she thought the four of us were dead.'

Dolores, Les and Brian drove home to their daughter. What they had been through had shattered their lives: 'We just drove home in a fog.' Les concluded, 'When you think about the day, we were denied everything. Messed around from pillar to post for seven or eight hours, treated like dirt.'

Jimmy Aspinall went to the game by car; his son James went with his friends by coach. Jimmy was in the side pen: 'You could sit down where I was. I knew well over half an hour beforehand . . . I was very worried and said to my brother-in-law, "That crowd's not normal in there, it's too tight." There was no sway in the crowd at all, just not right. I was a good way from there but the policemen were right on top of it and they did nothing.'

At home in Huyton, Jimmy's wife, Margaret, saw the disaster develop on television. 'I actually saw someone getting taken on to the pitch and laid on their back and I started panicking. I thought it was James and I was screaming, "That's our James."' She then saw a police officer push a young man back into the pen. 'You start panicking because you hear the commentators saying there is some sort of trouble . . .

'I didn't know anything about pens. I didn't know they were caged in like animals . . . You could see it was overcrowded just by looking. They gave emergency numbers and we wrote them down and, of course, you couldn't get through. Imagine you could not get through!' At about 6 p.m., Margaret's sister-in-law's son rang from Sheffield. He had seen James earlier, sitting on steps eating his lunch, but not since.

In the ground, Jimmy was kept back with all the other fans in the end pen: 'We were the last out. By the time we got out the back, everything had been cleared up. I had just heard that people had been injured. I saw a couple of people walking along the road holding each other's shoulder. I didn't know then exactly what had happened. I'd seen people on the pitch but not properly because there were that many people running around . . .'

Jimmy phoned Margaret at about 6.30 p.m. and asked if she had heard from James. 'I said, "No, Jimmy. Find our son. Wherever you find him, bring him home with you. Don't come home without him."' Jimmy went to the hospitals where he gave a full description. He was told that James was not on any lists. He repeated the trips, growing more anxious, until about 8.30 p.m.

Margaret, meanwhile, had contacted the coach company. 'They told me that they were all accounted for but the coaches had been impounded and would be arriving in Liverpool about twelve o'clock.' When Jimmy rang her again Margaret had said, 'He's okay. Come home and we'll go down and meet him in Liverpool.' She added, 'You can imagine the relief for Jimmy; for both of us. He came all the way back from Sheffield and got in about half an hour before we went into Liverpool.

'We went into Liverpool with James' friend, John. The coaches came in and everybody was getting off the coach. We were looking for James and Graham, no sign. The very last coach . . . and he wasn't on it . . . so the panic really set in . . . We went to the police station in Tuebrook and they said that no list had come through yet of the living or the dead . . . I said I can't wait any longer for a list to find out whether my son is alive. They said there was nothing else they could do.'

Jimmy decided to drive back to Sheffield with his brother, David. Margaret stayed at home with their other children in case James returned. They agreed that Jimmy would phone home every hour. Margaret managed to contact one of the hospitals and gave them a description of James. 'They said they had a list and he wasn't on it. I asked if it was for the living and the dead and they said it was . . . I thought that he couldn't be dead and must be alive somewhere.'

All the way back to Sheffield, Jimmy 'thought James might be in someone's house . . . I thought that right to the very last second.' He was directed to an office 'to talk to this social services fella. When I mentioned what James looked like, I should have put two and two together then. And he told me to wait, he would take me round to the . . . gym, it must have been.'

At home, Margaret had a call from Jimmy at about 3 a.m., 'when four o'clock came I said that he wasn't phoning me, he'd found James and something had happened.' Jimmy was at the gymnasium. 'When I went up there to identify James from the picture there was a woman screaming . . . sitting on the steps screaming . . . I remember those screams all the time. Then the police officer took the statement from you . . . and asked how many drinks, and that type of thing.' James had personal identification on him, yet had not been listed.

Jimmy returned home, devastated. Margaret was waiting. 'I decided to walk out the front door. God, something's happened to my son. Jimmy would've phoned . . . but he wouldn't phone me with bad news. I saw the car and I knew that if he got out of the car he was going to tell me that my son had died. So I ran away, screaming, knocking on people's doors, shouting, "Don't come near me and tell me because I don't want to know. Because if you tell me I'll know it's true." Jimmy caught up with me and said, "Marg . . ." I said, "No, Jim. It's six o'clock in the morning. How can you tell me he's dead at six in the morning when I've been waiting for him since three o'clock yesterday?"'

Later that day they travelled together to the Medico–Legal Centre. Margaret said, 'I just wanted to cuddle him. I had his coat for him and they wouldn't let me near him. They showed me him behind the glass. I said I wanted to take him home and they said he didn't belong to me, he belonged to the coroner.' It was the final cruel blow following an 'awful night – waiting and hoping J was alive – the most horrendous thing to put any mother through'.

* * *

Stephanie Jones travelled to Sheffield the night before the game to stay with her brother, Richard, and his girlfriend, Tracey, who were at Sheffield University. The plan was that on the Sunday, Doreen and Les Jones would pick up their son, daughter and Tracey and drive to the Snake Pass for a picnic. On the Saturday afternoon, Doreen had gone to visit her father at his home. 'I was in the back kitchen but my father shouted me to tell me there was trouble at Hillsborough.'

Doreen went through to the television. 'I saw people lying on the pitch and people coming over the fence . . . and I heard the man say it was Leppings Lane that the trouble was in . . . and I couldn't understand why these people seemed to be falling on to the pitch. For somebody who is very calm in herself . . . I started to panic and that was from the word go. I was shouting, "My three are in there. I've got to go home," and I started to cry. I hadn't seen anybody who'd died, who was really bad, but his voice was very serious . . . and I ran all the way home.'

Doreen rang Les at work where he was also watching the television coverage. He felt that the three would be safe because they would not have been near the front of the pen. Doreen was 'getting more and more upset watching the scenes' while Les 'was already quite aware that there were deaths in the crowd'. Some time before 5 p.m. Stephanie rang from Sheffield. She was in tears because she had lost both Richard and Tracey. With the help of another fan she had made her way back to the car where a local woman had taken her into her house to use the phone.

'She said she'd hurt her ribs, hurt her arm. I told her to go back to the ground and tell the police what she had told me. When she rang it all changed for me. I then became very calm and tried to instil some calmness in her.' Doreen thought that Richard must be hurt and was probably at the hospital. Contacting the police was the best option for Stephanie. Doreen then phoned Les and he returned home immediately. She contacted Tracey's mother in Wiltshire and 'promised that with every step of the way [they] would keep in touch.

'Les came home and got changed . . . Stephanie finally rang and said she was in a boys' club in Sheffield, right by the police station. She told her dad where it was and we told her we were leaving right away for Sheffield.' They gave Stephanie her other brother's phone number to reassure her that while they were on the road 'she wouldn't be totally on her own . . .'

As they set off, Les was sure that Richard was seriously hurt.

'There was no way he would have let Stephanie go missing and the fact that he was missing was conclusive proof that there was something wrong . . . The Snake Pass seemed to go on for ever and ever. It seemed a hundred miles long.' 'At first,' said Doreen, 'we were talking all the time about whether they were all right . . . slowly all this conversation petered out and the journey was in silence, the Snake Pass never ending . . .'

At the boys' club, they met Stephanie who was with Richard and Tracey's friends and a social worker. Doreen and Les were also assigned a social worker, 'provided with a cup of tea and nothing else . . . it must have been midnight when they got the phones on'. There was no information, no casualty list but a 'terrible atmosphere . . . slowly but surely the people in there were being taken over by dog collars . . . more priests and vicars than you could see people . . .'

Then towards 1 a.m. a senior police officer stood on a chair announcing names. 'We didn't know whether they were people who'd been injured or [whether] he was looking for people . . . no one seemed to react.' So Les went and asked. When he received no real answer he went to the police station and was 'chased back' to the boys' club. They were told to wait.

It was about 2.15 a.m. when another police officer announced that they 'were being taken to the ground to look at some photographs'. Doreen shouted out, 'Why? What are we going to look at photographs for? Why aren't we being taken to a hospital?' She continued, 'He knew what the photographs were and I suppose I did . . . but I didn't know what was going on, possibly I didn't want to accept what was going on.' But the point was they were never told.

They were taken outside – 'two priests, two social workers, Stephanie, Les and I' – and put upstairs on a double-decker bus. Les could not stop shaking, 'considering it'd been such a nice day, it was freezing . . . it was absolutely bitter in the middle of the night and we were all freezing. You were shaking anyway but you didn't know if it was the cold or the fear or what . . .' At the ground they were left on the bus in this state, 'the Salvation Army . . . throwing blankets around [their] shoulders to keep [them] warm'.

Queuing outside the gymnasium, the police reaction was 'aggressive . . . pushing and shoving [people]'. A Salvation Army officer approached and saw that Les 'was fuming' and asked, 'What's the problem?' Les replied they had not seen a casualty list. He could not believe it, told them not to worry and he would fetch one. 'He went away to get me one, but he never came back . . .'

Once inside, they realised the full horror of the gymnasium. Surrounded by gym equipment, and what looked like 'curtains hanging', they watched 'a guy standing there punching a brick wall . . . people screaming and God knows what . . . nobody even taking a blind bit of notice. I couldn't understand why this guy was punching the wall, blood pouring down his arm and nobody taking any notice . . .'

Les was asked to go and view the photographs. Doreen said, 'He's not going anywhere without me . . . the pair of us went hand-in-hand to stand in yet another queue . . . there were, like, partitions and this noise all around you of people sobbing and screaming . . . I couldn't keep still, I was just shaking from my head to my feet. I had this blanket on but I was still shaking and shaking. And this policeman – he had a helmet on – said, "Can't you just keep still?" I looked at him and tried my best to stop shaking.'

Stephanie had stayed in the room with the social worker. Doreen and Les then saw the photographs, 'pinned on to the divider . . . any old way'. Doreen said, 'They were only small Polaroid pictures and we seemed to go along loads of them. And then Les pointed out Richard without telling anybody that it was Richard . . . And then he said he couldn't find Trace. I said this was Trace . . . Les didn't recognise her at first.' The photographs were dark and poor quality and this caused real problems for the bereaved.

They were taken inside the door, 'and they brought us two trolleys together, pulled one out – unzipped it, just showed you the head and you just said, "Yes" and they pulled the next one forward . . . you've got no idea of size because they're in bags'. Doreen bent down, 'to cuddle Richard' but she never made it. 'I don't know who it was but . . . they hawked me up and told Les that they [the bodies] were the property of the coroner and we couldn't touch him. The next thing I know I'm sitting on a chair, so whether I blocked it out, I don't know. But I know I didn't touch him, I know I wasn't allowed to touch him and I know somebody forcibly stopped me.' Les said, 'They just quickly zipped the bag up, ushered us away and they were gone.'

Someone went to collect Stephanie and then an argument broke out. The police were demanding statements and Les said, 'I don't want to give you a statement now.' They replied, 'I'm afraid you're going to have to.' Social workers were arguing that the statements could wait and the police responded, 'No. We want them now.'

'I was absolutely fuming with rage but thought okay we've got to do it, I suppose they need identification, so let's get it over with.'

'Do you know whether he had a drink on the way up here? What time did he leave home? What did he do the night before? Do you know whether he went for a drink the night before? Did he usually have a drink before the match?' Sitting opposite and alongside police officers, Les 'was like a zombie, just staring ahead'. The questions felt like accusations. Accusations against loved ones just identified in the most appalling circumstances.

'The whole time this guy, in civvies, alongside me was tut-tutting, making noises. I don't know what he was saying, I just tried to blot him out but he was getting on my nerves. Eventually the guy asking the questions said, "Okay, that's great," and walked away and I thought that was it . . . then another bobby came and we had to go through it all again over Tracey. All the time, during these interviews, horrendous scenes were going on.'

When they finished answering questions about Tracey, they went to get up from the table and the plain-clothes officer said, 'I want a statement now, an overall statement.' Les sat down. 'I was so mad . . . I just stared ahead and he was asking me questions, like an overall statement. When it was over he sort of threw the statement at me and said, "Here you are, get that signed." I said, "No. I'm going to read it first." I started reading it and he had everything wrong, it was unbelievable, he had his [Richard's] age wrong, everything wrong.'

Doreen recalls the plain-clothes officer rocking his chair on its back legs, 'tapping his pen on the table'. He 'had a thick gold bracelet, and the whole time he was tapping he was swinging . . . and he kept saying, "I've just said, sign it. I've just said, sign it." Maybe he wanted someone to have a go at him. Stephanie was there, actively taking a part. I wasn't . . . I was sitting there just saying I wanted my son.

'All the time we were there, there was all this noise, all around you. You feel you're in a goldfish bowl and everyone's looking at you. The social workers tried to take over, "If she wants to see her son, she should be allowed to see her son." You were more or less trying to say "shush", if we behave ourselves they'll say none of this is true and Richard will be alive. It was like a conveyor belt and they wanted you out as quickly as possible after they'd got what they wanted.'

Later that day they went to the Medico–Legal Centre but were denied access to Richard's body. Doreen wanted to sit with Richard, as she had wanted to hold him at the gymnasium, but it was forbidden. Doreen reflects, 'I was made to feel that I was off my head for wanting to sit with Richard. I asked myself, "Is it me? Am I being macabre?" And then you ask yourself why you let them make you sit for so long at the boys' club – why I let them stop me when I wanted to hold Richard in the gymnasium, why I let them rule me . . .

'Why was I so weak? All these guilt complexes going through your head. That at one time in your life when you needed to be with your son . . . You've brought him into the world, for Christ's sake, you needed to see him out. Why the hell wasn't I strong enough to say all this?' Doreen knew why. Regardless of her actions, however hard she and Les had tried, 'there was no way they were going to let me be with him'. They were powerless.

But they were also shattered by the impact of sudden bereavement, exhausted by shock, their vulnerability exploited by a procedure which failed to recognise their basic needs and fundamental rights. Like so many others that night, Doreen, Les and Stephanie were beaten down by procedures that cast doubts on the good names of the dead, made criminals of survivors and victimised the bereaved. It was an exercise in the use of crude, unsophisticated institutional powers.

* * *

Pat and Peter Joynes had experienced deep personal loss before. Their son, Mark, was killed in South Africa and they had been through a dreadful time arranging the return of Mark to England. Advised, and told, not to view Mark's body, for some time Pat 'could weave these stories that it might not have been Mark that had died . . . eventually I did accept it'. For those prevented from identifying loved ones, Pat's experience is typical.

On the afternoon of the game, Pat was working at Marks and Spencer and knew that her son, Nick, had gone to the match. 'The first I heard that anything was wrong was at tea-break in the afternoon. Word went round that there'd been trouble . . . then rumours started circulating that some fans had died. Quite frankly, I couldn't believe it . . . It was gone four o'clock and a security guard came around asking if anyone had family at the match. If they had they were to go upstairs so that they could go home . . . there were a lot of people becoming very upset.'

Peter had just heard the news and went to pick up Pat from work. 'It was very quiet in Liverpool city centre. It was very unusual and quite eerie.' At home they switched on the television and began phoning the emergency numbers . . . 'they just rang out or were engaged'. Nick had not long been married and at about 6 p.m. Gill, his wife, rang Pat and Peter to say that according to the coach firm everyone on the mini-coach had been accounted for. It was an instant relief.

'We just sat down to eat and Peter was opening a bottle of wine when we had another phone call. It was about 6.30 p.m. It was Gill, to say it had been a mistake and Nick was the only one on the mini-coach who hadn't been accounted for. We went straight to Gill and I said that I was sure Nick would be all right. Basically I just thought it couldn't happen again. We couldn't lose another son in such horrific circumstances.'

Pat and Peter are both from Sheffield with family still in the city. They phoned relatives and tried to ring the emergency numbers. By 9.30 p.m. they had not heard from Nick and decided to go to Sheffield: 'doing something seemed the more positive action . . . Peter, myself, Gill's dad, and Nick's best friend – we all piled into the car. My last words to Gill were, "I will bring him back for you", because at that time I really believed I would do.'

They travelled over the Snake Pass and went to the Royal Hallamshire. 'People came with lists and we checked for Nick's name on their lists of dead and injured . . . some of the injured were in intensive care and hadn't been identified. Gill's dad and Nick's best friend went to the ward . . . he wasn't there. Then people started crowding round and I thought to myself that Nick was dead, that was it, he was gone.'

Social workers advised them to go to a temporary mortuary. 'They gave us a cup of tea in the hospital. By then I had lost any hope. I knew then. I think Peter was still quite hopeful. We followed the social workers in the car to Hillsborough. It was dark and cold.' At the gymnasium there were a lot of people outside, including journalists and photographers. They were told to join a queue but the social worker said, 'No, they're looking for someone.'

Inside Pat remembers the 'appalling noise, people screaming and crying, like walking into hell on earth'. Volunteers took them to an area where there was tea. Then Ian, Nick's best friend, went and returned to say that 'he had met one of Nick's friends from the minibus and he had identified Nick from the photographs. Then it was more or less confirmed that Nick had died . . . We sat at the table crying. It became really imperative then that I saw Nick to make sure he was dead.

'I was taken to see him with Ian. I remember these shutters and doors opening and there were three lines of bodies on the floor. It was very brief. They brought Nick on a wheeled stretcher and they opened the body bag and there was no disputing it was Nick, there was just a little graze on his face. Apart from that he just looked as though he was asleep. I stayed, talking to him and trying to get my thoughts together. I went back to Peter. He was distraught and didn't want to see Nick at that time.'

They then gave statements and were presented with 'all Nick's belongings in a plastic bag – his personal belongings, not his clothes, nor his ticket. We were in shock, it was very cold and there were a lot of press, taking photographs and wanting interviews.' Peter and Pat went to see Gill at her mother's house and visited their other son who was with their daughter. They then returned home distraught.

* * *

Andrew Sefton was the only one in the family keen on football. Neither his mum, Teri, his dad, Colin, nor sister, Julie, were interested. Andrew had told them he was off to watch the game in Sheffield having managed to buy a ticket from a friend who was going to a wedding on the day. Teri was at work when 'one of the patients was calling us to look at the TV. It was Hillsborough

– I'd never heard of it – I thought there was something wrong and all I could think was, "I'm glad Andrew's not there." For some reason I thought Hillsborough was down south.'

Eventually Teri discovered that Hillsborough was in Sheffield and that Andrew was there. She phoned Colin. On her break she took down the emergency numbers and phoned them through to Colin. By this time Julie had rung. They each tried to get through on the emergency numbers but it proved impossible. Between 5 p.m. and 6 p.m. Teri discovered that a friend had phoned Colin. Although there were many injuries and some deaths, Andrew was all right. 'I went into the rest room and must have been absolutely terrified because I just burst into tears . . .'

On finishing her shift at 8 p.m. Teri went home: 'As I turned into the road I didn't see Andrew's car and I thought they should be at home by now . . . Typical, worry the life out of you . . . I've just spent ages crying and they'll just walk in saying, "Did you hear what happened today?" . . . that sort of thing.' Then Colin told her that he had received another phone call. Two friends were safe, one was in intensive care and Andrew and another friend were missing. Although she thought that Andrew would be at the hospital, it was unusual for him not to ring. She was now very worried.

Julie's husband, Leo, arrived to take Teri and Colin to Sheffield. They left Skelmersdale at 9.30 p.m., arriving just after 11.45 p.m. 'We came across Hillsborough by chance . . . the only reason we stopped was because there were police cars, transit vans and loads of police outside and Leo stopped to ask directions.' As it happened they were by the gymnasium. They enquired if there was a casualty list and were told that 'no such list existed'.

Teri then asked what was happening and they were told that it was a temporary mortuary. 'You had better go inside, look at photographs and eliminate the possibility of him being among the dead.' Otherwise, the police officer suggested, they 'could spend all night looking and still end up at the gymnasium as more hospitals were now being used than the original two'.

'We went in and were met by someone who put our name on a list. Leo said that he would go and look at the photographs. The things that go through your mind are so peculiar. I thought, "They must think I'm terrible only just arriving, that I should have been there ages ago . . . his mum just arriving now." But there was something else in the back of my mind – why so many people were there.'

It was after 12.30 a.m. and there were 'loads and loads of people, not just us . . . people who had been at the match and were only just being allowed to identify their loved ones. Leo had to join this huge group and it was all going over my head . . . I was wishing he would come back and we could just go and find Andrew.'

Sometime after 1 a.m., having waited an hour, Leo picked out Andrew from the photographs. He said: 'I was immediately taken through to identify the body of the photograph I had identified. I was then taken to make a statement . . . during this statement I asked to go back and look again, as I could not be sure because the body looked so unnatural . . . I touched Andrew's face and noticed without actually saying that it seemed too warm for a body which had been dead for so long.'

Meanwhile, Teri went up to a police officer and asked why Leo had been away for so long. She was told that there were 'a lot of people to identify'. Then she gave a brief description of Andrew and 'he asked me which pub would he have stopped at on the way over. So I said he wouldn't have done because he was driving and besides which he doesn't drink and, not that it makes any difference, but he doesn't smoke either. He turned to the other officer, asking me how old Andrew was. I told him he was 23. He said, "She'll be telling us next he's a bloody virgin!" I was not in a position to say anything and went back and sat with Colin.'

Teri comforted two young boys, about 15 or 16 years old, who had identified their friend. They asked, 'What are we going to tell his mum?' She was about to find someone to help them when Leo arrived back and said, 'Teri, Andrew's photograph is in there.' Teri 'just went dead, I did not want to know . . . all I could think was that he's not and I must get to him.' Teri collapsed. 'I was standing opposite two policemen, another a few feet away when I fainted. They did nothing to help.'

She then went to identify Andrew. 'I couldn't believe the way he looked. This look of peace that people say [you have] when you are dead, but my son looked bewildered. I could hardly recognise him. It was awful. I tried to comfort Andrew and his face was warm and it was soft. I asked what time he died. At that point I thought they'd all been taken to hospital and Leo had been waiting for him to be brought back. Nobody knew.'

In the gymnasium, all that could be heard were the screams of women, 'usually mums', said Teri. 'It was like being in a death chamber' and 'the police had total control. They handled everything and gave nothing . . . There were a hell of a lot of police officers on duty and the nearest we got to sympathy was the chap on the door . . . he wasn't sympathetic but he was far better than the others, he was civil. The rest were dreadful, I mean dreadful.'

Giving statements, after the identification, Leo and Teri were again asked which pub Andrew would have stopped at on the way to the match. Teri replied, 'None.' Then, 'they turned to Leo and I, and said, "Which pub did you stop at on the way here?" We had literally raced there from home. These were not the sort of questions you ask if you're filling in a sudden death form.'

They stayed in Sheffield and early the next morning went to the police headquarters. There they discovered that Andrew had not made it to hospital. Teri was 'frantic, because I felt . . . there could have been something done to save him . . . a feeling which remained with me for an awful long time. I still believe that in the gymnasium they were dying and some were not dead until much later.' Because Teri felt that not enough had been done to save Andrew, she was left feeling guilty, that, in some way, 'it was my fault'.

* * *

Graham Roberts left home for Hillsborough at 10.30 a.m. He went to the match with a group of friends and was caught in the crush outside the turnstiles. When gate C opened they went through, down the tunnel and into pen 3. One of Graham's friends last saw him a few feet away from the perimeter fence.

Back in Wallasey, his parents, Stan and Daphne Roberts and sister Sue, became worried once they realised that there were deaths and injuries among Liverpool fans. Graham was reliable and so were his friends. They knew that he would ring home if he was safe. No news was bad news. Throughout the evening they made phone calls to Sheffield and to their local police station in Wallasey.

Each time they managed to speak to someone they gave a very detailed description of Graham, what he was wearing and his black onyx ring, worn on the middle finger of his right hand. In the early hours of the morning Stan was on the phone, 'speaking to a sergeant in Sheffield and he was telling me there was no one of Graham's description. We had already been told that three or four times an hour.' Sandra, Graham's fiancée, arrived and told them Graham had died. He had been identified by her brother-in-law at 1.40 a.m.

The Sheffield police sergeant, still on the phone, said to Stan, 'This cannot be, this is impossible.' Stan told him about the identification and that, 'before they [the brothers-in-law] had left Sheffield they pleaded with two senior officers to phone us before they got home and they promised they would. This they did not do.' At about 5.55 a.m. Stan went to the local police station to let them know of Graham's death. While he was there, the South Yorkshire Police phoned through. The Wallasey sergeant said down the phone, 'Yes, I already know. I've got Graham's father stood alongside me. What the hell are you doing in Sheffield?' and with that he 'slammed the phone down'.

The next day, without sleep and in a state of shock, Stan, Daphne, Sue and Sandra went together to a police station in Sheffield. It was Sunday lunchtime when they arrived. Stan felt that they were treated, 'like Saturday night drunks. We were told to, "Sit there", no help was given us.' They were then directed, unaccompanied, to the Medico–Legal Centre, and 'interviewed' twice by social workers. They asked how Graham's body would be returned home and were told, 'they'd all come home in the back of a lorry'. Then they were directed to the mortuary. 'That was something I find hard to explain,' said Stan, 'but it was disgusting. We were in a queue waiting to go and view Graham's body and up to a point Daphne was going to come in and a young boy came out with his parents and said [of their loved one], "He's been murdered, mum, he's been battered." '

At that moment Daphne felt that she could not go through with the identification: 'I said I couldn't see Graham if he's been battered.' Stan, Sue and Sandra went into a room, 'where there was a closed door, and this fellow wearing a white smock said to us, "Are you ready?" We said, "Yes." He drew the curtains and there was no body there. There was then an argument between the two blokes in white smocks.

'They closed the curtains and we heard one of them say, "Well, you'd better go and find the body." We were just waiting while all this was going on. How I kept my cool I'll never know. Minutes passed and then we were asked again if we were ready. The curtains were opened and Graham was there. Then they just ushered us out and that was it – no physical contact. We were like zombies, we didn't know what was going on.'

* * *

Steve Kelly had been working on the taxis throughout the night. He guessed that his brother, Michael, would have gone to the match, travelling from his home in Bristol with other supporters. Steve half-expected him to make a weekend of the trip by calling

162

over to Liverpool. The people Michael travelled with also assumed he would visit his family. So Michael was not immediately missed.

After about three hours' sleep, Steve woke. It was 7 a.m. and he felt 'something strange' was going on. He phoned a few people to find out if Michael had been in touch. Getting no response, he phoned the police. They told him not to worry because all the dead had been identified. He asked, 'Everybody?' They replied, 'Everybody.'

Steve gave them Michael's name and a detailed description which included an unusual ring and a fresh scar on his stomach from recent surgery. He then phoned hospitals and contacts in Bristol. Michael was nowhere to be found, so Steve contacted the police again in Liverpool and Sheffield. The South Yorkshire Police, apparently 'fed up' with Steve's persistence, told him that if they had any further information they would contact the Merseyside police at his local station.

By 2 p.m. Steve was so concerned that he drove to Sheffield. He went with his wife and arrived at Leppings Lane where an officer radioed for a police car which took them to the boys' club. They were interviewed by police officers and social workers and Steve repeated the detailed description of Michael: 'A police officer went away and soon returned, "No," he said, "everyone's been identified," and there was talk of going to some hospitals.' The police officer went and returned again, this time pulling a social worker to one side.

Steve saw 'the expression on her face change and knew there was something wrong'. He and his wife were asked to go to the Medico–Legal Centre. Steve asked what the point was if all of the bodies had been identified. He was told that two bodies still had not been: 'I actually tried to get out of the chair and couldn't.'

At the Medico–Legal Centre two photographs were shown to them. One was Michael. He was dead. About twenty minutes later they were taken to identify Michael through a glass screen. Steve had been looking for his brother all morning, had been reassured that he was alive, now he was devastated to see him lying there. 'The photograph was the only preparation we got.'

Before they left, Steve asked to spend some time with Michael, but again it was through the glass screen. Steve said he wanted to hold, to touch his brother. His request was refused. 'The next morning when my friend drove me back to Sheffield I saw him again, again through this glass screen. They wouldn't let us go in, because I did ask, I wanted to go in . . . just give him a kiss. He was my brother . . . I just wanted to hold his hand or something, let him know I was there, because he had been on his own all that time.'

* * *

Derek McNiven and Tony Curran, having watched the horror of the central pens from their stand seats returned to the car to meet up with Eddie and Adam Spearritt. They soon became increasingly desperate with worry. At 6 p.m., with no sign of Eddie or Adam, they reported both missing and were directed by police to the boys' club to register their names. They gave full descriptions, including ages and clothing. It was about 6.20 p.m. Social workers, clerics and volunteers were offering tea and cake.

Sarah Collins, a volunteer, had been there since 5.15 p.m. It was 'total confusion' with no one obviously in charge. Eventually she met Derek and Tony. At about 7.20 p.m., Sarah put it at 7.30 p.m., they remember a senior police officer, in his 'early thirties', standing on a chair on a raised platform. He held a loud hailer, microphone attached. It failed to work so he shouted names from a compiled list. Names of those reported missing but who were 'safe and well'.

'Halfway through the list of about a dozen names was Adam's. We were relieved but said nothing because we were hoping for Eddie's name to be read out.' Safe in the knowledge that Adam was alive, Derek phoned Adam's mother, Jan, to give the partly positive news. Their next priority was to find Adam and to trace Eddie: 'We went to a police officer and asked about the list . . . and were told the list could not be traced to source.'

Accompanied by Sarah, and other volunteers, Derek and Tony were taken to the gymnasium. 'There, amid confusion, cold and damp, and heavy distress, we were shown the photographs of all who died in the tragedy.' At least, that was what they were told. They were reassured that Eddie's photograph was not there. With Adam already safe it looked as though both had survived.

They were then taken to the Northern General where they were shown four young boys in the intensive care unit. None was Adam. About to leave, they mentioned Eddie and returned to the unit. He was there, unconscious but stable. It was now 1 a.m. on Sunday morning and they rang Jan again to tell her they had found Eddie but had no further news on Adam. They were so relieved. There was no reason to doubt the information about Adam and he was not among the photographs of the dead.

They travelled to the Royal Hallamshire hospital but none of the boys there was Adam. At about 2.30 a.m. 'we returned to Hillsborough to have another look at the photographs.' It was harrowing: 'The faces barely recognisable . . . we asked to see any males under 20 and were shown a body. It was not Adam. We asked to see the photos again but we were told it was not worth it because there was only one unidentified lad left and we had just looked at him.'

They returned to the Northern General where they met Eddie's brother, Robert. They reassured him that Adam was not among the dead at the gymnasium. But it was now six hours since they had heard the 'alive and well' announcement and there had been no further word on Adam's whereabouts. Concern was now mounting and on the advice of hospital staff they returned to Hillsborough with Robert.

Once there, according to Derek, a senior officer 'told Robert he could look at photographs – plural'. They told the officer that there could not be more than one photograph because earlier they were informed that there was only one unidentified body. 'The policeman told us more bodies had been brought in.' This came as a shock, as Derek, Tony and Sarah had been told that all who had died were at the gymnasium. 'There were about ten new photographs. Looking at them, we recognised a picture of Adam.'

Adam's body was brought to the door of the gymnasium where Robert identified his nephew. A senior officer apologised for the 'confusion' but his apology was rejected. He said there had been a 'lack of communication'. In fact, Adam was pronounced dead soon after his arrival at the Northern General. There was no explanation offered for the delay in transporting him back to the gymnasium, for the misinformation of the 'alive and well' list or for the continuing reassurances made to Tony and David that all who died were at the gymnasium. Whoever sent them back to the gymnasium from the Northern General just before 3 a.m. must have known that more bodies had been transported from the hospital.

By now, Jan was at the bedside of her unconscious husband. Relieved that Adam was alive, her immediate concern was that Eddie would pull through. Robert returned to the Northern General to give her the dreadful news. It came as a massive shock. She wanted to go to Adam: 'Robert hadn't long identified him at the gym. From the gym he had come straight to the hospital, so it would be about half an hour after.'

Adam, however, had already been transferred to the mortuary at the Medico–Legal Centre, 'which is where I went to see him . . . he was behind a glass screen'. Jan wanted to hold Adam, to be close, 'and they wouldn't let me'. She 'begged and pleaded and everyone else who was there did', but she was told by a mortuary official that it would not be possible. To be with him she would have to walk past other bodies. She replied, 'It doesn't matter, I'll walk through and I won't look. Just let me go through, guide me to the room were Adam is.' Jan was denied access and told, 'When you get him home you can hold him.'

The strain was unbearable. An hour earlier she believed Adam had survived the disaster, now she was looking at his body through a glass screen, forbidden to touch, caress, kiss or say goodbye. Like any other loving parent she felt a real need to have close contact just hours after he died. 'It's just instinct to want to hold them in your arms. It's as if, once someone's died, they no longer belong to you, they belong to someone else and it's up to them to decide what you're allowed to do with them. It's something that will always haunt me, really, something I should have done . . . I think now I should have kicked and screamed and I say to myself it was my own fault. I pleaded but I should have gone on and on and on . . .'

Jan's moving account is a clear illustration of the powerlessness felt by people in the face of inflexible and bureaucratic institutions. Like so many others bereaved, particularly by sudden death, she needed an immediate, physical closeness with Adam. It was a need frustrated ostensibly by the layout of the Medico–Legal Centre. Alternatives to her walking through rows of bodies could, and should, have been found. Whatever she had done, however much she had pleaded, access would have been denied. The decision was immovable, indefensible.

That moment should have been Jan's by right. It could not be reclaimed at some later time when Adam returned to Runcorn for his burial. She was left to carry the burden of that denial and a deep sense of guilt that she should have done more to challenge those who had the discretionary power to make arbitrary, ad hoc decisions, to change minds narrowed by professional convenience and personal intransigence.

Eddie regained consciousness later on Sunday. Jan was back at his side. It was a parent's worst fear; he had lived but Adam had died. His first reaction was to see Adam and eventually it was agreed that he could make the journey to the Medico–Legal

Centre. On the Monday he and Jan went together. 'What a fiasco that was . . . He'd come off the ventilator but still had drips.' Eddie was wearing ill-fitting hospital pyjamas, odd top and bottoms, 'No slippers, no socks, nothing on his feet, with a drip still attached to him.'

He was taken in a wheelchair to a car, rather than an ambulance, where a male nurse set up the drip. The wheelchair was left at the hospital so when they arrived at the Medico–Legal Centre, 'and he was shivering by this time', Eddie had to walk. 'He had this tatty old blanket round him, it was like cobblestones, what a sight he looked.' A vicar commented to Eddie that it 'was one of the most remarkable sights he had ever seen, walking across this rough ground, covered in loose chippings, a drip attached and no shoes or socks'.

Yet this was only two days after a disaster in which Eddie had nearly died. The lack of appropriate support for the Spearritts at such a time was evident in the conditions they were forced to endure. Apart from his last attempts to save Adam before losing consciousness himself, the visit to see Adam at the Medico–Legal Centre was the worst experience of Eddie's life. Once inside, Jan and Eddie sat together and waited, 'while they got Adam ready'. Again, physical access was denied and they viewed their 14-year-old son through a glass window. 'It was as if he was no longer our son.' And that's the issue. To the authorities, Adam was now *their* body.

Chapter Six

FROM DECEIT TO DENIAL

On a daily basis the police significantly affect the formal content of the news. Crime, conflict and disorder are news, often 'big news'. During morning briefings, at police headquarters the length and breadth of Britain, it is often difficult to tell police press officers and local journalists apart. They need each other. With the public's seemingly insatiable appetite for crime stories, the police are able to construct stories, control the flow of information: as one former Metropolitan Police commissioner put it, 'mould public opinion'. Locally and nationally, they are powerful definers.

After Hillsborough, the police strategy was to put as much distance as possible between the acts and omissions of their officers while pointing the finger of blame at the fans. Usually, in the aftermath of disaster, the police, as the lead emergency service, provide the first detached overview of the tragedy and its aftermath. While always informed by their professional judgements and interpretations, the police account is expected to be factually accurate. At Hillsborough, however, senior officers knew from the outset that the actions and decisions of their colleagues put them in the frame.

The early impact of Duckenfield's lie cannot be underestimated. It set an immediate tone, focusing attention on the allegedly unacceptable behaviour of Liverpool fans outside the stadium. More significantly, it established an agenda, shaping the inquiries and investigations that followed. The coroner's unprecedented decision to take blood-alcohol levels of all who died was plainly influenced by police allegations of excessive drinking. Confronting bereaved families and friends about the drinking habits of their loved ones while the bodies lay, still warm, on the gymnasium floor, was a harsh demonstration of the priorities of the South Yorkshire Police.

From the outset the media was influential in conveying the police interpretation of events. As early as 3.40 p.m. on the day, BBC's radio coverage broadcast 'unconfirmed reports that a door was broken down' outside Leppings Lane. At 4.15 p.m. Graham Kelly, the FA's Chief Executive, was asked if this was the case. He replied that the police had not given the impression that they had ordered any of the exit gates to be opened.

He went on to say that the Sheffield Wednesday secretary, Graham Mackrell, had spoken to the senior officer in charge and 'at about ten to three there was a surge . . . composed of about 500 Liverpool fans and the police say that a gate was forced and led to a crush in the terracing area . . . well under capacity, I'm told, there was still plenty of room inside that area . . .'

Later, the bulletin reported that the gates had been 'broken down' with 'large numbers of ticketless fans' determined to push their way in. In part, this came from Graham Kelly's comment that over-crowding was due to 'people coming in at one end of the ground who were unauthorised'. At the evening press conference, the South Yorkshire Chief Constable, Peter Wright, blamed the initial crush outside the turnstiles on 'the late arrival of large numbers of people', which was reported as: 'between three and four thousand Liverpool fans turned up just five minutes before kick-off'.

Effectively, the 'forced gate' theory was replaced by the 'conspiracy theory'. This implied that Liverpool fans, drunk and ticketless, planned to arrive immediately before kick-off, com-pelling the police to open exit gates. 'Hooligan hysteria', linked to the 'Heysel factor', turned Hillsborough into a public order issue.

From the next morning this portrayal dominated much of the press coverage.

The *Sunday Mirror* reported between 3,000 and 4,000 Liverpool fans, 'seemingly uncontrolled', trying to 'force through the turnstiles'. The gate, it continued 'was opened to stampeding Liverpool fans'. Even *The Observer*, despite a well-balanced account, repeated uncritically Wright's comments on fans' 'late arrival' as a 'danger to life'. Both ITN *News* and BBC's *Newsnight* made similar points about the 'impatience' of Liverpool fans rushing the ground.

Other influential responses came from 'official' sources. Mackrell, having visited Gate C and without any evidence to support the police allegation, told the media that a 'surge' by Liverpool fans had caused the disaster: 'Forest supporters were in the ground early. Liverpool's were not.' Joe Ashton, a Sheffield MP, identified the origins of the surge: once in the ground, Liverpool fans 'all ran to the entrance behind the goal'. Again the source was Peter Wright who, at a second press conference, talked of a 'direct connection between the surge inside the ground and the incident outside'.

At the very moment when football's key spokespeople needed to take a measured and calm view of a tragedy quickly embroiled in controversy, UEFA president Jacques Georges made an extraordinary intervention. He said that 'People's frenzy to enter the stadium, come what may, whatever the risk to the lives of others' had caused the disaster. Barely disguising parallels drawn with Heysel, Georges likened Liverpool fans to 'beasts waiting to charge into the arena', concluding that what happened 'was not far from hooliganism'. Although later retracted, Georges' comments added weight to the near universal rush to judgement. Born from Duckenfield's lie, Georges' unrestrained attack was a form of verification.

In Sheffield, the early coverage was unequivocal in directing blame. The *Sheffield Star* headlined its front page 'RACE TO

STADIUM', describing a 'crazed surge' of fans with 'up to 40 people' dying in the tunnel, 'the rest trampled underfoot'. The *Yorkshire Post* pulled no punches in proposing that the 'trampling crush' had been caused by 'thousands of fans' mounting a 'fatal charge'. They were 'latecomers', determined to 'force their way into the ground'. Across the Pennines the *Manchester Evening News* repeated the same allegations, concluding that the 'Anfield Army charged on to the terrace behind the goal – many without tickets'.

Within forty-eight hours, the allegations against Liverpool fans consolidated. Writing in the *Evening Standard*, Peter McKay argued that gate C had been opened only because there was 'risk of death or serious injury among the hysterically pushing fans'. The roots of the disaster were in the 'tribal passions of Liverpool supporters'. Without a thought for the suffering of survivors and the bereaved he condemned the fans: 'They literally killed them-selves and others to be at the game.' They were victims of the 'mindless passion, rage and violence that soccer attracts'.

Soon the uncompromising rush to judgement against the fans stood virtually uncontested. As prejudices and bigotry were unleashed, journalists went in search of 'yob' stories. Writing in the *Liverpool Daily Post*, John Williams argued that the 'gate crashers wreaked their fatal havoc . . . uncontrolled fanaticism and mass hysteria which literally squeezed the life out of men, women and children.' It was 'yobbism at its most base' with ticketless fans 'crushing to death their fellow scousers . . . Scouse killed scouse for no better reason than 22 men were kicking a ball.' Paul Middup of the Police Federation stated that fans arrived 'tanked up on drink', putting officers in a 'simply terrifying' situation.

But on Tuesday, 18 April, a quite different and more sinister story emerged. The *Sheffield Star* carried serious police allegations that Liverpool fans had attacked rescue workers and stolen from the dead. Its front page headline 'FANS IN DRUNKEN ATTACKS ON POLICE' introduced 'the sickening story the police are piecing together'. Not only had 'ticketless thugs staged the crush [at the turnstiles] to gain entry' but 'yobs' had 'attacked an ambulance-man, threatened firemen and punched and urinated on policemen as they gave the kiss of life to stricken victims'.

That evening, BBC's main news 'revealed' the focus of police evidence to the Home Office inquiry which was already under way. Repeating allegations against Liverpool fans, it used further quotes from a Sheffield MP, Irvine Patnick, and the Police Federation, concluding that the South Yorkshire Police had 'reiterated their belief that they will be eventually vindicated by the inquiry'. On ITV, Patnick said that he had spoken to the officers who had tried to save lives; 'they'd been attacked . . . kicked and punched even when giving mouth-to-mouth resuscitation and people were urinating on them from the balcony above . . .'

The next morning national newspapers lined up to report the story. Typically, the most lurid and offensive reporting was in *The Sun*, giving its front page to the headlines: 'THE TRUTH: SOME FANS PICKED POCKETS OF VICTIMS; SOME FANS URINATED ON THE BRAVE COPS; SOME FANS BEAT UP PC GIVING KISS OF LIFE'. It later emerged that Kelvin MacKenzie, *The Sun*'s editor, had wanted to use the banner headline 'YOU SCUM', eventually settling on 'THE TRUTH'.

While *The Sun* took the full force of the outrage on Merseyside, other newspapers were little better. The *Daily Star* led its front page with 'DEAD FANS ROBBED BY DRUNK THUG'; the *Mail* carried the police accusation 'vile fans fought us as we tried to help the dying'; the *Express* used the headline 'POLICE ACCUSE DRUNKEN FANS' followed by 'Police saw "sick spectacle of pilfering from the dying"'; the *Yorkshire Post* ran 'Liverpool pickpockets "pounced on the dead"'; the *Sheffield Star* had 'Yobs "in sex jibes over girl's corpse"'. The quotes, mostly unattributed, came from police or Police Federation sources.

The following day several newspapers carried responses to the allegations but their intensity had been so powerful they gained widespread recognition as fact. By the weekend, untruths and

173

half-truths became reality as columnists added their opinions. Auberon Waugh reported 3,000 Liverpool fans 'rioting outside the gate', many 'without tickets', having 'spent the time drinking'. Ticketless Liverpool fans were 'further excited by the prospect of not having to buy tickets' and 'charged in'.

Anthony Burgess put the deaths down to 'certain football supporters' who had 'behaved stupidly'. They had escaped one disaster only to provoke another. And Hugh McIlvanney, renowned for his reflective and well-balanced sports journalism, wrote of the 'seething throng' outside the turnstiles, 'a number of whom had been lingering in pubs, some of them still in search of tickets'. Perhaps the most irresponsible and damaging conclusions were drawn by Edward Pearce, who decided to applaud Jacques Georges' comments: 'did he say anything but the unpalatable truth? For the second time in half a decade a large body of Liverpool supporters has killed people.'

Within a week of Hillsborough, the 'Heysel factor' was comprehensively established. This time, the story went, 'they' had killed 'their own'. While counter allegations ran throughout the first few days, focusing unfairly on Superintendent Marshall as the 'man who opened the gate', nothing compared to the orchestrated campaign of vilification directed towards those who died and survived Hillsborough. Apart from provoking a sense of outrage it caused real pain and suffering among the bereaved, the survivors and their families. As one bereaved mother put it, 'We soon realised that we weren't only in a fight for justice for those who died but also to clear their names and the names of the fans who lived.'

Eventually it emerged that the appalling allegations had involved off-the-record briefings by South Yorkshire senior officers. With junior officers already encouraged not to write in their pocket-books and to submit 'recollections' of the day to their seniors, the implications were clear. If the force was to extricate itself from its responsibility for the circumstances in which the disaster happened it needed to use the media to construct the

'Truth'. It also needed to supply hard evidence, particularly the evidence of its officers, verifying the 'Truth' as reported.

* * *

Within 24 hours of the disaster the Prime Minister, Margaret Thatcher, visited Hillsborough. She also took the opportunity, well publicised in the media, of visiting the local hospitals. 'The last thing I needed was to wake up in a hospital bed to be patronised by Margaret Thatcher,' said one critically ill survivor later. Photocalls aside, Thatcher's visit presented the South Yorkshire Police with the opportunity to provide the Prime Minister and her entourage, including the Home Secretary, Douglas Hurd, with their version of events.

It would be naïve to believe that as she toured the stadium, visited the gymnasium, the Leppings Lane terrace with its buckled barrier and ripped-out perimeter fencing, the tunnel, the turnstiles and the scene of the crush outside, she was not given a running commentary. Neither was Thatcher an impartial observer. Only four years earlier she had rounded on 'football hooliganism', being directly instrumental in introducing special measures to deal with the 'national malaise'.

Thatcher was also committed to the introduction of a compulsory National Identity Scheme for supporters. The scheme formed the first part of the 1989 Football Spectators Act, going through Parliament in the months following the disaster. There is no question that she and her colleagues viewed the disaster through the lens of hooliganism. The South Yorkshire Police and other interested parties were not going to lose the opportunity for reinforcing that view.

This has since become starkly apparent in observations made by Sir Bernard Ingham who, at the time, was Thatcher's Press Secretary, and accompanied her on the visit. He was privy to the press briefings and off-the-record comments surrounding the visit: 'I visited Hillsborough on the morning after the disaster. I know what I learned on the spot. There would have been no Hillsborough

175

if a mob, who were clearly tanked up, had not tried to force their way into the ground. To blame the police is a cop-out.'

In replying to a letter from Dolores Steele, whose son Philip died at Hillsborough, Ingham reiterated his allegation that a 'tanked up mob' had 'stormed the perimeter wall "causing" your son's death and I believe 95 others'. He continued, 'They are the guilty ones. They caused the terrible disaster and I am astonished that anyone can believe otherwise.' It is fair to assume that his conclusions were influenced by the Thatcher visit, which the South Yorkshire Police and club/FA officials attended. The conclusions bore a remarkable similarity to Duckenfield's lie in all but the 'broken gate' theory.

* * *

Whenever a major tragedy occurs it engulfs and overwhelms those caught in the trauma of its aftermath. Ordinary people going about their everyday routines are suddenly 'survivors' or 'the bereaved'. The shock of sudden death and the pain of survival are mind-numbing, debilitating. Apart from dealing with the practicalities of the immediate aftermath, individuals and families try to find ways of coping, taking it 'one day at a time'. The law, the investigations, the inquiries, seem to operate in another world. As people struggle to cope with bereavement and survival they assume that the investigative and legal processes work for them, rather than against; they put their trust in the law.

The investigation and inquiry into a controversial disaster such as Hillsborough is a complex business. Inevitably, the police are expected to pursue a criminal investigation, gathering evidence on behalf of the Chief Constable which is then forwarded to the Director of Public Prosecutions. The DPP decides if there is sufficient evidence to prosecute any individual, group or organisation. After Hillsborough, because South Yorkshire Police officers were directly involved in the disaster, the investigating police had to come from another force. The South Yorkshire Chief Constable was also concerned to discover whether any actions by his officers contravened the force disciplinary code. As complaints were made against the police the independent Police Complaints Authority also had a significant role to play.

Apart from the criminal investigation, civil actions were mounted by the bereaved and injured to claim damages against a range of responsible authorities, particularly the South Yorkshire Police and Sheffield Wednesday Football Club. These actions involved an attempt to show to the satisfaction of the civil courts that the authorities had been negligent and, therefore, had contributed to the deaths and injuries. Effectively, in such actions, any damages won are paid by insurers. It is often in their interests to 'do a deal' and settle outside the court.

But controversial deaths also involve the local coroner in whose jurisdiction the tragedy occurs. Technically the coroner takes possession of the bodies, is responsible for the pathological investigation, postmortems and the identification of the deceased. The coroner alone decides on the release of bodies to families. What follows is an inquest which determines the medical cause of death, considers the circumstances and arrives at a verdict from a prescribed list. But the coroner's court, where the inquest takes place, is not concerned with liability. In practice, inquests are formally opened and immediately adjourned until all other investigations and inquiries concerning liability are resolved. So it was after Hillsborough.

Making matters even more complicated is the 'public inquiry'. While incidents are regularly investigated by agencies such as the Health and Safety Executive, there are often calls for a 'public inquiry' if the tragedy is considered to have wider implications for the 'public interest'. Usually conducted by a High Court judge and commissioned, complete with terms of reference by the Home Office, public inquiries are not part of criminal or civil proceedings. There is no accused and, therefore, no prosecution or defence; their findings being drawn from a wide range of written and oral evidence.

Public inquiries, by their very nature, are official responses to controversial cases. Inevitably, they are surrounded by allegations and counter-allegations, raising serious matters of responsibility and liability. Conducted by senior judges, serviced by appropriate 'experts' and provided with their own counsel, public inquiries are inextricably linked to the apportionment of blame. Consequently, 'interested parties' hire the 'best' barristers and legal teams to safeguard their interests and, where possible, deflect liability.

Evidence is not always given under oath, rendering it useless as established fact in subsequent court hearings. The judge takes written and oral evidence, calls for 'expert opinion', and can be supported by the investigations of a dedicated police inquiry team. It is not unusual for public inquiries to provide an initial, interim report, in an attempt to respond to key questions, followed by a more measured and less specific final report.

The perceived strength of a public inquiry is that its recommendations carry the weight of a costly and in-depth investigation drawing on a mass of unsolicited as well as requested evidence and opinion. Further, findings are derived in rigorous cross-examination of key witnesses by lawyers representing the interests of all parties. Seen as 'independent' and commissioned by government, the presumption is that their recommendations will be treated with respect and implemented.

What is not so positive, however, is the process through which a public inquiry's terms of reference are established. Those most affected by an 'event' or 'issue' have no input into the priorities and emphases of the inquiry. This decision lies solely with the Home Secretary, or another appropriate government minister, often reflecting the 'early view' of what happened.

The day after Margaret Thatcher's visit, Lord Justice Taylor, a judge with a well-known personal interest in football, was appointed by Douglas Hurd to conduct a Home Office inquiry into the disaster. His terms of reference were simply to 'inquire into the events at Sheffield Wednesday football ground on 15 April 1989 and to make recommendations about the needs of crowd control and safety at sports events'. In other words, Taylor could explore the full range of matters he considered relevant to the disaster and its immediate aftermath on the day, drawing conclusions and making far-reaching recommendations on any matter of crowd control, management and safety. The remit gave him immense discretion.

Geoffrey Dear, West Midlands' Chief Constable, was invited to oversee the criminal investigation into Hillsborough and to gather evidence for the Taylor Inquiry. Directly responsible to Taylor, he appointed his Assistant Chief Constable, Mervyn Jones, full-time to the inquiry. The West Midlands team also had the responsibility of taking forward the criminal investigation for the South Yorkshire Chief Constable and the Director of Public Prosecutions. Later, its officers also worked as coroner's officers for the inquests. In effect, the West Midlands investigators played the lead role in all three 'independent' inquiries: Taylor, the police/DPP and the coroner.

The day after his appointment, Taylor and his team visited Hillsborough. Just ten days later he held a preliminary hearing, announcing the date of the oral hearings and the intended procedures. In Liverpool the solicitors representing families met, forming the Hillsborough Solicitors' Group Steering Committee. Group members were informed that the evidence taken would be 'determined by counsel and solicitors to the inquiry' (the Treasury team) after their consideration of 'all witness statements submitted'. Any evidence submitted to Taylor was not to be disclosed.

Taylor 'accorded representation' to the bereaved and injured, the Football Supporters' Association, the Football Association, Sheffield City Council, Sheffield Wednesday Football Club, South Yorkshire Constabulary and South Yorkshire Fire and Civil Defence Authority. This list was later extended to include the South Yorkshire Metropolitan Ambulance Service and Dr Eastwood, consultant engineer to the club. In according representation to the bereaved and injured, Taylor authorised that costs for their counsel and instruction would be met from public funds.

The Hillsborough Steering Committee was simultaneously involved in trying to establish liability through civil actions. By early May the committee was confident that it would not be difficult to establish liability but that the 'apportionment between defendants may be the stumbling block'. In terms of the Taylor Inquiry, the committee's priorities were to 'ensure that all facts . . . come out', concentrating 'upon issues which will affect civil liability . . . issues of safety and crowd control'.

According to the steering committee, Taylor 'made it clear' that he intended 'to find facts and not apportion blame'. Whatever Taylor's intentions and hopes, the establishment of 'fact' in such a massively controversial and contested case could not be divorced from the allocation of blame. As each of the interested parties lined up to cross-examine witnesses, their intention was to apportion liability to the others involved.

On 15 May, a month to the day after the disaster, at Sheffield's town hall, the Taylor Inquiry hearings opened. The West Midlands Police investigation had been gathering evidence since 24 April. Members of the public were invited to call a freephone number to offer evidence. Overall, 28 lines were open for six days yielding 2,666 calls. These calls were evaluated by West Midlands officers using a questionnaire. From these they made judgements on the 'quality' of the evidence and based their eventual selection. The West Midlands team took 3,776 statements and Taylor read 1,550 letters. Interested parties were asked to put forward appropriate witnesses.

Taylor stated that, 'From this mass it was essential to select only sufficient good and reliable evidence necessary to establish the facts and causes of the disaster.' The South Yorkshire Police, however, submitted that, because the West Midlands Police investigation was only in its early days at the time of the hearing, all the evidence had not been collected, rendering it 'unsafe' for Taylor 'to make findings of fact' at that time.

While accepting that the 'witnesses called were only a small fraction of those from whom statements were or could have been taken', Taylor was 'satisfied that they were sufficient in number and reliability' to enable him 'to reach the necessary conclusions'. His priority was to produce a speedy interim report and to have waited for further statements would have delayed its publication. He was 'assured' by the West Midlands Chief Constable that it was 'most unlikely' that further evidence gathered would 'significantly alter or add to the history of events which emerged at the hearing'.

On 1 August 1989, less than four months after the disaster, Taylor published his interim report. For those expecting the South Yorkshire Police to be vindicated, their allegations about 'hooliganism' accepted, his findings were stunning. He established that the immediate cause of the disaster was the failure to cut off access to the central pens once gate C had been opened. Effectively, this caused the overcrowding which, in turn, caused the deaths.

The central pens were already over-full, with no means of controlling entry to each pen nor any effective method of monitoring crowd density. Build-up of pressure in pen 3 led to the collapse of the barrier, followed by a 'sluggish reaction and response' by the police. Lack of leadership, together with the restricted size and small number of perimeter fence gates, hampered the rescue.

Taylor considered that the dangerous congestion at the turnstiles should have been anticipated and planned for. Neither the club nor the police recognised that unless fans arrived steadily over an extensive period of time the turnstiles would not cope. Neither the Operational Order nor the policing strategy considered the possibility of an unmanageable build-up at the turnstiles just before kick-off. While accepting that there was a drunken minority of fans, it was not these fans who caused the congestion. And the problem at the turnstiles was exacerbated by inadequate signs and ticketing.

Taylor found that 'hooliganism' played no part in the Hillsborough disaster. Yet, the 'fear of hooliganism' led to an undue 'influence on the strategy of the police'. This created an 'imbalance between the need to quell a minority of troublemakers and the need to secure the safety and comfort of the majority'. The 'real cause' of the disaster 'was overcrowding'; the 'main reason . . . was the failure of police control'. Having laid the primary responsibility at the door of the South Yorkshire Police, Taylor went on to castigate senior officers.

He was emphatic that once Duckenfield acceded to Marshall's request to open gate C, the tunnel should have been closed. What was happening both in the pens and at the turnstiles could be seen clearly from the control box. Failure to close off the tunnel 'was a blunder of the first magnitude'. Duckenfield's 'capacity to take decisions and give orders seemed to collapse' after he received Marshall's request and then 'he failed to give necessary consequential orders or to exert any control when the disaster occurred'.

Worse still, Duckenfield 'gave Mr Kelly and others to think that there had been an inrush due to fans forcing open a gate'. Taylor continued, 'This was not only untruthful' but it 'set off a widely reported allegation against the supporters which caused grave offence and distress'. Further, 'reluctance to tell the truth . . . did not require that he [Kelly] be told a falsehood'. The 'likeliest explanation' for Duckenfield's 'lack of candour' was that he 'simply could not face the enormity of the decision to open the gates and all that flowed therefrom'.

Taylor concluded that Duckenfield's failure to face up to the consequences of his decision 'would explain what he said to Mr Kelly, what he did not say to [Assistant Chief Constable] Jackson, his aversion to addressing the crowd and his failure to take effective control of the disaster situation. He froze.' Taylor's judgement fell heavily on the shoulders of a match commander lacking experience in policing football and left vulnerable by an inexplicable operational policy decision.

Taylor did not limit his criticisms of the South Yorkshire Police to Duckenfield. He considered it 'a matter of regret' that, 'at the hearing, and in their submissions', senior officers 'were not prepared to concede they were in any respect at fault in what occurred'. Apart from Duckenfield apologising, under cross-examination, for blaming Liverpool fans for causing the deaths, 'the police case was to blame the fans for being late and drunk, and to blame the club for failing to monitor the pens'. He concluded: 'Such an unrealistic approach gives cause for anxiety . . . It would have been more seemly and encouraging for the future if responsibility had been faced.'

Sixty-five police officers gave evidence to the inquiry and Taylor found the 'quality of their evidence' to be 'in inverse proportion to their rank'. Some junior officers made 'alert, intelligent and open' witnesses. Of these, 'many . . . strove heroically in ghastly circumstances' on the day. In contrast, most senior officers 'were defensive and evasive witnesses . . . neither their handling of problems on the day nor their account of it in evidence' showing 'qualities of leadership expected of their rank'.

Taylor also recognised that there had been a police-led campaign of vilification against Liverpool fans. He listed the allegations: drunken fans had urinated on the police while they rescued the dead and injured, and on the bodies of the dead. They had stolen from the dead. He concluded, 'not a single witness' supported 'any of those allegations although every opportunity was afforded for any of the represented parties to have any witness called . . . those who made them, and those who disseminated them, would have done better to hold their peace'.

While Taylor was uncompromising in condemning senior

officers, their decisions or lack of them on the day, and their flawed planning, oddly he declined to criticise the operational policies of the South Yorkshire force. Conversely, he praised their 'many years . . . of excellent service to the public' and their 'sensitive' and 'successful' crowd management at 'major matches, during strikes in the coal industry and the steel industry . . .'

Taylor's unsourced opinion, particularly regarding the policing of strikes, was far from uncontested. There was considerable evidence that South Yorkshire's response to pickets during the 1984–85 coal dispute was anything but sensitive. Yet within months of the interim report's publication the Chief Constable, Peter Wright, reported to the Police Authority that 'The management training, appraisal and selection processes that exist . . . are all targeted to achieve a continuation of that excellent service to the public . . .' By seizing on faint praise, Wright sought to deflect the force of Taylor's damning indictment of his senior officers' performance. While Wright offered to resign, Taylor's general support for the force's broader crowd-related policies added weight and legitimacy to the Police Authority's decision not to accept his offer. Despite this, the shock, anger and bitterness of the South Yorkshire Police response to Taylor was barely concealed. His findings not only entirely rejected the police version of events, they gave credibility to the fans' version of police mismanagement.

* * *

Other agencies implicated in the disaster were spared many of the criticisms anticipated before and during the inquiry. Taylor defended the Football Association's decision to use Hillsborough because the 1988 semi-final 'had been considered a successfully managed event'. This denied criticisms levelled by several bodies, particularly Liverpool Football Club and the Football Supporters' Association, against the venue and its arrangements.

Taylor acknowledged that the FA should have been 'more sensitive and responsive to reasonable representations'. Further, he stated that the FA 'did not consider in any depth whether it [Hillsborough] was suitable for a high risk match with an attendance of 54,000 requiring to be segregated, all of whom were, in effect, among supporters lacking week-in-week-out knowledge of the ground'. Yet the choice of venue was not 'causative of the disaster' and Taylor did not accept that the Leppings Lane terrace 'was incapable of being successfully policed'.

Taylor considered that 'the club over the years . . . adopted a responsible and conscientious approach to its responsibilities', retaining the services of a consultant engineer, Dr Eastwood. Despite this acknowledgement, Taylor found a 'number of respects in which failure by the club contributed to this disaster'. This failure included the state of the 'unsatisfactory and ill-suited' Leppings Lane terrace. Although the club was aware of the problems, attempting solutions between 1981 and 1986, 'there remained the same numbers of turnstiles, and the same problems outside and inside them'.

Alterations inside the turnstiles and on the terraces had affected capacity 'but no specific allowance was made for them' and both Dr Eastwood and the club 'should have taken a more positive approach'. While monitoring the pens was a police responsibility, 'the club had a duty to its visitors and the club's officials ought to have alerted the police to the grossly uneven distribution of fans on the terraces . . . the onus here was on the club as well as on the police'.

The removal of a pen 3 barrier in 1986 should have reduced the pen's capacity. It also created pressure inside the pen; pushing 'fans straight down by the radial fence to the lowest line of barriers'. Consequently the 'pressure diagonally from the tunnel mouth' down to the front barrier which collapsed was 'unbroken by any intervening barrier'. In evidence, Eastwood accepted that the removal of the barrier was a likely cause of the front barrier's collapse, where so many people died. Taylor considered its removal, on the advice of Eastwood and the local authority's advisory group, 'was misguided'.

Taylor levelled further criticisms at the club over breaches of national guidelines, poor sign-posting and the 'unhelpful format' of the tickets. He recognised the confusion and difficulties experienced by fans on their arrival at the turnstiles and inside the ground. He constantly referred to problems being made worse because of fans' unfamiliarity with ground layout and established routines.

Sheffield City Council also had a statutory duty to issue, monitor and revise the ground's safety certificate. Both club and authority failed in their respective duties as the safety certificate 'took no account of the 1981 and 1985 alterations to the ground'. Incredibly, the certificate in force had been issued in 1979, a decade earlier. It had not been updated and there was no FA procedure for checking its validity.

In 1981, the Hillsborough semi-final between Tottenham Hotspur and Wolverhampton Wanderers narrowly missed disaster as a large number of fans escaped from the Leppings Lane terrace on to the pitch. At the time there were no perimeter fences. Following this incident, the police advised the club that the specified capacity was too high. Neither the warning nor the near-miss was heeded by the club, the city council or the FA. In conclusion, Taylor found the 'performance by the city council of its duties in regard to the Safety Certificate . . . inefficient and dilatory'.

In marked contrast to these scathing criticisms of the club, the safety engineer, the local authority advisory groups and the FA, Taylor considered 'no valid criticism' could be levelled against the St John's Ambulance Brigade, the South Yorkshire Metropolitan Ambulance Service (SYMAS) or the fire brigade. He criticised heavily a Liverpool doctor who had publicly condemned SYMAS for the slow arrival of ambulances, insufficient equipment and lack of triage.

Another doctor was also criticised for complaining that defibrillators were not deployed. Taylor accepted expert evidence that using defibrillators 'with people milling about would have been highly dangerous owing to the risk of injury from the electric charge'. This was an extraordinary conclusion given that lives might have been saved.

In the report, Taylor recorded that St John's, SYMAS and the fire brigade each 'responded promptly when alerted', bringing 'appropriate equipment' and efficient personal intervention. In drawing this conclusion, Taylor skated over any thorough assessment of 'basic provision' for first aid, professional medical attention or appropriate ambulance cover. Further, his minimal attention to the events at the gymnasium, as the dead and injured arrived, contrasted with that paid to the adequacy of the police response.

While noting that vehicles parked around the gymnasium hindered the ambulance operation, Taylor did not make any assessment of the implications for saving life. At Hillsborough, like so many other major sports or leisure venues, the preferred option was to use St John's volunteers rather than full-time professional cover. A senior SYMAS officer stated, '. . . no matter how hard they try they are a voluntary agency . . . there's no comparison, but football clubs are notorious for getting the cheapest deal – £1 per 1,000 spectators'.

In refuting the claim that ambulances were not on the scene sufficiently quickly, Taylor accepted the evidence of the SYMAS control superintendent that approximately 20 ambulances had been dispatched by 3.30 p.m. Yet an ambulance officer administering to the injured behind the Leppings Lane end stated that there were no ambulances at 3.21 p.m. He then treated several people before the first ambulance arrived. This evidence supported the Liverpool doctor's assessment of the situation.

Further, the major accident vehicle was not requested until 3.29 p.m., arriving at 3.45 p.m. Given that it was the only vehicle equipped to deal with large-scale incidents, why was there a delay? Taylor, apparently judging its potential irrelevant, made no attempt to answer this question. Yet in his final report, he concluded that a major incident equipment vehicle used by the Scottish Ambulance Service, 'goes a long way to meeting the criticisms raised after Hillsborough'.

Taylor also denied that triage, 'ensuring that those most likely to benefit from treatment are seen first', had failed. In contrast, the doctors working behind Leppings Lane argued that triage was absent until one of them initiated it. Further, most of the dead, dying and injured were carried across the pitch. Their selection was arbitrary and no one established a system of triage around the goalmouth. Worse still, some of these fans were left in the recovery position at the other end of the pitch.

Eventually, those assumed dead were carried inside the gymnasium and those with injuries taken to the ambulances. Because those rescued or recovered were carried in no particular order, evacuation to hospital was random. Consequently, triage was limited. The dead, dying and injured were put down inside the gymnasium without priority. People were also left outside the gymnasium.

While the gymnasium as an 'emergency area' was mentioned by Taylor, he provided no evaluation of effectiveness, and no comment on adequacy or operation; merely recording as a matter of fact that it became the temporary mortuary. His only criticism was implied: 'There was intense distress amongst the injured and the bereaved; relatives were reluctant to be parted from the dead and sought to revive them . . . there were scuffles. Some of these involved those who were the worse for drink.'

This was an insensitive remark which deeply upset bereaved families and survivors. He seemingly overlooked the obvious explanation that fans' behaviour was the product of shock and grief rather than alcohol. Many had suffered the trauma of their own survival, witnessing death all around them, only then to be confronted with the dreadful reality of bereavement. It was an implied criticism contrasting with the testimony of senior ambulance officers and doctors who stated that they could not have coped with the scale of the disaster without the intervention of selfless fans.

Rather than focusing on isolated examples of negative or disruptive behaviour by a few fans, Taylor would have been better advised to concentrate on the appropriateness of the decisions to designate the gymnasium a temporary mortuary and to take blood-alcohol levels from the dead. These decisions, ignored by the inquiry, drew significant criticisms from families, survivors, SYMAS officers and other caring agencies. Clearly, Taylor did not consider the immediate aftermath to be part of his remit. However thorough the interim report appeared, with its 43 recommendations, Taylor's failure to fully evaluate the level of medical care administered at the ground and at the hospitals, as well as the issues around the gymnasium as a temporary mortuary and blood-alcohol levels, amounted to considerable oversights.

* * *

While Taylor was writing his interim report, civil actions to determine liability were pursued. As the families' lawyers predicted, apportionment of responsibility between defendants became a 'stumbling block'. The insurers of both the club and the police denied liability but the 'general view' of the steering committee was that 'liability was not likely to be a problem in the fatal cases or in those cases where people had received physical and/or mental injuries while in pens 3 or 4'. By mid-July these defendants, the police and the club, insisted that liability, particularly the question of apportionment, should be settled in the civil courts.

On 26 July there was an appearance before Mr Justice Steyn for his directions in the civil action. He considered that the Taylor Report 'be admitted as evidence of facts . . . with the reservation that any party had the right to call evidence on any fact found within the report with which that party did not agree'. At the same time, neither the police nor the club were 'prepared to make a formal admission of liability'. Nor were they 'prepared to indicate that they are prepared to make a payment by way of compensation'.

The solicitors' steering group informed families that while it was not unusual in civil claims for liability to be denied, insurers often settled claims. However, 'It has been made very clear to us that such a course of action is not going to be voluntarily taken.' By September, and following the publication of Taylor's interim report, the defendants 'as anticipated' blamed 'each other for the various aspects of the disaster and no admissions of liability' were made.

Predictably the South Yorkshire Police attempted to deny liability in negligence for what happened at Hillsborough, arguing that there was no duty of care owed to the dead or the injured. On 30 November 1989 the South Yorkshire Chief Constable, Peter Wright, and his Police Authority offered an out-of-court damages settlement to the bereaved and injured. In conjunction with their insurers, the Municipal Mutual, they released a press statement that Wright intended 'to open negotiations with the aim of resolving all bona fide claims against him for compensation arising out of the Hillsborough disaster'.

The statement also made it clear that the 'other parties . . . named as defendants in the civil proceedings' had been offered the opportunity to join the police in the settlement but had declined. These were the club, the safety engineers and the city council. Wright's press release warned that he would 'pursue legal action against those parties to recover moneys paid out to the claimants pursuant to today's offer'. The offer carried no acceptance of liability.

In October 1990, the South Yorkshire Police launched a civil action to reclaim part of the costs of the out-of-court settlement. Before Mr Justice Jowitt at Manchester's High Court, counsel for the police argued that there were four key factors which together created an inherently 'unsafe system' at Hillsborough's ground: no means of controlling the capacity of pens 3 and 4 . . . 'the main cause of the disaster'; an 'unsafe system' of management by the club; an 'unsafe system' of escape; an 'unsafe system' of inspection and testing of the barriers. On this collective basis South Yorkshire Police claimed negligence and breach of common duty and care against the club, and negligence only against the safety engineers, Eastwood and Partners.

Within days, and following a weekend of private negotiations, a secret deal was struck between the parties. Having decided on a settlement and by spreading the cost of damages across insurers, the parties avoided a court ruling which publicly apportioned blame for the disaster. In the terms of the settlement was an agreement by each party not to disclose its details. While the deal had no effect on the amount of payments to the bereaved and injured, the families felt that any official ruling on responsibility once again had been denied.

Eventually, compensation payments were paid. By early 1998 there had been 36 settlements for loss of financial dependency, 50 fatal claims (restricted to funeral expenses and/or statutory bereavement payments) and 1,035 personal injury claims. While a fair number of claims remained outstanding, £13.5 million had been paid in compensation and legal costs. This was well short of the £50 million estimated in 1990.

The Chief Constable's agreement to settle in November 1989, put in writing by the police solicitors on 15 December, was widely reported as a settlement 'without liability for what happened'. Yet two years later, in a House of Lords ruling on a different but related claim, Lord Keith of Kinkel commented, 'The Chief Constable of South Yorkshire has admitted liability in negligence in respect of the deaths and physical injuries.'

The question of whether 'liability in negligence' represents a tacit acceptance of blame has resurfaced repeatedly throughout the last decade. Settling compensation claims out of court, and doing deals with other defendants behind closed doors, did not inspire confidence among families and survivors that the police and other parties were willing to accept, openly and without ambiguity, their part in causing death and injury.

* * *

Whatever the shortcomings of Taylor's interim report, there was no doubting his key findings. The build-up and crush outside the turnstiles were not the fault of the fans and were entirely fore-seeable. Once the decision was taken to open gate C, Duckenfield and Murray should have anticipated the consequences and sealed off the tunnel leading to the central pens. Taylor concluded that if they were not aware of the overcrowding in pens 3 and 4 prior to opening the gate, they should have been.

Faced with the enormity of what was unfolding before him, Duckenfield 'froze', responded ineptly and then lied. The main reason for the disaster was police mismanagement of the crowd. Culpability seemed to be restricted to certain senior officers on the day. Little was made by Taylor of force policy and the inherent risk of appointing an inexperienced match commander at such short notice.

While the South Yorkshire Police had to publicly accept Taylor's findings, they were far from impressed. Even though Wright offered his resignation, he continued to rail against the fans – promising, some interpreted it as threatening, that the inquests would reveal the full story and his officers would be exonerated. He also claimed that some of Taylor's comments had been 'harsh', even 'savage'. Among families and survivors the feeling was that Wright and his force would never accept responsibility.

Taylor's findings were important in establishing primary causation; indicating the clear chain of events which led to the crush and inhibited rescue and evacuation. Yet he failed abys-mally to explore fully the circumstances which surrounded the actual deaths of those who survived the crush in the pens.

Many families whose loved ones died on the pitch, at the back of Leppings Lane, in or around the gymnasium, in ambulances, or at the hospitals, sought answers to the specific circumstances of those deaths. They knew that the injuries which caused death were sustained in the fatal crush. What disturbed them was whether anything more could have been done to save lives once they had been rescued from the pens.

Within a month of the disaster, the Hillsborough Solicitors' Steering Group met with the bereaved families and their counsel. At the meeting a 'number of relatives were anxious to know precisely when, where and how those who died, died . . . This is a matter which will be dealt with at the inquests . . .' From the outset, then, there was an expectation among the families' lawyers that specific circumstances, particularly relating to appropriate medical care and attention, would be unveiled and cross-examined at the inquests.

Peter Wright also made it clear that he too was eagerly awaiting the inquests. There was, he argued, a 'very strong feeling of resentment and injustice in the force' because 'nobody seems to have grasped the full picture'. This implied Taylor was flawed. Finding difficulty in 'coming to terms' with Taylor's rejection of the hooliganism and drunkenness claims by the police as key factors in the disaster, Wright warned that 'a lot of additional evidence' would be presented to the inquests 'which may put a different complexion on the end product'.

Given Wright's widely publicised comments and the families' growing concerns about the precise circumstances in which their loved ones had died, the inquests grew in significance. Yet, they had to remain adjourned until the DPP had come to a decision over criminal prosecution. Then, in a wholly unprecedented move, the coroner took a decision which was to have far-reaching consequences.

Chapter Seven

VERDICTS BEYOND REASON

Coroners' courts are exclusive places in more ways than one. They deal only with death, and even then only with certain classifications of death. Sudden death. Deaths in custody. Unexplained death. Deaths in controversial circumstances. Very few deaths are processed through the local coroner's office and of these only a small percentage warrant a full-blown inquest before a jury. Yet this direct descendant of a twelfth-century institution exists throughout England and Wales. Every authority has a coroner's court but, thankfully, few people have to attend them.

In full session the coroner's court seems familiar. Scenes instantly recognisable from years of watching televised courtroom dramas. The raised stage from which the judge, in this case the coroner, conducts the proceedings; stood up for on entering, bowed to on addressing. Reverential acknowledgement of ascribed status. Court ushers, witnesses, lawyers, juries, transcribers, police officers, the press and the public. All the usual suspects.

It looks, feels, even smells, like any other courtroom. But it isn't. High-powered barristers, often the best money can buy, do battle over evidence taken under oath, cross-examining defensive witnesses rigorously, even harshly. Their efforts focus solely on establishing who, individually, collectively or corporately, was or was not responsible for causing death. Yet the inquest is not concerned with liability. While the atmosphere is often charged with blame and guilt, there is no one on trial, no prosecution and no defence.

Criminal and civil courts, regardless of who takes legal action and on whose behalf, are dedicated entirely to liability. Even in civil actions, where opponents agree to settle on the steps of the court, the settlement reflects a 'best deal' possible for both parties. Whatever the subtext, the agreement is derived in negotiating liability. In criminal cases the end-product, barring a hung jury, is 'guilt' or 'innocence', with the 'court' then administering punishment to the guilty.

In the coroner's court the objective is to establish the medical cause of death and, through consideration of the pathological evidence and the 'circumstances' in which the person died, to reach an appropriate verdict from a prescribed list. Verdicts are not supposed to indicate liability and inquests are held once all other criminal and civil avenues have been exhausted. The naïve assumption is that if someone has died through the actions or inactions of another individual, a group, an organisation or a dangerous procedure, then the adversarial courts will sort it out. Once sorted, the inquest deals with the pathology, the medical cause of death, reaches a verdict and releases the body for burial or cremation. This is a hopeful, but hopeless, counsel of perfection.

In controversial cases it rarely works like that. If a prosecution fails, or there is a decision not to prosecute, or families have neither the know-how nor finances to pursue a civil action, the inquest becomes the only forum in which the circumstances of the death or deaths will be raised and cross-examined. Often it affords the only opportunity for bereaved families to hear and test the evidence.

Yet the inquest is no more than an inquiry before a local authority appointed coroner: a doctor or a solicitor. The witnesses called are 'coroner's witnesses'. 'Interested parties', usually the bereaved and any individual or agency directly involved in the death, are designated solely by the coroner and cannot call witnesses. Once witnesses are sworn in, their evidence is examined by the coroner, who takes them through their previously gathered statements, and then cross-examined by lawyers representing the 'interested parties'.

No questions are permitted which might point the finger of liability and the coroner alone decides on the appropriateness of a line of cross-examination. Witnesses do not have to answer incriminating questions. The order of witnesses appearing before the court, the focus and style of cross-examination and the general conduct of the court are entirely at the coroner's discretion. Once the evidence has been heard, the coroner alone summarises for the jury. Lawyers cannot make speeches, address the jury or sum up the evidence from their or their clients' point of view.

The coroner's summary of the evidence inevitably reflects an opinion, however considered, based on interpretation and value judgement. It is often not difficult to identify the coroner's favoured version of the 'truth'. As well as summing up, the coroner also directs the jury towards a prescribed verdict based on the evidence, the legal test for each verdict and legal submissions made by the lawyers in the absence of the jury.

From the jury's perspective, it can be difficult to distinguish between the summing-up and the legal direction. Although coroners make the distinction, lay juries can easily confuse the coroner's interpretation of the facts with legal direction based on points of law; the certainty of direction becoming a straitjacket for reviewing complex and contrasting versions of events. Clearly, if the coroner passes an opinion on the facts it carries considerable clout; he or she is the map and compass on legal direction.

A range of verdicts is available to juries. Most contentious cases have occurred around three verdicts: 'suicide', 'accidental death' and 'unlawfully killed'. Suicide indicates that death was self-inflicted. Often that is clear from the case. What it does not indicate is whether a person was driven to suicide by the actions of others or their experiences of an institutional regime, such as a prison. Debates here have raged over the extent to which a duty of care is owed, by individuals or institutions, to those for whom they are responsible.

Duty of care, or lack of appropriate care, has also been central to cases in which people have died directly or indirectly through the negligence of others, their employers or service providers. There is no verdict of 'negligence'. In fact, there is no verdict which 'fills the gap' between accidental death and unlawfully killed. Because the legal test for unlawful killing is equivalent to manslaughter, and coroners instruct juries that they should be satisfied 'beyond reasonable doubt' in applying the test, cases involving a high degree of negligence often end with an accidental death verdict.

Throughout the investigation of deaths within the coroner's jurisdiction the procedure is serviced by coroners' officers, often local police officers on secondment. Coroners also work closely with pathologists. Usually the inquest hears the medical evidence, any other 'expert' evidence deemed appropriate by the coroner, and evidence from witnesses to the death and its circumstances.

If bereaved families feel short-changed by the criminal or civil investigations, the inquest is their last resort. It inspires a belief that it is 'their' inquest into the death of their loved one: 'their' time, 'their' right. Coroners invariably speak to the bereaved in that way, showing sympathy and concern. In their opening comments coroners also tend to emphasise that inquests set out to establish 'who' died, 'when', 'where' and 'how'. The first three are straightforward, but establishing 'how', the circumstances surrounding the death, is where difficulties often arise.

In controversial cases, families tend to know 'who', 'when' and 'where'. Their sole concern is 'how'. Yet immediately, behind the sympathetic words and sensitive acknowledgements, hangs the denial of their agenda: a spectre over the proceedings. 'How'

– the circumstances of death – can be pursued; it can be discussed; it should be established. But it is 'how' without liability, 'how' without blame. It does not take a sophisticated analysis to appreciate the contradiction. One eminent barrister likened the job of cross-examining at an inquest to working with 'both hands tied behind your back'.

This is the procedure, an adversarial wolf in inquisitorial sheep's clothing, to which the bereaved have to turn. This is the anachronistic, inadequate and dishonest forum which is left to carry the full weight of responsibility for resolving and revealing the circumstances of death, while giving not so much as a nod towards individual or corporate liability. Coroners' courts are places of illusion: one minute beckoning, the next rejecting. And they kick people when they're down. They are painful places, where those traumatised by sudden bereavement suffer the story of death in a vacuum of non-liability.

* * *

Like any other inquest where there might be a prosecution, the Hillsborough inquests were opened and adjourned immediately after the disaster. With the Taylor Inquiry and the criminal investigation under way, the inquests had to wait. The West Midlands Police investigation serviced not only the Director of Public Prosecutions (DPP) and Lord Justice Taylor but also the coroner; the police investigators eventually deputed as coroners' officers.

Once Taylor reported in August 1989, the bereaved were concerned about slow progress over prosecution and the delayed inquests. Their concern focused on the specific circumstances in which their loved ones died and the relevance of blood-alcohol levels. There had been so many allegations over drunkenness that families felt the taking of alcohol levels constituted a real threat to the integrity and reputation of their loved ones.

As early as July 1989, the solicitors' steering committee informed families that the coroner, Dr Stefan Popper, was thinking of holding 'one inquest covering the general facts and matters which gave rise to the deaths immediately followed by 95 individual inquests [at that time the death toll had not reached 96] dealing with the situation of each of the deceased'. Popper intended to hold a generic 'scene-setting' hearing, retelling the story of the disaster, taking both expert and more general evidence as to the events – a kind of Taylor rerun – followed by individual hearings with each family. It would move from the general to the specific. It seemed to make sense.

Following further written approaches from the solicitors' steering committee, Popper took the extraordinary decision to resume proceedings before the issue of criminal prosecution had been settled. Having sought advice from various sources, including the DPP, he met with Doug Fraser, the steering committee's nominee as the solicitor to represent the families for the duration of the inquests. A week later, on 6 March 1990, Popper held a pre-inquest review meeting attended by Mervyn Jones, the West Midland's Assistant Chief Constable heading the coroner's investigation, together with solicitors representing other 'interested parties'.

Jones emphasised that the DPP was still unable to rule on prosecution as all necessary evidence had not yet been gathered. Despite this, Popper was keen to progress on a limited basis. He had sought, and gained, the DPP's approval. Now he reversed the previously proposed sequence. Preliminary hearings, or mini-inquests, would be held with each family, then adjourned to await the DPP's decision on prosecution. Once the issue of prosecution was resolved, the inquests would resume on a generic basis. Mini-inquests would deal only with the medical evidence on each of the deceased, blood-alcohol levels, the deceased's location before death and subsequent identification. They would not address 'how' people died.

Popper was 'prepared to take some evidence to meet the legitimate needs of the bereaved' but, he argued, it was not in the interests of justice to 'muddy the waters and hinder other action'. So no controversial matters would be addressed. A general opening with 'expert' evidence overviewing blood-alcohol levels, documentation and general pathology would be followed by the mini-inquest on each of the deceased. At each mini-inquest, his objective was eight inquests per day over a three-week period, the bereaved would hear only from the pathologist and the police.

All evidence gathered in respect of each death, including witness accounts from the time of leaving home to, where possible, the moment of death, were to be summarised by West Midlands investigating officers. The summaries would be read to the court by the officers: their synopses, their words, their selection of material. It was an unprecedented decision as the evidence could not be cross-examined. Yet it would be heard by the jury, weighted by the personal interpretation of the officers.

On 9 March, Doug Fraser wrote to all families' solicitors. He stated that it was 'not possible' for 'all the information' to be released because of the possibility of criminal prosecution. Summaries, compiled by the investigating officers, would be 'scrutinised' by senior officers and the coroner before their release to families and in advance of the mini-inquests, 'to ensure they contain no controversial details and they are as accurate as possible in the circumstances'.

Incredibly, Fraser commented that once 'many families' had seen the summaries, they would be 'satisfied with the factual information . . . and not want to take any further action'. He went on to state that the mini-inquests would be 'low key . . . an exercise in distributing information to families about precisely how their loved ones died and where, and not an attempt to discover why or who was to blame'. The deal with the coroner had been sold to families on the basis that there would be satisfaction with 'factual information' and it would relate to 'precisely how' the deaths had occurred.

Fraser stressed that the mini-inquests amounted to an

'information dissemination exercise'. The senior pathologist, Professor Alan Usher, would give 'distressing' evidence but 'will hopefully clear up much anxiety and show that many fans simply "went to sleep" without any great discomfort because of lack of oxygen'. This was an extraordinary statement. Whatever the good intentions behind it, Fraser pre-empted evidence that was controversial and possibly had a bearing on liability. It was not for him to presume a lack of suffering.

He concluded, 'For our part we believe that this move by HM Coroner to impart information to families is to be applauded and we have taken the liberty of making that point in open court and through the press . . . we believe his stated intentions to assist families in any way he can by providing this information are entirely genuine and we trust that those families who you represent will accept this move on his behalf . . .'

With this endorsement won, Popper wrote to each solicitor reiterating the format: '. . . the intention is to take postmortem evidence together with a summary of the evidence as it relates to the location of the deceased, the time of death as far as it can be reasonably established and to clear up any minor matters such as the spelling of names.' He stressed that evidence would be presented in a 'non-adversarial' fashion and would be 'non-controversial'.

And so the scene was set. The inquests into the deaths of those killed in the biggest disaster in British sports history were to be resumed on a strictly limited basis. Those in control on the day would be conspicuous by their absence, as would the rescuers and medics. West Midlands Police officers would give oral summaries, selectively written at their discretion, of other people's evidence. No cross-examination, no contesting of the summaries, no testing of the evidence. It was an unprecedented move which resulted in families and the jury hearing evidence that was impossible to question.

Early in April 1990, just days before the first anniversary of the disaster, Popper wrote to families informing them of the date and time of 'their' mini-inquest. With a level of insensitivity characteristic of official organisations and their bureaucratic procedures, the date for the opening of the inquests was 18 April, just three days after the first memorial. Perhaps the second most distressing day in the lives of the bereaved was followed immediately by the opening of a most significant hearing. Many felt 'in no fit state' to attend. But they did.

*   *   *

As the inquests drew near it was clear that families had no idea what faced them. Why should they? Most people never have to sit through such an ordeal and many inquests are uncontested, lasting minutes rather than months. Yet with growing concern over the specific circumstances of each death and real anxiety over whether enough had been done to save lives, together with the South Yorkshire Chief Constable's statements that the inquests would set the record straight and exonerate his officers, the stakes were high.

In preparation for the inquests, a day-long seminar was held to brief all social workers directly involved. Contributions had been sought from people with first-hand experience. A Liverpool team social worker commented, 'We hadn't a clue, none of us had attended an inquest let alone one of this size and importance, yet we were supposed to be advising families and the survivors called to give evidence.'

Some members of the social work team requested advice from the Hillsborough Project researchers, given their well-established background in controversial deaths and inquests. 'We had their book,' said another social worker, 'and it was the only thing I'd read that spelt out the deficiencies and problems with inquests in big cases. We needed more on this to give families and survivors a clear picture.' The researchers were invited to the briefing seminar and accepted.

Just days before, however, the invitation was withdrawn. The training officer responsible stated that the decision had been reversed because the Hillsborough Project team had 'the potential to unsettle the delicate relationship between the social workers and the police' – the police in question being the West Midlands investigators. Consequently, these officers advised the social workers about the inquests, their organisation, their conduct and all other arrangements.

* * *

Outside Sheffield's town hall, on the first day of the mini-inquests, television crews, photographers and journalists jockeyed for position to gain the best shots or the most telling interviews with families as they arrived. It was a sad, distressing and intrusive moment as bereaved families arrived in minibuses accompanied by social workers, or simply tried to be inconspicuous having travelled by car or train. West Midlands officers, in civilian clothes, were everywhere, handling everything.

The early sessions, before the mini-inquests proper, were heavily stage-managed. In the Council Chamber, used as the 'court' for the first two days, Popper, accompanied by Mervyn Jones as his senior coroner's officer and introduced as the man who 'wears several hats', rehearsed and re-enacted their entrance to accommodate photographers and television. Camera crews seemed to be everywhere, relaying close-ups of families' tearful anticipation throughout the world. 'It was like a circus and no one cared about our feelings,' said a bereaved mother.

Popper introduced the proceedings, welcoming the various 'interested parties' and their legal representatives. Outlining the procedure, he repeated the formula agreed at the pre-inquest review meeting. It was a highly charged atmosphere. He described how summarised evidence would be presented, emphasising that it would be taken as a factual account. Further, he informed the court that selected extracts from statements in his possession would be used at his discretion. Again, the families' lawyers accepted this unusual arrangement although it denied the disclosure of evidence and prevented cross-examination.

Several witnesses were called to set the scene. A chemical pathologist, Dr Forrest, gave evidence concerning blood-alcohol levels. After much technical detail and listing the levels of all who died, the families' solicitor, Doug Fraser, made a regrettable comment: 'as a matter of fact it is about one-sixth who were effectively too drunk to drive'. This was a crass remark playing directly into the hands of tabloids eager to have their earlier allegations of drunkenness endorsed. It was as if the families' own lawyer was pointing the finger of guilt or responsibility at some of those who died.

While some newspapers reported the first day responsibly and fairly, *The Sun* predictably led with the headline, '15 Hillsborough Dead Too Drunk for Driving.' Its article stated: 'tests showed that 51 of the dead – more than half the total – had been drinking'. A national yardstick for assessing fitness to drive immediately became the assumed measure of drunkenness at Hillsborough and, by implication, of blame for the deaths. It was unfair, inappropriate and insensitive.

Blood-alcohol levels, and the media emphasis on drunkenness, dominated the first day of the preliminary hearings. It was a taste of what was to come. More serious still, it was a distraction from a crucial issue glossed over by the coverage. Also giving evidence on the first day was James Wardrope, the Northern General's accident and emergency consultant. In describing the injuries suffered by the deceased, the coroner was informed by Wardrope that 'traumatic asphyxia' was not a condition regularly presented at the hospital: 'But you had quite a lot on this day?' asked Popper. 'Yes,' Wardrope replied.

In a signed statement made by the senior pathologist, Professor Alan Usher, asphyxia was defined pathologically as 'some mechanical obstruction to normal breathing'. Consequently, 'oxygen in the air cannot be drawn into the lungs and passed into the blood', in turn starving 'body tissues which require it for their normal function'. He went on to state, 'Virtually' all who died at Hillsborough suffered 'compression of the chest wall', causing 'the condition of traumatic or crush asphyxia – the terms are synonymous'.

His opinion was unequivocal. Any distinction between crush and traumatic asphyxia was immaterial. In questioning Wardrope, the coroner referred only to traumatic asphyxia and the consultant seemed to accept this. Yet, writing in the *British Medical Journal* two years after the disaster, Wardrope and his colleagues made a significant distinction: 'Traumatic asphyxia is usually caused by a heavy weight falling on the chest or a violent crush between heavy objects . . . Crush asphyxia is caused by a gradually increasing and sustained pressure on the chest.'

According to the authors, while crush asphyxia presents 'similarities to traumatic asphyxia, the conditions differ in mechanism of injury, clinical findings, main complications and outcome'. Undoubtedly, those who died at Hillsborough asphyxiated; but how, and over what period of time, were essential questions. Wardrope and his colleagues were subsequently making a distinction apparently considered immaterial by the senior pathologist at the time of the inquests. Clearly, they favoured crush asphyxia as the appropriate condition in most cases. This also contrasted significantly with Wardrope's response at the inquests.

The distinction was highly relevant in interpreting the circumstances: a sudden impact as opposed to a gradual compression. In retrospect, Wardrope and his colleagues concluded that the disaster 'resulted in a gradual and prolonged crush, affecting large numbers of previously fit young people'. A sudden impact, such as the barrier collapsing and people falling on those trapped below, could cause traumatic asphyxia: the chest wall compressed with such force that people went into unconsciousness within minutes, dying soon after.

The ebb and flow of the crowd, however, in which compression gradually occurred, leading to crush asphyxia, raised the issue of whether earlier rescue could have prevented asphyxiation. As one of Britain's leading forensic pathologists, Iain West, was later to state, if 'compression of the chest had been intermittent' it was impossible to state 'with any certainty' that death occurred within a precisely defined time period. The medical evidence regarding asphyxiation was later to prove crucial to the limitations on evidence set by the coroner. From the outset it was treated as objective, a matter of fact, and therefore non-controversial.

* * *

With the preliminaries over, the mini-inquests moved to the coroner's court at Sheffield's Medico–Legal Centre. For families this was a painful return to the place where they last saw their loved ones in the days after the disaster. It became a conveyor-belt of the grief-stricken. Some arrived with their social workers, others met Sheffield-based workers at the centre. Inside the door was a waiting area not designed for a rapid turnover of grieving relatives.

Some were taken to a side-room where they saw the West Midlands' summary of evidence for the first time. An already stressful experience was heightened by having to digest harrowing information, in public and for the first time. Some families found mistakes in the summaries which added to their distress.

Waiting and grieving. Anticipating the unknown and fearing the worst. Wall-to-wall West Midlands Police officers, two assigned to each family, some known to them through repeated home visits. Occasionally a little light-hearted, nervous banter broke the subdued atmosphere of waiting. They waited in turn, enveloped by an overwhelming sense of sadness. For those administering the process it was an agreed procedure, a routine to be gone through. For each family it was a precious moment dedicated to their loved one. The only occasion on which those who died were given their time, their due.

When the court was ready, the waiting family was escorted in, social workers and police officers in tow, faced by the coroner alongside the West Midlands senior investigating officer, Mervyn Jones. In the modern courtroom sat the jury, the lawyers, a South Yorkshire Police officer monitoring all proceedings, clerks and transcribers. Introductory words of sympathy from the coroner were followed by the pathologist's evidence. Blood-alcohol levels were once again read out. Then a West Midlands officer took the stand and read his or her summary of the evidence. Another West Midlands officer completed the proceedings by showing on a map of the ground all appropriate sightings of the deceased based on photographs and video material.

Finally, following words of condolence from the coroner, the family left via another door to a small room. Here the pathologist gave words of reassurance, informally answering questions. The most vital question for families was whether their loved one had suffered before they died. In most cases, what had been stated in court was repeated: after the impact of the crush, the 'surge', they lost consciousness quickly and felt nothing. A quick death, almost peaceful, in the most traumatic circumstances.

Then it was over. The ordeal for each family seemingly had ended. They went down the stairs, out of the building and made the journey home. Due process had taken its course; each family given their time, their opportunity. This, however, was an illusion. Popper made it clear he would only accept questions on matters for clarification. Yet many families had numerous questions. Burning questions, particularly regarding the circumstances of death, remained unaddressed, let alone answered, discarded as being beyond the parameters of the inquest.

* * *

The mini-inquests had a devastating impact on most families. Many received information for the first time on their arrival in Sheffield. They were left to read and digest their contents minutes before entering the court: 'We had an appointment to meet two officers from the West Midlands Police in the bar of a hotel in

Sheffield on the evening prior to our son's mini-inquest timed for 9.30 a.m. the following morning. This was the only opportunity we had to go through the summary. Due to pressure of work, the police officers did not arrive.'

The public statement of blood-alcohol levels at the start of each hearing, set the tone and put families on the defensive. The emphasis on blood-alcohol levels confirmed the worst fears of the bereaved families and survivors, fuelling the press obsession with drunkenness and violence. Rather than exposing and challenging the decision to take blood-alcohol levels, the mini-inquests justified and legitimated this unprecedented and indefensible decision. Both the pathological and summarised evidence were given before the jury, unchallenged and as state-ments of fact. With no disclosure and no opportunity to cross-examine, these versions of what happened stood, and remained, uncontested.

Whatever the intended outcome of the mini-inquests, the pro-ceedings seriously disadvantaged the bereaved and undermined their rights to a thorough public hearing. The mini-inquest was the only forum in which evidence specific to those who died was presented, yet it was unrecognisable as an inquest. Not only were substantive witnesses absent, but those who addressed the court could not be questioned.

There was overwhelming dissatisfaction with the flow of information about the mini-inquests and their proceedings. While many families voiced their concern over the mini-inquests, they felt they were left with 'no option' but to proceed. One typical comment was that agreement was 'on the basis that ques-tions that would not or could not be asked at the mini-inquests' would be asked 'at full inquests' when witnesses would be called.

One mother, emerging from her mini-inquest, felt she had 'just been to the theatre . . . it was rehearsed'. Answers to questions did nothing to alleviate fears. According to another mother, 'It just made them worse . . . How is it possible to gauge the truthfulness of the [summarised] evidence . . . when no opportunity was given to cross-examine the individuals who were the source of the information?' Families, however, were reassured that unanswered questions would be raised at the generic hearing: '. . . when they [controversial medical questions] weren't answered adequately we were left with the impression that the questions would be dealt with at a later stage.'

What began as a procedure to provide information on the death of loved ones ended in confusion and disillusionment. The conduct and orchestration of the mini-inquests, the stage-management of the process and the choreographed presentation of evidence did little to ease the suffering and intimidation endured by families. What the families were left with was a distorted and half-told account of each death; accounts derived in the opinions, interpretations and vocabulary of investigating police officers interwoven with edited witness statements. It was extraordinary that all this took place in a court, under oath and before a jury.

According to one parent: 'Really speaking, to face the mini-inquests on the day was, to say the least, most upsetting . . . unreal and, to be quite frank, impersonal. No one should ever be subject to such proceedings.' One mother 'felt I had just lost him all over again. I couldn't stop crying, thinking about him. They played on our emotions and illness – it was so cruel.' Families' assessment of the mini-inquests went from 'bewilderment' to 'disgust' and 'outrage'. One brief reflection accurately portrayed the over-all feeling: 'Any trust I had went out of the window . . . like many other families I thought the mini-inquests insufficient.'

* * *

On 30 August 1990, just four months after the mini-inquests had ended, a Mr Cleugh, head of the Police Complaints Division, wrote a brief letter to the South Yorkshire Chief Constable. It stated that, following the 'most careful consideration' of 'all the evidence and documentation', the Director of Public Prosecutions had 'decided that there is no evidence to justify any criminal proceedings' against the South Yorkshire Police, the club, the city council or the safety engineers. Further, there was 'insufficient evidence to justify proceedings against any officer of the South Yorkshire Police or any other person for any offence'.

No elaboration, no disclosure of evidence and no reasons were given. Insufficiency of evidence meant simply that the DPP was not convinced that he had a more than 50 per cent chance of a conviction. Evidence, yes; enough for conviction, no. The decision not to prosecute senior police officers, taken by the DPP in consultation, it later transpired, with two independent senior counsel, seemed to fly in the face of Taylor's uncompromising indictment of the police.

While senior officers could still face internal force disciplinary charges, the door was firmly closed on criminal prosecution. The families and their lawyers were left, bereft of access, to second-guess the level and reliability of the evidence judged as 'insufficient'. Because of prohibitive costs, it was impossible for families to take a private prosecution. An intolerable weight was placed on the generic inquest. The bereaved now looked to the coroner, not only to address their unanswered questions, but also to uncover any breach or neglect of a duty of care by the relevant organisations and/or their senior personnel.

* * *

On 19 November 1990, in generic form, the Hillsborough inquests resumed at Sheffield's town hall. They ran until 28 March 1991, taking evidence from 230 witnesses. The longest inquests in history. Twelve 'interested parties' were represented, six comprising 'police interests'. One barrister represented 43 families, less than half of the bereaved. In contrast to the Taylor Inquiry, the survivors were not represented. With no legal aid available for inquests, they could not afford it. The bereaved paid from their own pockets.

Immediately, the coroner dropped a bombshell. He announced that while the generic proceedings would be extensive, hearing witness evidence up to and including the 'moment' of the disaster, no evidence would be heard concerning events after 3.15 p.m. A '3.15 cut-off' was to be imposed. The families' counsel, Tim King, argued that there had been 'no investigation directed to the global organisation of what happened immediately after they [the dying and injured] were brought off the terraces' and 'to ignore . . . concerns as to the adequacy of the attentions and the rescue efforts after 3.15' amounted to failing to 'investigate what could well have been a major reason for why somebody died and did not survive'.

Having taken contrasting legal submissions, the coroner returned to the medical evidence. The 3.15 cut-off was not arbitrary, he argued, but rational and logical. It was the point at which the St John's Ambulance arrived on the pitch: '. . . I did try to consider in the light of the evidence which we had heard [at the mini-inquests] what could have been the latest time when the real damage was done.' Popper's statement went to the heart of his perception of what happened: a belief that once 'real damage' had occurred, each individual was beyond help or rescue.

According to the coroner, 'overwhelming medical evidence, the pathological evidence, and that is the crucial one [*sic*] I am interested in, is the damage that caused the death was due to crushing'. Once the 'chest was fixed so that respiration could no longer take place, the irrevocable brain damage could occur between four and six minutes . . .' And so '. . . the latest, when this permanent fixation could have arisen would have been approximately six minutes past, which is when the match stopped . . .' He then added a further six minutes to accommodate the pathologist's assessment of a six-minute period for brain damage, taking the time to 3.12 p.m., and identified an established 'marker' close to that, the ambulance appearing on the pitch at 3.15 p.m., to establish his cut-off time.

Popper constructed a logic of convenience. First, he took the pathological evidence as 'crucial' and incontrovertible. Then he accepted the pathological opinion on asphyxia as fact: the relationship between the 'fixed' chest and 'irrevocable' brain damage. Finally, he assumed that the latest possible time for this was 3.06 p.m., just happening to coincide with the referee's decision to stop the game. Popper reasoned that the 3.15 cut-off simply reflected the medical evidence and that 'each individual death' was 'in exactly the same situation'. He concluded: 'The fact that the person may survive an injury for a number of minutes or hours or even days, is not the question which I as a coroner have to consider.'

He was adamant that crushing was the sole cause of death, that those who died did so through injuries sustained in the crushing. Each death, then, lost its individual circumstances to a collective interpretation of the events leading to the moment of disaster. The only conclusion to be drawn from Popper's ruling was that those who died did so regardless of medical attention received or denied. Equally, by this logic, those who lived did so regardless of medical attention. A defiant logic which defied reason.

The 3.15 cut-off remained the most controversial decision of the generic inquest. It guaranteed that those most directly concerned with rescue, evacuation and medical treatment would not give evidence. It prevented consideration of the circumstances surrounding each death, thus denying families the opportunity to raise the questions left unanswered by the mini-inquests. It suggested that all who died did so inevitably, regardless of the treatment they received or deficiencies in planning which might have saved lives.

As was his prerogative, the coroner, in consultation with others 'behind the scenes', selected the witnesses for the generic hearing. Following approaches from the families, he agreed to call some witnesses not on his original list. The 'order' of witnesses was also his decision: licensees and local residents, police officers, senior police officers, survivors and 'experts'. The coroner did not provide, nor was he obliged to, the criteria on which he selected the relatively small number of witnesses from the thousands of statements taken by the police investigators.

Within days a tide of allegations from selected licensees and local people washed over the court. Again the newspapers had a field day, as fans were portrayed as drunk, violent and ticketless. Despite much of this evidence being inconsistent, full of discrepancies and in some cases discredited, the themes of the first week's media coverage soon consolidated. Once again fans were condemned through unsubstantiated impressions and questionable assumptions.

Effectively, such 'evidence' from local residents and licensees reinforced an already established agenda. After the first few days it was trumpeted across Britain. Liverpool fans had arrived early to drink heavily. Many without tickets then rushed the ground. Their behaviour was reported uncritically as being reprehensible, showing reckless disregard for others. The police claimed it was an orchestrated, planned attempt to create mayhem outside the ground to force mass entry. This early evidence constructed a worst-case scenario: some who died, and many who survived, were to blame.

As the generic, selective story-telling continued, so the indictment of the fans continued unabated. Police evidence followed, peppered with comments about the 'unruly' behaviour of fans, their unacceptable and insulting responses and their wilful rejection of reasonable police requests. A typical statement reflected on 'abusive comments' and concluded, 'the facial expressions, the overall demeanour of the crowd was . . . quite evil'.

The fans at the turnstiles were described as being forceful in their sole 'intent to get in'. One officer stated, 'they had just this one obsession . . . and if they won't work with you, you cannot break it'. It was a 'loud-mouthed, arrogant, utterly selfish and physical' crowd which, according to another officer, 'had been drinking far in excess than what we would normally expect'.

Many police officers made it clear that, had this been a 'normal' crowd consuming 'usual' amounts of alcohol, the police would have established and maintained control. Two statements were typical. One officer had 'never seen [such] a quantity of a crowd in possession of drink'; another considered it was 'as if everyone had delayed the time that they were coming to the ground and all decided to come later . . .'

Yet Taylor had already rejected these very points. He stated unequivocally in his interim report that 'some officers, seeking to rationalise their loss of control, overestimated the drunken element in the crowd'. He also found few officers subscribing to the 'conspiracy theory' over tickets, concluding that the '. . . slender evidence upon which this theory rested came from two sources: overheard conversations in public houses and the ante- cedent history of Liverpool supporters at away matches'.

Given the persistent, almost ritual, vilification of Liverpool fans, it appeared that Taylor's version of events, and the findings that followed, were under a seemingly orchestrated assault. The combined evidence of some local residents and police officers provided a strong foundation for the accounts of senior officers responsible for crowd management and control on the day. It was a foundation upon which they were eager to build. Senior officers, in varying degrees, laid the blame for the disaster at the door of the fans. Marshall's 17-page 'recollections' from the day were read to the court by Mervyn Jones, the senior West Midlands Police investigating officer. It contained opinion, prejudice and unsubstantiated allegations directed towards Liverpool fans. There then followed a 'voluntary statement', also read to the court, which included criticisms of evidence presented at the Taylor Inquiry.

Given that the coroner had debarred evidence taken by Taylor from the inquest, it was inconsistent that Marshall was allowed to criticise the inquiry and its findings. Further, Marshall also made references to Hillsborough in the context of various 'riots', including the Trafalgar Square anti-poll-tax demonstration. At

Hillsborough, he claimed, the police were powerless to stop a crowd whom he likened to the 'advance of an army'. Marshall expressed openly his 'fairly jaundiced view of football supporters', alongside his belief that the 'reputation of Liverpool fans left a lot to be desired'.

At this point, proceedings were adjourned while a heated discussion took place between lawyers and the coroner. The families' counsel argued that Marshall's voluntary statement contained 'speculation, opinion, all about matters which have no relevance to this inquiry'. The counsel contested that they were so 'prejudicial' that the jury should have been discharged and the inquests stopped. The legal wrangle went on over two days, ending with the coroner inviting the jury back into the court and instructing them 'to totally forget, as far as you are able, everything that happened yesterday morning'.

Much of the evidence given subsequently by senior officers focused on responsibility for crowd management, foreseeability and communication between officers after gate C was opened. The Duckenfield–Murray relationship was central to the cross-examination of both men, focusing on division of responsibilities, the monitoring of the pens, the custom and practice of fans being left to 'find their own level' and the decision to open gate C and its consequences.

A final question, concerning his 'stated ignorance' and 'total inexperience' to take command of the event was answered by Duckenfield: 'I had the ability overall as a Chief Superintendent and I had a contribution to make.' It was an instructive reply, revealing the underlying problem of police responsibility and the failure of judgement at Hillsborough. Confronted with serious difficulties, the primary need was for incisive, informed and competent leadership. In retrospect all Duckenfield could offer was his rank, his support team and his 'contribution'. Lord Justice Taylor concluded that his management fell far short of the minimum standards expected of a commanding officer and nothing emerged from the generic inquest hearing to challenge that assessment.

Following the 'expert' evidence of those associated with the city council, the club and the Health and Safety Executive, survivors were called to give their personal accounts. Regardless of the trauma of survival and the pain of giving evidence, these 'fans' were subjected to hard and, often, harsh cross-examination. Having recalled the most horrific details of death on the terraces, many survivors left the court in tears. Many felt compelled to defend themselves from accusations and serious inferences drawn from innocuous replies. They had lost family or close friends and taken part in rescue and resuscitation. Giving evidence was itself traumatising, yet there was little consideration of their suffering.

It was at this point that the sheer imbalance in legal represent-ation became obvious. The survivors were cross-examined by as many as six lawyers representing different police interests. They worked as a team, able to co-ordinate their cross-examination. This was in marked contrast to the cross-examination of police witnesses when one barrister represented the interests of 43 families.

Survivors were left feeling that the disaster was their fault, that they were 'on trial'. One survivor stated: 'They didn't know what I'd been through. I'd lost someone dear to me, fought to survive and others died around me. People died before my eyes and no one helped. It was chaos and I know some could have been saved. They didn't want to know at the inquest. No questions about the first aid on the pitch, about carrying people on hoardings, about the police in the gymnasium. None of that. But I was there and I saw it with my own eyes. But they didn't want to know. It was all a sham.'

The treatment of survivors under cross-examination reflected ill-informed criticisms levelled previously by police officers, politicians and journalists. It was evidence from survivors of a dreadful disaster forced to justify their actions; fans under suspicion who had to live down the image of drunken, violent hooliganism. What was lost in the hostile questioning was that they were not passive observers of an event, but were, and remain, survivors of an appalling disaster. They witnessed death; against the odds they tried to save lives.

Hillsborough survivors, like those who survive other tragedies, talk poignantly about the desperate circumstances of slow death. In taking their evidence, in affording little protection from often bullying and blame-soaked cross-examination, the court denied them the dignity which was theirs by right. Yet, as many left the inquests hurt, frustrated and angry, their concern was that it was they, and not the procedure, that somehow had failed the bereaved. It was the ultimate irony that those who survived, who had lived with the 'guilt' associated with survival, had their guilt compounded by a legal process which treated their testimony with disdain.

* * *

Once the evidence had been heard, legal submissions to the coroner took two full days in the absence of the jury. Most of the oral submissions were also supported in writing and the debate almost exclusively turned on the possibility of a verdict of unlawful killing. Each submission relied on previous legal rulings. Central to 'unlawful killing' was a standard of proof demonstrating a failure of a duty which itself comprised a substantial cause of death. While much of the discussion was technical, going back over previous cases, the main point was whether there was an obvious and serious risk and failure to give such a risk due thought and consideration.

The families' counsel focused on the 'logical chain' of events set in motion by Duckenfield's decision to open gate C. Without diverting those who entered away from the tunnel, was there an 'obvious and serious risk of overcrowding and crushing' in the central pens which, in turn, gave rise to 'an obvious and serious risk of physical harm'? He concluded that if Duckenfield 'knew' of the risk, and ran it, then his act and omission could amount to unlawful killing. Opening gate C was a positive act; failure to divert was an 'omission'. Together, he argued, they constituted unlawful killing.

With the jury back in court, the coroner summed up the evidence and gave his legal direction. He stated that the 'criminal equivalent' of unlawful killing 'is one of the forms of involuntary manslaughter'. The 'kernel' of this verdict was 'recklessness' accompanied by an 'obvious and serious risk to the health and welfare of the deceased'. 'Foreseeability' was not the same as 'obvious' . . . 'mere failure to recognise the presence of . . . a risk is not sufficient'. Recklessness also had to be established 'beyond reasonable doubt'.

Considering the verdict of accidental death, the coroner advised the jury, 'the word "accident" straddles the whole spectrum of events . . . from something over which no one has control . . . where . . . no one could be blamed – to a situation where you are in fact satisfied that there has been carelessness, negligence, to a greater or lesser extent and that someone would have to make, for instance, compensation payments in civil litigation'. He added, 'bringing in this verdict does not mean that you absolve each and every party from all and every measure of blame . . .'

Of all that the jury had sat through over the previous months, this was possibly the most telling, the most significant, statement. South Yorkshire Police had already settled compensation payments in civil litigation for liability in negligence. With no verdict available between accidental death and unlawful killing, no verdict available indicating negligence or lack of care as contributory factors in the deaths, jurors were instructed that they could return a verdict of accidental death legitimately incorporating a degree of negligence. The jury was presented with the opportunity to subsume any possible concerns over liability, which might not have satisfied the unlawful killing tests, within the boundaries of accidental death.

Following his summing-up of the evidence, the coroner reaffirmed: 'negligence . . . is not the same as recklessness . . .' He continued: 'The fact that people made mistakes; that they might be liable for civil damages; that they may have made serious errors . . . they may have been incompetent is not the same as saying that a person is being reckless . . .'

Acts or omissions had to be attributable to individuals. There could be no aggregation of responsibility. Failure to 'be satisfied beyond reasonable doubt on any of the grounds' could only lead to an accidental death verdict: 'you should remember what I told you, that it straddles the whole spectrum from where you say, "Well, nobody can be blamed" to the position where in fact you may feel that there was negligence . . .'

At 12.33 p.m. on 26 March 1991 the jury retired to consider its verdict. Two days later, at 12.08 p.m., on the eightieth day of the generic hearings, the jury returned. It was a nine-to-two majority verdict on all who died at Hillsborough. The words, calmly spoken, reverberated around the hall: 'accidental death'. Bereaved families, survivors and witnesses, exhausted from the months of travelling, listening and waiting, broke down and cried. Some voiced anger and outrage. A few jurors were clearly upset.

The media portrayed families' anger and frustration as bitterness, acrimony and a desire for revenge. But the overwhelming, shared feeling was that a serious miscarriage of justice had occurred: 'The inquests were a farce from beginning to end . . . The coroner clearly directed the jury to an accidental death verdict. He got what he wanted'; 'I cannot be totally objective but it would seem that the jury could only arrive at one verdict after the coroner's performance'; 'How can it be construed as an accident in view of the overall emphasis on negligence so prominent in Lord Justice Taylor's report?'

By April 1991 the optimism following the Taylor Report had evaporated. The DPP had ruled against prosecutions and the inquest verdict of accidental death had been delivered. Claims for compensation for trauma suffered by those who died or, secondarily, by close relatives who witnessed the disaster on television had also failed. As Eddie Spearritt commented, 'It was as if every door was closing on us. To tell the truth I didn't expect anything else. It was too big an issue, too many top people, too much to lose. The inquest was a farce but we all went along with it – we had to, there was no choice.'

Chapter Eight

NO LAST RIGHTS

It was Robert Mark, then Commissioner of the Metropolitan Police, who made the claim that British police forces are the 'least powerful' and 'most accountable' in the world. As 'citizens in uniform' the police, at least in principle, are not above the law. As local government employees they are expected to be politically accountable to local authorities' police committees whose duty is to 'maintain an adequate and efficient police force'. Like other professions, they are also bound by a disciplinary code.

Over the years since the 1964 Police Act there has been constant debate concerning double jeopardy. Put simply, if police officers are prosecuted for an offence and acquitted, they still have to answer to the force disciplinary code. As both the criminal justice system and the force code must prove a case 'beyond reasonable doubt', police officers argue that once a criminal prosecution fails so should disciplinary action. Otherwise, officers are effectively tried twice for the same offence. In practice, double jeopardy is rare. Acquittal usually applies across both codes. Force regulations tend to be used mainly for less serious breaches of force discipline.

Once the Director of Public Prosecutions (DPP) decided that there was insufficient evidence to prosecute senior officers on duty at Hillsborough, and there was no evidence to act against the force as a corporate body, the 17 complaints made to the

Police Complaints Authority (PCA) by members of the public were considered for disciplinary action. The PCA brought in a case worker who went through material gathered by the West Midlands Police investigators, considering each complaint on its merits. He was assisted by another PCA member.

In two cases, those of Duckenfield and Murray, the PCA concluded that there was sufficient evidence to pursue disciplinary action for 'neglect of duty'. The PCA was convinced that both senior officers had failed in their duties. South Yorkshire's Chief Constable disagreed and, given Hillsborough's public profile, the PCA's chair and deputy chair became involved. Behind the scenes there was a major dispute between the PCA and the South Yorkshire Police.

It was resolved on 11 July 1991 when the PCA directed that Duckenfield and Murray should face a disciplinary hearing charged with 'neglect of duty'. While not an indication of guilt, the charges demonstrated that the PCA considered there was sufficient evidence to support this action. 'Neglect of duty' has no direct counterpart in the criminal justice process.

At the time, the South Yorkshire Chief Constable strongly opposed the action, although it has since been portrayed that he 'wanted the discipline process to be worked through' given the 'significance of the disaster'. Duckenfield, however, was on sick leave, 'too ill to be amenable to the disciplinary process, let alone face the necessary tribunal'. Early retirement through ill-health is not unusual in cases where officers face disciplinary charges. With proceedings abandoned, their index-linked pension rights and personal reputation remain intact. It is an expensive process and does little to encourage public confidence in force accountability. On 10 November 1991 Duckenfield retired early on medical grounds.

The charges against Murray, however, stood. It seemed unfair that Murray should be left to shoulder the burden of what was a 'joint charge'. The PCA took judicial advice and, following considerable discussion, on 13 January 1992 decided not to proceed against Murray. Effectively, this ended the disciplinary proceedings. Once again the families and survivors were devastated. Although the DPP had ruled against criminal prosecution for manslaughter, the PCA identified a clear case against the senior officers for neglect of duty. But the proposed action failed and the case was abandoned. Murray later retired. That there was a case for neglect of duty to answer, however, raised again the apparent anomaly of the accidental death inquest verdicts.

* * *

Six crucial issues undermined public confidence in the Hillsborough inquests. First, the separation of the inquests into mini-inquests and a generic hearing limited disclosure and prevented appropriate cross-examination. Second, the 3.15 p.m. cut-off curtailed any examination of the circumstances surrounding many of the deaths. Third, the instruction by the coroner to the jury to wipe from their minds Marshall's statement to the court not only revealed his error in allowing it, but demanded the impossible. Both the 3.15 p.m. cut-off and the error over Marshall's evidence gave grounds for a judicial review of the inquests. At the time the families were advised against a judicial review and told to await the outcome of the inquests. This was not necessarily the best advice since High Court judges are reluctant to quash inquests once verdicts have been returned.

Fourth, as is so often the case at inquests, interested parties had no detailed information as to the criteria used in the selection of witnesses. Fifth, there was considerable concern, particularly among the bereaved families, over the coroner's weighting of evidence in his summing-up. His direction that accidental death could incorporate a degree of negligence certainly was open to debate. If there was negligence, did it breach a 'duty of care' owed to the fans? Sixth, survivors were not represented and the families were restricted to one barrister while six lawyers represented the different police interests.

On 6 April 1993, after extensive preparation, six bereaved families were granted an application for a judicial review of the inquest verdicts under Section 13 of the 1988 Coroners' Act. Grounds for appeal to the High Court include irregularity of proceedings, insufficiency of inquiry and the emergence of new facts or evidence. Each of the six claimed irregularity and insufficiency. They were, in effect, test cases for all who died.

In winning leave to challenge the verdicts of accidental death the barrister for the six families, Edward Fitzgerald, stated that, 'whatever else this death was, it was not accidental and it would be some assuagement of feelings if the verdict was struck down'. In giving his consent to the judicial review, Mr Justice Macpherson concluded that, 'a case can be sensibly argued'. Amid scenes of relief and optimism the families felt that at last someone in authority was listening.

But Mr Justice Macpherson sounded a cautionary note: 'I don't know what will happen in the end. I don't know how desirable it is that these agonies be prolonged.' And Christopher Dorries, the new South Yorkshire coroner, played down the significance of winning leave: 'All that has happened today is that the families have gone along and won the right to a full review. No one else was in court.'

Winning leave, however, was a significant achievement, a success against considerable odds. Nineteen months after the initial submission to the Attorney-General, the judicial review opened in the Divisional Court before two judges. 'In many respects,' argued Alun Jones, QC on behalf of the families, the inquests were 'empty'. There had been an 'appearance of bias' towards the police and authorities by the coroner, particularly in the withholding and suppression of evidence. These claims were strongly contested by the coroner's barrister.

On 5 November 1993, following detailed submissions on behalf of the six families, the judges ruled in favour of the coroner. Lord Justice McCowan considered that Popper had 'made a full inquiry' and that the 'allegations against the investigating police officers' provided no grounds for quashing the verdicts and ordering a new inquiry. Both McCowan and Mr Justice Turner considered that the inquests had been conducted properly. No evidence had been suppressed. Far from criticising the coroner's performance, Lord Justice McCowan stated that not only was the inquest 'correctly completed' but also the 'direction to the jury as to the manner in which they should approach it completion was impeccable'. Mr Justice Turner concurred; there was, 'nothing to show any lack of fairness or unreasonableness – there was no error'.

'What would be the purpose of fresh inquests?' asked McCowan. 'To get a verdict criticising the police?' Answering his own question, he argued that the police had been criticised already in the Taylor Report. They had 'admitted fault and paid compensation'. He continued, 'To get a verdict criticising the emergency services?' There was 'no evidence to justify such criticism, and in any event it would be irrelevant if all six were brain dead by 3.15 p.m.' Finally, he asked, 'To obtain further examination of the last minutes of their lives?' He doubted that 'anything more would have been learned' but, 'the process would be a harrowing one involving large numbers of witnesses and lasting if not for 96 days, for not far short'.

Lord Justice McCowan's conclusion was that the inquests had been conducted and concluded properly; the police had already accepted fault and, accordingly, paid compensation. Despite hearing persuasive and authoritative medical arguments to the contrary, he accepted the coroner's dubious reasoning that all who died were clinically 'brain dead' by 3.15 p.m. Implicitly, then, the emergency services had saved all who could possibly have been saved. It was a level of certainty wholly inconsistent with the facts and other informed professional opinion.

Further, it was McCowan's opinion that 'irrespective of whose fault, if anyone's . . . four and a half years have already passed since the tragedy occurred'. To quash the 'existing verdicts, leaving nothing in their place' would be 'absolutely valueless'. He recognised that the bereaved families had a 'deep instinct to know the circumstances in which their relatives died'. While respecting this 'motive', he had 'to take an objective view . . . considering the interests of all concerned'. Consequently: 'I would in my discretion conclude that this is not a case in which it will be right to order fresh inquests.'

Understandably, the families were floored by the force of the rejection, especially the resounding endorsement of Popper. It was put to them that the costs incurred would not be levied but that a further appeal to the House of Lords 'would bring massive costs'. It was, seemingly, the end of the road. Doreen and Les Jones, one of the six families, concluded: 'Having exhausted the legal process, not one of the questions regarding the death of our son was addressed and this points to the inadequacy of the legal system which needs radical reform.'

* * *

The medical opinion ignored by the Divisional Court judges came from two doctors. Each contested the pathological evidence given at the mini-inquests. Dr West stated that it was not possible to establish how long consciousness could, or would, have been sustained after crushing. Victims 'could well have survived for a considerable period, well after 3.15 p.m.' Dr Burns agreed. Even in severe cases of traumatic asphyxia 'it is by no means certain that . . . death necessarily ensues three or four minutes after the compression begins'. The crucial factor was 'whether the compression' had been 'sustained'. He concluded that 'intermittent pressure' could delay death 'for a considerable length of time'.

Both highly respected forensic medicine specialists cast serious doubts about the medical evidence presented at the inquests and the cast-iron conclusions drawn from it. While some of those crushed would have experienced severe and sustained compression, this could not be taken as a rule-of-thumb for all who died. It was

226

not possible to conclude with certainty that everyone who died endured constant severe compression followed by the rapid onset of unconsciousness and death in three to five minutes.

In one of the six cases reviewed there was evidence that the deceased, Kevin Williams, had lived for a considerable time after 3.15 p.m. On 2 June 1994 this case featured in television's *The Cook Report*. Interviewed for the programme, the coroner confirmed that evidence to the inquests had been selective. On 26 October 1994, in a House of Commons adjournment debate, Sir Malcolm Thornton, the Williams's MP, argued that the judicial review had paid 'scant attention' to the medical opinions of both Dr West and Dr Burns.

Speaking in the debate the Labour MP for Knowsley, George Howarth, highlighted the problems caused by the 3.15 p.m. cut-off. He stated, 'despite everything that has been said and all the conclusions that may have been drawn, exactly what happened in . . . individual cases has not been covered'. No stone should be left unturned, he argued, in ensuring for the bereaved that 'everything that can be done has been done'.

Replying, the Attorney-General commented that while the broadcast was 'an absorbing, fascinating programme on a tragic subject', it did not constitute 'evidence in itself'. He noted that the Divisional Court had looked at the case and the medical opinions, ruling that the new evidence was 'far too tenuous . . . to justify ordering a new inquest'.

Echoing Lord Justice McCowan's ruling, the Attorney-General concluded that it would take 'really cogent and persuasive' arguments to achieve fresh inquests. He considered that the programme added nothing to the evidence presented to the judicial review. Lord Justice Taylor's inquiry had been 'painstaking and thorough' and had 'placed the blame for the tragedy fairly and squarely on the police handling of crowd control at the event. The police had admitted fault and paid compensation.'

* * *

During the week of the House of Commons debate a massive controversy blew up yet again over fans' behaviour at Hillsborough. Extracts from Brian Clough's autobiography appeared in the *Daily Mail* on 22 October 1994. The former Nottingham Forest manager boomed, 'I will always remain convinced that those Liverpool fans who died were killed by Liverpool people. All those lives were lost needlessly.' It was insensitive and typical of Clough, long regarded as a maverick with uncompromising opinions.

Unsurprisingly, the book was ghost-written by a *Sun* sports columnist, but the extracts appeared in Ian Wooldridge's *Mail* column. Wooldridge, a well-respected sports writer, saw Clough as a 'close witness' at Hillsborough who was only stating publicly what many who 'remained silent at the time for a variety of motives' believed. Clough had 'enormous sympathy' for the police who 'bore the brunt of the blame' because 'they were so outnumbered'.

The next day, James Reeve covered the issue on Radio 5 Live. He suggested there had been 'scenes of behaviour that were at best irresponsible', what happened being 'within striking distance of Heysel'. After Heysel, he claimed, the fans should have learned, yet some 'were drunk and behaving ridiculously at Hillsborough'. Maybe Clough's 'description of these people' was 'nearer the mark than people like to admit'.

Within days the row had gathered momentum. In an incredible misinterpretation of what had happened, the *Daily Star* reflected that 96 people had died 'in a stampede after the gates were locked'. Andrew Forgrave, writing in Liverpool's *Daily Post*, attacked the 'maudlin indignation' and 'knee-jerk reaction' of Liverpool people who had dared to challenge Clough. Liverpool had 'been molly-coddling its own tragedy, like an over-protective mother . . . a city wallowing in the past'.

A bereaved mother responded, 'Clough's remarks are sick and just go to show he has no heart. Mothers lost sons and wives lost husbands that day, and his comments just bring the memories flooding back.' The father of a survivor stated that his son was 'still trying to come to terms with the Hillsborough disaster and Clough [had] brought back all the old ghosts'. Jan Spearritt wrote that Clough's 'knowledge' of the disaster was limited to what he had been told by a 'biased senior police officer'. Eddie and Adam, her husband and son, had witnessed the 'chaos at the turnstiles, caused by poor police organisation'.

Jan continued, 'My son died that day and my husband ended up in intensive care and as for blame, yes, my husband does blame himself and will continue to do so for the rest of his life for not being able to save our lovely son despite his desperate efforts . . .' She condemned Clough and the media for their 'continued incorrect portrayal of the disaster' suggesting that they would receive 'the eternal gratitude of the South Yorkshire Police'.

When confronted with the full force of criticism Clough simply replied, 'I do not regret what I said. Liverpool people killed Liverpool people.' Of those who had boycotted the book he retorted, 'half of them can't read and the other half are pinching hub caps . . .' Not only was he unrepentant but Clough boasted that he 'would have got into more trouble' if all he wanted to say had been published. It was in this climate that Sir Bernard Ingham, Press Secretary to Margaret Thatcher at the time of the disaster, chose to attack Lord Chief Justice Taylor, who had 'whitewashed the drunken slobs who caused the Hillsborough football disaster by storming the perimeter wall . . .' costing the lives of their fellow fans.

In February 1995 the Liverpool and Nottingham Forest clubs, together with both city councils, issued a statement concerning the 'considerable efforts' made by 'certain individuals to dismiss or distort the findings of Lord Justice Taylor . . . by placing the blame on Liverpool FC supporters, despite overwhelming contrary evidence gathered by the judicial investigation'. While the organisations reiterated the nine 'principal factors' which caused the deaths, Clough, Ingham and their supporters had returned many of the bereaved and survivors to a state of profound misery. Vicious and false allegations had been thrown, like salt, into the wounds of sudden bereavement and desperate survival.

* * *

The row over Clough and Ingham was a cruel but pertinent reminder, if one was needed, that many people beyond Merseyside remained unconvinced by Taylor's findings; their bigotry and prejudice fed and fuelled by the media's continuing obsession with hooliganism. Without first-hand experience of watching football, most people relied on newspapers as their only source of information. Clough played to a primed audience, both captive and captivated, via a press high on deceit and conjecture yet low on facts and investigative journalism.

In November 1995, after six years of painstaking research, the Hillsborough Project published *No Last Rights*. Subtitled *The Denial of Justice and the Promotion of Myth in the Aftermath of the Hillsborough Disaster*, the 375-page analysis of the legal procedures and the media coverage condemned the institutional structures as 'corrupt' and the operational practices as 'dishonest'. Hillsborough, the authors argued, constituted a 'grave miscarriage of justice' in which the due process of law had denied the bereaved and survivors 'human rights and social justice'.

Three lengthy chapters detailed the 'dishonesty' and 'inadequacy' of the inquest process endured by the bereaved. It remained a 'serious concern that the same investigating officers supported all three inquiries into Hillsborough . . . the "independence" of each inquiry was compromised . . .'

Without disclosure, the bereaved 'were forced to go to the inquests with no knowledge of the evidence held by the police or seen by the coroner'. While the coroner 'set the agenda', the South Yorkshire Chief Constable 'had access to the results of the police investigation', enabling his legal team to prepare accordingly. As police liability was a central issue, unequivocally endorsed by

Lord Justice Taylor, 'such differential access was wholly inappropriate'.

Without legal aid, the bereaved families had to find over £150,000 for their collective legal representation. But corporate bodies and professional associations provided lawyers for their members, some of this coming from the public purse. Senior police officers, including the former Chief Constable, 'were fully represented as individuals and the Police Federation provided representation to cover the interests of the other officers'. The authors of *No Last Rights* found the 'inequality in access to legal representation . . . unacceptable', severely inhibiting 'the fairness of the process . . . it skewed the Hillsborough inquests, denying all fans, and those families who could not afford it, any legal representation'. Finally, it 'unbalanced the cross-examination of witnesses and prejudiced the outcome'.

One barrister represented 43 families, instructed by the solicitors' steering committee. While the steering committee co-ordinated the case and its progress, it also suffered serious drawbacks. The authors noted that bereaved families 'did not receive information consistently or thoroughly . . . Different solicitors, with different experiences or knowledge of the process, provided different information, both in quality and in quantity.' Once the inquests were in motion, many families felt that they had 'little or no control over the progress or priorities of their cases . . . the organisation of representation did not operate efficiently, effectively or fairly'.

No Last Rights was scathing in its criticisms of the inquests. The mini-inquests were 'misguided' and 'effectively prevented any significant cross-examination of key witnesses'. Families, 'processed through in minutes', were denied 'the opportunity to ask questions significant to the circumstances in which their loved ones died'. Stage-managed and under the claustrophobic direction of the West Midlands Police, the mini-inquests were 'more akin to a conveyor-belt line of production than a sensitive review and exhaustive questioning of the facts of the case'.

The 'only possible explanation' for the taking of blood-alcohol levels of all who died, according to the authors, was that the coroner had been 'unduly influenced by early police allegations that drunkenness had played a contributory part in the disaster'. They continued: 'Even so, it did not constitute sufficient reason' for such an unprecedented act. It was 'a decision lacking in sensitivity which not only caused much additional pain but also led directly to misinformed speculation and untruths in the media'.

While providing a catalogue of other errors of judgement and insensitive official responses, *No Last Rights* reserved its most exacting criticism for the coroner's decision to impose the 3.15 p.m. cut-off on evidence. The 'quality of emergency care and treatment received in specific cases in order to establish whether some of those who died might have been saved' had been dismissed as irrelevant by the coroner. His interpretation of the questionable medical evidence was that all who died were beyond help by 3.15 p.m. regardless of the actual time of death.

The selection and order of witnesses at the generic inquest was determined solely by the coroner and the 'imbalance of legal representation' unfairly weighted their cross-examination. Police counsel not only worked hand-in-glove throughout much of the cross-examination, they also did so throughout the legal submissions at the close of the inquests. They adopted 'each other's submissions . . . adding or developing arguments around specific [previous] cases and their rulings'. These were 'polished and refined performances from a range of highly experienced counsel, each with their own supporting team'. *No Last Rights* demonstrated, chapter and verse, the 'definitive repercussions' of these submissions for 'the coroner's interpretation of the law'.

With prescribed verdicts guided by rulings in previous case law, coroners are guided by legal submissions. But, as has been shown earlier, it is often difficult to disentangle coroners' legal, technical directions, which bind juries, from their interpretation of the evidence, which has no binding status. *No Last Rights* showed clearly how the coroner 'selected the evidence which he considered to be significant, often passing opinion on reliability or even the style or presentation of certain witnesses', turning his summing-up into 'a highly subjective process' of 'opinion rather than fact'.

'Whatever the coroner's direction,' concluded the authors, 'it is only an interpretation and distillation of previous cases . . . themselves interpretations of other cases.' But directions stand as 'objectifying, defining principles' and 'when they are presented by a coroner to a jury they carry a powerful, determining weight'. Undoubtedly the coroner favoured accidental death which 'could incorporate a degree of negligence by individuals or corporations'. Effectively, argued the authors, 'this ruling enabled the jury to accommodate any concerns about negligence, or failures in any duty of care, within the verdict of accidental death.

'At Hillsborough it was indisputable that a sequence of seriously negligent acts by individuals and corporate bodies led to the deaths of 96 people, yet the inquest verdict records that those deaths were accidental. The verdict, both in substance and in impact, remains indefensible in any terms other than those constructed within the law.' The authors of *No Last Rights* indicted an 'antiquated, unfair and structurally deficient process run by coroners who possess discretionary powers in excess of their knowledge or capability to use them'. Worse still, it was inevitable that there would be no redress through judicial review as the Courts of Appeal 'dance to the same tune . . . trapped in procedural precedent'. Meanwhile, 'in determining the rights of the deceased and the bereaved', the Hillsborough inquests amounted to an 'institutional denial of the principles of equality, fairness and justice enshrined in international conventions'.

No Last Rights made 87 detailed recommendations for institutional reform in handling the aftermath and legal processes following disasters. These included: 10 recommendations concerning crowd safety, policing and citizen's rights at sports and leisure events; 19 on official bodies' responses in the immediate aftermath (mortuaries, identification, rights of the bereaved, inter-agency conflict); 8 on the role and constitution of official inquiries; 33 on the role and function of inquests. It constituted the most thoroughly researched review of the procedures ever written.

The launch of *No Last Rights* was attended by over 50 families and many survivors. Despite the acres of newsprint devoted to Hillsborough over the previous six years, only three national newspapers covered the detail of the findings and recommendations. Within 48 hours it was as if the book had never been written. Effectively, despite unreserved support from families and survivors, *No Last Rights* was buried. Distributed widely to Merseyside MPs and Labour Party shadow ministers, response was minimal. Interest in Hillsborough seemingly had waned. Clearly, the truth was hard to swallow.

* * *

Academic research, however close to people's daily experiences, rarely catches the attention or imagination of mass audiences. In contrast, television is a powerful medium not asking its viewers to make a long-term commitment, delivering its message sharply, literally between cups of tea. With television, people do not have to actively seek out the story. As *No Last Rights* was in production Jimmy McGovern, the much-acclaimed Liverpool writer, was commissioned to write *Hillsborough*, a two-hour drama-documentary. Both *No Last Rights*, and a previous report by the same authors, *Hillsborough and After: The Liverpool Experience*, informed McGovern's initial bid. His intention was clear, to raise 'a question of truth and justice' which would lead to a mass audience being 'appalled at the things which were done, before and after the tragedy, by our public services in our name'.

During the summer of 1996 occasional references to the making of *Hillsborough* were carried in newspaper reports. It emerged that the programme had a budget of £1 million and that it would focus on the build-up to the disaster and the immediate aftermath. A *Daily Mirror TV Weekly* 'exclusive' revealed that the reconstruction would centre on the experiences of three families: the Glovers, the Hicks and the Spearritts. The intention was to 'enlighten' people. According to Jimmy McGovern: 'We went to enormous lengths to be accurate.'

As the early December screening approached, journalists realised the story's full potential. The combination of the controversy surrounding Hillsborough, Jimmy McGovern and a prime-time two-hour networked slot was in itself a story which caught the imagination of features and news writers alike. Added to this was Jimmy McGovern's commitment to 'tell it like it was' and the promise of new evidence uncovered by the programme's researchers.

From mid-November, newspapers ran features on *Hillsborough* which factually revisited the disaster and its aftermath, using interviews with families, while examining the dynamics and intentions of making *Hillsborough*. Some of this coverage included debate over the 'validity of the form' of drama-documentaries in covering highly sensitive and unresolved miscarriages of justice. Ian McBride, the co-executive producer, argued that the research for the programme was 'every bit as stringent as we would do for a network documentary'.

The coverage certainly indicated that *Hillsborough* was to be a ground-breaking production. Robert Crampton's feature for *The Times* commented: 'How *Hillsborough* came to be written and filmed, is actually about people being able to recognise and face up to responsibility.' He concluded that everyone involved 'decided that their responsibility was to the dead and to the truth'. Jimmy McGovern, in a *Sunday Telegraph* interview, did not think that the programme 'would change anything' but argued 'there's a truth that needs to be told'.

A week before screening, the 'new' evidence to be revealed in the drama-documentary was leaked, probably deliberately, to the press. It centred on a reference to Roger Houldsworth, a civilian video technician employed at Hillsborough, in the Taylor Inquiry transcripts. It was clear from the reference that Houldsworth should have known which of the cameras deployed at Hillsborough to monitor the crowds were operational and, from his own monitors, precisely what the police, including the match commander, could see on their control box monitors. Potentially this was vital information as part of the police explanation of their failure to respond to the crushing in pens 3 and 4 was that one camera was faulty and the monitors provided limited coverage.

Roger Houldsworth had made a full statement to the police investigation and this evidence apparently contradicted the police explanation. Yet his statement had never seen the light of day and someone, if not several people, had taken decisions that Houldsworth would not be called either to Lord Justice Taylor's inquiry or to the inquests. Houldsworth considered that, on the day, the police cameras and Hillsborough's own CCTV cameras gave 'views which ought to have been available to officers in the police control box'. To him it was 'obvious' that pens 3 and 4 were full to capacity when the decision was taken to admit over 2,000 people into the stadium through exit gate C.

The programme makers traced Houldsworth, who made a further statement suggesting that the police could see, but chose to ignore, the state of the pens or, alternatively, that they were seriously negligent in not registering what was before their eyes. As Trevor Hicks, the chairman of the Hillsborough Family Support Group, stated, 'I have always had trouble coming to terms with the police claim that they could not see anything before they opened the gate. This evidence shows that the cameras were working.' Houldsworth also revealed that two tapes were stolen from the club's control room on the night of the disaster. They had been locked away.

These revelations provided a flavour of the 'hard facts' documented in *Hillsborough*. The tabloids anticipated the screening in their usual style: 'It's the most shocking TV drama ever'; 'TRAGEDY ON THE TERRACE'; 'CHRIS RELIVES A DAY OF HELL'; 'DARKEST DAY NOW RIGHT FOR TV TRIAL'. Curiously, the press produced a champion of the cause. Despite ambivalence at the time of the disaster, and its contribution to the promotion of myths surrounding fans' responsibilities, the *Daily Mirror* launched a campaign just three days before the screening.

Several factors came together for this unlikely alliance. Most important was that Brian Reade, a former *Liverpool Echo* reporter whose coverage at the time went against the tide of Fleet Street myth-making, had moved to the *Mirror*. He was personally committed to the story. Piers Morgan, the *Mirror* editor, was not so easily convinced that a drama-documentary, nearly eight years after the event, warranted extensive national news coverage, let alone a nation-wide campaign.

In the tabloid wars, however, the market-place is the bottom line of most decisions. Newsworthiness, whatever the relative strength and merits of a story, is worked out not on the back of an envelope but on the front of a pocket calculator. Circulation and sales are the driving forces. With the exception of special events, newspaper readership is finite, predictable and constantly market-researched. In the context of Hillsborough, the *Daily Mirror* could not fail. Its arch-rival, *The Sun*, was a prisoner of its own history. If *The Sun* covered and went along with the drama-documentary, it would have to face up to its own lies and distortions. If it challenged the factual basis of the programme, it would compound the felony. *The Sun* had no alternative. Caught in its own web of deceit, it had to remain silent.

Piers Morgan did not have to be the most adept opportunist to realise that in the *Mirror–Sun* circulation war, with *Hillsborough* he had the stage to himself. He could even accommodate national cynicism, if necessary, simply by running regional front pages.

What would appear on Merseyside as the lead, full-frontal campaigning exclusive, would be carried inside, less blatant, in other regions. Not only would this consolidate *The Sun*'s long-term demise on Merseyside, it would also recruit new readers to the *Mirror* throughout the region.

On 2 December, three days before the broadcast, Brian Reade's 'exclusive' was published. The previous day he had attended a 'private' showing of *Hillsborough* at Liverpool's Neptune Theatre along with 300 family members. His report respectfully commented on the 'weeping' relatives, noting that their 'anger had been re-ignited'. Jimmy McGovern had received 'his most special ovation ever'. He had been truthful 'for the sake of the dead'; calling the aftermath of Hillsborough 'quite simply the biggest injustice in British history'.

While the *Mirror* front page carried a brief comment, the private screening was covered inside followed by an exclusive interview with Eddie Spearritt filling two further pages. Under the headline 'POLICE DID NOTHING AS MY SON DIED IN FRONT OF THEM', Eddie told the story of a police officer's refusal to open the perimeter track gate, just an arm's length away, as Adam lost consciousness in his arms. The message throughout the piece underlined the importance of another headline, 'HILLSBOROUGH FAMILIES IN CALL FOR NEW PROBE'.

On Thursday, 5 December, the day of the broadcast, the *Daily Mirror*, using four dramatic stills from the drama-documentary, led with a front-page headline 'HILLSBOROUGH THE REAL TRUTH', parodying *The Sun*'s April 1989 front page. The *Daily Mirror* attached the instruction, 'All Britain must watch the most harrowing TV programme ever made' to its masthead. Seven years on, *Mirror* reporter Brian Reade thanked 'God and Jimmy McGovern, that someone had the guts and the talent . . . to expose the lies. To tell it like it was.' He fiercely attacked the police and defended the families and survivors. The leader comment proclaimed it was, 'Time to end this cover- up.'

The *Daily Mirror* argued that 'the real truth will come out' only through reopening the inquests. It claimed that this was what the families wanted and called for a readership campaign, based on a telephone vote, to persuade the Attorney-General to reopen the inquests. It listed 20 'questions no one has answered'. What it failed to consider was whether the Attorney-General could reopen the inquests given the decision in the Divisional Court to support the inquests and their findings. There was no consideration given to which of the questions could be addressed by reopened inquests. The campaign, as with so many tabloid responses, was under-researched; revealing a flawed understanding of the issues and how they might be resolved. With some justification it was high on indignation but, as the families had experienced time and again, the legal process would not respond appropriately, however sound and convincing the argument. There was no recognition that, as ever in such cases, the families and survivors were trapped within a justice system and legal procedures based not on reason but tradition, precedence and protocol.

Having published its exclusive prior to the screening, the *Daily Mirror* followed up with the announcement that, even before viewing the drama-documentary, 10,000 readers had demanded the inquests be reopened. Its 6 December front page ran the headline 'COP-OUT' accompanied by a photograph of Duckenfield being door-stepped by a *Mirror* reporter. Asked to apologise for 'bungling' the police management of the semi-final, he replied: 'I have no comment to make.' Among the *Mirror*'s five pages of coverage was a statement from Tony Edwards, the South Yorkshire Ambulance Service paramedic who drove his ambulance on to the pitch at Hillsborough. After the disaster, he claimed, there had been a 'huge cover-up' involving the Ambulance Service: 'There have been lies told.'

On Saturday, 7 December, the *Daily Mirror* regionalised the debate by publishing a 'special Merseyside edition'. The story of

John Major's 'crisis' at losing his House of Commons majority was reduced to second place as the banner front-page headline demanded 'SIGN YOUR NAME AND GIVE THEM JUSTICE'. With the 96 who died listed under the Liverpool Football Club crest, the campaign for a 'new inquest' was in full swing. Quotes from the readers filled four columns as the *Mirror* called for the police to 'come clean', to 'stop covering up' and 'stop avoiding responsibility – not just for the disaster but for their behaviour after it'. The leader concluded, 'We only want what the families of the victims want. Justice.'

However inappropriate the call for new inquests, the response to *Hillsborough*, given that much of what was in the programme had already been researched and published, was extraordinary. It illustrated well the fusion between television and the press in illiciting a major response from a viewing audience/readership. But it also demonstrated the potential of television in using drama to develop an argument. Jimmy McGovern's achievement was in the selection of key moments, blending actual footage with acted scenes, and using the dialogue to make the argument while balancing a complex range of issues.

Inevitably, Richard Wells, the Chief Constable of South Yorkshire, was unconvinced by what he saw, commenting that there was 'nothing new' in the programme. While giving a 'very solemn undertaking' to pursue any new evidence raised by the programme, he concluded that, 'Material has been laid before two inquiries and that hasn't satisfied the families and I am not sure what more we can do because we are bound by the criminal justice system.' However ungracious this comment might have seemed, at the time it was instructive. Richard Wells was indicating strongly that it was the broader administration of the legal process which set the limits to inquiry and investigation. Any new initiative, then, required a strategy which would challenge that process. Simply demanding new inquests, while an effective rallying call, carried no weight when set against the formal mechanisms of the law and its procedures.

The media coverage of *Hillsborough* continued to personalise the stories. Inevitably, as the screenplay featured three families, journalists sought to 'follow up' their lives, pursuing 'human interest' and 'personal tragedy' storylines while discussing the possibility of a further inquiry. Meanwhile, other journalists, like Jeff Powell writing in the *Daily Mail*, warned that if the programme 'is unlikely to result in a prosecution – any more than the official inquiries did – I fear it will end in further frustration, a prolonging of the agony and possibly a lingering sense of having been used'. He concluded, somewhat arrogantly, that it was 'time to let these poor people rest in peace'. Julie Fallon, whose brother died at Hillsborough, responded sharply to such criticism. She commented, 'Well-meaning people sometimes say: "Poor you, they're dragging it up again." But we don't feel like that. We have to expose what we believe to have been the corruption of the police and judicial process.'

By 10 December the *Daily Mirror,* reinforced by 32,000 calls for a new inquest, had another exclusive. The Home Secretary, Michael Howard, admitted that he had not seen *Hillsborough*. The *Mirror* accused him of being a 'complete flop at staying in touch with ordinary people', instructing him to 'set aside a couple of hours today' to understand why the drama had 'swept the country and led to demands for action against the police'. The following week Peter Kilfoyle, Labour MP for Walton, announced his intention to propose to the Commons the need for a 'fresh look at the tragedy'. While David Maclean, a Home Office minister, was initially expected to make the Government's response in the House of Commons debate, the Home Secretary was left in no doubt as to the strength of public feeling on the matter.

* * *

On 17 December many of the bereaved made the journey to Westminster to hear the debate. It was 10 p.m. when Peter

Kilfoyle, a Merseyside Labour MP, rose to speak. The Home Secretary had decided to attend and reply on behalf of the Government. Peter Kilfoyle recalled 15 April 1989, focusing particularly on the 'train of events that led to the tragedy'. He noted the Attorney-General's earlier observations that the Taylor Inquiry had been 'painstaking and thorough', placing 'the blame for the tragedy fairly and squarely on police handling of crowd control at the event'.

Kilfoyle roundly condemned the police, the press and others, including Brian Clough, for orchestrating and then delivering 'wholly partial versions of events emanating from police sources, blaming the fans and fuelling a climate of cynical disregard for the facts'. *Hillsborough* had corrected this 'wholly erroneous version of events', while raising the important question of 'the allegedly faulty video camera and this missing tape'. He referred to a previous statement in the House made by another Merseyside MP, Gerry Bermingham, just two days after the disaster, in which he had encouraged the Home Secretary to secure and make available all film coverage to the Taylor Inquiry, stating 'unless we move quickly, that footage may be lost and it contains evidence that may be of great value to the inquiry'.

Kilfoyle then listed other 'outstanding questions' which required answers: 'Why was Chief Superintendent Duckenfield put in charge of a major semi-final only 21 days before the game when he was relatively inexperienced at policing football matches? Why, unlike in 1988, were there no barriers or cordons to filter the crowd outside the Leppings Lane end? As the danger unfolded, why was the kick-off not delayed? Why did police not recognise the build-up in pens 3 and 4 when television commentator John Motson and the video technician, Roger Houldsworth, clearly saw what was happening? Why was the lethal tunnel not sealed off as it had been in 1988? Why did Chief Superintendent Duckenfield tell the Football Association that fans had forced gate C when he had ordered it to be opened? Why did it take until 3.30 p.m. to make an address on the public announcement system to inform or instruct fans and to seek medical personnel to help the dying or injured? Given that 42 ambulances reached the ground, why did not more of them get on to the pitch to provide expert medical help? Why did only 14 of those who died get to hospital? Why was the city's major medical disaster plan never put into effect?'

It was, argued Kilfoyle, the responsibility of the House to 'raise the burden on the survivors and on the families of the victims, who wish only to see that justice is done'. He concluded his hard-hitting speech with the comment that the 'dead, their families and survivors cry out in the name of justice to be answered'.

In reply, Michael Howard offered his 'deepest sympathy' to the families. Their loss was 'made all the worse by the fact that it arose from an event that should have been a normal family outing'. He had watched the drama-documentary, finding it 'harrowing'. However, his primary concern had to be 'a consideration of all the relevant facts'. There had been 'four independent investigations': Taylor; the inquests; the police investigation under Police Complaints Authority supervision; the judicial review. Howard then detailed the Taylor findings, concluding, 'There were a number of reasons for that dreadful disaster, and no single person or organisation was held to blame, but Lord Taylor did clearly put a significant portion of the blame at the door of the police.'

The ambiguity within the Home Secretary's account had dogged versions of the disaster from the publication of Lord Justice Taylor's findings onwards. On the one hand the 'main reason' was police mismanagement, yet on the other 'no . . . organisation was held to blame'. It was a curious double-speak given that Howard went on to quote extensively from Taylor's 'strong criticism' of senior officers. He then went further, commenting on statements made by the 'present Chief Constable of South Yorkshire, Richard Wells . . .'

Wells had 'admitted that once the gates were open, the police should have foreseen where the fans would go', accepting that 'they might have reduced some of the pressure by changing the kick-off time' and 'that officers did not recognise soon enough the distinction between disorder and distress'. Howard concluded that the 'South Yorkshire Police have accepted that they were at fault in those respects and the South Yorkshire Police authority has paid compensation to the families of those who died'.

The Home Secretary also covered the inquests, reminding the House of the 'purpose of an inquest'. Without commenting on the problems associated with the selection of evidence, the use of summarised evidence, the denial of any opportunity to cross-examine important evidence at the mini-inquests, the imposition of the 3.15 p.m. cut-off and the coroner's direction of the jury, he simply recorded that 'the cause of death was accidental death'.

He reviewed the West Midlands Police inquiry, under the supervision of the Police Complaints Authority, and its sub-missions to the Director of Public Prosecutions, 'who concluded that the result did not indicate that anyone should be made the subject of criminal proceedings'. In fact, the DPP stated that his decision not to prosecute any officer was based on insufficiency of evidence. 'For any other person apart from a police officer,' stated Howard, 'that would have been the end of the proceedings, but for a police officer there remained the question of whether they had failed in their duty.' He went on to explain why the disciplinary proceedings against Duckenfield and Murray were abandoned.

Finally, Michael Howard discussed the judicial review of the inquests in the light of 'dissatisfaction with the verdict'. He stated that Lord Justice McCowan's ruling clearly showed that there were no grounds for intervention by the Divisional Court. In particular, the 3.15 p.m. cut-off had not been 'an unreasonable decision' and there was 'no criticism of the coroner's directions to the jury'.

The Home Secretary emphasised that he 'would not take a decision to reopen the inquiry lightly'. For such a move he would have to be 'convinced that it would be in the public interest . . .' He noted the 'charge' that 'there has been a cover-up, an attempt to pervert the course of justice'. Had 'new evidence' emerged and been put before Lord Justice Taylor or the coroner, would it have affected the 'outcome of the Taylor Inquiry or the verdict of the jury?' Howard stated his commitment to 'searching for the truth'. This included concerns over the video camera and the apparent conflict of evidence, '. . . it is perhaps inevitable, though deeply distressing for the families, that there will be confusion about some details'.

In all, the adjournment debate took 26 minutes. Seven and a half years of legal proceedings, information gathering, in-depth research and campaigning covered in 26 minutes. While Howard did not close and bolt the door on the issues, he laid the ground for what was to follow. A clear line ran through his response. First, he went to great pains to establish that previous inquiries had been thorough, exhaustive and impartial. Second, that every opportunity afforded by law had been taken and that the judicial review of the inquests had found their conduct beyond reproach. Third, that 'new evidence' meant that which had not been placed before Taylor or the coroner. Fourth, that such evidence would have to be persuasive in that it would have changed the outcomes of the inquiry or the inquest had it been presented. Effectively this ruled out questions concerning the reliability of the evidence before the inquiries and those related to the processes of selectivity adopted by Lord Justice Taylor and the coroner. Yet the main concern of the bereaved families and their lawyers remained. Without disclosure of the existing evidence, they were unable to make an informed assessment of its quality or reliability.

Chapter Nine

IN WHOSE INTEREST?

On 1 May 1997, the Labour Party swept to victory in a massive landslide. Michael Howard had given no indication that he had made any decision. The issue was inherited by his successor at the Home Office, Jack Straw. On 30 June 1997, over 40 Hillsborough families were back on the road to Westminster. This time it was to meet the new Home Secretary and a group of Merseyside MPs. After eight and a half years campaigning, the Hillsborough families had woken to many false dawns and the mood on the London-bound coach was cautious optimism, tinged with nagging cynicism. 'I felt we might get somewhere this time,' said Eddie Spearritt. 'You know, a new government and public opinion right behind us . . . but you always have your doubts. Hillsborough's a big issue with reputations at stake.' And there was a world of difference pursuing the debate in opposition and being on the receiving end in government.

As the families met with jubilant Labour MPs and the Home Secretary, Eddie's words seemed over-cautious. Jack Straw stated his concern as to 'whether the full facts have emerged'. He sympathised with the bereaved, whose pain had been 'exacerbated by their belief that there are unresolved issues which should be investigated further'. There would be, he told the hushed and expectant group, an independent judicial scrutiny 'to get to the bottom of this once and for all'. Further still, he had invited a senior Appeal Court judge, Lord Justice Stuart-Smith, to conduct the scrutiny of new evidence and to consider any 'further material that interested parties wished to submit'.

The mood was buoyant. 'It seemed to us,' said a bereaved mother, 'that he was saying he'd looked at the case, wasn't impressed and this judge would come in and get it sorted.' Certainly that was the impression reinforced throughout the media. Within minutes, news bulletins were announcing 'a new judicial inquiry', an 'independent review of the disaster' and so on. While newspaper headlines proclaimed a 'NEW LOOK AT CRUSH' and 'A FRESH INQUIRY' as a victory for the families' campaign for justice, the key questions were not even asked: What on earth was an independent scrutiny? What were its powers? What was the extent of Stuart-Smith's discretion?

As with his predecessor's comments to the House, the warning signs were already evident in Jack Straw's House of Commons statement. He noted the most recent evidence submitted and its careful consideration by the Home Office, the Attorney-General and the Crown Prosecution Service. The conclusions had been unequivocal. There was no justification for criminal proceedings, for further review of the inquests or their accidental death verdicts. Despite this, Straw wanted to 'ensure that no matter of significance [was] overlooked'. Accordingly, Lord Justice Stuart-Smith would examine the 'new' evidence.

Stuart-Smith's scrutiny, therefore, was tied tightly to reviewing evidence previously 'not available' to the Taylor Inquiry, the Director of Public Prosecutions, the Attorney-General or the South Yorkshire Chief Constable. 'New' evidence would have to be 'of such significance' that it could lead to criminal prosecutions or disciplinary charges. The scrutiny's limited remit seemingly contradicted the Home Secretary's commitment to a 'once and for all' inquiry.

The status and conduct of the scrutiny was never properly clarified. It had no precedent. While the media continued, mistakenly, to portray it as a judicial inquiry, it soon became evident that the scrutiny's focus was a matter for Stuart-Smith's discretion. Although the terms of reference were tightly defined, they included the rider 'and to advise whether there is any other action which should be taken in the public interest'. Potentially this gave Stuart-Smith immense scope. Whatever his priorities, the South Yorkshire Police knew that their archives would be central to his deliberations.

The South Yorkshire Police held all information gathered by the West Midlands Police investigation into Hillsborough. All statements, documentation, video footage and photographic evidence gathered for the criminal investigation, the Taylor Inquiry or the coroner became the property of the South Yorkshire Chief Constable once the inquiries were over. Effectively, his co-operation was essential to any further investigation into the conduct of the South Yorkshire force on the day. Once the scrutiny was announced the South Yorkshire Police went to considerable lengths to prepare for the judge's visit. Rooms were set aside at police headquarters and an officer who had monitored the progress of the inquests, Ken Greenway, became the liaison contact.

Stuart-Smith took August off for his annual vacation and the Hillsborough Family Support Group began to plan its submissions. While their solicitor for some time had been seconded from Liverpool City Council, it was necessary to brief a top barrister, Alun Jones, QC. A highly successful rock concert held at Anfield, Liverpool Football Club's stadium, raised substantial funds towards the Family Support Group's campaign and legal costs. Much of the information-gathering in preparation of the Family Support Group's submissions to Stuart-Smith focused on the 'new' evidence of the video technician, Roger Houldsworth, revealed in the drama-documentary *Hillsborough*. It also concerned what appeared to be 'new' evidence contradicting medical opinion given at the inquests and challenging the 3.15 p.m.

cut-off. Serious claims concerning improper conduct by the police investigators, first raised in the judicial review and reiterated in *The Cook Report*, were also pursued.

What followed, to say the least, was incredible. The Family Support Group made representations to the South Yorkshire Police to access statements, photographs and video footage relating to the circumstances in which their loved ones died. After eight years, and despite a Home Office inquiry and the longest inquests in legal history, families had still not seen most of the witness statements. Gradually, through pressure from Stuart-Smith's office, 'body files' containing detailed statements on each of those who died, were released. Reading the statements for the first time, many families' worst fears were realised. Statements were contradictory, confused, partial and, in some cases, blatantly inaccurate.

* * *

On the morning of 6 October 1997, bereaved families met on the steps of Liverpool's Maritime Museum in the heart of the city's gentrified docklands. The independent scrutiny, having experienced the hospitality of Sheffield Wednesday Football Club and the South Yorkshire Police, had moved across the Pennines to spend three days listening to a handful of families raising their concerns before Lord Justice Stuart-Smith. Invitations had been sent to all families to attend a 10 a.m. general meeting at the museum. Reception was from 9.30 a.m. onwards.

As 10 a.m. approached, families congregated outside the museum's main entrance. With no reserved parking available there was considerable delay in getting from the car park to the museum. Local and national journalists mingled with the growing crowd. Trevor Hicks, Phil Hammond and others from the Hillsborough Family Support Group were interviewed for radio and television, each stating their hopes for the scrutiny and its outcome. Then Lord Justice Stuart-Smith appeared for a photo call. Obviously it was 'good PR' for the scrutiny to have the judge greeting families and providing a brief comment on its progress.

Unexpectedly, the judge turned to Phil Hammond and, with a wry smile, asked: 'Have you got a few of your people or are they like the Liverpool fans, turn up at the last minute?' Phil Hammond was taken aback, not believing his ears. But there was no mistake. Stuart-Smith's outrageous comment was on tape, word for word. The remark spread among the families like wildfire. Jaws dropped open and there followed a collective outpouring of anger. How could a senior judge come to Liverpool to meet bereaved families and make such a crass and insensitive comment? It had taken over eight years to successfully combat the hurtful and unsubstantiated rumour that Liverpool spectators deliberately conspired to arrive late at Hillsborough; yet there it was, the judge's first words to the families.

Up in the reception area the families were in no mood to negotiate. With typical dignity and remarkable restraint they discussed abandoning the meeting. It was a difficult situation. To participate in the meeting would appear to accept the judge's insensitivity, but leaving would mean exclusion from what was their only chance to hear and respond to the judge in person. Eventually it was decided that the meeting should go ahead, with a demand that he retract the comment and offer a full apology for the hurt that it had caused.

The families filed into the lecture hall. No journalists or others, not even Hillsborough survivors, were invited. Tension filled the air as Chris Bone, secretary to the scrutiny, opened the morning session, introducing the judge familiarly as 'Sir Murray'. Lord Justice Stuart-Smith went straight to the point, stating that within the terms of reference he was compelled to 'look at all the information that people are now coming forward with to see whether it is fresh evidence about the disaster'. He then had to 'decide whether to recommend that any fresh evidence that [he found justified] a new public inquiry, new inquest or any other kind of legal proceedings or action by the authorities'.

The judge was unambiguous over 'fresh' evidence. It had to be 'evidence which was not available or was not presented' to the inquiries, the courts or the prosecuting authorities. Even then it had to 'lead somewhere and . . . show that the outcome of the legal procedures that have taken place might have been different or that those responsible for instituting criminal or disciplinary proceedings might have taken different decisions'. Anything 'broadly in line' with that previously put to the inquiries, regardless of which conflicting position it supported, would 'not be of much help . . .'

Echoing Michael Howard's 1996 statement to the House of Commons, the judge went over the 'broad conclusions' of the previous inquiries and proceedings. In discussing Lord Justice Taylor's findings, he reminded the families that the failure to block the tunnel and divert fans to the end pens once gate C had been opened constituted 'a blunder of the first magnitude'. He noted that Taylor had been 'highly critical of the police operation' but had extended criticism to the city council, Sheffield Wednesday Football Club and the safety engineers. It was 'not difficult to discern what happened', he said, accepting without reservation the findings of his former colleague.

He reviewed the inquests, emphasising that the 96 verdicts of accidental death, as directed by the coroner, were 'in no way inconsistent, with the deaths having been caused by negligence or breach of duty'. Many of the criticisms levelled against the inquests had been subject to judicial review in the Divisional Court and all had been rejected. He concluded, 'I cannot act as a Court of Appeal for the Divisional Court.' He could, however, establish 'whether there is any fresh evidence which might show that some or all of the verdicts of accidental death should be quashed and a fresh inquest ordered'.

'Fresh evidence' also concerned the decisions made by the prosecuting and disciplinary authorities, 'namely the Director of Public Prosecutions and the Police Complaints Authority'. If 'fresh' evidence existed and was of such significance, in his opinion, to have 'caused them to reach different decisions', he would invite them to reconsider. 'Fresh evidence', then, was the cornerstone of the Stuart-Smith scrutiny. It had to be new, not considered at all by the previous inquiries, and it had to be so significant that, in his judgement, it would have changed the Taylor, DPP or inquest outcomes.

At the meeting, Stuart-Smith reminded families that the South Yorkshire Chief Constable had 'paid compensation to those who were injured and the families of those who were killed on a basis of full liability'. While he had 'not seen any formal admission of liability by the police . . . they have never contested that they are liable'. Stuart-Smith was not talking about criminal liability but 'damages for negligence or breach of duty', reflecting the Chief Constable's responsibility 'in law for the acts or omissions of his junior officers'.

Compensation payments reflected the collective 'faults of the police, their negligence overall'. In Stuart-Smith's opinion there was 'no difference in principle between accepting liability and paying on a 100 per cent basis than there is making a formal admission of liability . . . no distinction between the two'. That the South Yorkshire Police had never contested civil liability amounted to an acceptance: 'It is a distinction without a difference.'

Stuart-Smith's discussion of liability demonstrated the tangled web in which the law and its procedures ensnares those who attempt to understand what are apparently straightforward issues. He responded exactly as expected. No senior officer was identified as 'criminally' liable, as that would have meant that he had been guilty of manslaughter beyond reasonable doubt. And negligence could not be aggregated to a charge of manslaughter against the force. Yet, civil liability could be aggregated for the negligence or breach of duty of a number of officers. Once damages had been paid, even if the police claimed against other organisations which had contributed to the disaster, civil liability was established.

In concluding, the judge apologised for his earlier 'flippant remark', which he realised had caused offence. He reassured families that it was 'not in any way an indication of my thinking up to now'. As the morning session ended, it was difficult for families to accept his reassurance. On leaving the building all the media wanted from families was their reaction to the remark. For his part, Stuart-Smith issued a statement of 'deepest regret' for an 'off-the-cuff' remark 'without any intention to offend'. The incident deflected attention from the real issues, elevating a side-show to the main event.

Even before receiving written submissions, or taking oral statements, Stuart-Smith had set out his stall. Lord Justice Taylor had successfully completed a thorough and exhaustive inquiry. The police had accepted, albeit indirectly, liability in negligence and paid damages. The inquests had been exemplary, according to the judicial review ruling, and the scrutiny could not be an appeal court for that ruling. While accepting that the use of summarised evidence at the inquests might not have been appropriate, it was an arrangement – like the use of mini-inquests – which had been accepted by the families through their solicitors. Finally, the judge was satisfied that the DPP's decision not to prosecute was sound.

Lord Justice Stuart-Smith's sole objective was 'fresh evidence'. It followed a central tenet of appealing against the reliability of verdicts in criminal cases – appeals granted on the basis of 'new' evidence. 'New' evidence, however, as was pointed out to the judge, is only one way of redressing a miscarriage of justice. Another exposes the unreliability of the old evidence in terms of how it was gathered, used or selected. As families accessed 'body files' and other statements, contradictions and conflicting accounts emerged; graphically illustrating the folly of limiting the scrutiny to 'new' or 'fresh' evidence.

* * *

During his three days in Liverpool, Stuart-Smith met 16 families, each for approximately 40 minutes. How or why families were selected to meet the judge was never made clear, although he later stated he 'met all those families personally who wished to see me'. The meetings were unusual and dramatic, giving families a rare opportunity to raise personal issues and concerns about the circumstances in which their loved ones died. Stuart-Smith, accompanied by the scrutiny's secretary, Chris Bone, and occasionally by another official, sat alongside families at a table. The meetings were transcribed.

Judges rarely have 'informal' contact with the public, certainly not at such close quarters. Some families had written submissions prepared by the Family Support Group solicitor, others did not. Inordinate and inexplicable delays by the South Yorkshire Police in supplying body files meant that families met the judge without access to key documents. Those who had read statements for the first time felt that the anomalies and inconsistencies in their cases constituted 'new' evidence. It was new to them. Yet it was not new evidence in the context of the scrutiny's terms of reference because it had been available to all previous inquiries.

Occasionally the pain of the process, together with the frustration of its limited remit, developed into anger. For years, significant questions had remained unanswered as families were denied disclosure of witness statements relating to the circumstances in which their loved ones died. Now, suddenly, they were receiving thick 'body files' including enlarged A4 photocopies of the Polaroid photographs which, on the night of the disaster, had been pinned to the screens in the Hillsborough gymnasium.

Other statements, photographs and video footage were also circulating among families. Trying to make sense of so much material, in such a short space of time, so that a coherent case could be presented to a High Court judge was near impossible. As he listened to families' concerns, while they recounted their tragic stories, the overwhelming sense from him was one of sufferance. While the judge undertook to chase up statements, make further enquiries and try to resolve some of the anomalies, he continually reminded families that much of what they were asking was beyond the scrutiny's scope.

While some families, with incredible self-control and dignity, told him of their determination to fight on, regardless of the scrutiny's outcome, others were reduced to silence by their personal grief and the growing realisation that their primary concerns would remain unresolved. As she stood to leave her family's meeting, Teri Sefton told the judge in no uncertain terms of her dissatisfaction with the entire legal process. The families, she said, would not be defeated in seeking justice, they would 'not go away'. She spoke for many others. Curiously, her comments were not recorded in the transcript of the meeting.

Of the 34 families who made written submissions, 18 eventually met the judge. He met a further 14 witnesses and drew on 16 others for assistance, 'on various aspects' of the scrutiny. While the scrutiny was in process, there was regular telephone contact between the scrutiny office and families, including 'off-the-record' comments which occasionally were, at best, ill-conceived.

* * *

The week after the judge's visit, a group of families asked me to meet with them to discuss the scrutiny's progress and potential outcome. I had attended the main meeting in Liverpool and several of the families' meetings. By now it was clear that Stuart-Smith considered the Taylor findings flawless, the DPP's decision not to prosecute appropriate and the failure to progress internal force disciplinary actions unfortunate. It was also apparent that Stuart-Smith accepted the reliability of the medical evidence and, it followed, the coroner's decision to introduce the 3.15 p.m. cut-off on evidence.

I discussed these issues with the families and told them that because the Divisional Court had ruled on the inquests, Stuart-Smith would require significant new evidence to make any recommendations about their conduct or verdicts. More broadly, acts or omissions of police officers on the day were covered, in Stuart-Smith's opinion, by the police acceptance of 'liability in negligence'. Considerable time was devoted to discussing the relationship between civil liability in negligence and criminal liability.

While Stuart-Smith had conceded that there had been procedural problems and difficulties, particularly concerning the inquests, he warned that the families' lawyers had accepted the coroner's arrangements at the time. 'No full scale investigation,' said Stuart-Smith, 'will resolve these problems.' Effectively, Stuart-Smith's public rejection of the criticisms levelled against the legal process meant that 'new evidence' to the scrutiny had to be watertight and convincing.

I stated my concern that, however significant the 'new' evidence appeared, much of it had actually been available to the inquiries. Although witnesses had not been called, their statements were on record, thus putting the evidence technically outside the scrutiny's remit. While Stuart-Smith would examine recent statements by witnesses, even meet them, he would rely on original statements made by them shortly after the disaster.

My meeting with the families lasted nearly three hours, covering all aspects of the scrutiny. Families were anxious and angry over the conduct of the scrutiny, unsure of its powers and critical of the discretion afforded to the judge. They felt that many issues of concern were being overlooked. The last thing I wanted to be was the bearer of bad news but the warning signs were obvious as Stuart-Smith closed the door on each possibility for further review. His opening address to the families had set a fixed agenda towards a conclusive, negative outcome.

I concluded that the scrutiny was a prisoner of its terms of reference, trapped within the narrow confines of Stuart-Smith's search for 'fresh evidence'. Worse still, I had told the Home Secretary this would happen in an exchange on BBC's Radio 5 the day after he announced the scrutiny. While there might be some recommendations for reform, particularly regarding police retirement on the grounds of ill-health and the confusion over inquest procedures, I suggested that the scrutiny would not enable families to move any closer to resolving the injustices they had suffered.

* * *

On 18 February 1998 the bereaved families yet again made the trip to the House of Commons. Jack Straw met them, along with Merseyside MPs, before going to the House to announce the outcome of Stuart-Smith's scrutiny. In hushed silence the Home Secretary told the families that, despite the judge's 'thorough' and 'impartial' scrutiny, nothing had emerged of such significance that challenged any previous decisions, judgements, rulings or, in the case of the inquests, verdicts. Straw was satisfied that Stuart-Smith had done an excellent job. There would be no further review. It was over.

Minutes later, speaking to a packed House and to the nation, the Home Secretary noted that the scrutiny was the 'latest in a series of lengthy and detailed examinations' of Hillsborough. Stuart-Smith had written a 'comprehensive report' which went into 'immense detail to analyse and reach conclusions on each of the submissions . . .' Each allegation made, each piece of suggested 'new' evidence, had been examined and handled 'with great care'.

Straw went on to summarise Stuart-Smith's findings 'on the key allegations relating to video evidence and the cut-off time of 3.15 p.m. for the inquests and allegations of interference with witnesses'. Video tapes stolen from the club's control room 'would have shown nothing significant' and Stuart-Smith was 'satisfied that all police tapes were made available in their entirety to Lord Taylor's inquiry and to the coroner'.

'Allegations' that the 'police had blamed their failure to see overcrowding in pens 3 and 4 on camera 5 being defective, when it was not; that evidence of the video tapes taken by camera 5 was deliberately suppressed and concealed; and that two police officers gave deliberately false evidence that camera 5 was not working correctly' were each 'unfounded'. Stuart-Smith also rejected any reconsideration of the 3.15 p.m. cut-off as it 'did not limit the inquiry of the inquest' and neither was the inquest 'flawed'.

Stuart-Smith, stated Straw, concluded 'that there was no improper attempt' by the West Midlands Police investigators 'to alter the evidence' of witnesses. The scrutiny report 'also deals comprehensively . . . with the ten questions posed by the Granada Television programme [*Hillsborough*]'. Straw continued, 'Taking those and all other considerations into account, the overall conclusion that Lord Justice Stuart-Smith reaches is that there is no basis for a further public inquiry . . . for a renewed application to quash the verdict of the inquest' and 'no material that should be put before the Director of Public Prosecutions or the police disciplinary authorities . . .' None of the evidence that Stuart-Smith had considered 'added anything significant to Lord Taylor's inquiry or the inquests'.

The Home Secretary, the Attorney-General and the DPP had examined Stuart-Smith's findings and had 'no reason to doubt his conclusions'. Jack Straw stated that he knew the outcome of the scrutiny would 'be deeply disappointing for the families of those who died at Hillsborough and for many who have campaigned on their behalf'. He continued: 'I fully understand that those who lost loved ones at Hillsborough feel betrayed by those responsible for policing the Hillsborough football ground and for the state of the ground on that day.'

Quoting from Stuart-Smith's report, Straw noted that the judge accepted 'the dismay that they [the families] have that no individual has personally been held to account either in a criminal court, disciplinary proceedings, or even to the extent of losing their job'. What Hillsborough had revealed, argued Straw, were 'serious shortcomings in the police disciplinary system'. It had also shown the inappropriateness of holding both public inquiries and inquests and going over the same ground twice. On both counts the Government was examining and developing the case for reform.

Straw endorsed Stuart-Smith's findings, accepting them as 'dispassionate' and 'objective'. He concluded, 'We cannot take the pain from them [the bereaved], but I hope that the families will recognise that the report represents – as I promised – an independent, thorough and detailed scrutiny of all the evidence that was given to the committee.' As Merseyside MPs rose to demand a full debate on the scrutiny's outcome, bereaved families were united in their rejection of the report and in their criticisms of its findings.

* * *

As Jack Straw noted, much had been made in Jimmy McGovern's drama-documentary of Roger Houldsworth's evidence. He was the Sheffield Wednesday video technician who had made a statement soon after the disaster but was never called to give evidence to the Taylor Inquiry or the inquests. Interviewed during the research for *Hillsborough*, Houldsworth challenged police accounts of both the condition and usefulness of the CCTV cameras, particularly camera 5 which overlooked the Leppings Lane terrace.

Duckenfield, in particular, was adamant that there was no reason to believe that the central pens were full immediately before gate C was opened. Camera 5 had a zoom facility and was capable of transmitting close-up shots of the crowd. How could officers in the police control box claim ignorance of the packed pens if camera 5 was transmitting detailed pictures?

The officers directing the cameras and monitoring the screens told both the Taylor Inquiry and the inquests that camera 5 was faulty and had not been used as normal. Close-ups were not possible and the camera angle gave a 'false impression' of crowd density. At the inquests, police officers stated that the faulty camera 5 was the only camera covering the central pens from 2.05 p.m. onwards. But this did not fully explain why there was no coverage prior to 3.02 p.m. available on video.

When interviewed in 1996, Houldsworth's account contradicted the police version. He had fixed camera 5 earlier in the day. It was, he claimed, in perfect working order. On the club control room monitors he was 'able to see what the police could see on their monitors . . . the pens were full to the point of overcrowding'. What was more, camera 5's zoom was so powerful it could pick out facial features. He rejected the police perception that it gave a false impression of crowd density.

Houldsworth also stated that camera 5 was not the only camera covering the Leppings Lane terrace. Camera 2, a colour camera, was also used prior to 3 p.m. giving a clear view of the packed pens prior to gate C being opened. It had powerful magnification. Further, camera 3 was also sufficiently powerful to 'give a clear picture' of the pens.

The Family Support Group submitted that Houldsworth's account showed that the police evidence had been deliberately false and misleading. Video evidence from camera 5, it was alleged, had been deliberately suppressed and concealed by the South Yorkshire and/or West Midlands Police, constituting a prima-facie perversion of the course of justice. The coroner, it was claimed, had failed to pursue the question of the missing tapes. In addition, police officers had lied about the condition of the cameras and Houldsworth's evidence had been withheld from the inquest jury.

These were serious allegations, each in its own right. Taken together, if proven, they amounted to an orchestrated attempt to suppress or change evidence. Stuart-Smith was unconvinced. He rejected the claim that Duckenfield and Murray had relied on cameras in forming their judgements about crowd density in the central pens: 'They could see the West terraces but they did not realise that the central pens were becoming overcrowded. They thought the numbers were normal for a big match.' In other words, camera 5's reliability was irrelevant because the police did not attribute their failure to identify overcrowding on the state of the monitors.

Stuart-Smith rejected as 'completely unfounded' the submission that 'police hid video footage'. The vital tapes, he stated, had been '. . . at all times, together with the schedule of their contents, available to be seen by legal representatives of the families'. Because he denied that video footage had been suppressed or was missing, the submission that the coroner failed to pursue the question was untenable. In Stuart-Smith's opinion, the coroner 'dealt perfectly properly with the jury's request to see the camera footage of the terrace'.

Whether or not the police had exaggerated the defects in camera 5 was immaterial, argued Stuart-Smith. The difference in evidence between police officers and Houldsworth was no more than a 'difference in opinion'. This, and other matters raised by Houldsworth, were of 'little consequence'.

Houldsworth claimed in his 1996 account that at 2.50 p.m., prior to the opening of gate C, he could see from cameras 3 and 5 that the central pens were already overcrowded. Stuart-Smith went back to Houldsworth's original 1989 statement. In this Houldsworth stated that he left the club control room to go to the pitch at 3.05 p.m. 'Like almost everyone else,' noted Stuart-Smith, 'he thought he was looking at a pitch invasion', the inference being that he was witnessing crowd disorder. Stuart-Smith concluded that Houldsworth would not have reached that conclusion had he identified serious overcrowding some 15 minutes earlier.

Finding Houldsworth's evidence inconsistent, and revealing discrepancies over timings, Stuart-Smith discarded the 1996 version of events in favour of the contemporaneous statement of 1989. The judge was 'unable to accept that his [Houldsworth's] recollection of events is now accurate', rendering the key submissions 'untenable'. Nothing in the submissions gave grounds 'for any further inquiry or consideration'. Stuart-Smith dismissed the much-publicised significance of Houldsworth's evidence with the damning conclusion that it had been 'exaggerated out of all proportion'.

* * *

As previously stated, only 14 of the 96 who died at Hillsborough made it to hospital. Most of the 14 were dead on, or soon after, arrival in casualty. Asphyxiation causes oxygen starvation and the body cannot function for long without a regular and sufficient supply of oxygen. It is well-known that oxygen deprivation does not always end life but can leave people 'brain damaged' or what has been defined as in a 'persistent vegetative state' (PVS). The controversy over the medical evidence after Hillsborough concerns the relationship between asphyxiation which fixed the chest to the extent that recovery was rendered impossible and asphyxiation which did not fix the chest so that resuscitation was possible.

Initially, and at the inquests, the case was made that all who died suffered traumatic asphyxia, their chests fixed and their destiny sealed within minutes. The message to the families, repeatedly delivered by a coroner anxious to emphasise that loved ones did not suffer, was that once consciousness was lost death followed quickly and inevitably. In other words, nothing could be done to save them: no amount of medical technology or personal care. Even to the lay-person this was not convincing.

Some of those who lost consciousness regained it in minutes. People were resuscitated. Had they been left they would probably have died. Others, like Eddie Spearritt, remained unconscious for 24 hours or longer. A young boy, Lee Nicol, died two days later. Two young men, Tony Bland and Andrew Devine, were diagnosed as being in a persistent vegetative state. In 1993, after much anguish, Tony Bland's courageous parents and his dedicated consultant, Jim Howe, shared the painful decision to cease

262

mechanical feeding and allow him to die peacefully. Andrew Devine remains alive. From these cases it is clear that death did not occur inevitably in minutes.

As discussed earlier, this raised the dreadful possibility that, if more had been done to rescue and resuscitate the dying earlier and more efficiently, fewer people would have died. The coroner, however, later supported by the Divisional Court, refuted this claim. In a nutshell, once they had fallen victim to asphyxiation, death was inevitable, following within minutes. Hence his decision to impose a 3.15 p.m. cut-off on evidence; all who died, he ruled, had received their fatal injuries and lost consciousness well before that moment.

It was an argument which repeatedly and fiercely surfaced once the coroner announced his intentions to restrict evidence. It was central to the 'miscarriage of justice' claim made by the authors of *No Last Rights*. It was only after the screening of Jimmy McGovern's *Hillsborough*, however, that an off-duty hospital doctor who had rushed to the Northern General at the time of the disaster came forward with what appeared to be disturbing 'new' evidence.

Dr Ed Walker, who in 1989 worked as an anaesthetist at another hospital, treated the first emergency admissions to arrive at the Northern General from Hillsborough. Yet, in a letter to Mr Wardrope, the Northern's accident and emergency consultant, sent on 8 February 1997, he stated that he had not been 'contacted by West Midlands Police to provide an official statement nor asked to appear at the inquest'. This seemed an extraordinary oversight given that Walker had arrived at the hospital 15 minutes ahead of Wardrope and, initially, was the only doctor in casualty with anaesthetics training.

During the Taylor Inquiry and the inquests, Walker had never been acknowledged by name but simply referred to as an 'unidentified doctor'. He found this curious because he was known to Wardrope and had submitted a hospital report after the disaster in which he raised several matters of concern. Walker had treated at least nine admissions, each of whom was critical. Some died, others lived. Some responded to intensive treatment, others didn't. In other words, some recovered. Death was not inevitable.

While accepting that all who died did so from the injuries inflicted in the crush on the terraces, Walker's informed medical opinion, based on administering care in the immediate aftermath, was that appropriate and swift medical intervention had saved lives. Conversely, inappropriate decisions taken by non-medically trained people could easily have cost lives. This led to the Family Support Group submission that the 3.15 p.m. cut-off 'was predicated on a number of unrealistic assumptions about the time it took for the deceased to be asphyxiated and unconscious'.

The submission regarded Walker's 1997 claims as 'new' evidence. He could show from his interventions at the Northern General that some who died were alive on admission and at least one who lived would otherwise have died. The jury, the submission argued, had been denied knowledge of such cases just as they had been misled over the inevitability of death. Further, the decision not to present Walker's evidence was 'fraudulent concealment', the verdicts of accidental death 'procured by fraud, suppression of evidence or insufficiency of inquiry'.

Stuart-Smith was adamant that criticisms of the 3.15 p.m. cut-off showed a 'complete misunderstanding of the coroner's reasons for its imposition'. Even before dealing with the submissions, the judge outlined his unqualified agreement with the coroner whose 'reasoning . . . has been widely misunderstood and misinterpreted'. First, it was irrelevant whether a person 'died instantly at the scene, or some time later, after medical or unsuccessful treatment'. There were no 'new intervening cause[s]' breaking the 'chain of causation between crushing injuries and death'.

All who died, Stuart-Smith stated, received their fatal injuries before 3.15 p.m. and 'once the chest of the victim was fixed . . . irreversible brain damage would occur after between four and six minutes'. Finally, the inquest had to be kept 'within reasonable bounds and to this end a time cut-off' was necessary. The coroner, he concluded, had never intimated that 'all those who died did so before 3.15 p.m., or that the medical evidence was to this effect . . . he has been widely misrepresented'.

People died, according to Stuart-Smith, through traumatic or crush asphyxia (a 'semantic' difference) caused by overcrowding in the central pens, not 'because first aid or medical attention failed to resuscitate them'. That people lived beyond 3.15 p.m. 'was well-known to the coroner and legal representatives of the families, and also to the inquest jury'. That some survived unonsciousness and recovered, however, did not affect the coroner's reasoning. Walker's evidence added 'nothing to the evidence given at the inquest'.

In discussing the relationship between the crush and the fatal injuries, Stuart-Smith established a direct 'chain of causation'. To challenge this the law demands that other 'intervening acts' have to be present, suggesting another cause. But the law is concerned with 'omissions' as well as 'acts'. No one doubts that crush injuries caused the deaths. The crucial issue all along was whether negligent or ill-conceived acts or omissions condemned to death some of those who might otherwise have lived. Without having the opportunity to examine the circumstances of the deaths, the bereaved could not address this question. Stuart-Smith took them no closer to a satisfactory resolution.

The bereaved families submitted that the inquest verdicts were untenable because 'new' evidence showed that a more prompt and efficient response by the emergency services would have saved lives. Stuart-Smith rejected this, arguing that the evidence in no way undermined or affected 'the coroner's decision not to have a wide-ranging inquiry' into the emergency response. The judicial review, he noted, had clearly ruled that it was 'a matter for the coroner's discretion at what point he chose to confine the inquiry'. It was a 'reasonable and sustainable' decision given Lord Justice Taylor's 'exhaustive public inquiry'. Submitting that there had been deliberate suppression or concealment of evidence, that 'those concerned acted in bad faith', was 'wholly irresponsible'.

In the course of the scrutiny it also emerged that Dr Walker had, in fact, made a full statement, hand-written on West Midlands Police headed paper. Dated 20 July 1989, it was signed by Walker and witnessed on each of its seven pages by A.R. Dicks and Julie Appleton. When challenged by Stuart-Smith, Walker, who had claimed that he had never been asked to make an official statement, replied that he had 'completely forgotten' having made this statement. In retrospect, he had 'no arguments' with its contents.

What was of concern, however, was the appearance of Julie Appleton's name as a witness to the statement. Mr Dicks, a hospital staff nurse, had been the sole witness. Walker had never met Julie Appleton. She was a member of the West Midlands Police investigation team. But the addition of her name seemed to be of no concern to Stuart-Smith: 'Well, presumably it [the statement] got back to the West Midlands Police, and I imagine Miss Appleton was dealing with it. I don't think we need lose any sleep about that.' An investigating police officer retrospectively signed her name as a witness throughout a doctor's statement, the two never met, and the judge slept soundly.

Whatever the confusion over Dr Walker's 1989 statement, no satisfactory explanation emerged from the scrutiny as to why he was referred to at the inquests as an 'unidentified doctor' when his identity was well-known. His evidence was significant in that his medical opinion was at odds with other doctors and he had played a crucial role in administering medical aid to the first casualties at the Northern General. In publishing his interview with Dr Walker in the scrutiny report, Stuart-Smith merely demonstrated further why that evidence was significant. Certainly it cast doubts on the reliability of the medical evidence heard by the inquest jury.

* * *

When Eddie Spearritt regained consciousness the day after the disaster his only thoughts were for his son, Adam, who he had last seen unconscious, held in his arms. The intensity of his grief was overwhelming: an unrelenting, unimaginable pain. As discussed earlier, the visit with his wife, Jan, to see Adam at the Medico–Legal Centre was an appalling example of the insensitivity shown by authorities to the bereaved in the immediate aftermath of the tragedy.

In the days that followed, Eddie, Jan and their other son, Paul, mourned Adam, like so many other families, in the media glare and under the public's gaze. These were not appropriate times to raise searching questions. But, within their trauma came the realisation that Eddie had 'gone missing' for two hours after he lost consciousness. It was 3.06 p.m. when he collapsed, it was 5 p.m. when he was admitted to the Northern General. 'I suppose I could have crawled, unconscious, to the hospital. That would've taken about two hours,' stated Eddie with bitter irony.

Eddie Spearritt's case remains crucial because he was crushed, lost consciousness, received no treatment for two hours, yet lived. Where was he? Laid out on the pitch and carried on advertising hoardings? Left, assumed dead, on crash mats in the gymnasium? Carried through the tunnel and put with the dead behind the West Stand? No one remembers.

How did he get to hospital? Like others, did he stir, show some sign of life among the dead? Did someone examine him, find a pulse? Eddie was the invisible man. He's in none of the police or ambulance officers' statements so far released. Yet he was, and remains, distinctive in style and looks. So close to death, someone must have worked on him. No one remembers.

The one consistent 'fact' is Eddie's arrival, unconscious and fitting, in the Northern General's casualty department at 5 p.m.

Case notes, hurriedly scribbled on blank paper, note his condition. Within 45 minutes he was transferred to intensive care, his notes then entered on headed paper.

Eddie's case summary classified him as an emergency, 'agitated, cyanosed and only responding to painful stimuli'. His disaster patient number was 96. He was diagnosed as suffering from cerebral oedema through asphyxiation; developing 'epilepticus . . . treated as a matter of urgency . . . sedated and paralysed to be put on a ventilator.' From the notes there is no hint of any delay in treatment from entering casualty to his transfer into intensive care.

On 12 May, almost a month after the disaster and a week after Eddie's case summary was written, he returned to the Northern General. With him was his wife, Jan, and a social worker. They met a consultant, the hospital's assistant general manager, nursing staff and a minister. Much of their discussion centred on the vain attempts to save Adam. Contemporaneous notes made by the social worker confirm that Eddie was 'admitted to the Northern General at about 5 p.m.'. Fitting, heart beating, 'he was showing obvious signs of lack of oxygen'.

Two years later James Wardrope, the senior accident and emergency consultant, co-authored a *British Medical Journal* article about Hillsborough. Between 4 p.m. and 5 p.m., it noted, 24 people were admitted. Case 96, male aged 41, was admitted at 1700 hours, 'agitated, responsive to pain'. Forty-five minutes later he 'developed status epilepticus' and was then 'sedated and ventilated for 24 hours'. Four others were admitted unconscious between 4 p.m. and 4.40 p.m. Case 96 was Eddie Spearritt.

Another possible explanation for the missing two hours was that he could have been assumed dead at the hospital, put to one side. Was he put in the plaster room, used temporarily to house the dead? Did someone notice a flicker, feel a pulse? Had he arrived earlier but only been admitted to casualty at 5 p.m.? No one knows. Or, if they do, they are not saying.

A meeting, several years later, with Wardrope was instructive. He had no dispute with Eddie's case notes. They had been written, albeit under some duress, at the time. Wardrope felt that Eddie was 'deemed as not being seriously ill and put to one side'. Did this suggest that the first hospital examination had been administered before 5 p.m.?

Eddie's survival, against the odds, raised the awful possibility that others who died might have lived had they been rescued earlier and been given necessary care and treatment. It drove a horse and cart through the coroner's decision to impose a 3.15 p.m. cut-off on evidence heard by the inquest jury.

Stuart-Smith rejected the importance of Eddie's experience in just two bald paragraphs. The judge was 'unable to ascertain at what time Mr Spearritt reached hospital, though according to Mr Wardrope it was *before* 5 p.m.' Where did this new estimate come from? Nine years on it seemed that Wardrope was doubting the times recorded and recalled by him and his staff at the time.

Stuart-Smith continued, 'Most of the serious cases, of which Mr Spearritt's was one, were taken to hospital well before this.' The inference being that Eddie had been admitted much earlier than 5 p.m. There had been no 'detailed inquiry or evidence . . . collated in respect of victims who, like Mr Spearritt, were crushed but survived'. And so it was not possible 'to conclude on the evidence that Mr Spearritt was at any time "left for dead"'.

Two sentences and a case dismissed. Exactly the opposite conclusion was equally tenable. From the evidence, especially the missing two hours, it was not possible to conclude that Eddie had *not* been left for dead. All the indications were that he had. Perhaps the most alarming features of Eddie's case were the silence of witnesses, the absence of records prior to 5 p.m., the new estimated time of arrival at the hospital.

Following publication of the scrutiny, Stuart-Smith wrote to Eddie's MP in answer to a request for information: 'I recall that there was some doubt, I believe from the hospital records themselves as to precisely when Mr Spearritt arrived at hospital; some records suggested it was 5 p.m., *others* that it could have been earlier. I therefore took the matter up with Mr Wardrope who told me that it was before 5 p.m., but he could not say how long before.'

And so, on 15 July 1998, over nine years after the disaster and following Stuart-Smith's supposedly exhaustive scrutiny, it transpired that *another* set of records existed. Why were they not revealed earlier? Why were they not included in the case notes? Why had Wardrope not taken notice of them in his *BMJ* article? Why was no reference made to them in Stuart-Smith's two paragraphs on Eddie's case? Where were they?

Chapter Ten

SANITISING HILLSBOROUGH

Disasters make good television. The wreckage of the aftermath triggers the imagination: how the victims died, how anyone survived. Dramatic accounts, sometimes live from the scene, provide a graphic insight into the horror and the heroism. Some of the coverage is thought-provoking, informative, even inspiring. Much is gratuitous, intrusive and ghoulish: the pornography of tragedy. Occasionally, there is a programme made with compassion, providing carefully edited insights into worst-case scenarios.

Towards the end of an intense programme on how rescuers suffer post-traumatic stress a former South Yorkshire Police officer talked with depth and integrity about his realisation of the damage done to him at Hillsborough. Living with what he felt was the personal guilt of failing to breathe life back into those he attempted to save, the experiences had overwhelmed him. But his suffering was not solely related to his efforts on the terraces.

Speaking quietly, and with carefully chosen words, he said, 'The police lost a lot of dignity and pride that day. People tried to alter the truth and embellish certain bits and just not admit to certain bits, so that it could be more of a hygienic day for all concerned. It was devastating, completely, and you almost feel after that day you were never clean again and can never be clean again.' As the camera rose over the deserted Leppings Lane terrace, the credits rolled.

271

It was a breathtaking comment. The truth altered? A more hygienic day? Tainted by embellished accounts? No one had said this before. Who was the former officer and what was he getting at? The questions were profound but their relevance was missed. A police officer, traumatised by his experiences at Hillsborough whose suffering, according to the programme, was compounded by 'senior police officers' attempts to cover up their mistakes', had spoken out and no one was listening.

Months later, on a cold early winter's day high in the hills above Hathersage, the former officer recalled the dreadful moments in the pens as he fought to save lives. He remembered the pain and sorrow, the anger and insults, the sense of failure. But he also detailed the aftermath. The moment when a young officer with eight years' service was asked to change his statement.

Like every other officer on duty at Hillsborough, sent away by senior officers to write their 'recollections' of the day, he 'wrote it like it was', warts and all. Their brief: to provide full and detailed accounts including feelings, emotions and impressions. These were not usual police statements, which were bland, factual and written on Criminal Justice Act forms. They were handwritten on blank A4 sheets. Officers thought it had something to do with counselling, like 'getting it out of your system'.

Not so. Walking through the first snows of winter, the former officer recounted how he received back a word-processed version of his recollections. It was annotated, sentences scored out, words altered. His most personal comments, his experiences, deleted. Someone had systematically gone through his recollections and reshaped them. He was devastated: the implication was that 'recollections' had been taken and turned into 'statements'. It was an incredible story and a most irregular practice.

Months later, he produced a box-file of papers. He took out the six pages of word-processed recollections, altered exactly as he had described. The 154 sentences or phrases from his original hand-written recollections were all there. But 57 had a line through them. A further 28 were substantially edited. The statement was fronted by a letter: a solicitor's letter from one of the north's leading firms, Hammond Suddards, the South Yorkshire Police solicitors. Referenced in the initials of a senior partner, Peter Metcalf, it was addressed to Chief Superintendent Denton of South Yorkshire Police Management Services.

Dated 15 May 1989, the letter read: 'We have the following further comments on statements requested by the West Midlands inquiry. As before, the mention of a name without comment indicates that the statement has been read and we have no suggestions for review or alteration.' The words 'review' and 'alteration' were stunning. They implied that officers' recollections, self-written and unwitnessed, had been sent to the solicitors where they were scrutinised as part of a process of transformation into formal statements.

The letter named three officers under the heading 'Serial No. 21'. Attached to the name of a sergeant were the words: 'Good statement, but he may wish to reconsider some of the comments on pages 3/4, as to his views prior to realising the seriousness of the incident.' In fact, the phrase that was eventually edited out read, 'We were near the corner flag by now but still no understanding of panic or alarm from supporters on the pitch . . .' There followed another officer's name without comment.

Then came the former officer's name. It stated, 'This is a personal and graphic account, which we would suggest is not necessarily suitable in its present form for submission as a factual statement to the West Midlands inquiry.' The advice was unequivocal. Without major modification, his recollections did not make the grade; the amended recollections, received by him, from his senior officers, seemingly did.

From that moment on, he felt 'betrayed' by the force, the uniform. Other officers had discussed the procedure and were unhappy about having to alter their recollections. Usual practice had been abandoned. Told not to write up a record of the day in their pocket-books, then given sheets of paper to write personal emotional accounts, none of the Criminal Justice Act procedures had been followed. To the former officer, Hillsborough was being 'sanitised'.

Years later, having left the police and struggled with the legacy of post-traumatic stress, he told his story to the nation on television. The moorland walks which followed coincided with the broadcasting of *Hillsborough* and the massive publicity surrounding the programme. When Jack Straw announced the judicial scrutiny, despite reservations over its remit, the former officer agreed to give evidence.

His meeting with the judge took place at the Home Office on 24 October 1997. Until his arrival, Lord Justice Stuart-Smith did not know which former officer he was meeting. Stuart-Smith was presented with the altered statement and its accompanying letter. He sat and read them, occasionally stopping to clarify a word unrecognisable beneath the alterations. Stuart-Smith stated that it was his understanding that officers had been asked to write a personal 'description of what happened that day', in their own words, 'with all [their] feelings and emotions at the time'. Would he have 'included all those matters' had he been asked to make a witness statement? Would he 'have wanted this original statement to go in as it was, as a witness statement . . . ?'

The question went to the nub of the issue. Of course officers did not expect their personal recollections to go forward as official statements. No one had anticipated that they were gathered for that purpose. But neither had they considered the possibility that their recollections would become the template for their final statements. The former officer commented, 'If you asked me to sit down and write you a police witness statement as a professional witness, obviously it would be very different to this [his personal recollections]. But at no stage was I asked to do that.'

Stuart-Smith seemed oblivious to the response, continuing to press the former officer to indicate what 'ought not to have been cut out' of his original recollections. Unmoved, he replied that he failed to see why Criminal Justice Act statements had not been taken at the outset. The procedure, said the judge, was 'for the benefit of the South Yorkshire Police and their solicitors'. Had Stuart-Smith ever 'known this to happen . . . as regards police officers giving evidence?' Evading the question the judge responded, 'I have not had experience of a disaster of this sort.'

The former officer was convinced that the removal, 'wholesale', of any criticisms of senior officers or their lack of organisation was the force's objective. Officers met with senior officers and were 'asked/impelled to sign things, that they didn't want to [sign] that had been changed'. Whether or not they went along with these 'requests' he 'couldn't say'. But he recalled that a few days after the disaster a 'certain Chief Superintendent' took him and fellow officers out for a drink; 'we were basically told, "Look, unless we all get our heads together and straighten it out, there are heads going to roll." And we were told in no uncertain terms to . . .' Stuart-Smith cut him off mid-sentence, seemingly uninterested in the specifics of South Yorkshire's unprecedented exercise.

Stuart-Smith was informed that there had been considerable anger among officers 'about the way this was dealt with afterwards' but that they were not willing to speak out. Many officers felt that the procedure was an organised attempt by senior management 'to sanitise the whole event and protect themselves'. Any 'honour' attached to the South Yorkshire Police, 'which . . . at the time was considerable, disappeared for me'. He could no longer 'wear the uniform with any pride'; what happened was 'not what I believe in . . .'

There had been a general feeling of cynicism among officers: 'we were asked to do it in this way so that alterations could be made and then submitted'. It was, said the former officer, 'unprecedented'. He doubted if changes would have been made had statements been taken formally and witnessed. At the time he expected it to 'be done fairly and squarely and above board . . . I don't believe it was.' The judge's concern appeared to be with content rather than process, outcome rather than intent. Focusing only on precisely what was changed, he seemed unconcerned about the irregularity of the practice. Indeed, he endorsed it.

* * *

So, what went on inside the South Yorkshire Police in the days and weeks that followed the disaster? How extensive was the practice of reviewing and altering officers' recollections? And, who knew? Within the South Yorkshire force, senior officers were anxious to prepare their case. They were well aware that the police operation on the day was under scrutiny, particularly the decisions and actions of senior officers.

At a meeting in October 1997 with one of the families, Stuart-Smith confirmed that police officers had not used pocket-books – the usual procedure after an incident: 'What they were asked to do when they got back to the station or wherever . . .' was 'to write out a statement in their own handwriting . . . of what they had done that day'. Stuart-Smith's assessment verified the former officer's account. In his report, Stuart-Smith noted that at a meeting of South Yorkshire senior officers two days after the disaster it was agreed that officers 'principally involved' at Hillsborough should draft their recollections and pass them to their line managers.

According to Stuart-Smith's account, the practice quickly became institutionalised. Chief Superintendent Wain of the South Yorkshire Police instructed supervisory officers to obtain their officers' recollections on plain paper – 'not' to be 'taken under Criminal Justice Act rules'.

'Our job,' it was stated, 'is merely to collate what evidence South Yorkshire Police officers can provide their Chief Constable in order that we can provide a suitable case, on behalf of the force to subsequent enquiries.' Wain's instructions were distributed throughout the force. Stuart-Smith, although not reproducing them in his report, concluded that they 'appear to call for a factual account'.

At a meeting of South Yorkshire senior managers, the force solicitors and barristers, the QC advised that the 'evidence-gathering operation' was solely for the 'information of legal advisers'. Thus, 'any statements taken for this purpose would be privileged', meaning that they would not be subject to disclosure. It would be 'a sort of catharsis': a confidential process through which 'legal advisers would choose what they wanted to leave in or leave out'. Peter Metcalf of Hammond Suddards, the force solicitors, recalled that the 'statements were intended to be used for the purpose of Lord Justice Taylor's inquiry' but not, as far as he was aware, 'intended to form Criminal Justice Act statements'.

While this was going on within the South Yorkshire Police, the full police investigation by an outside force, the West Midlands, was already under way. Investigating officers were gathering evidence, including statements, for the Taylor Inquiry and the criminal investigation. A week after the disaster the West Midland investigators were told that the South Yorkshire Police had started to collect 'self-serving statements' from their officers. In other words, the West Midlands investigators knew of the 'recollections'.

Just two weeks later, counsel for the Taylor Inquiry, via the West Midlands investigators, requested approximately 120 of the recollections gathered by South Yorkshire. A letter, dated 7 May 1989, was sent from the head of the West Midlands investigation team to the South Yorkshire Chief Constable which made reference to officers' 'recollections in writing'. By then, Chief Superintendent Denton of South Yorkshire's management services department was heading an internal review team charged with vetting and reviewing the recollections as they were gathered. He met with Peter Metcalf to discuss the Taylor Inquiry's request. According to Stuart-Smith it 'was agreed that many [of the recollections] might be suitable to be handed over as they were, but some might include comment and speculation and might have to be redone'. Denton sent a first batch to Metcalf under a cover-note which read: 'no doubt you will advise me on the propriety of supplying these documents to the West Midlands Police'.

Metcalf, in a letter to Stuart-Smith, commented: 'With the passage of time it is difficult to say why this approach was adopted. Rereading the file I think that it followed on from the procedure adopted with the senior officers and in particular the officers who had borne the brunt of the press criticism following the disaster . . . these men had been the subject of severe criticism and might well expect to be further criticised at the inquiry.' Accordingly, Metcalf concluded that the procedure adopted was 'entirely appropriate'.

Stuart-Smith records that in five weeks over 400 recollections went to the solicitors. Of these he reckoned 253 passed without comment and 60 were 'slightly' amended. Over 90 statements were recommended for alteration. It did not end there. As further statements were requested by the West Midlands investigators, South Yorkshire's review team approached officers to make alterations which fitted the pattern of review adopted by the solicitors.

In the course of his scrutiny, Stuart-Smith examined 'approximately one hundred amended statements where on the face of the comments by the solicitors something of substance might have been referred to'. He concluded that 74 were 'of no consequence'. In the remaining 26, 'comment and opinion' had been excluded, mainly officers' criticisms of the police operation. These concerned lack of radios and poor communication, shortage of police at Leppings Lane and 'lack of organisation by senior officers in the rescue organisation'. As matters of 'comment and opinion', Stuart-Smith felt that the solicitors 'could not be criticised for recommending their removal'.

Stuart-Smith expressed concern over just ten statements. Five had 'factual matters' edited out 'which arguably should not have been'. Four had 'implicit' factual matters edited. The tenth, which strongly criticised the command structure, the control room's 'paralysis', reduced manpower, failure to delay the kick-off and complacency over policing Hillsborough, was dismissed by Stuart-Smith. The criticisms were 'matters of opinion and comment'.

In considering the deletion of 'factual matter', Stuart-Smith accepted 'that the solicitors had to exercise judgement as to whether material unhelpful to the police case should be excluded'. After all, the South Yorkshire Police 'perceived themselves to be on the defensive' and this was a 'perception' shared by their 'legal advisers'. Stuart-Smith considered it 'understandable' that the police should not 'give anything away'. Nevertheless, he concluded that 'at least in some cases it would have been better' had some of the deletions not been made. This was 'at worst . . . an error of judgement' and the judge did not consider that 'the solicitors were guilty of anything that could be regarded as unprofessional conduct'.

Stuart-Smith acknowledged that what happened was 'well-known to Lord Taylor's inquiry team', as it was to the West Midlands Police investigators. In his opinion, the West Midlands investigators 'could not have taken the statements in time' for the Taylor Inquiry. Taylor was 'clearly well aware that the original self-written statements [recollections] were being vetted by the solicitors and in some cases altered'. Stuart-Smith was in 'no doubt' that Taylor 'knew or suspected that criticisms of the police operation or conduct of their senior police officers were being excluded . . .'

In fact, the sensitivity surrounding the alterations came to a head during the Taylor Inquiry. A South Yorkshire Police officer was cross-examined on the contents of his recollections. It transpired that an issue raised during his cross-examination centred on comments which had been removed from his original statement. In other words, the officer's original, unedited recollections had been forwarded in error to the inquiry. The head of the West Midlands investigation, Mervyn Jones, considered this a breach of the arrangement he had 'made with the Chief Constable of South Yorkshire'.

The dispute centred on a deleted paragraph which read: 'The crush outside the ground could have been better controlled with more police officers and a better regulation of the flow of fans . . . knowing the ground as I do and how the Leppings Lane end fills up it might possibly have been better to direct the fans coming in through the open gates into the flank areas [side pens].'

In a letter written to Mervyn Jones on behalf of the Taylor Inquiry, the Treasury solicitor commented that there was 'absolutely no reason' to exclude 'expressions of opinion' by South Yorkshire officers, 'when they touch on matters relevant to the public inquiry . . .' But he conceded that 'in view of the personal undertaking which you have given to the Chief Constable of South Yorkshire', the counsel for the inquiry 'agrees that it would not be appropriate to use the original statement for the purposes of the inquiry when this has been superseded by a subsequent statement'.

* * *

The interpretation of what happened over the review and alteration of South Yorkshire Police recollections presented by Stuart-Smith in his scrutiny report seems not wholly accurate. Chief Superintendent Wain's request, distributed throughout the force via senior officers, actually emphasised that the information-gathering 'exercise' had 'no connection with the investigation . . . conducted by a team headed by Mr Dear, Chief Constable of West Midlands'. Little wonder that officers who, as requested, submitted their recollections were surprised to learn that they were used as the basis of formal statements to the West Midlands investigators.

Officers had not been informed that 'legal advisers would choose what they wanted to leave in or leave out', yet this had already been decided. As for calling for what Stuart-Smith was satisfied was a 'factual account', Wain's request included additional questions over and above times, duties and responsibilities: 'What was the mood of the fans?; Actions of the stewards – were they doing their job?; Was there any breakdown in radio transmissions?; Did you handle any bodies? In what part of the ground? Did you move a body, if so, where to? Did you hand the body to another officer, if so, who?' It asked for a brief description of bodies handled by officers, concluding: 'Officers should include in their statements, their fears, feelings and observations.' Without doubt, Wain's questions and direction went well beyond 'factual' matters. They expected, even demanded, personal comment and opinion.

In assessing the significance of deletions or altered statements, Stuart-Smith was concerned solely with establishing whether they amounted to 'comment or opinion'. Reading through the hundreds of statements submitted to the West Midlands investigation, all vetted, many changed, the inescapable fact remains: they were riddled with comment and opinion. Hardly any of the sometimes scurrilous attacks on Liverpool fans were amended. In fact, every mention of fans' behaviour, alcohol or aggressiveness was underlined and annotated.

Stuart-Smith knew this. In his November 1997 meeting with Richard Wells, then Chief Constable of South Yorkshire, the judge commented that 'there was a tendency to remove opinion and intemperate language about senior police officers but leave in similar material about misbehaviour by Liverpool fans'. It was, he continued, 'a matter of concern that there seemed to be a pattern of changing this material in this way'. Stuart-Smith also met former Chief Superintendent Denton. The solicitors, suggested Stuart-Smith, 'were seeking to cut out . . . comments, speculation and bad language'. Denton added, 'opinions and emotive statements'. It struck Stuart-Smith that there tended to be 'a removal of criticisms of senior officers but no corresponding removal of criticisms of the fans'.

So Stuart-Smith was well aware that officers' recollections had been vetted and altered to reflect well on the police response yet badly on fans' behaviour. While he stated in his report that the South Yorkshire Police were on the 'defensive', he failed to record his concern as strongly as he had in his meetings with Wells and Denton.

Neither did the force or content of additional exchanges with Denton find their way into the scrutiny report. Stuart-Smith challenged Denton: 'some of these alterations do seem to alter the factual position', adding, '. . . it is not your function, is it, to change factual matters?' Denton replied, 'No it isn't, and I didn't change it either, sir . . . Mr Metcalf suggested all the changes. There were no changes suggested by the police at all.'

Yet many annotated statements not only carried comments by Denton's review team, as discussed above, but the changes were written in their handwriting. Stuart-Smith let this go, replying that Metcalf, the force solicitor, had confirmed that he 'merely gave advice' and no 'indication that any particular alteration should be made'. In a letter to Stuart-Smith, Metcalf confirmed that he 'read through the statements and made comments by fax' to Denton. He 'did not amend any statements' but 'suggested changes . . . principally removal of comment or impression'. Denton disagreed, commenting that Metcalf had even suggested changes to specific words.

Certainly at least one letter to Denton from Metcalf covering officers' statements referred to 'suggestions for review or alteration'. Stuart-Smith did not develop this point, but asked Denton how the alterations were made: 'Did you cross out what you thought should not be in and then invite the officers to sign them?' Denton replied that it 'was very much a joint affair'.

He continued, 'This was a huge task because there were

upwards of a thousand statements . . . The things that came back from Mr Metcalf, in a word, went to that team who suggested amendments, and who then went out . . . and saw the individual people [officers]' to discuss 'their revisions to the statement, and came back with a signed statement and that was sent to the West Midlands Police'.

It was inevitable, according to Denton, that the South Yorkshire Police would vet, review and alter police statements to their best advantage. They 'had their backs to the wall' he said, and it was 'absolutely natural for them to concern themselves with defending themselves'. This was a telling quote from the man at the epicentre of the storm. It was conspicuously absent from Stuart-Smith's report.

* * *

When Jack Straw announced the outcome of the Stuart-Smith scrutiny to the House of Commons he devoted just three sentences to the review and alteration of police statements, noting that the judge was satisfied that 'Lord Taylor's inquiry was not in any way inhibited or impeded by what had happened'. He also told the House that the material considered by the scrutiny would be placed in the Commons library: 'Let me make it clear that the material that will be published will include all the original statements made by South Yorkshire police officers, together with the amended versions submitted to the Taylor Inquiry.'

Eleven uncatalogued boxes containing over a thousand handwritten documents at different points in their transition from recollections to statements were placed in the library. Not all statements were included. From the material, it is clear that the primary function of the South Yorkshire review team was not to improve presentation or to remove all comment and opinion. It was about damage limitation: taking out criticisms, explicit or implied, of senior officers. Suggested alterations ranged from a few significant words to whole pages.

Denton's team appear to have been thorough. Even accounts of

Superintendent Marshall's radioed request to the control box to open gate C were scrutinised and altered. Many officers stated that Marshall's requests, as Duckenfield failed to reply, became increasingly desperate. Typical of the comments deleted were: 'The message passed became more and more frantic . . . a note of real fear and panic was in the voice of the officer requesting this'; 'each time it was more frantic'; 'seemed highly agitated'; 'sounded extremely agitated and upset'. The latter was changed to: 'I noted there was a sense of urgency in his voice.' In another statement, 'virtually screaming' became 'shouting'. Numerous references to 'panic' and another to 'pleading' were deleted.

The lack of leadership and direction shown by senior officers, as the fatal crush occurred, featured regularly in officers' recollections. Typical deletions were: 'Certain supervisory officers were conspicuous by their absence'; '. . . in the absence of instructions . . .'; 'There were no senior officers present . . .'; '. . . and therefore received no direction'; 'Throughout the time I was on the pitch or at the rear of the stand I saw no officer above the rank of sergeant . . . .'; '. . . and did not receive any instructions from any commander'; 'I could see no supervisory officers'; 'Other senior officers were on the pitch but appeared in as much confusion as many other officers.'

A lengthy passage deleted from an inspector's recollections recounted that during the pre-match briefing 'no mention was made about the tunnel gates being used to control ingress of the crowd'. He continued, 'Although, on rare occasions in the past I have used the gates nearest the concourses to control flow away from the tunnel around to the south pen.' Similarly, a question raised in another officer's statement was also removed: 'Why were the sliding doors at the back of the tunnel not closed at 2.45 when those sections of the ground were full as at the Manchester United match this season?'

In some cases entire passages were removed and replaced by versions which significantly changed their meaning. An officer on the perimeter track, realising that fans were dying in the pens, recorded a confrontation with a senior officer: 'I moved along the fence towards the gate. I then saw another PC begin to open one of the gates and he was arguing with an inspector who was telling him to close it again. The PC turned away from the inspector and opened the fence gate. I couldn't hear what was said because of the noise inside the ground. Once the fence gate was opened people just poured out . . .' Altered, this read simply: 'I moved along the fence towards a gate which, once open, people just poured out . . .'

On the pitch, officers stood around 'without any further orders or deployment from anyone'. This account continued: 'there was [sic] no directions given to me/us by any senior police officer present . . . There seemed to be a number of inspectors present but no one giving orders or instructions to anyone. We seemed under-employed . . .' This entire passage was removed together with a later comment, 'I was surprised at the delay in this [public address] announcement and felt relief that someone had at last given some instruction about the seriousness of the incident.'

Officers were scathing in their criticism of the lack of organised response. This extended to comments prior to the disaster. An officer, reflecting on the high police presence around the perimeter track well before the kick-off, stated, 'This was somewhat excessive from 10.30 a.m., the manpower could have been put to better use until, for instance 12.30 p.m., monitoring public houses close to the football ground. To have 20 police officers stood around for two hours with hardly anyone in the ground was a bit of a waste.' The passage was removed and replaced with, 'We had nothing much to do at this location at this time.'

Later, as officers realised the full extent of what was happening, communications became strained. 'We remained there several minutes and following what appeared to be confused radio messages, we were then requested . . .' was changed to, '. . . a number of radio messages which we found difficult to hear

285

because of the noise in the ground, we were requested . . .' Another officer recalled, 'There seemed to be no information to either the officers in our serial nor the Nottingham Forest fans as to what was occurring.' This was replaced by, 'At this stage, we were uncertain as to what had occurred.'

This form of deletion was repeated in many statements, for example, 'Still we received no confirmation of what was occurring either by radio or tango . . .'; '. . . fans were more aware of what was happening'; '. . . yet we still weren't told from official channels what exactly had occurred'; '. . . and all we were receiving [over the radio] was garbled and incomprehensible'. Again, the deletions changed the meaning of passages. An officer in the West Stand stated: 'People were very aggressive because no information was forthcoming. Nobody seemed to know what was happening and there was total confusion throughout the rear of the stand.' This was altered to read: 'People were very aggressive.'

Even though senior officers understandably made errors of judgement in the confusion of the rescue operation, any hint of criticism was removed. A typical deleted passage read: 'A supervisory officer requested that supporters be moved back into the terracing. This, however, was protested against by other officers as being a very dangerous and unsuitable action at the time. This idea was then forgot [sic].'

Another officer up in the West Stand stated, 'Both PC [name] and myself commented to each other that whatever was happening down there, police officers who were there, about three, were going to lose the situation.' Outside, an officer could 'remember saying to the officers in the van that we were starting to lose this one . . .' Another officer stated: 'The control room seemed to be hit by some sort of paralysis.' All three references to loss of control were removed.

At the gymnasium, a sergeant told a senior officer what was happening on the terraces. As to be expected, the senior officer, 'looked at me in disbelief when I told him that I had seen several dead. He immediately regained composure . . .' This reference was deleted. So were comments about conditions in the gymnasium at the height of the chaos that followed: 'One half of the gymnasium seemed to be full of dead bodies and together with the numerous police officers present, there seemed to be little organisation initially.' This became, 'One half of the gymnasium seemed to be full of dead bodies and the police officers there were working hard to organise a temporary mortuary.' Another officer's reference to 'utter confusion during the event' at the gymnasium was taken out.

The vetting officers occasionally attached notes to the recollections, specifying alterations or requesting further consideration. For example, attached to one officer's recollections was the comment: 'Panic and hysteria – I believe he refers to the mood of the fans and not police management?' The more senior vetting officer noted, 'Seen. Agreed as above. Okay.' Attached to another statement was: 'Chaos and panic. I believe this relates to state of fans and not police management of events.' 'Seen. Okay.' Another note instructed a force investigating officer to 'speak to the officer with regard to the attached statement, and to review areas of particular concern to us at pages 2, 3 and 4.' The next entry, a month later, replied 'P4 amended' and was signed off.

Attached to a statement in which an officer described his distress, and that of his colleagues, was the instruction: 'Last two pages require amending. These are his own feelings. He also states that PCs were sat down crying when the fans were carrying the dead and injured. This shows they were organised and we were not. Have PC [name] rewrite the last two pages excluding points mentioned.' Other covering notes commented on issues that were 'of interest' in the statements or remarked, 'Good statement for SYP [South Yorkshire Police]'.

On one attached note the first comment read: 'PC [name] is making an assumption we can manage without'. The senior officer agreed, stating that one of the vetting team would arrange for a force investigating officer to meet the officer concerned 'with a view to reviewing the paragraph, or, preferably deleting it altogether'. The next entry noted that the officer had been seen but was 'adamant' that his statement was 'correct' and had refused 'to alter or delete it'. They decided to take it no further, noting, 'There is plenty of evidence to show that he was under a false impression. I don't think that the remark he makes is sufficiently critical to warrant pursuing it further.'

An officer who criticised the lack of personal radios and poor command structure stated that he was 'sure many [officers], like me, felt like headless chickens running about'. He concluded, 'I am not concerned with apportioning blame in this matter but I felt ashamed for quite a while that the police did not respond professionally after the deaths etc were established.' The attached instruction read, 'FIO to see the officer and ask him to review the above. The officer's views and sentiments expressed are understood and have been noted elsewhere.'

Finally, in an unusual set of recollections, an officer recorded that his 'actions were, from then on, compatible with those of Inspector [name] and outlined in his submission. I have therefore copied his report, signed the appropriate part of the papers, and attached it hereto.' Rather than insisting that the officer submit his own account, over six pages, word for word, were identical to those of the inspector's statement. Only the names were altered, giving the appearance that it was the officer's personal statement.

It was ironic that in the course of a House of Commons adjournment debate on 8 May 1998 the Home Secretary, Jack Straw, stated that, 'Lord Justice Stuart-Smith also unearthed the fact that some of the original statements made by individual police officers had been edited by solicitors acting for the South Yorkshire Police.' Had the former officer remained silent it is doubtful whether the scrutiny would have known about the South Yorkshire Police procedure of review and alteration, let alone addressed it.

Despite a 'whispering campaign' aimed at discrediting his vital evidence, its significance could not be denied. Yet, three months after Stuart-Smith's report was published, the Home Secretary still laboured under the misapprehension that 'some' statements 'had been edited by solicitors'. He said nothing about Denton's review team and its collaboration with the solicitors.

During the House of Commons debate a Liverpool MP, Maria Eagle, accused the South Yorkshire Police of behaving 'abominably' prior to the Taylor Inquiry. She stated that they had 'orchestrate[d] what can only be described as a black propaganda campaign which aimed to deflect the blame for what had happened on to anyone other than themselves'. She argued that they had engaged in 'preparing a defence' with the fans as 'the main target'. She noted that a 'liaison unit' of six senior officers, including the Chief Constable and his deputy, 'appears to have . . . orchestrated that campaign'.

Maria Eagle, herself a former solicitor, attacked the 'systematic attempt to change police statements to emphasise the slant on the defence that the police wanted to develop'. Despite Taylor's unequivocal condemnation of South Yorkshire's senior officers, the 'campaign', Eagle stated, 'continued' as did 'the life of the liaison committee . . . beyond the end of the inquiry to the generic inquest'. Its primary role throughout being 'to deflect blame'.

Eagle's account was not entirely accurate. In fact the six officers she named appeared on a force distribution list much later, at the time of the inquests. Shortly after the disaster the South Yorkshire Chief Constable did set up a unit under the direction of Chief Superintendent Wain. While the extent and details of its role and responsibilities have never been made public, part of the remit of Wain's unit was to prepare the force's response to the Taylor Inquiry, including the review and alteration of officers' recollections.

In initiating and carrying out the review and alteration of police statements, the South Yorkshire Police senior management did not act illegally nor were they guilty of professional misconduct. What is more, the West Midlands investigators, the Taylor Inquiry and, seemingly, the Director of Public Prosecutions and the coroner were aware of and accepted the procedure. After all, other agencies, such as the South Yorkshire Ambulance Service, gathered their officers' statements internally and submitted them, via their solicitors, to the investigators. Yet this unprecedented, institutionalised and 'orchestrated' transition of police officers' personal 'recollections' into formal statements is not without wider implications.

The law protects citizens from being pressured into making formal statements which could implicate them or might not be in their best interests. Under investigating procedures, at least in theory, both suspects and witnesses have the right to legal advice. But, as the examples quoted show, the procedures adopted after Hillsborough regarding police evidence were quite different. The protected interests were those of the South Yorkshire Police, not the individual officers.

* * *

As the criticisms of the Stuart-Smith scrutiny mounted it must have been obvious to Jack Straw that Hillsborough's unresolved issues, unanswered questions and inherent contradictions were not about to evaporate. In announcing the judicial scrutiny just weeks after the election, he had been seen to act swiftly and responsively. Given its unfamiliar form, its limited scope and its ambiguity as an inquiry, perhaps he had acted too quickly; advised and directed, as he must have been, within the Home Office. Worse still, he had committed himself and the fledgling government to a pledge of 'once-and-for-all' discovery and disclosure. Nothing of the sort was delivered. For all the parliamentary bluster in trumpeting its 'findings', Stuart-Smith's scrutiny raised more questions than it answered, introduced more doubts and further compounded the failures of a legal process which denied access, disclosure and openness.

The irony was that in office, Jack Straw was surrounded and informed by Merseyside MPs – now in positions of influence, if not direct ministerial responsibility – who in opposition had been among the harshest critics of the post-Hillsborough response. George Howarth, Peter Kilfoyle, Jane Kennedy and Colin Pickthall each had constituents who died and they had all met with bereaved families and survivors. The new Sports Minister, Tony Banks, a genial politician and much-publicised football fan, in opposition had repeatedly expressed his concern over the circumstances and aftermath of the disaster, the appalling treatment of the fans and survivors and the disregard for the bereaved.

When Jack Straw introduced the full morning session's adjournment debate on 8 May 1998, he again accepted Stuart-Smith's report without question or qualification. It had been 'thorough', 'impartial' and conducted within 'very wide terms of reference'. In fact, despite including a directive 'to advise whether there is any other action which could be taken in the public interest', Stuart-Smith's remit, as shown in Chapter 9, was tightly drawn in conception and remarkably narrow in interpretation. Referring to the Scrutiny Report, Straw recognised that the inquest system was 'unsuitable' for dealing with disasters, stating that a 'comprehensive public inquiry' which addressed questions usually covered by the inquest would lift disasters out of the coroner's responsibility. He committed the Government to reforming the law when a 'suitable legislative opportunity' arose.

Straw continued: 'I have often been asked, if the police were to blame, why has no officer been brought to book?' The 'only answer' was 'far from satisfactory: police disciplinary procedures have been so defective that individual senior police officers have been able to utter "disgraceful lies", act with contemptible incompetence and incur no penalty'. It was a state of affairs 'plainly unacceptable to the whole House and to the whole country'. While concurring with Stuart-Smith that there was no 'new evidence' to be placed before the Director of Public Prosecutions or the Police Complaints Authority, 'in the light of Hillsborough . . . there is a compelling case for reform of the police disciplinary system'.

The Home Secretary stated that the standard of proof in police disciplinary cases, where officers had allegedly breached the force disciplinary code, should be changed from the criminal to the civil test. In other words, officers would be judged on the 'balance of probabilities' rather than 'beyond reasonable doubt'. Further, police officers could face both criminal prosecution and disciplinary action for the same offence. This would end 'double-jeopardy' protection, with fast-track dismissal introduced in the most serious cases. The 'serious defect' of allowing officers 'to retire on medical grounds before disciplinary hearings can be completed' would be remedied: 'when accused officers claim that they are unable, through ill health, to appear at disciplinary hearings, matters can and will be decided in their absence . . .'

While these 'lessons' of Hillsborough would bring policy change and legal reform, nothing in Stuart-Smith's scrutiny or Straw's response took the Hillsborough bereaved and survivors further towards answering their questions, resolving the contradictions, establishing unequivocal culpability or securing accountability. 'None of us,' stated the Home Secretary, 'can begin to understand the anguish that is felt by the families who lost their loved ones in such tragic circumstances, but we have shared their determination to establish, to the fullest extent possible, why and how their relatives died.' For Straw, that 'determination' had brought about the scrutiny and its thoroughness was beyond doubt. Consequently, 'no purpose could be served by [a] further inquiry . . . We as a Government have done everything that is possible on their [the families'] behalf.'

Following Jack Straw's address, eleven Merseyside MPs, including Maria Eagle, spoke at length of their direct experiences of contact with the bereaved and survivors of Hillsborough. Drawing on the detail of their constituents' cases, they collectively submitted the catalogue of failures within the legal process that had dogged the long-term aftermath of investigating, examining and prosecuting culpability. There was universal condemnation of the South Yorkshire Police and deep concern over the institutionalised process through which statements had been collected, reviewed, altered and presented to the inquiry teams. There was concern about the failure to bring prosecutions and calls were made to refer the case back to the DPP. The MPs produced a litany of unanswered questions, some specific and many universal, raised by their constituents.

Summing up the debate, which lasted over four hours, Home Office Minister George Howarth pledged that if 'people are missing information they should rightly have, it will be sent to them'. He stated that the Home Office attitude to 'disclosure of documents has been simple. We believe that anything relevant or material – anything that throws light onto any of the events of that day – should be made available unless someone can demonstrate a very good reason why it should not be, although I have not so far come across such a case. I hope that access will be provided to *everything that is required*.'

Howarth noted that 'the system' had 'failed to provide adequate means for blame to be seen to be apportioned' and 'for injustices to be remedied'. A governmental response was necessary 'by putting into words the consequences for those left behind as a result of the failures' of 'the system'. He concluded: 'The reasons why those 96 people died had nothing to do with where they came from or who they were . . . It was not their behaviour or their alcohol intake that caused the tragedy, and nobody should be left in any doubt about that simple truth . . . One organisation, above all, was responsible: the South Yorkshire Police.'

While Howarth's condemnation of the South Yorkshire force concluded the debate, effectively the Government drew a line under Hillsborough after the judicial scrutiny. Despite George

Howarth's pledge, Jack Straw had already foreclosed further inquiries or full disclosure. While MPs had their say, and most of the burning issues were aired, the end of the parliamentary road had been reached. Nowhere was this more apparent than in two letters, one signed by the Home Secretary to a bereaved family, the other written to the author by Tony Banks, Minister at the Department for Culture, Media and Sport.

The letter from Jack Straw included the following passages: 'I am satisfied that Lord Justice Stuart-Smith has conducted a thorough scrutiny of the evidence and considered its significance carefully. His report covers in detail the matters put to him by the families and others and the reasons for his conclusions. He has considered all the material allegations about missing or concealed videotape evidence, the alleged interference with witnesses and witness' statements and concerns about the use of the 3.15 p.m. cut-off time at the Inquests . . . The Home Secretary [meaning himself] has indicated that he shares the sentiments expressed by Lord Justice Stuart-Smith in Chapter 7 of his report when he says: "*I understand the dismay that they [the families] have that no individual has personally been held to account either in a criminal court, disciplinary proceedings, or even to the extent of losing their job*" [italics in the original].'

There followed a lengthy paragraph on the 'profound short-comings of the police discipline system'. Significantly, Tony Banks, writing from a different department on a different but related issue, reproduces those entire passages verbatim as his own. While each letter addressed specific issues raised by the correspondents, both contained identical core passages. Not only had the line been drawn under Hillsborough, a very precise and agreed line was established and then communicated by ministers. Tony Banks, such a strong critic of the authorities when in opposition, now had no problem in quoting Stuart-Smith's con-clusions over the review and alteration of police statements. The Taylor Inquiry had not been 'in any way inhibited or impeded';

the 'outcome of the Inquests' and the decision 'not to bring criminal charges' had been unaffected; and there was no question of misconduct 'either by the solicitor who gave the police advice upon the statements or by the police officers who suggested alterations to the statements without referring the statement [*sic*] to the solicitors'.

* * *

Just five months after making her claim in the House of Commons that the South Yorkshire Police had engaged in a 'black propaganda campaign', Maria Eagle's allegations returned to the headlines in extraordinary circumstances. Following the retirement of Jim Sharples as Merseyside Chief Constable, the Police Authority announced his replacement: Norman Bettison, the Assistant Chief Constable of West Yorkshire. To those familiar with the aftermath of Hillsborough the name was instantly recognised. A Norman Bettison had been Chief Inspector, later Superintendent, at the headquarters of the South Yorkshire Police throughout the immediate aftermath of the disaster. On 14 October 1998, the day after his appointment to Merseyside, the same Norman Bettison came under fire from 'outraged Hillsborough families' in the *Liverpool Echo*. Calling for his resignation, the front-page story repeated the quote from Maria Eagle, reporting that he had been 'part of a South Yorkshire Police team set up in the wake of the disaster preparing for the Taylor inquiry'.

As the story broke, dominating the local broadcast and print media, fact was lost to myth, with accusations and recrimination dominating the headlines. Of particular concern was the public disagreement within the nine-person Police Authority appointments committee over whether they had been fully and appropriately briefed about Bettison's Hillsborough connection. Within days of the appointment Councillor Dave Martin, committee member and also Leader of Sefton Metropolitan Borough Council, stated that he had been unaware of Bettison's involvement within South Yorkshire after Hillsborough. Councillor Frank Prendergast, the Labour Leader on Liverpool City Council, also a member of the appointments panel, echoed Martin's opinion.

On 16 October, David Henshaw, Clerk to the Merseyside Police Authority and Chief Executive of Knowsley Metropolitan Borough Council, issued a statement contradicting Martin and Prendergast. It was an unusual move for a serving council officer, regardless of his status. The statement confirmed that the appointments panel had been supplied with a full set of papers on each candidate at a short-listing meeting in September. These papers 'indicated Mr Bettison's experience, both in South Yorkshire and West Yorkshire Forces', including 'a specific reference to his involvement in the team set up within South Yorkshire Police Force following the disaster'.

Henshaw stated further that the appointment panel retained the papers for three weeks until the interview date; they 'had information in front of them during the whole of the process, from short-listing to final appointment, which indicated Mr Bettison's involvement in the team set up after the Hillsborough disaster'. Carol Gustafson, the Police Authority Chair, went further, stating that panel members 'were aware of Mr Bettison's operational responsibilities in connection with Hillsborough *through the application form*' (emphasis added).

There followed a bitter five-hour emergency meeting of the appointments committee. David Henshaw was heavily criticised. The well-known Liberal Democrat Lady Doreen Jones considered that the matter had been 'extremely badly handled', with members put 'in a bad light with both the press and public'. She railed, 'I think that really you [Henshaw] are protecting yourself in this. I take exception to the panel being referred to on the radio as "a bunch of twits".'

Despite the internal rifts, the public outcry and intense pressure from the Hillsborough Family Support Group, a meeting of the full Merseyside Police Authority confirmed Norman Bettison's appointment by an eleven-to-three majority. The nine-hour meeting was addressed by a number of outside interested parties, including Hillsborough families' representatives. Soon afterwards, Councillors Martin and Prendergast resigned from the Police Authority and, on 16 November, Norman Bettison, in a blaze of local media publicity, took up office as Merseyside Chief Constable.

Interviewed 'exclusively' by the *Liverpool Echo*, the Home Secretary, Jack Straw, fully endorsed Norman Bettison's appointment. He made it clear that, in keeping with his office as Home Secretary, he had approved Bettison's short-listing. His approval carried the recommendation of Home Office officials. While refusing to state whether or not Bettison's links were known to him at the time of giving approval, Jack Straw strongly criticised the appointments panel for not fully reading the papers before them. He stated: 'Mr Bettison was appointed by the authority under proper procedures. The authority – because I have seen the papers – were given a biographical summary about his membership of the group that had something to do with Hillsborough . . . anyone who read them could have asked Mr Bettison any questions they wanted to ask. He has my full confidence. Everyone should now let him get on with the job.'

The issues raised by the disaffected councillors, however, require some scrutiny. At the short-listing stage Dan Crompton, Her Majesty's Inspector of Constabulary, did provide a note on all candidates, including Norman Bettison. This is standard procedure for the appointment of Chief Constables. In Bettison's case the note comprised twelve, mostly inconsequential, bullet points. The fourth point noted his 'varied career from Chief Inspector' and his membership of 'a small inquiry team reporting to the Chief Constable (of South Yorkshire) on the Hillsborough incident'. That was it. Not another reference to Hillsborough-related duties.

Further, Bettison's application listed four periods of duty: three at South Yorkshire and, most recently, as a West Yorkshire Assistant Chief Constable. He mapped his career history from October 1989, following promotion within South Yorkshire to Superintendent. This was six months after the disaster. In outlining and discussing his previous relevant experience the application claimed 'proven ability to bring order out of chaos', noting his significant roles after the 'Leeds bombing' and in the 'Yorkshire side of the investigation . . . linked to the Aintree incident'. Illustrating 'leadership skills', he referred to taking command 'throughout the Bradford riots in 1995'. Norman Bettison's application contained not a single reference to Hillsborough. Clearly, Carol Gustafson – the Police Authority Chair – had been mistaken.

So what was Norman Bettison's role following Hillsborough? The day after his appointment he released a press statement outlining his duties at the time of the disaster. He had attended the Liverpool–Nottingham Forest semi-final as a spectator. He watched the tragedy unfold from the South Stand, close to the Leppings Lane Terrace. At 3.25 p.m., while the pens were still being evacuated, he went to the local police station and put himself on duty. He had no involvement at the ground. 'A few days later,' he stated, 'I was assigned with other officers to a unit which was set up under a Chief Superintendent and two superintendents . . . tasked with looking at what happened on the day of the disaster, making recommendations about policing of the remaining football matches at Hillsborough . . . and reviewing policing arrangements for football at Hillsborough . . .'

This unit 'also liaised with and passed information to West Midlands Police, who were undertaking the formal and independent police investigation into the disaster'. In fact, the West Midlands Police investigators serviced Lord Justice Taylor's Home Office Inquiry, the criminal investigation and the Coroner's inquiry. Once the 'immediate work of the unit was complete',

Bettison was 'given a specific role to monitor the public inquiry and brief the Chief Constable on progress'.

While Bettison *was* a member of a unit set up in the immediate aftermath of the disaster, Maria Eagle, in her House of Commons speech, misidentified the unit. She confused it with a list of six senior officers, including the Chief Constable, to whom details of the inquest proceedings were circulated a year later. Bettison appears on that list, by then a superintendent. Throughout his initial post-Hillsborough duties he remained a Chief Inspector. His appearance on the later distribution list reflected his reassignment by the Chief Constable to monitor the Taylor Inquiry and, eventually, the inquests.

This confusion brought further speculation around his appointment as Merseyside Chief Constable. On 2 November he made a second, more fully developed statement to the Police Authority. He reiterated that he had 'never sought to hide my involvement in Hillsborough'. But he emphasised that it had been only 'a *peripheral* link' as 'a relatively junior officer'. South Yorkshire Police had assisted the West Midlands Police investigators 'with documentation', his unit providing 'a sort of mail room'. The unit also was expected 'to try and make sense of what happened on the day'.

Bettison was at pains to stress that his work 'contributed to only a small part of the jigsaw' – an example being the review and comparison of police operational orders for previous Hillsborough semi-finals. On completion, the unit's work was passed to the West Midlands investigators. He denied engagement in any 'black propaganda campaign' or 'historical revisionism'. Such allegations were 'utter nonsense . . . simply not true.' References to Hillsborough were absent from his application because 'in the two or three months immediately following the Hillsborough disaster' his work 'would not have been significant in addressing competences for Chief Constable'.

What enveloped Norman Bettison's appointment was the

relatively recent disclosure of the review and alteration of police recollections/statements in the immediate aftermath of the disaster. The picture, fresh in people's minds, was of a force on the 'defensive' yet also on the attack. What had been his role at headquarters, not necessarily as a 'definer' or 'protagonist', but as a participant? In responding to the issues of public concern, Norman Bettison described his status at the time as 'relatively junior'. This was as unhelpful as it was ambiguous. Already a Chief Inspector, he was promoted to superintendent within six months of the disaster. Similarly, it seems incongruous that he defined himself as a 'peripheral link': a status confirmed by Her Majesty's Inspector of Constabulary, who also considered Bettison's role as 'peripheral'. What emerges from closer inspection of the available documentation certainly stretches the definition of 'peripheral'.

Two days after the disaster the Chief Constable of South Yorkshire, Peter Wright, held a meeting of senior officers at police headquarters. It was at this meeting that the decision was taken to ask all officers for their hand-written 'recollections'. The meeting was not attended by the force solicitors, but Peter Metcalf commented, in a letter to the Stuart-Smith scrutiny, that the 'only record' detailing the request to officers 'will be in Chief Inspector Bettison's note of the meeting . . .' The clear inference was that Norman Bettison had responsibility for minuting the meeting. Subsequently, Norman Bettison has strenuously denied that he had such a role, stating that Peter Metcalf has reconsidered his comment to Stuart-Smith and had been mistaken.

Nevertheless, he accepts that he was one of a group of officers which formed the unit under Chief Superintendent Wain, whose signature appeared on the initial memorandum distributed to officers requesting submission of their recollections in writing. Members of Wain's unit actively participated in the process of review and alteration. There is nothing in the material housed in the House of Commons library which directly associates Norman

Bettison with reviewing or altering statements and he remains unequivocal that he had neither knowledge nor involvement in that process.

Once the 'immediate work of the unit' was complete Bettison was given, in his own words, 'a specific role to monitor the public inquiry [Taylor] and the inquest and brief the Chief Constable on progress'. Bettison attended the entire Taylor hearings, providing the Chief Constable and the Deputy Chief Constable with his 'analysis of the way the Taylor Inquiry was going'. Bettison claims that this 'enabled the Chief Constable to be in a position on the day that Taylor published his findings to publicly accept blame on behalf of South Yorkshire Police for their failure of public control . . .'

Months after Taylor reported, Bettison was telephoned by Wain, who had been asked by the Deputy Chief Constable to establish a case to recover contributions from other parties following the award of damages against the police. Bettison claims he was so busy that he appointed a Detective Inspector to carry out Wain's request 'on a day-to-day basis . . . I didn't have any involvement in completing those tasks.' Once the Detective Inspector had completed the job, Bettison 'wrote back . . . to the Deputy Chief Constable pointing out that they had been done'.

In fact, the memorandum – dated 12 July 1990 – is a substantial two-page briefing paper from Bettison to the Deputy, headed 'Preparation of Case for Hillsborough Contribution Hearings'. The first section notes that the 'mini-inquiry team, formed to assist Hammond Suddard [sic] in the preparation of the Contribution Hearing case, has completed the tasks it was set in May . . .' It then reports on nine key points. The second section notes a meeting between Bettison, Metcalf and the Detective Inspector on 11 July, listing five points arising from the meeting.

Within these points is the comment: 'Peter Metcalf is re-reading the Inquiry [Taylor] transcripts in relation to evidence provided by police officers . . . [He] anticipates a short list of officers who are to be asked to "clarify" a part of their evidence. For example, one or two officers talk of having a responsibility to monitor the pens. What do they mean by monitoring? Surely nothing more than keeping a weather-eye out. If this evidence goes unchallenged [unclarified] then another party might adduce that the police accepted a responsibility to count people into the pens.' Finally, Metcalf 'was informed that the inquiry team would revert to normal duties pending further requests', but would 'continue to be at their [lawyers'] disposal'.

Finally, Bettison's name appears on a distribution list relating to the monitoring of the inquests. This group, including the Chief Constable, the Deputy Chief Constable and Chief Superintendent Wain, was circulated by PC Kenneth Greenway, who attended the inquests and provided a daily account of progress. In a *Liverpool Echo* interview on 16 November 1998, Bettison stated that Greenway was 'a gopher for the West Midlands Police team who had been doing the inquiry and who subsequently presented the evidence to the coroner's court'.

Bettison continued: 'I can only assume [that] because he felt that he ought to justify the role he was performing he did reports on what was happening at the inquests and circulated them to people that he thought might be interested. For the most part, I used to receive those reports, read them because of course I was interested, and throw them in the bin.' What Bettison suggests is that Greenway took it upon himself to create a distribution list, that it was somehow arbitrary and that it had no recognised constitution or mandate. Yet in Bettison's press statement, a month before the *Echo* interview, he revealed that part of his 'specific role' was to 'monitor . . . the inquest and brief the Chief Constable on progress'. He made no mention of this in his lengthier statement to the Police Authority in early November.

On his first day in office, Norman Bettison repeatedly referred to the benefits of '20/20 hindsight', commenting that had he realised the potential intensity of controversy over his appointment, he might have approached his application and appointment slightly differently. At best, he was left appearing naïve, since it was inevitable that any officer of seniority who played even a minimal role after Hillsborough would be closely scrutinised on Merseyside. As the above discussion illustrates, Bettison's role, whatever he or Her Majesty's Inspector of Constabulary claimed, hardly qualified as minimal or peripheral. Even discounting Metcalf's earlier statement to Stuart-Smith, concerning Bettison's attendance as minute-taker at the initial headquarters meeting, his role was significant. He was part of Wain's unit, some of whom engaged in the review of and alteration of statements. He reported daily on the progression of the Taylor Inquiry. He prepared documentation on the contribution hearings. Finally, he monitored the inquests. These were tasks of importance and consequence to a force on the 'defensive', a force reeling from the realisation that it could be held primarily responsible for the disaster at Hillsborough.

What the Bettison affair illustrates is that the key questions concerning South Yorkshire's damage-limitation exercise in the aftermath were never adequately or appropriately answered. The sequence of events has remained hidden from view or scrutiny. While Maria Eagle's House of Commons allegations could not be sustained as they stood – with the specifics open to dispute – nagging doubts persisted over the roles, responsibilities, relationships and functioning of Denton, Wain and their fellow officers. There has never been full disclosure of the agendas, minutes or outcomes of the meetings held at South Yorkshire headquarters. While the controversy surrounding Norman Bettison's appointment could be viewed as the unfair pursuit of a very capable senior police officer and manager who had the misfortune to be caught up in the aftermath of Hillsborough, this is not the case. The saga of his appointment and the highly public row that followed went beyond Norman Bettison. It revealed, still only in part, the indefensible sequence of events which unfolded within the South Yorkshire force in the months following the disaster.

In 2002, Norman Bettison was reportedly offered a post at Her Majesty's Inspectorate of Policing, but he remained Chief Constable of Merseyside. Two years later, he became Chief Executive of Centrex, the Central Police Training and Development Agency. Knighted 'for services to policing' in 2006, he was appointed Chief Constable of West Yorkshire in 2007.

Chapter Eleven

A CASE TO ANSWER

In July 1998, just weeks after the final House of Commons adjournment debate, Richard Wells retired as South Yorkshire Chief Constable. Publicly acknowledged and acclaimed as an innovative leader who had 'restored the battered image' of the force and 'rebuilt bridges', he regretted that major issues concerning the Hillsborough disaster remained unresolved. That 'nobody carried the can', he considered, was the significant difference in perception between the police and the bereaved families. He said, 'Chief Superintendent Duckenfield, now retired, carried the can. His career was prematurely curtailed.' This perception was not shared, even by government ministers who had made it clear that avoidance of professional and personal accountability had remained a running sore. Wells, however, considered the problem to be one of perception and interpretation rather than culpability and liability: 'I wish I had been able to achieve more for the Family Support Group in terms of understanding. We've expressed remorse. I would have hoped for some expression of forgiveness to match that.'

Coming from a police officer heralded as one of his generation's most able, perceptive and progressive Chief Constables, these comments illustrate the gulf between the police and the bereaved and survivors of Hillsborough. From his first days in office, inheriting the poisoned chalice from Peter Wright, Wells seemed committed – as was his predecessor – to redistributing the blame for Hillsborough. As early as January 1992, Wells criticised some of Lord Justice Taylor's findings as 'hasty and based on a less than full account of the different perspectives'.

In the same month Wells wrote: 'There were many parties to blame that day and the police were just one of them. Our responsibility was to help prevent people arriving late and in droves and, where unable to prevent it, to react to it. The supporters' responsibility was to arrive on time (as, of course, the majority of them did), with tickets, sober, and prepared to accept, if not in possession of a ticket, that entry was impossible. They didn't discharge that responsibility and we didn't discharge ours.' The 'cause' of the disaster was 'shared between many, including ourselves'. This was the context in which Wells, according to one of his Assistant Chief Constables, 'accepted that the force made mistakes and . . . expressed his profound regret'.

That other organisations – the club, the FA, the local authority and the safety engineers – contributed to the Hillsborough disaster is beyond doubt. Richard Wells had every justification, supported by the Taylor Report, to point this out. But to blame fans for not 'discharging their responsibility' was, and remains, unacceptable. To the world beyond South Yorkshire Police headquarters, his comments smacked of denial. A denial not of some responsibility, but of primary responsibility. Little wonder that the bereaved and survivors were in no mood to match his declaration of 'remorse' with one of 'forgiveness'. Duckenfield retired prematurely, his pension secured, and he was eventually followed by his assistant, Superintendent Bernard Murray. Neither faced the disciplinary charges recommended by the Police Complaints Authority.

* * *

When Richard Wells made his parting comments about 'can-carrying' he was acutely aware that a private prosecution, initiated by the bereaved families, against Duckenfield and Murray was under way. Wells was keen to emphasise that what amounted to corporate liability shared by several organisations including the police should not be laid at the door of one man. As far as the families were concerned, senior officers had taken key decisions, on the day, which not only put their loved ones at risk but actually set in motion the fateful sequence of events that led directly to the 96 deaths. While other individuals and organisations had some responsibility for the context in which the disaster occurred, the bereaved families considered that primary liability could and should be attributed to the police officers in charge. The private prosecution was not about scapegoating or vengeance, but about establishing appropriate criminal liability in a court. There was no overwhelming desire to see individuals punished, but a shared need to have culpability recognised through a guilty verdict.

Private prosecutions are rare. While the Crown Prosecution Service recognises in its code that 'private individuals' have the right to bring private actions, there are inhibitions and limitations. Individuals are often restrained because they have neither the personal finance nor necessary skills to meet and fulfil the initial requirements of putting a case together. Invariably they are also operating in circumstances where the Crown Prosecution Service has decided that the evidence is not sufficiently persuasive to secure an eventual conviction. Beyond this, the Crown Prosecution Service has the right to intervene in a private prosecution solely for the purpose of ending it: where there is clearly no case to answer; where public interest factors 'tending' against prosecution clearly outweigh those 'tending' in favour; where the prosecution might damage the 'interests of justice'. While these circumstances are broad and discretionary, there is a reluctance to intervene solely because the Crown Prosecution Service previously discounted prosecution through insufficiency of evidence.

The decision, taken by the Director of Public Prosecutions (DPP) in August 1990, not to prosecute any officer of the South

Yorkshire Police because of insufficiency of evidence had remained a constant frustration for bereaved families. It suggested that there was some evidence, but they had access neither to the evidence nor to the reasoning behind the decision. It took eight years for an explanation to be offered and, even then, it was scant. They were told that the Crown Prosecution Service had to be satisfied that sufficient evidence was available to give a 'realistic prospect' of securing a conviction. For the families this was not news. What they required was an explanation as to how, and on what grounds, the decision not to prosecute had been reached. In the course of his scrutiny Stuart-Smith had stated that in making his decision the DPP had received a joint legal opinion from two senior Queen's Counsel.

Their opinion finally came to light in February 2000 when the judge for the private prosecution, Mr Justice Hooper, delivered his final ruling prior to the private prosecution. The 1990 opinion considered the possibility of prosecuting David Duckenfield, as the match commander, for manslaughter. It singled out Duckenfield because he had taken the decisions not to delay the start of the match and to open gate C without first sealing off the tunnel access to the already full central pens. While there was never any suggestion that Duckenfield deliberately put people's lives at risk, the focus of the opinion was involuntary manslaughter. There are two definitions of involuntary manslaughter. First, when an intended act, knowingly or unknowingly, is unlawful or dangerous because it is likely to cause direct personal injury. Second, when an intended act creates an 'obvious and serious' risk of causing personal injury. The person committing the act might not think about, or even recognise, the risk. Alternatively, they might recognise some risk but take a chance on running it. In the law, which is by no means hard and fast on this issue, this amounts to recklessness. The act itself, or the failure to act, does not have to be the sole cause of death, but a significant contributing factor. The parameters of 'significance' are for the jury to decide, based on the evidence presented and cross-examined.

The two QCs' opinion also discussed death caused by omission. There are grounds for a prosecution for manslaughter, they stated, where death is caused by not carrying out an act when there is a duty to do so. This amounts to gross negligence. Again, throughout the last two decades there has been considerable debate over the appropriateness of a manslaughter charge – a serious criminal offence – arising from negligence, however 'gross'. The two QCs agreed that regarding 'the circumstances of Hillsborough' it was correct 'to approach the evidence on the basis that the gross negligence test is sufficient to establish the offence of manslaughter . . .' Yet they were also clear that previous case law had established that 'when gross negligence or manslaughter by neglect is alleged against the police' a distinct and more detailed test of liability is necessary.

First, it has to be established that the police have a duty concerning the health and welfare of the deceased. Second, that there is a failure to act with regard to that health and welfare. Third, that the failure contributes significantly to the cause of death. Fourth, that the failure amounts to recklessness. The test of recklessness is that a police officer can be shown to have been indifferent to an obvious and serious risk, or to have recognised the risk and decided to take it. Failure to 'appreciate' a risk would not be enough to amount to recklessness.

The QCs considered that in not postponing the kick-off or in failing to seal off the tunnel before opening gate C, Duckenfield committed no intended act 'which created an obvious and serious risk of causing personal injury'. Further, there was 'grave doubt', given the 'complexity of the disaster', that Duckenfield's possible omissions 'created a risk which was obvious to anyone at the time'. Thus there was 'insufficient evidence on which to found a charge of recklessness' and there was no evidence that Duckenfield 'was grossly negligent in failing to act . . .' Put simply, given the requirements of the detailed test of liability regarding the police, there was 'no evidence that Mr Duckenfield was wilfully neglectful of his duty or was culpable so as to have committed the offence of culpable malfeasance' (an unlawful act in public office).

The legal opinion on which the decision not to prosecute Duckenfield was based demonstrated the problems associated with a prosecution for manslaughter. What constitutes an 'obvious and serious' risk, 'recklessness', gross negligence, duty of care, failure to act, indifference and their relationship to the definition and scope of a 'serious criminal act' have emerged as the key elements in involuntary manslaughter cases. On 20 August 1998, Duckenfield and Murray walked into the Leeds Magistrates' Court to hear a range of charges against them, including manslaughter. As far as the former officers were concerned, not only was there no case to answer – and this, it was proposed, had been established in 1990 by the DPP and reiterated by Stuart-Smith – but, given all that had happened since the disaster, including the relatively recent screening of Jimmy McGovern's *Hillsborough*, there was no possibility of a fair trial. Their claim to have the prosecution discontinued on the grounds of 'abuse of process' centred on the proposition that it was a malicious prosecution long after the event, that media coverage had been massive and influential on potential witnesses and that it would be difficult (if not impossible) to find a jury whose members were oblivious to the criticisms and the controversy.

On 11 February 1999 the DPP refused the defendants' request to intervene in the case with the purpose of discontinuing the prosecution. A month later an application for a judicial review of the DPP's decision was dismissed. In July 1999 there followed a five-day hearing before a Leeds stipendiary magistrate who dismissed an application by Duckenfield and Murray to 'stay' (abort) the proceedings against them. Again, their submission was based on the claim that, given the intensity and extent of publicity surrounding the case, they could not receive a fair trial. Their submission was rejected and Duckenfield and Murray were finally committed for trial.

On 3 September 1999 Mr Justice Hooper conducted the Pleas and Directions Hearing at Leeds Crown Court. He ordered that an application on behalf of the defendants, once again to stay the proceedings, should be heard by him on 4 January 2000. The grounds for the submission were: that the prosecution constituted a breach of the defendants' rights to a fair trial under Article 6 (1) of the European Convention on Human Rights; that it was 'so oppressive' to the defendants and 'so unfair' and 'so wrong' it should be discontinued; that pre-trial publicity was such that a fair trial was not possible; and that the delay in bringing the prosecution made a fair trial impossible. Mr Justice Hooper received the submissions and on 16 February 2000 he issued his ruling.

Mr Justice Hooper's 38-page ruling opened with a brief account of the charges. Both defendants were charged with manslaughter and with misconduct in a public office. Duckenfield was also charged with misconduct 'arising from an admitted lie told by him at the time to the effect that the gates had been forced open by Liverpool fans'. A further charge against him of perverting the course of justice had been withdrawn following the Attorney-General's intervention.

The judge summarised the prosecution and defence cases as follows: 'It is the prosecution's case that the two defendants are guilty of manslaughter because they failed to prevent a crush in pens 3 and 4 of the West Terraces [Leppings Lane] by failing between 2.40 and 3.06 p.m. to procure the diversion of spectators entering the ground from the entrance to the pen [and] that police officers should have been stationed in front of the tunnel leading to the pen to prevent access. It appears, at this stage, to be the defence case that neither of the officers, in the situation in which they found themselves, thought about closing off the tunnel or foresaw the risk of serious injury in the pen if they did not do so. The prosecution submit that they ought to have done. This is likely to be the most important issue in the case. There may well be a further issue: if the risk had been foreseen, would it have been possible or practicable to have closed the tunnel?'

According to the judge, not only were the bereaved left with 'an enduring grief ', but they also retained 'a deep-seated and obviously genuine grievance that those thought responsible' had not been prosecuted or 'even disciplined'. In response to the defendants' submission for a stay of proceedings, he provided an initial chronology of events, from 15 April 1989 to the Pleas and Directions Hearing – over ten years later – which had given rise to the ruling. He quoted extensively from Lord Justice Taylor's report, particularly on the police operation, Duckenfield's 'misinformation', the 'blunder' on opening the gates, the summary of causes and the police case at the Inquiry. He also quoted extended extracts from the legal opinion provided by the two QCs to the DPP and summarised the inquest proceedings and verdict, together with the judicial review that followed.

Mr Justice Hooper also outlined the terms of reference of the Stuart-Smith scrutiny, briefly indicating its key findings. He quoted one paragraph: 'The causes of the disaster were many and complex. So far as [the defendants] were concerned, the prosecution would have to prove, to the high standard required for a criminal conviction, that the failure to give the order to close off the tunnel when gate C was opened amounted to a serious degree of recklessness necessary to constitute manslaughter.' Mr Justice Hooper noted that the Home Secretary had expressed concern that 'no individual has been personally held to account in a criminal court'. He then quoted Jack Straw: 'I share the anger that no one has suffered punishment or has been disciplined for what happened at Hillsborough.'

The judge focused on the media influences on the case – specifically Jimmy McGovern's drama-documentary, a song written and recorded by the Manic Street Preachers and the publication and a review of *Hillsborough: The Truth*. He dealt in detail with the previous applications by the defendants to stay proceedings. Finally, he presented preliminary observations and a ruling on the latest application. Having referred briefly to the legal test for manslaughter, he noted that the stipendiary magistrate had concluded that both Duckenfield and Murray had a case to answer and the DPP had decided not to intervene in the case.

He declined the defendants' submission that the delay had been such that no fair trial was possible primarily because there was substantial video evidence – 'an invaluable and objective account' – and because it was 'not a case where anyone involved that day, witness or defendant, is going to forget what happened'. On the issue of the 'massive amount of adverse publicity about the role of the police and senior police officers' he detailed previous cases. 'Ever mindful of the obligation to ensure a fair trial,' he said, 'I have reached the conclusion that the defendants have failed to prove on the balance of probabilities that the adverse publicity will prevent or impede a fair trial. I go further. I am quite satisfied they will have a fair trial.'

Mr Justice Hooper voiced 'some reservations about the manner in which the prosecution has been conducted'. He took into account submissions from the defendants that the prosecution was 'oppressive, unfair and wrong', commenting that both defendants 'must be suffering a considerable amount of strain'. Both had resigned from the police force and conviction would be of little financial consequence. Further, they were 'receiving the best possible legal representation thanks to the South Yorkshire Police'. The 'thought of being convicted for a serious offence must be a strain on anybody', but the 'greatest worry' was 'the thought of going to prison'. This had more significance for police officers. He concluded: 'These two defendants, if sentenced to prison for the manslaughter of, in effect, 96 people, would necessarily be at considerable risk of serious injury if not death at the hands of those who feel very strongly about Hillsborough.'

Set against this concern for the defendants, however, was the 'public interest'. Quoting from the 1999 Divisional Court ruling, he emphasised that 'one extremely important factor in favour of prosecution' was the 'very serious nature of the alleged offences, in particular, the alleged offences of manslaughter'. For Mr Justice Hooper, his task was 'to resolve the competing interests of the defendants and the public . . .' He ruled: 'I conclude that the oppression is not such as to prevent the trial from taking place, but that I should now reduce to a significant extent the anguish being suffered by these defendants. I do that by making it clear that the two defendants *will not immediately lose their liberty* if convicted. This is, I accept, a highly unusual course; but it is a highly unusual case.'

While for many of the families the imprisonment of Duckenfield and Murray was not the objective, Mr Justice Hooper's decision to guarantee that punishment would not include prison if convicted was extraordinary. It was a decision taken not to alleviate the strain of conviction, but because of the violence – assumed by the judge to be inevitable – they would endure at the hands of other prisoners through their status as police officers. Once again, it appeared that police officers were receiving special, if not favoured, treatment. Whatever the outcome of the trial, neither police officer would go to prison. Mr Justice Hooper's ruling could not be published or disclosed until the verdict had been delivered. Eventually the trial date was set for 6 June 2000 at Leeds Crown Court. It was expected to last eight weeks.

* * *

A sombre mood prevailed in Court 5 as the prosecution of David Duckenfield and Bernard Murray opened at Leeds Crown Court. In contrast to the winter hearings, it was a sunny June day. Most of the bereaved families travelled together by coach, leaving Liverpool just after 7 a.m. They arrived outside the modern court

314

buildings to a phalanx of media reporters and broadcasters. Already they had been informed of a hitch. The judge was hearing another case throughout the morning, so their case had been postponed to the afternoon. A feeling of anti-climax pervaded as the families – most of whom had been up since 5.30 a.m. if they had slept at all – waited patiently for the trial to begin.

Court 5 is large, accommodating well over 70 people. The press occupied the rear of the court, in three rows, overspilling to the right, alongside the seats reserved for the jury. The three barristers took up the centre of the court, junior counsel behind them and solicitors and support staff behind them. Duckenfield and Murray sat with their solicitors. A large area of seating was reserved for the Hillsborough Family Support Group to the left of the court and facing the judge. More seats were reserved for the public, the defendants' relatives and members of the Hillsborough Justice campaign. The first afternoon was taken up with discussion of the arrangements for the forthcoming weeks and argument about breaches of the judge's ban on any aspect of the trial being publicised. He emphasised that there should be no display of badges or banners, no public expression of opinion in the vicinity of the court and no publication of any aspect of the case other than the reporting of the evidence heard by the jury.

Mr Justice Hooper stated that any display of campaigning, written or verbal, would constitute intimidation and be considered contempt of court. Having called the police officer responsible for public order outside the court, he affirmed that any demonstration would jeopardise the trial. This also applied to material posted on websites and to media coverage. While he was keen to ensure there could be no grounds for appeal on the basis of intimidation, his direction was harsh given that no demonstration had occurred or was threatened. His instructions created the clear impression that some form of disruption was anticipated, again feeding the myth of bad behaviour and unruliness which had come to dominate the experiences of the bereaved since the disaster.

There followed legal submissions and argument concerning the charge of misconduct against Duckenfield based on the 'admitted lie', told to Graham Kelly and Glen Kirton of the Football Association, that Liverpool fans had broken down a gate and caused an inrush into the stadium. The dispute centred on whether he had been referring to gate C or a gate in the perimeter fence outside the ground; and whether, in the circumstances, it was a purposeful attempt to mislead in order to deflect blame. Further, it was proposed that Duckenfield's intention had been a considered decision to protect public order – more an error of judgement than a deliberate lie. The exchanges between Duckenfield's counsel, the families' counsel and the judge relied on Duckenfield's statement and his cross-examinations at the Taylor Inquiry and the Inquest. It boiled down to the definition of a 'lie' and eventually led to the withdrawal of the charge. The remainder of the first week was lost to legal submissions and the jury of eight men and four women was not empanelled until 13 June.

Potential jurors were asked whether they supported Liverpool or Nottingham Forest or had a friend or relative who had attended the fateful match; if any friend or family were serving officers within the South Yorkshire Police; whether they had any recollection of the Manic Street Preachers' album *This is my Truth, Tell me Yours* or had seen the drama-documentary *Hillsborough*; if they had been to Hillsborough stadium; whether they felt able to consider impartially the evidence to be heard in court; if they had heard, seen, or read anything which might influence them during the trial; and if they had any holidays booked or urgent medical appointments between then and August. Once selected, the jury was addressed by Mr Justice Hooper. He instructed the jurors as 'judges of fact from the evidence' who must 'judge fairly'. They were not to discuss the case with anyone and he advised them against reading media coverage of the trial.

Alun Jones, QC, the families' barrister and prosecuting counsel, rose to make his opening speech. The case for the prosecution, he stated, could be 'described simply'. People died in the crush because they could not breathe. This was the physical cause of death. The crush was due to overcrowding 'caused by the criminal negligence of the two defendants' who, between 2.40 p.m. and 3.06 p.m., 'having ordered the exit gates to be opened . . . failed to take the obvious step of blocking off the narrow tunnel' which fed the pens where the fans died. From the 96 who died, two 'representative victims' had been selected. John Anderson died in pen 4, James Aspinall in pen 3. David Duckenfield and Bernard Murray were charged with the unlawful killing of both victims by 'gross negligence'. Further, both officers 'wilfully neglected . . . to ensure the safety of supporters'.

Alun Jones outlined the key issues: the pens and fences; gate C; inadequate signposting; the tunnel; the crush barriers; the turnstiles; the police policy of fans 'finding their own level'; the build-up at the turnstiles and the 'obvious danger' outside the ground. He then dealt with the significance of Duckenfield's lie: 'whatever the exact words, Mr Duckenfield deceitfully and dishonestly concealed from those men [Graham Kelly, Glen Kirton and Assistant Chief Constable Jackson] that he himself ordered the exit gates to be opened because the crush at the turnstiles had become so severe; that he and Mr Murray, in a criminally negligent application of the 'let them find their own level' thinking, had failed to divert people away from the tunnel round the sides to the empty wing pens.' It was 'extraordinary' that Duckenfield claimed he had misled his senior officer and the others because 'he feared crowd disorder if he said he had given the order'. In fact this indicated that 'he himself was in no doubt what had caused the deaths: the entry of spectators in great numbers through gate C into the tunnel'. What he did was 'immediately to deflect the blame from himself and place it on the spectators'.

Alun Jones accepted that opening gate C was 'understandable as an urgent measure', but suggested that had the tunnel been closed, 'the tragedy would not have happened'. Such a decision was the responsibility of the senior officers who had taken, to quote Duckenfield, the 'drastic step to open the gates'. Both officers 'owed a duty of care to those in the pens, adults and children alike, and those entering the ground, to prevent them from being crushed'. Failure to take the 'simple and obvious step' to prevent access to the tunnel 'caused death, and amounts to manslaughter'. As the decision had been taken not to postpone the kick-off, it became 'more important to be conscious of the safety of spectators, given the tight timescale involved in getting people into the ground'.

The decision to open gate C without closing the tunnel lay, ultimately, with Duckenfield and Murray. There was no provision either in the police operational order or at the police briefings for opening exit gates. It was a decision 'wholly out of the ordinary – such an obvious crisis measure – that failures to act, when the exit gates were opened, to prevent a disaster, cannot be blamed on general police failings, previous commanders, the Chief Constable or the club'. The defendants took the decision 'as men "commanding" the game that day; they were of high "command" rank, and correspondingly high responsibility'. Using references to photographs and CCTV, Alun Jones provided a detailed account of the context surrounding the build-up at the turnstiles through to the game's abandonment at 3.06 p.m.

The prosecution, he stated, would call over 20 witnesses selected from thousands. They would provide 'live evidence' which 'supplements and fits in with the video evidence', making 'the events real again'. Witness evidence collectively would show: the build-up at the turnstiles was gradual; on opening gate C there was no surge of people; the tunnel was the only obvious route; numerous officers were in the concourse area and could have been detailed to divert people to the side pens; diversion was a practical possibility; those who had been to Hillsborough previously could not recall access or lay-out of the ground; overcrowding in the central pens was obvious at the time gate C was opened. On this latter point Duckenfield had previously stated that at the time he 'was looking intently at the terraces, but could see nothing untoward'.

In providing an overview of the substance of the defendants' previous interviews, statements and evidence, Alun Jones commented that the prosecution did not 'know of any pocket-book entry made shortly after the events'. Each defendant had indicated that they saw videos prior to 'giving evidence for the first time in late May 1989'. That evidence was to the Taylor Inquiry. Again, this raised the contentious issue of privileged access to recorded material afforded to senior police officers prior to the Inquiry and further investigations. Without contemporaneous notes it was impossible to test the veracity of the eventual testimony.

In concluding his opening address, Alun Jones stated that the prosecution 'does not say that these men's inertia, their abject failure to take action, was the only cause of this catastrophe'. The ground was 'old, shabby, badly arranged, with confusing and unhelpful signposting [and] there were not enough turnstiles'. There existed a 'police "culture" . . . . which influenced the way in which matches were policed'. Yet the 'primary and immediate cause of death' lay with the defendants' own failures. And the prosecution had to demonstrate that each defendant 'owed the deceased a duty of care', 'was negligent', 'his negligent actions or omissions were a substantial cause of death' and that the jury believed that 'his negligence was of such gravity as to amount to a crime'. Each of these issues was disputed, but together they constituted the test for finding Duckenfield or Murray guilty of manslaughter. Alun Jones told the jury that if they considered that the defendants owed the deceased a duty of care and had been negligent, but their negligence was not a substantial cause of death, then they should return a verdict of wilful neglect rather than manslaughter.

Addressing the issue of 'hindsight', Alun Jones proposed that 'every evaluation of things past is an exercise in hindsight . . . the courts are constantly dealing in hindsight . . . it is our stock-in-trade . . .' What had to be avoided was the 'unfair exercise of hindsight'. Reflecting on the events on the day, the actions and omissions of the defendants were 'not a mere error of judgement' derived in 'spur-of-the-moment' reactions. The 'critical omission' occurred 'over 20 minutes'. To answer the key questions concerning the packed pens, the failure to close the tunnel and the failure to divert fans, the prosecution did not have 'to prove exactly what was in the minds' of Duckenfield and Murray throughout the 20 minutes.

Were Duckenfield and Murray 'simply indifferent', failing 'to give any thought to an obvious risk'? Clearly, from their previous statements their mindset had been disorder, with Duckenfield presuming a pitch invasion as fans in pens 3 and 4 climbed on to the perimeter track fences. For Alun Jones, this represented a 'powerful indication' of their response: 'these defendants appear to have regarded the spectators not as a group of individual, vulnerable men, women and children, but simply as part of a threatening, impersonal and hostile mass'. Pouring scorn on the defendants' accounts, he argued that they gave 'no coherent explanation for their failure to act', raising 'more questions than they answer'. He invited 'the defence to take on the real issues in this tragic case and to rise to the challenge presented by our evidence . . . the simple logic of this case'.

As Alun Jones ended his opening speech there was quiet satisfaction among the many bereaved families who filled the court. For the first time the essence of the case had been articulated in full and in public, without interruption. This was the 'day in court' that so many had anticipated for so long. Duckenfield and

Murray sat a few seats apart, impassive throughout. 'Whatever happens now,' said a bereaved mother, 'I have the satisfaction of seeing those men brought to court and listening to Alun Jones because it has been decided that there is a case for them to answer.'

Between 14 and 20 June the prosecution called 24 witnesses including three of the bereaved who had attended the match. Graham Kelly, cross-examined mainly on the allocation of crowd safety responsibilities between the police and football clubs, and Glen Kirton gave evidence about their conversation with Duckenfield in the police control box. Roger Houldsworth – whose evidence had been presented as 'new' to the Stuart-Smith scrutiny, only to be rejected – was also called. He had been the CCTV technician in the club's control box and claimed it was clear from the CCTV monitors that the central pens were full prior to gate C being opened.

David Duckenfield did not give evidence, but considerable time was devoted to considering the contents of his evidence to the Taylor Inquiry. On Monday, 26 June Mr Justice Hooper announced that he would call Mr Mole, Duckenfield's predecessor as match commander and the author of the police operational order. This enabled cross-examination by the defence and prosecution barristers. Mole was presented as a 'national expert' on crowd safety. Much of his evidence, heard over three days, concentrated on the 'key issues' from the build-up at the turnstiles through to the monitoring of the pens. He referred to the tunnel as a 'natural regulator' of the crowd. Opening gate C had been 'a textbook way' of resolving the build-up at the turnstiles. Yet he expressed serious reservations about allowing a mass, unregulated entry of fans into the ground. It contradicted a major policing objective: that of searching individuals for weapons.

Referring to 'hooliganism' as the 'darker side of football', Mole remained adamant that the 'main contributory factor to the disaster was the presence of ticketless fans and the manner of their entry'. Alun Jones told him that he 'had decided on behalf of the South Yorkshire Police to play the hooliganism card', being no more than a 'yes man' for the force. In the absence of the jury, Mr Justice Hooper commented that he considered Mole to be a partial witness. Soon after Mole had completed his evidence, and following legal argument and deliberation with the jury out, the charge against the defendants of misconduct in a public office was dropped. All that remained against both was the charge of manslaughter.

As expected, the defence pursued the theme of hooliganism, using evidence from a few local residents to establish a picture of ticketless fans running to the ground, carrying four-packs of beer, urinating in gardens and creating mayhem. Under cross-examination 'cans' became 'one can' and 'all of the crowd' became 'some of the crowd'. Several turnstile operators and a retired police officer briefly gave evidence about the build-up at the turn-stiles and the alleged 'late arrival' by fans. To one defence witness the rush to the ground was 'as though a train had pulled in'. The image created, as at the Taylor Inquiry and the Inquest, was that of an out-of-control crowd hell-bent on getting to the match, drunk and rowdy.

On 10 July Bernard Murray gave evidence. What he had heard in court over the previous weeks he had not 'seen before . . . People pushing into gates, hundreds of ticketless fans . . . Whether it manifested itself inside [the ground] I don't know.' Concerning the disaster, he had 'been haunted by the memory' that he could have taken action to save lives. 'That is the way I have felt ever since. I feel a great deal of sympathy and sadness for the people I see here every day . . . I know how they must feel and I know a lot of them must blame me. I just hope that they can be a little understanding because it does affect me.' Closing off the tunnel was 'something that did not occur to me at the time and I only wish it had'.

Responding to video evidence of the fullness of the pens between 2.38 p.m. and 2.52 p.m., the point at which gate C was opened, Murray said he had not recognised how full the central pens were. In retrospect he thought the pens were full: 'I wouldn't have liked it . . . I wouldn't take my son there . . . I wouldn't take my son to a semi-final.' Shown the video recording of the crush in the pens after gate C had been opened, he denied being 'indifferent to the scenes'. He replied, 'I did not see anything occurring on the terrace which gave me any anxiety.' His thought processes and decision-making had been affected by the late arrivals after 2.50 p.m. outside the ground.

On 11 July, following further witnesses for the defence including character witnesses, the evidence was complete. Over a month after the start of the case, Mr Justice Hooper turned to the jury. He stated that there were four questions on which the case rested.

Firstly, 'Are you sure that, having regard to all the circumstances, it was foreseeable by a reasonable match commander that allowing a large number of spectators to enter the stadium through exit gate C without closing the tunnel would create an obvious and serious risk of death to the spectators in pens 3 and 4? *If the answer is "yes" then go to question 2. If not, your verdicts must be "not guilty".*'

Secondly, 'Are you sure that, having regard to all the circumstances, there were effective steps which could have been taken by a reasonable match commander to close off the tunnel and which could have prevented the deaths through crushing of spectators in pens 3 and 4? *If the answer is "yes", go to question 3. If not, your verdicts must be "not guilty".*'

Thirdly, 'Are you sure that the failure to take these steps was negligent? The failure would be negligent if a reasonable match commander would, in all the circumstances, have taken those steps. *If the answer is "yes", go to question 4. If not, then your verdicts must be "not guilty".*'

Finally, 'Are you sure that, having regard to the risk of death, the failure to take those steps was so bad in all the circumstances as to amount to a very serious criminal offence? *If the answer is "yes", your verdicts must be "guilty". If not, your verdicts must be "not guilty".'*

As the jury filed out, the implications of what the judge had said hit home to many of the families for the first time. The tests applied to securing a conviction for manslaughter, particularly in cases where there exists a range of intervening, mitigating and contributory factors, are necessarily complex and stringent. Each question had to be contextualised 'in all the circumstances' in which both defendants had acted. In other words, did the circumstances of chaos and confusion impede or mitigate their decisions? Was an obvious and serious risk of death in the central pens 'foreseeable' by a 'reasonable' match commander – not a match commander of exceptional experience and vision, but an 'ordinary' or 'average' match commander – on opening gate C? In itself the first question posed a difficult hurdle, combining 'circumstances' and 'foreseeability'.

Question 2 was not so complex, relating solely to the possibility of sealing off the tunnel. But, as question 3 posed, could the jury be *sure* that not taking such steps, given the *circumstances*, amounted to negligence? And establishing negligence, even *gross* negligence, was not sufficient to secure a conviction for manslaughter. What had to be concluded beyond doubt was that the failure, the negligence, was so bad that the jury were satisfied that in the *circumstances* a serious criminal offence had been committed. Put another way, gross negligence can cause death but it does not necessarily amount to a serious criminal act. It was now up to the prosecution and defence counsel, in their closing addresses, to persuade the jury of the strength of their cases.

* * *

Alun Jones began his closing speech to the jury with a couple of preliminary points. The first related to a previous discussion which centred on Mole's curious assessment that 5,000 people had entered through gate C. The lower estimate was 2,200 but, as Alun Jones pointed out, the higher figure led to 'even more horrifying conclusions' concerning the eventual compression in the central pens. The second point concerned the previous day's cross-examination of Murray by Alun Jones in which he suggested that the defendant did not care. The 'prosecution's case' was not that the defendants had witnessed suffering and turned away, but that they 'did not think'. The 'mindset' throughout was that of a 'security problem' rather than safety, 'best summed up in the word "neglect"'. It was 'not hatred . . . not wanting to punish people . . . not hoping they suffer' but it was 'a failure'.

The 'mindset' was 'hooliganism', continued Alun Jones, as if it bore no relation to safety. But 'public safety and public order are just other sides of the same coin'. Order was maintained on the terraces to guarantee the safety of spectators: 'if people are safe, you have order'. What the case revealed was 'a regard by the defendants for only one side of that coin: a failure to think, a failure to consider consequences over a period of 26 minutes'. From the 'major crisis at the turnstiles' at 2.30 p.m., the disaster began to emerge and consolidate. It was not a failure in the demanding circumstances of a 'split-second' decision but 'a case of slow motion negligence'. The prosecution maintained that Duckenfield and Murray had enough time to respond to the simple questions regarding the consequences of opening exit gates: where people would go, what would happen on the terrace and who would organise the crowd in such an unusual situation.

It was instructive from the evidence, noted Alun Jones, that while the crush was worsening at the turnstiles, the two senior officers in the police control box did not request the ground commander, Greenwood, to move from dealing with a minor problem at the other end of the ground. Further, from the perspective of the control box the crisis at the turnstiles was 'foreseeably emerging' for a full 15 minutes. The 'thinking time', the 'build-up' and the 'slow development of this crisis' were significant issues relating to the question of negligence.

Alun Jones then turned to the prosecution witnesses' evidence. The first two witnesses commented on their experiences of the tunnel. One stated that 'the actual steepness, the gradient . . . plus the sheer numbers . . . combined and carried [me] off my feet maybe 30 or 40 feet'. Had just one person told him 'not to go down the tunnel, I wouldn't have done so, one person'. The other witness described the experience in the tunnel as like 'being hit in the back by an express train'. Neither they, nor any of the witnesses who followed, experienced crowd disorder or misbehaviour. One, a judge, stated that at 2.30 p.m. outside the ground there was some 'moaning'. A few people had been drinking 'and were behaving in a mildly boisterous fashion'. The defence did not challenge his evidence.

Drawing on the evidence of other prosecution witnesses, Alun Jones demonstrated a 'clear, cogent, overwhelming and unchallenged picture from all four corners of the ground'. Each witness had identified the seriousness of the overcrowding early on and had commented on it to friends, expressing serious concern. An off-duty police officer at the other end of the stadium typified the collective opinion of the witnesses called: 'By 2.45 to 3 p.m., the crowd wasn't moving. No movement in the crowd. Usually there's a swaying motion backwards and forwards. There was none at all. These people were just absolutely jammed in . . . I knew I was looking at something that was extremely danger-ous.' This evidence was not cross- examined, nor was it challenged. Seemingly, it was accepted by the defence.

Once the system of monitoring entry and recording numbers through the turnstiles had been 'invalidated' by the opening of gate C, Roger Houldsworth in the club control room was aware of the danger. The tunnel drew the crowd 'like a magnet'. Despite having an 'incomparably worse' view than that from the police control box, he knew that those entering through gate C would head down the tunnel into the back of the already packed central pens. Thus, stated Alun Jones, the problem was clear to many in the ground – especially those familiar with its layout – so it should have been obvious to Duckenfield and Murray.

But Duckenfield in his statements was adamant that club stewards should have managed the crowd more effectively and directed the fans away from the tunnel. He had not attempted to inform the club's security officer directly and he had left the police response inside the ground to the officers on duty. Alun Jones portrayed Duckenfield's approach as leaving the crucial decision – to seal off the tunnel and redirect fans – to those officers on the concourse. While Duckenfield explained this as delegation, Alun Jones saw it as abrogation.

The prosecution's case, responding to the first of the judge's questions, was this: in the prevailing circumstances a reasonable match commander, being reasonably attentive, would foresee that if you allowed a gate to open and hundreds of people to enter in behind that pen leading to the tunnel without supervision, there would be an obvious and serious risk of death to spectators in pens 3 and 4.

Dealing with Graham Kelly's evidence, Alun Jones noted that five comments had been made to him by Duckenfield. 'He [Duckenfield] said the gate had been forced, there had been a forced entry. There had been an inrush. He showed me a television screen which he said depicted the gate which had been broken through. He said there had been fatalities. He said the game would have to be abandoned.' Duckenfield sought to deflect blame solely onto the fans. When Graham Kelly arrived in the control box, Duckenfield 'knew what he had done, he knew what the cause was and he played the Heysel Stadium card, the hooliganism card, a card which is likely to gain credence outside . . . The same card that has been played in the court disgracefully by Mr Mole . . .'

As for Mole's 'expert evidence', Alun Jones commented that the jury 'might have spotted not a single answer he gave which was not clearly telegraphed by the defence as the one they hoped he would give'. In response to a question concerning the crowd's possible reaction to the police preventing access to the tunnel, Mole had stated: 'I think in the circumstances outlined in the determined entry in that way, the number of officers we are talking about, unless it was a real arm-linked unit for public order matters, would have little or no effect'. Having previously accepted that sealing off the tunnel was a realistic option, he then 'backed away'. According to Alun Jones the jury might have been 'driven to conclude that Mr Mole . . . is not a "yes" man . . . he is a stooge.'

Given the time that Duckenfield and Murray had to consider the build-up and development of the crush at the turnstiles, the 'seriously and dangerously full pens' and the location of the unpoliced and unmanaged access to the tunnel, the obvious and serious risk of people being crushed to death was foreseeable. Effective steps – and this was conceded initially by Mole and also by Murray – could have been taken to seal off the tunnel before opening gate C. A 'reasonable match commander' would have acted accordingly and the failure to act amounted to negligence. The prosecution, stated Alun Jones, was 'not alleging the equivalent of careless driving'. There had been considerable 'thinking time', there were 'no competing considerations' and 'no dilemma'. Deciding not to postpone the kick-off 'intensified the responsibilities of those who had taken the decision to get it right'. The negligence amounted to a serious criminal offence because 'thousands of people' had been affected by the breach of trust in the senior officers whose negligence contributed significantly to the disaster.

* * *

William Clegg, David Duckenfield's counsel, opened his speech to the jury with the comment that his client 'never unlawfully killed those 96 victims that afternoon any more than anyone else in that control room did'. The events on the day were 'unprecedented, unforeseeable and unique'. How often 'must those touched by the tragedy have lain awake at night saying, "If only" ... "if only I realised something was wrong in those pens" ... "if only someone had told me it was overcrowded" ... "if only I'd not won promotion".' The trial was 'misconceived' with the prosecution 'thrashing around ten years later trying to pin the blame on one or two men'.

No 'reasonable match commander' could have 'foreseen an obvious and serious risk of death', that would mean being able to 'imagine the consequence'. He continued, 'It couldn't have been foreseen or it wouldn't have happened'. David Duckenfield was a person of sound character with a 'proud record' who 'protected people from danger all his professional life'. William Clegg argued that the tragedy was unforeseeable because the terraces 'were perceived to be inherently safe ... used for the best part of 100 years without mishap ... all approved by experts ... The police, the club, everyone believed it to be safe'. Fans 'finding their own level' was routine procedure at football grounds and Hillsborough had been chosen for the 1989 semi-final because of the previous year's success. It was, he stated, 'a physical phenomenon that no one could have predicted and, to this day, no one has been able to explain'.

He turned to the prosecution's first witness. Here, he stated, was a grown man of substantial build who, in the tunnel, had been lifted off his feet and projected for 30 or 40 feet on to the terraces. The sole reason that deaths occurred was 'that people left the tunnel with force ... with such speed and momentum ... that they carried grown men airborne and crushed people to death'. Duckenfield could not be guilty unless it was 'reasonable for him to foresee that people could exit the tunnel with that force'.

William Clegg asked what had created such a 'unique, unforeseeable, physical phenomenon' that had 'never been seen before'. Commenting that no relevant expert witnesses had been called by the prosecution, he stated that one theory was that the gradient in the tunnel had generated the force and momentum. It was implausible because the tunnel had been used for nearly a century. Another prosecution witness felt he had been hit by an 'express train'. How could the gradient alone have caused such a blow? Referring to Mole's 'expert' evidence, William Clegg noted his opinion that the tunnel should act as a crowd regulator, slowing access rather than accelerating it. Mole 'had never foreseen or encountered' such a force, otherwise he 'would have done something about it'.

Given that the gradient alone could not have caused such a powerful surge, William Clegg asked what had happened in the tunnel that created the force. The possibility was that a 'tiny proportion' of the crowd who had caused problems outside the ground 'behaved in the same manner in the tunnel'. If they had done, their actions could not have been foreseen. Quoting defence witnesses' evidence of mayhem at the turnstiles, he said, 'I am not suggesting that people were pushing in malice': there was no deliberate attempt to put people in danger or 'cause loss of life'. But there was a 'tiny minority of supporters, frustrated by the lack of turnstiles' who pushed. The situation was aggravated by late arrivals . . . it was a hot sunny day . . . more pleasant to have a pint outside a pub than to stand on a dry terrace.'

Warming to his central theme, William Clegg suggested that perhaps the 'tiny percentage outside included some without tickets, some who had been drinking, some of whom arrived late'. Here lay a possible explanation of what occurred in the tunnel. 'I am not saying that they were hooligans. I am not playing what Mr Jones calls the "Heysel card" or that anyone that day drove anyone to their death . . . It would never have crossed their minds. They just wanted to watch the match and didn't think . . . No deliberate attempt to cause danger or any risk to life . . . no malice, just irritation, urgency, a natural desire to watch the match and a failure to realise the consequences of what they did.'

Having dealt with the issue of foreseeability, William Clegg was clear that 'no one in their worst nightmares could have anticipated' the outcome. While the case against the defendants fell at the first question, he moved on to deal with the remaining questions. He stated that no one noticed that the pens were dangerously overcrowded until after 3 p.m. There had been nothing in the build-up to suggest 'anything untoward in the pens'. When realisation hit home, he argued, the time-span for reaction was minimal.

His client had not been negligent, because he 'had to make a decision in the agony of the moment', relying on 'the experience of his senior officers'. Perhaps the plan was deficient, or 'the police in general were negligent', but Duckenfield had inherited and accepted an operational order 'written by a man [Mole] with far more experience than he'. Further, 'a reasonable man like David Duckenfield isn't required to possess the accumulated knowledge and foresight of his junior officers'. He was entitled to delegate and to 'rely on the knowledge and foresight of others in that team'. The test for the jury, then, was to be sure that Duckenfield 'had sufficient personal knowledge to realise for himself the consequences of the fatal crush on the terraces'.

On the final question, William Clegg asked, 'Did David Duckenfield show such a disregard for the lives of the public that it is right to brand him a criminal, attaching to him criminal responsibility for the deaths of 96 people?' This would amount to 'turning an error of judgement, an honest mistake, into a crime with all that that entails'. Returning to the circumstances, William Clegg assessed the opening of gate C as a 'moment of crisis', a decision taken in 60 seconds and then only because lives were at risk: 'This is the agony of the moment, a unique situation.' It was a crisis compounded by problems at gate A. Further, the control box was not focused solely on the one area. There was a wider responsibility both inside and outside the ground. 'All that goes into the melting pot.'

William Clegg concluded: 'This case is a tragic combination of events that combined together to cause one of the worst disasters that anyone could imagine. Nothing can be done about the disaster now. You have to decide the fate of David Duckenfield. He's a good, honest man, has devoted his life to public service [and] any one of us would be pleased to have him as a friend and neighbour.'

Finally, on the issue of the 'lie' told to Graham Kelly, Duckenfield 'accepts that it is possible that Mr Kelly may have had the wrong impression . . . There are good, sound operational reasons why you would not want the public to know that the police had ordered the opening of the gates.'

* * *

'Hillsborough is everybody's nightmare . . . children not back on time, minibus late . . . All anxieties came true. Nothing I say is intended to diminish the recognition of that hurt. I have a task to invite you to conclude it is wrong, wrong, and wrong again to seek solace in the prosecution of the man I represent.' These were the words with which Michael Harrison opened his speech to the jury on behalf of Bernard Murray. His client had given evidence, provided statements and made 'a deeply sincere attempt to speak to the people who now bring charges against him and to tell them of his regret, his sorrow, his remorse'.

Despite Muray's 'sincerity' and 'decency', the prosecution had been 'tempted towards' making an allegation against him 'nothing short' of showing 'a callous indifference to the plight of people in the pens'. It was a proposition implied by Alun Jones, but one he 'never dared put into words'. It was both 'contemptuous' and 'outrageous'. Moving on, he asked the jury if they were clear in their minds exactly how 96 people could have lost their lives at Hillsborough. He rejected the prosecution's view as 'simplistic' and 'superficial'. It was a view derived in a 'tide of emotion springing from the genuine hurt' of those whose relatives had died but who could not explain why and how.

The evidence showed that the state of the pens prior to kick-off had been no different to the previous year. He rejected any suggestion that they were dangerously full. Adopting William Clegg's argument, he stated, 'Nobody knows for certain how many people got on to those terraces . . . how many went through the tunnel.' But it was not a '26-minute case' amounting to 'slow-motion negligence'. The lack of concern that anything untoward was happening was universal; it 'was a disaster that struck out of the blue'. It was both superficial and wrong to assume that because 'a lot of people got on to the terrace . . . those who didn't stop it must have been negligent and, therefore, must be marked as criminals'.

Warning the jury not to reject Mole's evidence on the prosecution's proposition that he was merely a 'yes man', Michael Harrison insisted that he had been right to raise the issue of hooliganism. It had been hooligans who had 'created a situation in which administrators and politicians created pens . . . these death traps' and it was they who 'should have these 96 deaths on their conscience'. Those who had tried to gain entry on the day were not necessarily 'the sort of hooligans in the same class as real hooligans'. They 'probably thought it a bit of a scam'.

Again adopting William Clegg's argument, Michael Harrison agreed that the prosecution fell at the first hurdle. An obvious and foreseeable risk was not created by opening gate C. Further, it did not constitute negligence 'to make an error of judgement, to make a mistake'. Negligence had to relate to the duty a person has responsibility to perform, an error that 'no person reasonably could have made'. It related to the 'exercise of the ordinary skill of an ordinary competent person'. He continued, saying that a 'police superintendent should not be a prophet or a mastermind . . . The law does not require unattainable standards'. Furthermore, 'errors of judgement in an emergency where circumstances are stressful do not amount to negligence,' as they are not what the law is looking for: 'They have to fall below ordinary, reasonable competence.'

He asked, 'Was death obviously and seriously on the cards here?' Nobody in the ground 'foresaw those deaths as a consequence of relieving the pressure at the turnstiles . . . You can only pin it on somebody if you use hindsight . . . It was not foreseeable on the day.' If the build-up and potential outcome had been so obvious, why had the club control room, the club's head of security, not noticed and intervened? What really happened, he proposed, was that senior officers were caught up in 'doing their level best . . . to restore and maintain control over entry to the ground . . . It was one crisis on top of another'. Because Murray had been preoccupied with responding to an emergency, deploying officers to gate A, it 'doesn't mean that he didn't care what was happening on the terraces'.

Taking the issue of personal responsibility further, he said to the jury: 'You might say that the police operation in general had so many deficiencies [and] as a whole was defective, but you can't single out Mr Murray, and of course Mr Duckenfield, to carry the can. It seems so unfair.' Michael Harrison stated that Murray was not a steward, his duty for safety was maintaining order and he had wide-ranging and diverse tasks to perform both inside and outside the ground. Historically the terraces were not seen as 'carrying any inherent dangers' and 'all authorities thought they were safe'. On the terraces the policy and practice of 'find your own level' was generally accepted, taken for granted: 'Mole's policy, Mole's custom and practice'.

On the day, the build-up in the pens had been anticipated and at 2.50 p.m. it was normal. The police worked as a team and Murray relied on officers on the ground to feed back any problems. At 2.52 p.m. the focus in the control room was the crisis at the turnstiles, a blockage that itself had been unforeseen. The club had 'no contingency plan to cope with the build-up at the turnstiles' and this was a clear deficiency. Because opening exit gates to allow entry ran contrary to policing policy and planning, the decision 'created pressure in the minds of those taking the decision' – particularly as the numbers that would gain entry could not be monitored. But the senior officers outside had their responsibilities and made decisions themselves; this was not Murray's job.

The 'initial entry into the ground was orderly and gave no cause for concern'. Not all entering through gate C would go down the tunnel, which would act as a regulator. Thus the disaster could not be foreseen. Events 'of the magnitude of Hillsborough do not usually happen for one single reason', but it is 'natural to pin the blame on one single scapegoat'. Quoting the Archbishop of York's memorial address soon after the disaster, that 'mistakes, misjudgements and missed chances come together', Michael Harrison considered the cleric to have been 'absolutely right and the evidence proves it'. To convict Bernard Murray, he concluded, 'would be making him a scapegoat'.

* * *

The jury lies at the heart of the criminal justice process. In serious criminal cases, and occasionally less serious prosecutions, defendants retain the right to be judged by their peers. It is, for lay people called to jury service, an onerous and demanding task. One minute, people are going about their day-to-day business, their work and leisure routines, responding to the demands of family, friends and community. The next minute, they are plucked from their homes and workplaces and deposited in a court alongside people they have never met before to listen attentively to, deliberate on and conclude a complex adversarial case – in which fact is mixed with fiction and evidence is measured against a background of previous cases. Throughout, they are not allowed to talk about the very issues that consume their lives. Finally, following tense, formal debate, they decide on the factual evidence that beyond reasonable doubt a person is guilty as charged. Given the slightest hint of doubt, a verdict of not guilty must be returned.

The prosecution and defence counsel had had their say. Now,

on 17 July, after weeks of evidence and legal submissions, it was left to Mr Justice Hooper to summarise the evidence, consider the interpretations by counsel and direct the jury on points of law. There is no question that the judge, particularly in prosecutions where the law is complicated, ambiguous or even contradictory, plays a vital role in guiding the jury. It is a necessary role, yet it remains a fine line separating opinion from fact. Inevitably it is an interpretative role.

Mr Justice Hooper began by instructing the jury that they could not decide the case on sympathy, but 'on the evidence and only the evidence'. He presented them with both interpretations of Duckenfield's response to Graham Kelly and Glen Kirton, warning that they should take great care with the evidence. 'Expert' opinions had come from Mole and Kelly as 'part of the evidence', but it was of limited importance and the jury did not 'have to act on it'. He reminded them that Alun Jones had referred to Mole as a 'yes man' and a 'stooge'.

The defendants had to be judged 'by the standards of 1989'. At that time caged pens were accepted', having the 'full approval of all the authorities as a response to hooliganism'. The jury should 'adopt the pre-Hillsborough mindset'. Further, the delay in bringing the case created the possibility of real prejudice against the defendants: 'People's recollections change over the years . . . It is a risk.' The jury must not hold Murray's inabilities to remember conversations at the time against him. And nor should Duckenfield's failure to give evidence be held against him.

In terms of the first key question put to the jury, Mr Justice Hooper asked what the law defined a 'reasonable professional' to mean. He defined it as 'an ordinary competent person exercising that particular role'. Mole, it might be concluded, 'was a highly qualified match commander', but Duckenfield should not be judged by those standards. 'The law', he continued, 'doesn't require a person to be a paragon or a prophet' but 'ordinarily competent'. So, what skills should have been expected of the defendants, and what significance did delegation play? Duckenfield was a new appointment, his skills limited by inexperience, but he had experienced junior officers and a 'tried-and-tested' operational order. It was not appropriate to judge him 'simply because of lesser experience'.

The standard applied had to be reasonable competence 'at the relevant time' and 'not with the wisdom of hindsight'. He reminded the jury that the 'Hillsborough disaster has had a profound educational effect on all of us and has led to significant changes'. Regarding the circumstances, he noted that the defence proposed that, ordinarily, crowd management was the responsibility of the club rather than the police. While the police role was primarily to retain order, it did not mean 'that if they order the opening of the gates they should ignore the consequences'. The division of responsibility between the club and the police was an important and relevant circumstance for the jury to consider.

The ground itself was thought to be safe by all appropriate authorities, although, in contrast to Lord Justice Taylor, Mr Justice Hooper failed to recognise that the safety certificate was well out of date. According to Graham Kelly, Hillsborough was 'one of the best-appointed grounds in the country'. Concerning the policy of 'find your own level' adopted by the police and club stewards in filling the terraces, it was now known to be 'fatally flawed'. But it was 'not known then'. It was 'part of the atmosphere of the game'.

The operational order prepared by Mole and adopted without change by Duckenfield did not consider the possibility of opening exit gates for entry; 'in fact, it went against the conditions of entry'. Opening exit gates was not part of the plan but 'death was not in the reckoning of those officers'. It was a decision which responded to a 'life-and-death situation' outside the ground. The jury had to 'take into account that this was a crisis' and he instructed them to 'be slow to find fault with those who act in an emergency'. Both the 'extent of the crisis' and the 'thinking time' available to Duckenfield and Murray were 'hotly contested issues'. Put simply, 'what reaction should properly be expected by a reasonable person in a crisis?' This constituted 'a very important circumstance' because it was 'a severe crisis and decisions had to be made quickly'. Both defendants' counsel had proposed 'that if you concentrate on the decision it is more difficult to think about the circumstances'.

The build-up at the turnstiles and the filling of the pens were, according to the defence, the responsibility of the commander outside the ground and police spotters inside. Nothing was transmitted to the control box concerning the respective dangers until Marshall requested the opening of the gates. Inside, the spotters had not recognised overcrowding or discomfort. A further indication of the 'failure to recognise what was happening' was that the universal response to the fans climbing on the perimeter track fences was the police misjudgement that a pitch invasion was about to happen. Was it necessary for the jury 'to resolve whether [the pens were] full or grossly overfull? What matters is whether it was full and the consequences that flowed from that.'

In the control box no one 'foresaw the dangers to spectators in pens 3 and 4 . . . foresaw injury and certainly not death'. This also applied to the club officials, including Houldsworth. Mr Justice Hooper then summarised the defence and prosecution positions concerning the tunnel and the force generated within, propelling still more people into the central pens. On the one hand there was no expert evidence on the issues concerning the tunnel, on the other there was no 'direct evidence' supporting the defence theory that 'those who were pushing outside . . . got into the tunnel and started pushing'. The judge asked the jury to stand back from 'the precise mechanics of the disaster' and consider simply the issues of the full pen and the opened gate.

Could effective steps have been taken to close the tunnel? Here the dispute had centred on the capability of officers on the concourse to prevent access and redirect all who entered through gate

C. This was doubted by the defence but the prosecution was clear that it could have, and should have, happened prior to the opening of gate C. Moving on, the judge echoed defence counsel in instructing the jury of the 'huge difference between an error of judgement and negligence . . . Many errors of judgement we make in our lives are not negligent.' He continued, 'The mere fact that there has been a disaster does not make these two defendants negligent.' The jury should not be concerned whether the South Yorkshire Police had been negligent, but should concentrate on the acts or omissions of Duckenfield and/or Murray.

Establishing negligence, however, would 'not finish your deliberations'. Consideration had to be given to whether such negligence, if found, constituted a serious criminal act: 'We do not punish negligence normally. To turn it into a serious criminal offence you would have to take the steps "that it was so bad" as to warrant a conviction for manslaughter.' Yet again the judge reinforced the point that the 'defendants were in a crisis situation'. A guilty verdict would mean that negligence had been established and was 'so bad to amount to a very serious criminal offence in a crisis situation'.

It was not a case in which people had considered a risk and decided to run it regardless of the consequences. It was 'about not thinking of the consequences of a decision taken in an emergency'. Mr Justice Hooper then asked the jury if a criminal conviction would 'send out the wrong message' to those who have to react to an emergency and take decisions: 'Would it be right to punish someone for taking a decision and not considering the consequences in a crisis situation?' Clearly these were questions of policy rather than evidence. Effectively, he invited the jury to consider the consequences of a criminal conviction, not for the case, not for the defendants, not for the bereaved – but for people coming afterwards whose decisions and actions could not be anticipated. It seemed an extraordinary comment to make, and was seen by the families to defy the jury to return guilty verdicts.

He reminded the jury that 'the fact that 96 people died does not mean that a criminal offence has been committed by these officers'.

Mr Justice Hooper spent the afternoon of 17 July and part of the following morning taking the jury through the evidence of each witness, reminding them of the key points raised. At 10.55 a.m. he directed the jury to reach a unanimous verdict. They were, he stated, under no time constraints. That afternoon, people rushed back to the court believing a verdict had been reached. The jury, however, had sent out a note that a technical breakdown had prevented the viewing of a video. At 3.15 p.m. the following day the jury sent a further note asking for clarification between negligence and a criminal offence as it related to question 4. Mr Justice Hooper instructed the jury that a failure to act had to be 'so bad' that it amounted to a very serious criminal offence. It also had to take account of all the circumstances which he had already outlined at length.

Repeating his previous instruction, he stated that a person might consider the consequences of an act but decide to take a risk: 'If one takes the risk and causes death then one has no difficulty in concluding that it is a very serious and criminal offence.' For example, a driver choosing to consume excess alcohol would know the risk and if he caused death there would be 'no difficulty concluding this a very serious and criminal offence'. But this was 'not the case; the defendants [Duckenfield and Murray] did not think of the consequences'.

Mr Justice Hooper emphasised that the crucial decision to open gate C had been taken in a crisis. Had it not been opened, severe injury or death would have occurred at the turnstiles. 'How much of a crisis' and 'how long they had to consider the consequences is up to you'. He reminded the jury that the prosecution's case was that the defendants' actions and inactions amounted to 'slow-motion negligence', while the defence had argued that the real time period was significantly shorter and under the circumstances of much else happening.

Mr Justice Hooper yet again instructed the jury to reflect on the 'message' a guilty verdict would send out. 'You are entitled to ask whether it would send out the wrong message for those who have to act in an emergency . . . dealing with incidents like this all the time . . . in crisis situations. That is, to avoid death and injury to others. To label it so bad is a matter for you, it is your decision, but you must be sure. The mere fact that 96 people died does not in itself mean it is a very serious criminal offence.'

Finally, he expressed concerns regarding Duckenfield. Given that the jury had reached question 4, it appeared that they had not accepted William Clegg's argument as to what constituted a 'reasonable match commander'. The judge instructed that this was a matter, at this stage, on which the jury should focus – particularly regarding Duckenfield's competence and inexperience. It was important to accept that the role of match commander went with the posting to Hammerton Road. Duckenfield had been appointed just two to three weeks before the semi-final and this was the decision of the South Yorkshire Chief Constable, who would have been aware of the implications. These were matters that the jury was 'entitled to take into account'.

The judge's portrayal of the deaths of 96 men, women and children as a '*mere*' fact was crass and insensitive. It was a fact, certainly, but not one to be diminished. Further, to emphasise to the jury that a guilty verdict based on the evidence before the court could be influenced and mitigated by its implications for others acting in good faith, seemed to breach the spirit of establishing guilt on the basis of fact. It suggested that guilt could be cancelled on the potential of its consequences. Finally, the judge's parting comments on Duckenfield certainly directed the jury to reconsider question 1 if – and the judge had no way of knowing – they had already agreed that Duckenfield had been negligent.

At 3 p.m. on 20 July, after 16 hours' deliberation, the jury was told that a majority decision would be accepted. At 2.15 p.m. the following day, after 21 hours and 26 minutes deliberation, the jury returned a verdict of not guilty on Bernard Murray. An hour later the judge asked if there was a 'realistic possibility' of returning a verdict, on which ten jurors were agreed, on Duckenfield. The foreman stated that with a 'little more time' there might be a majority verdict. On Monday, 24 July at 11.55 a.m. the jury, still unable to reach a verdict, was discharged. A blanket ban was imposed on reporting, 'to ensure that at all times Mr Duckenfield has a fair trial'. The judge retired to contemplate the implications of the hung jury.

On Wednesday, 26 July Alun Jones, on behalf of the bereaved families, applied for a retrial of David Duckenfield to be conducted by a different judge. He expressed concern that Mr Justice Hooper's direction on gross negligence with regard to manslaughter had been wrong. This centred specifically on the distinction between 'foresight' and 'not thinking'. He was highly critical of the judge's repeated comments on the implications of a guilty verdict for future actions of emergency workers. This was, he argued, a public matter and as such had no direct bearing on the case. Mr Justice Hooper asked Alun Jones if he was alleging 'bias' against him. Alun Jones replied that it was neither an attack nor an allegation of bias, but the judge's directions to the jury had been 'wrong and this matter should be dealt with by another judge'. Mr Justice Hooper refused the application for retrial, delaying giving his reasons for two days.

On Friday, 28 July the judge returned to explain why he had decided to stay the charges of manslaughter against Duckenfield. He stated that the history of the case included a public inquiry at which Duckenfield gave evidence, a police inquiry after which the DPP decided not to prosecute, a coroner's inquest and the publication of a CD including a track labelling Duckenfield a mass murderer. The seven-week trial of the former police officer and his deputy had been 'very public' and the defendants had 'faced the public humiliation that accompanied it'. Forcing David

Duckenfield 'to undergo another trial would constitute clear oppression'. He concluded, 'I have an overriding duty to ensure a fair trial for the defendant. That, I am firmly convinced, is no longer possible.'

The Assistant Chief Constable of South Yorkshire, Ian Daines, expressed hope that the judge's decision would help people 'move on'. He said, 'Blame has been attributed and some of it, quite rightly, at the feet of South Yorkshire Police and various organisations. Nothing more can be gained by continuing to think that anything more can be learned about the disaster. It happened in public and has been scrutinised in public.' This was a sentiment universally rejected by the bereaved families. Daines's claim to a full public scrutiny of the disaster, particularly the immediate aftermath and the review and alteration of police statements, was both dismissive and flawed. If anything, the private prosecution, concentrating on events between 2.30 p.m. and 3.06 p.m., had been even more limited in focus than the inquests. A bereaved father summed up the feelings of the families: 'I never expected we would get a conviction, especially after I heard the judge's direction. But people on that jury held out. The case went all the way but we will never know the full extent of what went on afterwards.'

In completing his comments Mr Justice Hooper paid tribute to the bereaved families: 'Notwithstanding that much of the evidence was inevitably very emotional, their behaviour was impeccable. I would like to thank them very much for that. It made my task and, much more importantly, the task of the jury an easier task to perform, albeit that the questions facing the jury were very difficult.'

It was a sentiment clearly not shared by the police. As the families left Leeds Crown Court for the last time their external composure hid inner turmoil. Their pain and deep sorrow had been expressed in private; their support for each other was clear in public. Mothers and fathers, brothers and sisters, sons and daughters, and other relatives and friends had borne the daily vigil at the court with fortitude. They shared a decade's struggle for justice which had been institutionally denied.

Outside the court there awaited a reception from a West Yorkshire Police video-surveillance team which filmed their dignified, calm yet unbowed departure. The police explained: 'We had some officers there as evidence-gathering because we had some intelligence about some threat to Mr Duckenfield and a potential threat for some disorder.' How ironic, given the judge's comments on the 'impeccable' conduct of the families throughout. To the families it was yet another slur on their reputation and that of their loved ones. 'We felt like criminals' was the common response.

* * *

When Mr Justice Hooper instructed the jury to judge the defendants against the 'standards' which applied at the time of the Hillsborough disaster, he reminded them of the 'profound educational effect' of the tragedy. As he listed the custom and practice which governed the management and regulation of football crowds in 1989, it was as if, to quote one of the defence counsel, Hillsborough had happened 'out of the blue'. But the problems were clearly evident: failure to filter the crowd's approach to the stadium; a well-established and threatening bottleneck outside; entry for half the capacity crowd via a known bottleneck; aged and malfunctioning turnstiles; woefully inadequate directions inside; tunnel access to the central pens in breach of the Green Guide; pens no more than cages; lack of efficient and effective monitoring and management of crowd distribution between the pens; and a clearly reckless shared 'policy' of fans 'finding their own level'.

That these deficiencies were not covered by the police operational order inherited by Duckenfield and Murray from Mole, the 'national expert' on crowd management, was taken to mean that they were not perceived as deficiencies at the time – the logic being that if they could be established as dangerous deficiencies only in hindsight, literally because 96 people died, they could not be judged so at the time. Thus they could not be foreseen. Yet, as Chapter 1 demonstrates, the 1946 Burnden Park disaster and the Moelwyn Hughes report that followed set a clear safety agenda for all sports grounds where large crowds could be anticipated. It was a safety agenda at first eroded and then neglected as the 'mindset' of crowd control institutionally replaced the good intentions of crowd safety. Judged against the Moelwyn Hughes recommendations, the custom and practice at Hillsborough and most other premier sports venues constituted an unacceptable risk. The policing and stewarding practices operated in the context of unacceptable risk, inheriting and reinforcing the mindset of control. Inherent and obvious dangers became masked by regulatory objectives and arrogant complacency.

None of these issues, either individually or in sum, invalidated the private prosecutions of Duckenfield and Murray. Both were senior officers whose shared role, regardless of knowledge and experience, included the maintenance of order and safety through effective crowd management outside and inside the ground. Whatever the responsibilities of the club, its officials and its stewards, part of the police function was to manage the crowd inside the ground. The police were also responsible for their actions, particularly any deviation from the procedures laid down in the operational order. While defence counsel attacked the prosecution as 'simplistic' and 'superficial' in its reasoning, Alun Jones emphasised that the case was simple and uncomplicated. To agree to and order the opening of gate C and other exit gates, for whatever reason, given adequate thinking time for considering the consequences, without sealing off the tunnel, put those in already full pens at risk of serious injury and death.

That this decision was taken outside the procedures of the operational order and in a crisis meant, according to the prosecution, that even more care should have been taken not to shift the life-threatening crush of the bottleneck outside to the tunnel and the terraces inside. Of course, the range of contributory factors has to be identified and accepted if the complexity and context of the disaster is to be understood. But that range of factors did not mitigate or remove the professional responsibilities of senior officers for their decisions and actions. The private prosecution of Duckenfield and Murray was not about attributing *all* blame and *all* responsibility to two men. It was about establishing culpability for their part in the disaster.

It was instructive that in presenting their cases, both defence counsel raised hooliganism as an issue, but in muted and more subtle tones than at previous public hearings. At the Taylor Inquiry hooliganism was presented by those representing all police interests, individual and corporate, as the single cause of the disaster. When Taylor discounted it, the then Chief Constable, Peter Wright, warned that irrefutable evidence would be produced at the inquests to show the full extent and overwhelming impact of crowd disorder, drunkenness and violence. And that is what happened, with survivors who gave evidence suffering a torrid time under cross-examination by police counsel. But this was played down by the defence counsel in the Duckenfield–Murray trial. What a decade earlier was portrayed as the most violent and uncontrollable crowd in football history became reconstructed as late arrivals who had stopped for a pint on a hot spring day. They arrived alongside a few ticketless fans and were understandably frustrated by the delay at the inefficient turnstiles. It was selfishness, frustration and eagerness to watch the match which caused them to push and shove – not malice, not 'real' hooliganism. And, perhaps, argued the defence, it was this same group, having entered through gate C, who released their full physical force in the tunnel – thus causing a grown man to be lifted and carried 30 to 40 feet. Maybe, speculated William Clegg, they were the 'express train' and the 96 who died were its victims.

Apart from a 'softly, softly' approach to the hooliganism issue, the defence case rested on an invisible, unprecedented and, therefore, unforeseeable physical force generated in the tunnel. The defendants could not be held responsible for the institutional deficiencies and neither could they be held responsible for the 'unknown' dynamics within the tunnel. Against this highly dubious line of argument, the prosecution made the relatively straightforward point that Duckenfield and Murray together had the opportunity (in time) and the capacity (in police availability) to secure the tunnel and redirect the fans to the side pens. This was the least that could be expected of a competent senior officer, given the circumstances of allowing uncontrolled access to the stadium. Their failure amounted to gross negligence so bad, given the visible state of the central pens, that it constituted a serious criminal act.

Mr Justice Hooper's direction reviewed the evidence and revisited the debates over circumstances, hindsight, foreseeability, negligence, obvious and serious risk, and what constituted a serious criminal act. While questions remain over his interpretation of the appropriate legal tests, it was his comments to the jury – about how manslaughter convictions would impact on the future actions and responses of emergency services' professionals – that caused the most surprise and concern. While not necessarily signifying 'bias', it was undoubtedly a direction, repeated when the jury returned for clarification of the relationship between negligence and serious criminal act, which conflated and confused a policy matter with legal direction. Alongside this were his comments to the jury which reminded them of the difficult 'circumstances' in which Duckenfield and Murray were operating, suggesting that he was leaning towards not guilty verdicts.

Yet it was the judge's casual remark to the jury, that the 'mere fact' that 96 people had died did not necessarily suggest that a serious criminal act had occurred, which caused the most offence and deepest hurt to the families. Immediately afterwards, families gathered in the carpeted area outside Court 5. They held each other, some sobbing uncontrollably while others were physically sick in the toilets. A bereaved mother, in tears of anger and of sorrow, spoke for all: 'How could anyone who has listened to the evidence in front of us all, knowing what we're going through, call it a *mere* fact? I felt he [her son] had died again.'

The private prosecution of David Duckenfield and Bernard Murray by the bereaved families was possibly the most significant in recent times. For many outside the case it was seen as wrong to prosecute two senior police officers so long after the event. Yet, given the circumstances of the longer-term aftermath, the state's rejection of prosecution and the failure to disclose most of the evidence, the families had little choice. It remains highly instructive that at the conclusion of both the inquest and the private prosecution the juries requested further clarification of negligence. Such a verdict is not available at an inquest, but negligence troubled the jury. It also appears to have been the focus of the trial jury's mammoth deliberations as they struggled to establish its relationship to 'serious criminal act'. The fact that there was a case to answer and, in the end, the jury was deadlocked over Duckenfield's culpability, demonstrated that the families' pursuit of limited justice was not misconceived.

* * *

Yet there was a broader case to answer. On 16 April 1989, within 24 hours of the Hillsborough disaster, Margaret Thatcher flew by helicopter to Sheffield. Her Home Secretary, Douglas Hurd, recalls a briefing by a 'pale and inarticulate' South Yorkshire Chief Constable, Peter Wright. It was at this time that the Prime Minister's Press Secretary, Sir Bernard Ingham, formed the impression (from which he never wavered) that a 'tanked-up mob' of Liverpool fans had caused the deaths and injuries.

Visiting the hospitals, according to Hurd, Thatcher was 'shaken, but remorseless in her compassion'. She approached the bed of a dying boy whose family was in 'great anxiety'. She 'went straight up . . . took control of the situation, talked to them in a way I wouldn't have dreamt of. But she was right. They will remember that all their lives; not just a bossy Margaret Thatcher coming in and making a nuisance'.

However sincere her compassion on the day, throughout the previous decade the policies of successive Thatcher administrations, driven by moral righteousness and rigid dogma, had contributed to the Hillsborough deaths. An unswerving commitment to the principles of free-market economy actively promoted a market-place unrestricted by the state and its institutions. The economy seemed to boom. With instant returns on investment, risk-takers quickly becoming profit-makers. 'Deregulation' became the watchword in a 'popular capitalism' where ordinary people could live the illusion of 'share-holding' in former state-run industries. In the 1980s Britain became a chancer's paradise.

But taking so-called financial risks, in a market let loose from its usual restraints, meant an increase in physical risk. Cross-channel ferries, frantically cutting turnaround times to meet the demands of profitability in a market with a finite number of customers, put to sea with their bow doors open. Overcrowded commuter trains sped along under-maintained tracks, attempting to meet impossible schedules. Pleasureboats on the Thames vied for water with unsafe industrial vessels. Years of rubbish gathered beneath stands in football grounds, and escalators on the London Underground, just waiting for ignition. Each day on most building sites, in most factories and on all forms of transport, carrying people or freight, deregulation increased danger.

With inspectorates seriously under-staffed and poorly resourced, the task of regulating industry became impossible. As people lost their lives in disasters, tragedies and industrial accidents the response from the inspectors was 'give us the funding, we'll do the job'. It never happened. Football, like so many other forms of entertainment, was a case in point. Breaches of the Green Guide were commonplace.

Hillsborough, supposedly a top venue, typified the problem: an out-of-date safety certificate, unsafe terracing with dangerous access and limited escape, antiquated turnstiles, the Leppings Lane bottleneck and minimal medical cover. Yet the Football Association, football's governing body, hired the stadium for prestigious semi-finals. The local authority, whose responsibility it was to issue the ground's safety certificate, seemed unconcerned that it was a decade out of date. And the club appeared complacent that its stadium, in part, was poorly maintained.

As Taylor stated in his final report, football suffered from a deep-rooted structural and organisational malaise. Loyal fans paid their money to risk injury, even death. They had no voice, no constituency and little support in high places. The Football Supporters' Association, founded after Heysel and still in its infancy at the time of Hillsborough, was alone in opposing club directors more concerned with corporate hospitality than with providing basic facilities for paying customers.

Another priority in the Thatcher project was 'law and order'. To the Prime Minister, and some of her senior colleagues, 'football hooligans' were part of the 'enemy within'. The Conservatives' attack on 'youth lawlessness' made football an even bigger target for heavy, uncompromising policing. It remains a dreadful irony that in relentlessly pursuing policies of crowd control – supposedly geared to eliminating violent disorder – the Government, the police and the clubs created the very conditions which, in part, killed people.

The obsession with policing by force and coercion, treating fans not as citizens but as an 'enemy', consumed vast resources and finance. Of course some fans, a small minority, would be violent and aggressive. Of course some fans, a small minority, would be drunk and abusive. Policing by containment, from corralling to penning, not only 'upped the stakes', it fatally neglected fundamental safety provisions while promoting a high-profile control agenda. Not only were lessons not learned, they were recklessly ignored. Unqualified attention was devoted to controlling and containing. So it was at Hillsborough, where the Operational Order was committed to regulation and enforcement rather than safety and management: the police as a *force* rather than a *service*.

The Hillsborough disaster was as inevitable as it was shocking. The appalling terror of the pens which left 96 dead, hundreds injured and thousands traumatised could, and should, have been anticipated and avoided. Without doubt, the full responsibility for the disaster lay with those organisations which owned, ran, maintained, hired and managed the stadium. Each had a primary role in ensuring a safe venue. Put simply, both legally and morally, they owed a duty of care to the fans.

* * *

'But perhaps the greatest tribute to those who tragically lost their lives, and the firmest indication that the deaths were not in vain, lies in the transformation of football stadia.' This comment, made in March 1998 by Ian Daines, Assistant Chief Constable of the South Yorkshire Police, graphically and tellingly reveals an unwitting, crass insensitivity towards the suffering of the bereaved. His naïvety defies credibility. Premier League football clubs, the beneficiaries of massive cash injections by Rupert Murdoch's media empire, built all-seater stadia on the back of Taylor's recommendations and made unprecedented returns on their investments. And this is supposed to be *the* greatest tribute to the Hillsborough dead.

There is not the slightest acknowledgement that it took a disaster, with men, women and children being killed, to shake the reckless complacency that had infected football, its ownership, its organisation and its policing. There is no appreciation that, while the bereaved and survivors of Hillsborough would want to prevent a repeat of the tragedy, the 'transformation of football stadia' is not their highest priority. In May 1997, when tens of thousands of Liverpool supporters, joined by a much wider national constituency, demanded 'Justice for the 96', their public demonstration represented something significantly more profound than the provision of all-seater stadia.

It was a recognition that no individuals or corporate bodies had been formally held responsible for the circumstances in which 96 people were killed. It was a groundswell of concern that, despite Taylor's clear message over liability, no prosecutions followed, no one was disciplined and inquest verdicts of accidental death' had been returned. It was a cry of outrage that families and survivors were treated with contempt and disdain in the immediate aftermath and, subsequently, were denied a full, public hearing including all evidence relating to each death.

None of these wrongs could be corrected, or even addressed, by the bricks, mortar and steel of refurbished grounds. How could a senior police officer talk of deaths being 'not in vain' when the operational policies, professional practices and legal processes which contextualised Hillsborough and the aftermath had not been overhauled? *No Last Rights*, based on six years of research, made 87 recommendations for reform. Ten of the recommendations dealt with crowd safety, policing and citizens' rights at sports and leisure events. Eight concerned the role and constitution of official inquiries and 36 focused on a full review of the deficiencies inherent in the inquest system. Other recommendations concerned the role and function of the media, and responding to the needs of the bereaved. The scope of the research, its findings and recommendations, broke new ground and had implications for reform well beyond Hillsborough.

In 1997, *Beyond Disaster: Identifying and Resolving Inter-Agency Conflict in the Immediate Aftermath of Disasters* was published. Based on in-depth research into the aftermath of Hillsborough, the *Marchioness* and Lockerbie/PanAm Flight 103, it submitted a full report and 55 recommendations to the Home Office. These related to the role of local and central government departments in the immediate aftermath of disasters; guidelines for inter-agency cooperation; and effective crisis support for families. Twenty-three recommendations laid down a protocol and procedure for responding to the needs of the bereaved and survivors.

The findings called on the Government to initiate the 'fullest possible consultation, involving bereaved and survivors' campaign and advocacy groups' to establish a charter for the bereaved. The charter would provide a 'clear overview of the statutory role and obligations of the police and the coroner, distinguishing between such obligations and discretionary practices'. It would present a 'statement of rights for the bereaved', covering: information; viewing of the body; identification; post-mortems; return of the body; return of personal effects; access to the disaster site; and crisis support.

The charter would be made available to all 'who suffer sudden bereavement in controversial circumstances, in disasters or related tragedies'. Finally, it would recognise that 'those bereaved, injured or affected by disasters have a right to privacy and a right to be protected from further suffering occasioned by intrusive journalism'. The call for a charter was based on overwhelming evidence that, in the aftermath of disasters and other tragedies, the needs and wishes of the bereaved have been barely recognised, always subordinated to the priorities and requirements of the investigating agencies. What the scope of the recommendations in both publications shows is that piecemeal reform cannot deliver adequate, appropriate and supportive procedures and practices.

* * *

Many of those involved in the Hillsborough disaster, including police officers, were – and remain – traumatised by their experiences. But the burden carried by the bereaved and survivors extends beyond the horror of death and the desolation of bereavement. As fans were being dragged from the pens, Duckenfield told his detestable lie: fans had forced entry. Hours later while the dead, still warm, lay in body bags on the gymnasium floor, the decision was taken to take their blood-alcohol levels. Throughout the night families and friends endured the screams of bereavement, the barely recognisable Polaroid photographs and the crass insensitivity of an identification process built around professional convenience rather than the priorities of grieving. Then, in public, intimidated by an overwhelming police presence, shocked relatives and friends sat through a statement-taking procedure more akin to an interrogation, subjected to the callous indifference of some investigating officers.

Within days, police officers made malicious, off-the-record and unattributable allegations to the press in an attempt to confirm that fans' behaviour caused the deaths. This was the climate of deceit and hostility in which the dead were laid to rest and the Taylor Inquiry was conducted. It took nearly ten years for the story of how the South Yorkshire Police reviewed and altered their officers' recollections to emerge. Much that went on was never recorded and will remain hidden from public scrutiny. Much that is already known 'on the grapevine' remains impossible to verify. The feeding of information, including vetted police statements, to the West Midlands investigation, along with the internal monitoring of the Taylor Inquiry and the inquests, represent an unsavoury chapter in the history of the South Yorkshire Police. More broadly, the process illustrates the serious limitations of police accountability.

Taylor, despite sanctioning the review and alteration of police statements, was unimpressed. Although levelling stern criticism against the city council, the club and the safety engineers, he directed his most uncompromising judgement towards the police. Failure in police control was the primary reason for the disaster. He castigated senior officers for being 'defensive' and 'evasive' and the force for not being 'prepared to concede' that it was 'in any respect at fault for what had occurred'. Given the strength of these findings, and the technical acceptance of liability by the

South Yorkshire Police in paying damages, it was assumed that criminal prosecutions would follow. When this did not happen, the bereaved sought redress through the inquests – a court of inquiry unable to resolve matters of liability.

Hillsborough, perhaps more than any other tragedy, exposed the serious deficiencies and inadequacies of the coroner's court and the discretionary powers of the coroner. As detailed earlier, the lack of disclosure of witness statements, the summaries of evidence written and presented by investigating officers, the selection of witnesses, the 3.15 p.m. cut-off on evidence, the uneven legal representation and the weighting of the coroner's summing-up, together undermined the credibility of the inquests and the accidental death verdicts. Imposing the 3.15 p.m. cut-off, a time when many who died were still alive, denied the bereaved the opportunity to hear and cross-examine evidence directly relevant to the circumstances in which death occurred. They were unable to determine whether the rescue response and medical treatment was adequate, and whether some who died might have lived.

Denying the bereaved this opportunity breached the spirit, if not the letter, of international conventions: the right to a 'fair' and 'public' hearing. Without disclosure, much of the evidence was not brought into the public domain. Without cross-examination it was never tested. The adopted procedure was neither 'fair' nor 'public'. Yet the demand for a full hearing to secure disclosure and cross-examination of all evidence was over-shadowed by the Home Secretary's decision to establish a judicial scrutiny confined to 'new' evidence.

It was entirely predictable that, given its restricted terms of reference, Stuart-Smith's scrutiny would raise more questions than it answered. Without significant 'new' evidence he was able to challenge neither the DPP's decision not to prosecute police officers, nor the Divisional Court's endorsement of the inquests and their verdicts. Consequently, the families were left with anomalous accidental death verdicts, no prosecutions or disciplinary actions and, worse still, apparent support from Stuart-Smith of the procedures adopted by the South Yorkshire Police in preparing their case for the various inquiries. The families also had to come to terms with the details contained in 'body-files' on their loved ones, many of which were full of inconsistencies and inaccuracies.

Hillsborough's aftermath, perhaps more than any other, demonstrates the necessity for change in professional cultures and attitudes, discretionary powers, public inquiries, inquests and police disciplinary codes and their application. It also emphasises the urgent need to review strategies for gathering police evidence in controversial cases. It is only when the full significance of these issues is realised and accepted, when they lead to a recognition of – and apology for – the added suffering inflicted on those bereaved in controversial circumstances, and when there is an explicit admission of culpability by all involved, that there can be some move towards reconciliation.

The deep pain and persistent distress endured with dignity and resolve by the bereaved and survivors can only be imagined by those not directly afflicted by the Hillsborough disaster. Compounding their suffering has been, and remains, the torment of injustice. Paltry compensation payments, flawed coronial procedures, inappropriate inquest verdicts, questionable police practices and the failure to prosecute or discipline those responsible, raise serious questions about the institutional, structural and embedded deficiencies in the law and its administration. What the bereaved and survivors have discovered, to their financial and personal cost, is that the theatre of the 'law' has little to do with the discovery of 'truth' and the realisation of 'justice'.

Chapter Twelve

ENDLESS PRESSURE

As an FA Cup semi-final, the Liverpool v Nottingham Forest match in Sheffield was one of the highest-profile domestic football games of the season. A rerun of the previous season's semi-final, with the prospect of meeting Everton in the final, it carried added significance. Liverpool had been long established as the premier club in England and one of the top teams in Europe, although the club was serving a long ban from European competition after the Heysel tragedy. Consequently, the media, print and broadcast, were there in force, including international correspondents. Sports journalists and photographers transformed into disaster reporters, and the film and photographic record was extensive. This immediacy led to false allegations being broadcast around the world following Chief Superintendent David Duckenfield's widely published allegations about fans' forcing entry into the stadium. Confronted by reporters and film crews, a senior Liverpool director made an unfortunate remark regarding the potential damage to the club's chances of returning to European competition.

Extensive press coverage the following morning carried explicit, close-up photographs and graphic descriptions of the dead and injured. Decisions to film, photograph and interview distraught fans were taken in the heat of the moment, but production and editorial decisions to broadcast or publish graphic material had the benefit of measured consideration. Over the following days, intrusive journalism included: attempts to photograph the dead as bodies were transferred; accessing hospital wards without permission; doorstepping; posing as social workers to gain entry into the homes of the bereaved; and using long lenses to photograph personal grief at funerals. Mass loss of life on the scale of Hillsborough, occurring at a managed and policed event, demanded in-depth investigative journalism 'in the public interest', yet media coverage rushed to judgement.

Within days, unqualified blame was directed against Liverpool fans. As discussed earlier, 'police sources' alleged that Liverpool fans were drunk and violent, attacked rescue workers, and urinated on police officers while abusing and stealing from the dead (*Sheffield Star*, 18 April 1989). Along with Sheffield MP Irvine Patnick's allegations, this led to the *The Sun*'s infamous front page: 'THE TRUTH: Some Fans Picked Pockets of Victims; Some Fans Urinated on the Brave Cops; Some Fans Beat Up PC Giving Kiss of Life'. Eight newspapers carried the allegations. These unrelenting, unsubstantiated and inflammatory accounts reinforced Duckenfield's initial lie. They were consolidated by senior police officers in 'off the record' briefings. The bereaved and survivors bore the brunt of condemnation, and the apparent reliability of the allegations determined the course of events in the immediate aftermath, setting a longer-term media and political agenda. Written twenty years on, this chapter considers the 'endless pressure' of discredited but persistent allegations, attributable to a concerted campaign by the police and transmitted regularly and effectively through compliant media coverage.

On Merseyside, a mass boycott of *The Sun* reflected the depth of feeling towards the newspaper and its editor. Its front page was the most extreme example of many unfounded allegations, which, had they been made against named individuals, would have resulted in libel actions. Consequently, Hillsborough became synonymous with soccer-related violence and hooliganism. These themes dominated news coverage of the Taylor Inquiry and the coroner's inquests. While Taylor rejected all such allegations, the police continued to deflect responsibility by reiterating claims of hooliganism. Simon Heffer's response to Taylor was headed 'BLAME THE HOOLIGANS, NOT THE STADIUMS'. He claimed Taylor was 'reluctant' to accept that '95 Liverpool fans were killed by the thuggishness and ignorance of other Liverpool fans crushing into the ground behind them' (*Sunday Telegraph*, 4 February 1990). John Naughton had 'sympathy' for the dead but asked, 'What about the other fans – the ones who milled round the gates and stampeded down the tunnel into the pens simply because they couldn't bear the thought of missing the kick-off?' (*The Observer*, 11 February 1990).

Others in authority, well connected to the media, relentlessly repeated the allegations. Former chairman of Sheffield Wednesday Football Club, Bert McGhee, diverted attention from Taylor's scathing criticisms of the stadium's safety, its flawed stewarding and poor policing by arguing that 'many, many hundreds of people came to Hillsborough without tickets in the knowledge that if they created enough mayhem the police would open the gates. And that is exactly what happened' (*Liverpool Echo*, 16 March 1990). Peter Wright, South Yorkshire Police Chief Constable, heavily criticised Taylor for rejecting 'mass drunkenness' as a main cause (*Daily Mail*, 6 February 1990). He remarked, 'Other factors in the disaster [will] emerge at the coroner's inquest and give people a different view of what happened' (*The Guardian*, 6 February 1990). Bereaved families made formal complaints to the South Yorkshire Police Authority against its Chief Constable. The *Yorkshire Post*'s Bernard Dineen (30 April 1990) responded, 'Everyone with a scrap of sense knows that drink was a contributory factor at Hillsborough: why crucify the police for saying so?' He doubted that Liverpool fans rarely 'indulge in alcohol' or that they 'spend their entire leisure time sipping bitter lemon and debating the finer points of philosophy'.

The coroner's unprecedented decision to take blood-alcohol levels of all who died, including children, was portrayed as further confirmation that drunkenness was a primary cause. It implied that fans had contributed to their own deaths and to the deaths of others. As each inquest opened, the recorded blood-alcohol level of the deceased was announced, creating a kind of league table of blame through which the victims were named and shamed. A consequence of this persistent, cynical misrepresentation was a growing concern, voiced by the bereaved and survivors, that those who died were being held responsible for the disaster. And so it proved. In an off-the-cuff remark during an interview with Bobby Charlton, Terry Wogan commented that unlike soccer's other disasters, Hillsborough was 'self-inflicted'. David Evans MP commented that the Hillsborough disaster, as 'everyone in football knows although they won't say it, was caused by thousands of fans turning up without tickets, late and drunk' (BBC Radio Four, 14 October 1993). As discussed earlier, Brian Clough – Nottingham Forest's manager at Hillsborough – and Sir Bernard Ingham – Margaret Thatcher's Press Secretary – also attributed primary responsibility to violent, drunk fans. Thus police allegations of hooliganism became entrenched within a mindset that lived on.

Duckenfield's initial lie, the police allegations and the coroner's decision to record and make public the blood-alcohol levels of the deceased together constituted a profound deceit resulting in a massive national and international impact. In his book, *Understanding Soccer Hooliganism*, John Kerr notes the 'chaotic horror at Hillsborough' caused by a 'late inrush of spectators' who 'had run into an already full enclosure of Liverpool fans, causing a desperate crush'. Kevin Young lists Hillsborough as one of 13 international 'noteworthy incidents of sports-related collective violence' between 1955 and 1989. He states, '94 fans [*sic*]' had been 'crushed to death as fans arriving late attempted to force their way into the game'. Writing on the 'psychological and political consequences of disasters', David Cohen attributes allegations about Hillsborough to Heysel: 'Some fans . . . urinated on the dead, on police and on ambulance men'. Using 'behavioural categories' to analyse 'crowd behaviours', Jerry Lewis and Anne-Marie Scarisbrick-Hauser review evidence presented in football-crowd safety reports, proposing 'new' categories: 'climbing, falling, kicking and public urinating'. They consider 'surging', 'jogging', 'climbing', 'falling' and 'public urinating' to have occurred at Hillsborough.

Journalists and academics were not alone in publishing casual, under-researched commentaries on Hillsborough. In her novel, *Acid Row*, first published in 2001, bestselling author Minette Walters failed in attempting to locate fiction in 'fact': 'Gaynor, who had seen footage of the Hillsborough Stadium disaster, when football fans had been mercilessly crushed by a stampede of people behind them, was terrified that a catastrophic surge would cause the people against the wall to be suffocated'. In November 2007, a conversation between two characters, one a Liverpool supporter, in the BBC soap *EastEnders* included the comment, 'Five years out of Europe because of Heysel, because they penned you lot [Liverpool fans] in to stop you fighting on the pitch, and what did we end up with? Hillsborough!' In January 2009, *Daily Mail* reporter John Edwards wrote that deaths were caused by a 'surge of late arrivals' who 'crushed' their fellow fans 'against railings at the front' of the pens.

* * *

The negative reputation ascribed to Liverpool fans in these diverse commentaries about Hillsborough provided fertile ground for a broader attack on Merseyside as a region inherently violent, militant and arrogant. Psychologist David Cohen, for example, considers Hillsborough symptomatic of Liverpool's 'darker side: a massive drugs problem, endemic unemployment and a resultant capacity for mass disorder'. In this volatile context, Liverpudlians had developed a 'ferocious reputation' bearing 'the hallmarks . . . of Neanderthal man'.

Public demonstration of sympathy and compassion for the dead and solidarity with the bereaved and survivors was recast as pathetic self-indulgence, self-pity and mawkishness. Untruths about fans' behaviour at Hillsborough were matched by untruths about the people of Liverpool.

In 1993, following the tragic killing of two-year-old James Bulger by two ten-year-old boys, the prevailing image of Liverpool was a place in which violence, fear and a disdain for authority were not only dominant but encouraged and promoted. Writing at the time, Auberon Waugh seemed fixated on a diminishing gene pool in which low intelligence was linked to pathology:

> It is said that Liverpool's problems are all due to unemployment. I wonder what Liverpool's unemployment is due to. I fear it may be due to the stupidity as much as the unpleasant habits of the people who live there. All the clever people left it long ago.
>
> (*Daily Telegraph*, 3 March 1993)

Connecting the Bulger case to Hillsborough was exemplified by the headline 'HEYSEL, HILLSBOROUGH AND NOW THIS' (*The Guardian*, 20 February 1993). In his article ' A CITY ACTS UP', Ian Jack proposed that Liverpool possessed a unique 'capacity to turn a deep but very particular and personal tragedy into a wake' (*Independent on Sunday*, 28 February 1993). Its people acted out a script 'as if they expect it now, mugged by one disaster after another until a peculiar kind of martyrdom has become part of the municipal character'. Writing in the *Sunday Times* (28 February 1993) under the headline 'SELF-PITY CITY', Jonathan Margolis explored the 'dark and ugly side' to that character 'which has belied the cheeky Scouse image it loves to promote'. He continued that the 'most liberal of people can turn out to hate, or at least be irritated by, Liverpudlians . . . however much you like the city, Liverpool culture seems nevertheless to combine defeatism and hollow-cheeked depression with a cloying mawkishness'. Focusing insensitively on a pre-match tribute paid to the dead by Liverpool football supporters, Margolis simply asked, 'Does anyone dare wonder how many of the Anfield faithful solemnly observing a minute's silence at last week's home match were, to put it crudely, getting off on the "city in mourning" theme?' Jack and Margolis, alongside numerous other journalists, suggested that Liverpool people wallowed in tragedy in their communities. Their commentaries on 'self-pity', 'martyrdom' and 'cultural mawkishness' preceded references to Heysel and Hillsborough, then linked to the Bulger killing. Margolis wrote:

In what one liberal commentator described post-Hillsborough as the 'world capital of self-pity', everyone tells you that the atmosphere after the Bulger murder was just like Hillsborough. Indeed, Hillsborough is mentioned in every conversation. Yet in two weeks, the name of Heysel, where bad behaviour by Liverpool fans helped lead to the deaths of 39 Juventus supporters, was never brought up. The inevitable taxi driver, oddly enough a coloured South African, explains without apparent irony, 'That's because no Liverpool lives were lost at Heysel.'

Quoting an 'anonymous' sportswriter, Margolis continued, 'Looking back, the way the Heysel boys were treated was monstrous. All those Italian fans were dead, and the Liverpool boys were heroes.' He offered no evidence to support such an inflammatory claim. Collapsing together Heysel and Hillsborough, Jack pursued a similar theme:

The first incident [Heysel] produced collective guilt, the second [Hillsborough] – for which Liverpool people were not to blame – collective anger and self-pity. The victims were said to have 'died for football' or at least 'not died in vain' . . . Thus Liverpool learned to dramatise itself, to show its stigmata.

Margolis saved his most vindictive, spiteful comments for his conclusion:

> The tragedy is . . . that Liverpool is stuck in a groove, refusing to listen to criticism, clinging to past charms and triumphs, desperate not to be seen as provincial but managing to appear just that by cutting itself off from the world. When the world is against you, how gratifying it must feel to know that you really do walk alone.

These articles failed to recognise that after Hillsborough most people on Merseyside knew a bereaved or a survivor's family and many were aware they could have suffered a similar fate. They also understood that the bereaved and survivors had been treated disgracefully by the authorities in the aftermath. Thousands visited Anfield and laid wreaths as tokens of remembrance and respect to relatives, friends, workmates and school friends. Self-pity was the last thing on their minds. Their grief was dishonoured by journalists who sacrificed knowledge and understanding to prejudice and arrogance. Again, the negative portrayal consolidated over time.

In October 2004, the Margolis/Jack portrayal of the city and its people was reawakened. British hostage Ken Bigley was executed in Iraq. There was a minute's silence before an international football match, and the editor of *The Spectator* and Conservative MP Boris Johnson criticised 'the mawkish sentimentality of a society . . . hooked on grief . . . wallow[ing] in a sense of vicarious victimhood'. The public's 'extreme reaction' to Ken Bigley's death had been 'fed by the fact that he was a Liverpudlian'. He represented Liverpool as a place confounded by a 'tribal sense of community'. It had endured 'economic misfortune' combined with 'an excessive predilection for welfarism', which together 'created a peculiar, and deeply unattractive, psyche among many Liverpudlians'. They 'see themselves whenever possible as victims . . . resent their victim status; yet at the same time they wallow in it' thus producing a 'flawed psychological state'. Always eager to blame others, 'they cannot accept that they might have made any contribution to their misfortunes'.

Having attacked the city and its inhabitants, Johnson turned his attention to Hillsborough:

> The deaths of more than 50 [*sic*] Liverpool football supporters at Hillsborough in 1989 was undeniably a greater tragedy than the single death, however horrible, of Mr Bigley; but that is no excuse for Liverpool's failure to acknowledge, even to this day, the part played in the disaster by drunken fans at the back of the crowd who mindlessly tried to fight their way into the ground that Saturday afternoon. The police became a convenient scapegoat, and *The Sun* newspaper a whipping-boy for daring, albeit in a tasteless fashion, to hint at the wider causes of the incident.

It was a remarkable commentary, using a single tragic death and public expressions of sympathy as a vehicle for condemning collective 'mawkish sentimentality' while resurrecting the false allegations about Hillsborough. A week later, Johnson published an apology for 'mistakes of facts and taste'. While 'welfare-addicted Liverpudlians' might exist, 'it was wounding and wrong to suggest that this stereotype could be applied to the city as a whole'. Further, he admitted to 'sloppy' journalism in stating that 'the Hillsborough tragedy was caused by drunken fans, when the inquiry report found no evidence for this whatever'. It was a 'mistake [that] caused real offence and hurt'.

Yet Johnson repeated concerns about 'bogus sentiment, self-pity . . . and our refusal to see that we may sometimes be the author of our misfortunes'. His initial editorial dramatically revealed the depth and permanence of the myths of Hillsborough. It was corrected only because he received a 'huge [amount of] mail' and an embarrassed Conservative Party leader, Michael Howard, ordered Johnson to visit Liverpool to repent. Typically flippant, Johnson labelled his visit 'Operation Scouse-grovel'. His grave error of judgement appeared not to harm his political career. In 2008, he was elected mayor of London.

* * *

The campaign on Merseyside against *The Sun* newspaper and its former editor Kelvin MacKenzie continued unabated. In July 2004, Liverpool-born Wayne Rooney, at the time an Everton player, accepted a reported £250,000 for a series of exclusive interviews. Realising the severity of the backlash against Rooney, The Sun published an editorial stating that its coverage of Hillsborough had been the 'most terrible mistake in its history'. Fifteen years after the disaster, it admitted that 'carelessness and thoughtlessness following the blackest of days made the grief of their families and friends even harder to bear'. It concluded:

> We long ago apologised publicly to the victims' families, friends and to the city of Liverpool for our awful error. We gladly repeat that apology today: fully, openly, honestly and without reservation. *The Sun* of 2004 no more deserves to be hated on Merseyside than Wayne Rooney does.
>
> (*The Sun*, 7 July 2004)

Photographs of Wayne Rooney were published alongside the editorial, leaving an impression that he supported the apology. Phil Hammond, chair of the Hillsborough Family Support Group, commented, 'They [*The Sun*] think that because they've got a big name on board, people in Liverpool will now start to buy the paper, but we're not that stupid' (*The Guardian*, 8 July 2004).

Following the Rooney affair, Graham Dudman, managing editor of *The Sun*, met members of the Hillsborough Family Support Group in an attempt to resolve the long-running boycott.

He offered support to the families' campaign on condition that they accepted the apology. The group, however, refused him a full meeting. Margaret Aspinall reflected the feelings of many: 'People believe what they read. When we had the trial, all we heard was drink, drink, drink. James [her son] didn't even have a drink that day . . . mud sticks. That article [in *The Sun*] made me have to defend my son.'

The underlying suspicion was that *The Sun*'s 2004 apology and Dudman's subsequent visit were contrived solely to revive newspaper sales on Merseyside. Describing the initial coverage as a 'mistake', caused by 'carelessness' and 'thoughtlessness', portrayed the infamous 'Truth' edition as unintentional, a consequence of innocence and unthinking naivety. Yet the circumstances in which Kelvin MacKenzie published scurrilous allegations suggest a different story – a decision taken neither lightly nor carelessly. It was considered and deliberate. Charting the 'rise and fall' of *The Sun*, journalists Peter Chippindale and Chris Horrie suggest MacKenzie 'did an enormously uncharacteristic thing'. Far from acting as usual, with 'instant decision-making', he 'sat for fully half an hour thinking about the front-page layout'. Rejecting his first inclination, the headline 'YOU SCUM', he decided on 'THE TRUTH', causing a 'collective shudder . . . through the office . . . an instant gut feeling that it was a terrible mistake'.

MacKenzie's colleagues were 'paralysed'. His 'dominance was so total that there was nobody left in the organisation who could rein him in except Murdoch, who was not there'. Chippindale and Horrie continue:

The error staring them [the staff] in the face was too glaring and too terminal to be possible. It obviously wasn't a silly mistake; nor was it a simple oversight . . . and it certainly wasn't a typographical error . . . they just took one look and went away shaking their heads in wonder at the enormity of it . . . [MacKenzie] was convinced he knew what the real situation was. The police obviously couldn't be totally to blame . . . The time he had spent deliberating had been solely about the headlines – the details did not concern him.

The Press Council described *The Sun*'s front page as 'insensitive, provocative and unwarranted'. Rupert Murdoch, owner of *The Sun*, was contrite – the coverage had been 'uncaring and deeply offensive to relatives of the victims'. On radio, MacKenzie accepted that 'with hindsight . . . most of the newspaper coverage of Hillsborough had been a mistake'. While it had been 'one-sided, misleading, insensitive', he denied responsibility for the allegations. It had been his 'decision alone to do that front page . . . and I made a rather serious error'. His grudging recognition that a 'mistake', an 'error', had been made fell short of an apology. It was assumed that MacKenzie had been instructed by Murdoch to make a statement, as *The Sun* had lost nearly 40 per cent of its regional circulation, some 200,000 readers, worth an estimated £10 million a year in lost revenue.

In his autobiography, Kenny Dalglish, then manager of Liverpool, recalls a phone call:

> They knew the story had no foundation. Kelvin MacKenzie even called me up. 'How can we correct the situation?' he said. 'You know that big headline – "The Truth"?' I replied. 'All you have to do is put "We Lied" in the same size. Then you might be all right.' MacKenzie said, 'I can't do that.' 'Well,' I replied, 'I cannot help you then.' That was it. I put the phone down . . . The shameful allegations intensified the anger amidst the trauma.

MacKenzie informed a House of Commons select committee that he regretted his 'fundamental mistake' but 'would not have gone with it' without authoritative sources. Eventually, he moved from The Sun, and it was widely assumed that he stood by his initial judgement, as became evident over a decade later.

In November 2006, speaking at a business lunch in Newcastle, MacKenzie reportedly stated:

> All I did wrong there was tell the truth. There was a surge of Liverpool fans who had been drinking and that is what caused the disaster. The only thing different we did was put it under the headline 'The Truth'. I went on *World at One* the next day and apologised. I only did that because Rupert Murdoch told me to. I wasn't sorry then, and I'm not sorry now.

Responding to the story, Phil Hammond told the *Liverpool Daily Post* (1 December 2006):

> It has been proven that the story was a pack of lies, yet here he is all these years later peddling his lies on the after-dinner speaking circuit. Why doesn't he come and tell the families this to their faces? If he really believed he was printing the truth and stood by what he said, then why didn't he walk away when Rupert Murdoch supposedly made him make this apology?

On 7 January 2007, Liverpool played Arsenal in an FA Cup game at Anfield. The BBC broadcast the tie at peak-viewing time. Agreed by the club, the Liverpool fans' group Reclaim the Kop organised a protest directed at MacKenzie and the BBC for employing him as a presenter. At the kick-off, the entire Kop, approximately 12,000 fans, held a mosaic above their heads in red and white. It spelled 'The Truth'. For six minutes, precisely the length of time played at Hillsborough before the match was abandoned, the Kop chanted 'Justice for the 96'.

A few days later, MacKenzie was a panellist on the BBC programme *Question Time*. Asked about the sincerity of his earlier apologies, he remarked that the bereaved and survivors should 'find somebody who actually caused the disaster'. He claimed that a key 'aspect' of the disaster was the determination of ticketless fans to force entry. The front-page allegations had originated 'from a Liverpool news agency . . . a Tory MP and an unnamed senior police officer'. He did not know whether allegations that fans urinated on the police or stole from the dead were true. Another panellist, Clare Short MP, told MacKenzie that he 'should apologise – you've hurt so many people'. He replied, 'That story has become so caught up in a battle between the Liverpool Football [sic] or some of the fans and me that actually no matter what I said would resolve the issue.' He refused to apologise. Jenni Hicks, whose two daughters, Sarah and Victoria, died, regrets that 'after all that has been established it is that one deceitful article in The Sun that's remembered – that's the myth that's believed'.

* * *

Lord Justice Taylor's Interim Report focused on the background to the disaster, the build-up on the day and the evacuation of the pens. It did not provide a detailed account of medical care in the stadium, at the hospitals or during the days that followed. Neither did Taylor consider the failure of the emergency plan or the appropriateness of the procedures for identifying the dead and dealing with bereaved relatives. As discussed earlier, the subsequent decision by the coroner not to hear evidence beyond 3.15 p.m. on the day seriously limited any inquiry into the circumstances of the deaths of those who died after that time. His unreliable assumption was that all who died suffered irreversible, fatal injuries before 3.15 p.m., thereby resolving doubts that appropriate medical treatment, administered quickly and effectively, might have saved lives.

The experience of Eddie Spearritt, discussed in earlier chapters, is a tragic and dramatic illustration of the severe limitations of the inquiry and inquests into the Hillsborough disaster. His precise whereabouts between losing consciousness some minutes before 3 p.m. and his first recorded treatment at the Northern General

Hospital nearly two hours later are unknown. Even in the chaos of multiple admissions to accident and emergency, it is inconceivable that Eddie was left unconscious and without treatment. This raises the possibility that, at some point, he was presumed dead. There were several fans initially considered to be dead who soon after regained consciousness. Given that few who died were taken to hospital, it remains a significant concern that inadequate medical care and treatment in the immediate aftermath might have contributed to some deaths.

There are two significant issues. First, Article 2 of the European Convention on Human Rights (ECHR) places a duty on the state to protect the right to life of all individuals. There is a right to 'effective investigation' for any potential breach of Article 2. It should be independent, thorough and attribute responsibility where appropriate. While it is often assumed that breaches of Article 2 by state institutions relate mainly to 'unreasonable' use of direct physical force, the 'right to life' includes circumstances where the state fails, through act or omission, in its responsibility to protect individuals. Second, Article 6 establishes that 'everyone is entitled to a fair and public hearing within a reasonable time by an independent and impartial tribunal'. If, as has been suggested, some who died at Hillsborough did so as a consequence of ineffective or inappropriate treatment, or through neglect, the failure by both Taylor and the coroner to extend their inquiries to include a rigorous appraisal of the medical care administered in the immediate aftermath could amount to breaches of Articles 2 and 6.

In this context, the most significant and well-publicised case concerns the circumstances in which Kevin Williams died. Kevin's mother, Anne, campaigned for two decades following disclosure that a special police constable suggested Kevin was alive at 4 p.m. and had mumbled 'Mum'. Another officer stated that after 3.15 p.m., while attempting to resuscitate Kevin on the pitch, he located a pulse and Kevin convulsed. Seemingly, both statements were ignored by the pathologist who conducted the post-mortem. He concluded that Kevin would have been dead before the special police constable arrived on the scene. This assessment was supported by another doctor who estimated that Kevin probably died in the crush on the terrace. The second officer subsequently revised his statement, confirming that Kevin was dead on the pitch.

After the inquests, both officers claimed that they had been pressured into changing their initial statements by the investigating officers from the West Midlands Police. Subsequent opinions given by three highly regarded pathologists confirmed that Kevin might well have been alive at the times first noted by the officers. Given the controversy surrounding the officers' statements, the persuasion to alter them and the conflicting medical opinions regarding the possible time of death, the potential breaches of Articles 2 and 6 were clear. If Kevin was alive, however barely, was the emergency response adequate and appropriate? Were there failures in the duty of care by those responsible for activating the emergency response? Given that Taylor and the coroner decided against a thorough inquiry into events beyond 3.15 p.m., did the state fail to provide a 'fair and public hearing'? As Anne Williams argued consistently and tirelessly, the case for due consideration of the evidence and medical opinions concerning Kevin's death was, and remains, compelling.

Following a special edition of the investigative television programme *The Cook Report*, Anne Williams wrote a book *When You Walk Through the Storm*. Having exhausted all domestic legal remedies, the case was submitted to the European Court of Human Rights on 12 August 2006. In a subsequent press release, she stated:

> Europe is the last chance for any sort of justice . . . I have sent all
> the evidence that I have uncovered over the years, evidence from
> some of the highest forensic pathologists suggesting that Kevin

would not have died by 3.15 p.m. and would be alive today if oxygen had been supplied. I have sent evidence that West Midlands Police interfered with witness statements and suppressed vital evidence. I tracked all the Liverpool fans that carried Kevin that day. I just hope Europe will give us justice.

As Anne Williams stated repeatedly, her campaign has major implications for the families of all who died at Hillsborough. It is beyond question that through the limitations of its Home Office Inquiry and coroner's inquests, the state failed to investigate thoroughly the precise circumstances in which people died. Such an investigation should have focused on the failure to operationalise the emergency plan, deficiencies in the on-site medical provision and procedures for evacuation of those in need of immediate treatment. For a 'duty of care' to have been realised, each of these requirements should have been met. The available evidence suggests that there was an institutional failure in that duty and some of the fans that died might have been saved. In March 2009 Anne Williams' case was rejected by the European Court. Still campaigning, she died in April 2013.

* * *

During the early phase of the inquests, families attended the Sheffield Coroner's Court to hear synopses of the evidence concerning their loved ones read to the court by investigating officers from the West Midlands Police. Pathologists also gave evidence on each case, focusing on the relationship between traumatic asphyxia and crush asphyxia. One of the pathologists stated that after 'the compression of the neck or chest has occurred . . . unconsciousness occurs very rapidly, certainly within a few seconds . . . there is no discomfort and no pain. Death then occurs after approximately three to five minutes.' As discussed earlier, it was this line of reasoning, seemingly incontrovertible, that informed the coroner's decision not to hear evidence of events beyond 3.15 p.m. on the day.

Yet the pathologist's medical opinion was contested by two forensic specialists, Dr Iain West and Dr James Burns. Dr West stated that a victim 'could well have survived for a considerable period, well beyond 3.15 p.m.' There were several factors that could influence survival, particularly in cases of crush asphyxia, where pressure might not be continuous. Dr Burns noted that 'it is by no means certain that even in cases of traumatic asphyxia', when pressure would be sudden, violent and sustained, 'death necessarily ensues three or four minutes after compression begins'. The most 'important factor . . . is whether the severe compression is sustained. If the pressure is intermittent, then death may not ensue for a considerable length of time.' While the pathologists' evidence at the inquests might have reassured families that their loved ones died quickly, relatively free from pain and suffering, it was a debatable opinion. Although in many cases death might have occurred within minutes of losing consciousness, this condition could not be generalised.

Considering the broader evidence regarding fans who lost consciousness and recovered, including those presumed dead, the only reliable conclusions are that they survived because compression was intermittent, the particular physical circumstances were different and the speed with which individuals were rescued and received proper medical attention was inconsistent. Yet the coroner's insistence on a 3.15 p.m. cut-off fixed in the public's mind that those who died were beyond rescue and survival. Medical opinion was transformed into scientific fact, with the bereaved reassured that nothing more could have been done to save their loved ones. Given the disparity in recovery, this was not a sustainable position. In fact, not all who lost consciousness recovered fully and two young men were diagnosed as being in a 'vegetative state'. One was Tony Bland, chronologically the ninety-sixth person to die, almost four years after the disaster on 3 March 1993.

Tony's family and medical team went to the courts to apply for artificial feeding and hydration to be withdrawn, as he had no potential for recovery. The ground-breaking legal case drew widespread media attention, focusing particularly on public and political debates about 'persistent vegetative state' and 'euthanasia'. When it was announced that an application was to be made to the courts, the hospital was picketed by campaigners alleging 'medical cleansing' and 'murder'. The protest extended to the Blands' home. The well-known journalist Melanie Phillips compared the decision to 'Nazi euthanasia'. Since Tony's death, 'pro-life groups' have continued to portray the case as an example of a 'slippery slope' to non-voluntary 'euthanasia'. Emotive and hurtful commentaries that he was 'kept alive' only to pursue a test case, that he was 'starved to death' and that the case is representative of a 'silent Holocaust' are illustrative of contemporary campaigns demonstrating little understanding of the individual circumstances or medical condition. In 2006, Tony's neurologist at the centre of the protests, Dr Jim Howe, published a full account of the case.

Having been crushed on the terraces, 18-year-old Tony endured severe anoxic brain damage. He was admitted to the Northern General Hospital in Sheffield, where he was ventilated. Able to breathe, his condition seemed consistent with being in a 'vegetative state'. He was transferred to Airedale Hospital, close to his home in Keighley, where he was treated by a team headed by Jim Howe. Tony received excellent care from the rehabilitative and nursing team, but, as Jim Howe noted:

> There was no improvement. He remained unresponsive. There was no eye contact and no sign of communication. After three months, his family could see there had been absolutely no change and said so.

Eventually, after full consultation among the medical teams and the Bland family, Jim Howe decided on withdrawal of treatment, including nutrition and fluids supplied by tubes direct to Tony's stomach:

> It seemed to all of us that no purpose would be served by continuing treatment, including artificial nutrition and hydration . . . Tony was not conscious, and was extremely unlikely to recover consciousness, so could never have any semblance of normal human life . . . We set a date to withdraw all life-prolonging treatment, including artificial nutrition and hydration, while continuing comfort, care and support.

Jim Howe recalled the decision being taken amidst the 'furore' surrounding Hillsborough, not least the impact of media allegations about fans' behaviour. He informed the coroner of the intended course of action. The response was unexpected: 'It is difficult now to convey my shock in receiving his intimidating reply . . . advis[ing] me that I would risk a murder charge should I withdraw treatment.' The coroner warned:

> I could not countenance, condone, approve or give consent to any action or inaction which could be, or would be, construed as being designed or intended to shorten or terminate the life of this young man. This particularly applies to the withholding of the necessities of life, such as food and drink.

The coroner copied his letter to the Chief Constable of the West Midlands Police heading the investigation, the Yorkshire Regional Health Authority solicitor and Howe's medical defence society. Jim Howe was interviewed by the police and advised that he would be charged with murder should treatment be withdrawn. Faced with this unequivocal threat, he was well aware of the consequences – suspension from work, a protracted trial, a professional conduct hearing before the General Medical Council and the pressures of an ill-informed media. Yet his concern lay primarily with the family:

The Blands could not understand why the courts should be involved . . . Their sadness at the appalling circumstances that had taken their son, their anger at the handling of the aftermath of the Hillsborough disaster, was so profound that they just could not contemplate any further involvement with authority or the media. Tony's care and treatment continued. Gradually, his limbs became more contracted, but at no time was there any sign of communication. His mother and sister began to find it difficult to visit. His father had nightmares about his son, and the care team became disheartened.

Having taken legal advice, the family eventually agreed that a legal application should be made to withdraw treatment. The case was heard in the High Court Family Division. It was concluded that withdrawal of treatment would not be unlawful. The official solicitor appealed the ruling, and the case was heard in the House of Lords. The initial ruling was upheld and treatment withdrawn. Jim Howe stated:

The law relating to withdrawal of life prolonging treatment in PVS [Persistent Vegetative State] was clarified and guidance given for future cases, including a requirement for rehabilitation before making an application. It was affirmed that artificial nutrition and hydration are medical treatments . . . that in common law the doctrine of the sanctity of life gave way to personal autonomy . . . that existing in a vegetative state was of no benefit to Tony and implied this was not a life worth living.

It was clear to Jim Howe and to the medical carers that 'Mr and Mrs Bland believe that their son died at Hillsborough in 1989'. Seeing Tony freed from the medical equipment that had maintained his condition, his family felt it was 'the first time he has looked like Tony since the day he left for Sheffield'. The case made legal history and remains central to debates in moral philosophy and medical ethics. Responding to the criticisms that Tony's passing would be 'hideous' as a result of 'starvation' and that the family and medical staff would suffer 'severe stress and guilt', Jim Howe stated that 'treatment limiting decisions' are made daily by those caring for the terminally ill. He concluded, 'At the time, we all felt, and still feel, that it is an affront to human dignity to keep a body with no person in it alive for years.'

Jim Howe's medical care for Tony, supported by colleagues, was guided by sensitivity, integrity and compassion. The courage he showed at the time was matched by writing a deeply personal and professional account of the tragic circumstances 13 years on. Characteristically, he reserved his greatest 'praise and admiration for Mr Bland, whose plain good sense and determination never wavered. He was never angry or difficult with our staff, and he dismissed the protestors with the comment that they clearly did not understand what they were shouting about.' The family's strength and resolve remains all the more remarkable given their suffering over the months and years, from the first realisation of Tony's condition through to his funeral. They endured Tony's 'living death' within the context of inquests with which they had no involvement, through media coverage and other commentaries that blamed victims, and during prolonged legal action that exposed their private grief to public scrutiny and criticism.

* * *

In media coverage of bereavement, particularly in controversial circumstances receiving a high public profile, much is written and broadcast about 'closure', about 'coming to terms with the past', about 'moving on'. The shallowness of popular psychology places the bereaved under immense pressure to reassure others of their 'recovery' – that they are 'dealing with' their loss. Taken literally, the word 'closure' implies that there comes a time when pain and suffering diminish, leaving the bereaved and survivors to live 'normal' lives. In the aftermath of the private prosecutions, a time when it appeared that all legal remedies had been exhausted, family members reflected on their personal experiences of Hillsborough's legacy. There was a sense that friends and acquaintances who had shown care and sympathy in the early days had withdrawn over time. A bereaved father stated, 'They just dropped away. They couldn't cope with our sadness, even though we tried not to talk too much about him [their son] or the case.' Consequently, many bereaved families and survivors talked of keeping their emotions to themselves, effectively silenced by their consideration of others. There was also a feeling that not 'moving on' was seen as inadequacy: 'I find myself apologising for not coping better and inflicting my despair on others.'

'Closure', particularly in the context of inadequate investigations, unreliable evidence, flawed inquests and an inconclusive private prosecution compounded by hostile media coverage, is an imposed expectation for the benefit of others. Experiencing a disaster on the scale of Hillsborough, through bereavement or survival or both, generates mixed, deeply felt emotions of loss, anger, guilt, failure, inadequacy. Coping should not be confused with recovering. As Margaret Aspinall, mother of James, stated, 'They took away our children, and they took away our grandchildren, what they would have become . . . you can't stop that hurt or that anger.' Jenni Hicks' daughters, Sarah and Victoria, both died: 'My anger is still there, just beneath the surface.' People 'died so unnecessarily' and the investigation, inquests and lawyers 'let us down'.

Doreen Jones, 'just a Mum who tried desperately to get some kind of justice for Rick and Trace and all the victims of Hillsborough', had 'no desire to be seen as a sad or angry person . . . I get on with my life.' But 'how are you supposed to feel when it all gets raked up? I have a smouldering anger, we all have it. You only have to scratch the surface and I erupt. It shouldn't be like this. I should be able to mourn.' Doreen highlighted how ill-informed journalism, often reflected in everyday conversation, denied 'the injustices that remain to this day'. Then 'I have to tell people what happened.' Peter Joynes, father of Nick, felt the 'depression and despair over 20 years' was exacerbated by the continual misrepresentation of Hillsborough: 'Anything like this gets to me, and I can't sleep at night until I put it right.'

Misrepresentation comes in various forms. In November 2002, the Australian edition of the men's magazine *FHM* published a profoundly distasteful and hurtful feature under the heading 'World of Disasters'. Inexplicably, it published six photographs of the disaster accompanied by appalling captions, meant to be amusing. A photograph showing distressed fans waiting to carry the dead and dying on advertising hoardings was captioned 'Pitch invaders: Lazy'. Phil Hammond, chair of the Hillsborough Family Support Group, responded angrily that treating the victims as the 'butt of a very cheap joke' was 'sickening', especially as families had 'lost sons the same age as the young men that read this magazine'. Replying to *FHM*'s offer of a donation, he stated, 'Copies have been sold already and it's gone too far. It is sick. It's like me making a joke about Bali – it's the pits.' The *FHM* photographs and callous comments emphasise the vulnerability of the bereaved and survivors to ignorant and insensitive portrayals of their suffering. Unsurprisingly, they provoked a deeply hurtful mix of anger, resentment and further injustice.

The notion of 'justice', given its prominence in the campaigns, brought mixed responses. Margaret Aspinall stated, 'What makes me so angry is I can't abide this word justice. There's no justice for a life. I don't believe in the word.' Her anger was a consequence of witnessing the authorities' manipulation of the criminal, civil and inquisitorial legal processes. She continued, 'I still cry over the way we were all treated and the way the dead were treated. They had no rights; we had no rights.' While Julie Fallon, whose brother Andrew died, welcomed changes in legal processes, safety policies and inquest procedures, she maintained that anger is a rational response: 'The topmost issue for me is that should anything like Hillsborough happen to my family again, I would take the law into my own hands.' Reflecting on her experiences of the investigation and the courts, she stated, 'I would never again hand the responsibility for justice to the police, the coroner or the judiciary, but with absolute certainty I would take direct action.' Her conclusion was not based on a desire for revenge but an informed judgement of 'how the judicial system fails to its core'.

Brenda Fox, mother of Steve, recognised that 'not all' South Yorkshire Police officers 'were at fault' and remained grateful to those who responded positively, who 'helped to carry the make-shift stretchers across the pitch' and to the one officer who blew the whistle on changed statements. Yet she had a different response to 'officers who heard the fans scream for help, who observed and shrugged their shoulders and turned their backs and did nothing, and the senior officers in the control box who did the same and produced this lie which resulted in the slur on our city and its people'. They 'brought shame to the uniform they wore and the officers who served under them'. Would she 'forgive' them? 'I only have one simple message: No. Never. May the shame of the day always be with you and the guilt on your conscience be with you for ever and ever.' She had no wish for revenge but saw no reason to forgive those who collectively denied their personal and professional responsibility.

The outcome of the private prosecution created profoundly contradictory emotions. That it went ahead, through to a verdict, showed there was a case to be answered. Yet the trial judge's direction of the jury, the failure to reach a verdict on Duckenfield and the acquittal of Murray brought dismay. Families felt that in directing that a guilty verdict would send the 'wrong message . . . to those who have to act in an emergency of this kind', the judge confused possible consequences with the factual case against the officers. Given that the jury requested guidance, Doreen Jones challenged the impartiality of a direction that was 'daunting and seemingly impossible to overcome'. She remained dissatisfied that having taken the private prosecution so far, the families' lawyers refused to apply for a retrial: 'It should have been lodged even if we didn't get it . . . but off they [lawyers] went back to London, leaving nothing but despair behind them. We felt let down.' Jenni Hicks agreed: 'We didn't appeal, and historically that will look like we agreed with the verdict . . . At least an attempt to go for a retrial would have registered we objected.'

On leaving Leeds Crown Court for the last time, Doreen 'looked around at the faces of the families – so much sadness – and I was deeply dismayed to see armed police behind us . . . Was there any need for that? And to this day, I ask myself why, what on earth they thought we could or would do. It left a bitter taste.' Returning home after the private prosecution, Doreen initially 'felt utterly dejected and wanted to sit in a corner. I thought this would last a short while, but I was on my knees for a long time. It left me feeling inadequate, and I had a deep feeling of despair.'

Jenni Hicks questioned how 'something so simple, so obvious, was turned into something so complicated'. Revisiting the immediate context of the disaster, she stated, 'If the tunnel had been closed before the exit gate was opened, we wouldn't have had the deaths and injuries.' She rejected as 'nonsense' claims that fans 'having a few drinks' or 'going to a big match without tickets' were 'unexpected': 'It was a regular feature at all major events.' The 'simple fact' was that when the decision was taken to admit fans via the exit gate, 'they [police] didn't provide a safe place for them to go. I will never come to terms with Hillsborough because of that.' Peter Joynes remained astounded that 'given all the evidence, it's impossible to believe or bear' that 'twenty years on no-one is held responsible for one of sport's biggest disasters'. Following the first memorial service at Liverpool Cathedral, 'Pat and I were introduced to Mrs Thatcher. Telling her of our concerns, she tried to reassure us by saying there would be no cover-up, no whitewash . . . she should have continued by saying there will be no justice.' The Taylor Inquiry, the inquest evidence, the civil cases and the private prosecution 'all pointed the finger of culpability at senior police officers'.

Despite the circumstances of the disaster, the appalling treatment of the bereaved in its aftermath, the calculated review and alteration of police 'statements', and the outcome of the private prosecutions, there was little appetite for revenge among the bereaved. Margaret Aspinall commented, 'I don't want vengeance. I don't believe in an eye for an eye. Nineteen years ago, it was different . . . but not now. I felt vengeance then and realised it was eating me up.' For Julie Fallon, the implication that 'closure is on a higher plane that you have failed to reach because you are still angry' was actually imposed on the bereaved and survivors 'as a judgement'. It extended beyond individuals to the community, the city: 'So it's continually said that Liverpool gets very angry, is very easily provoked, its nose is constantly out of joint. But anger is an appropriate and reasoned response. Other people might not like it, but it is a correct response. Then people pass judgement that we haven't moved on. I might have to temper my anger, articulate it, put a thin crust over it, but it's still a real and rational response. If the source of the anger doesn't disappear, then the anger won't disappear.' The source was about recognition, acknowledgement and responsibility.

Julie believed her emotions, however extreme they might appear to others, could not be reduced to bitterness but 'are about personal awareness'. She continued, 'Absolutely, unequivocally, [as a consequence of Hillsborough] I realise there are aspects of my personality that are at an extreme. At its outer reaches, I feel I could be capable of violence, willing and capable of real personal sacrifice. I know that with certainty. Hillsborough has provoked in me an awareness of what I am capable of, and for that I'm grateful. In normal, everyday life, this is never tested. When it is, you find out about yourself with certainty. In a way, that's a gift.'

Dolores Steele felt that the loss of her son, Philip, was a constant. Yet 'you learn to live a different life', accommodating but not recovering from grief. She stated, 'The authorities all thought we were after money, big claims, but all we wanted was the truth and for someone to say, "We made a terrible mistake. Ninety-six died and we are sorry." And it never came.' Peter Joynes thought that families were 'pushed towards getting over it or building a new life while we have been through the pain barrier so many times, and we continually hope that one day someone will stand up and admit their mistakes'. Margaret Aspinall believed that while 'there can be no conclusion' to her grief, along with other families, her determination remained undiminished. They demanded 'acknowledgement and accountability . . . for them to stand up and say, "We got it wrong." All I want now is the truth to come out, from them.'

Sue Roberts, whose brother Graham died, also emphasised lack of acknowledgement and its consequences for families: 'Personally, I'm just upset that so many parents and other family members are passing away without ever having had an apology or any other form of justice. The names of our loved ones remain tarnished, with some members of the public still believing it was other fans that caused their deaths. The insight we've had over the past 20 years into the cover-ups that have gone on is appalling and still needs addressing. They say time heals . . . but in our case it hasn't.' Brenda Fox agreed: 'We are approaching the 20th anniversary, and it still feels like only yesterday when it happened . . . When I'm asked if I will ever forget it, the answer is no. I will never forget my son and that Hillsborough robbed me of him.'

Twenty years on from the Hillsborough disaster, many bereaved families and survivors, their friends and relations, collectively demonstrated remarkable resilience and resistance. Yet, as can be seen from the comments above and from the moving accounts regularly written on websites, beneath the surface of strength in adversity lay the complex mix of loss, guilt and an overwhelming sense of injustice. That this gave rise to anger directed towards those responsible for the disaster, to those who made deceitful allegations and to those who perpetuated the myth of hooliganism should have come as no surprise. It was a rational response. Against the considerable odds of the authorities' privileged access to formal procedures, their lack of accountability and their continued unwillingness to acknowledge their responsibilities, the bereaved and survivors maintained a dignified opposition. The sheer scale of physical and mental ill-health and of premature death cannot be measured with clinical certainty. Yet, without doubt, they are serious consequences of the disaster and the injustices that followed. However strong are individuals, however supportive are alliances and however determined are campaigns, in examining the disaster and all that followed, the evidence presented in *Hillsborough: The Truth* indicts a system that privileges the interests of the powerful over the rights of the powerless. When major institutions are under threat, however, it remains a system that sacrifices, rather than realises, the principles of natural justice.

Chapter Thirteen

TWO DECADES ON

The previous chapter acknowledges the consistently dignified manner in which the Hillsborough families and survivors conducted their campaign for truth, seeking acknowledgement and justice in the face of seemingly endless pressure inflicted by their critics, often in the most public circumstances. As more bereaved relatives and survivors suffered physical and psychological illness, many forced into early retirement through trauma-related stress, it was clear that the destructive impact of Hillsborough extended beyond the deaths of the 96. It was a debilitating combination rooted in the tragic circumstances and immediate aftermath of the disaster, the deep-seated failings and injustices of state investigative and legal processes, and the prevalence of the view, widely held outside Merseyside, that the horror of death and survival was self-inflicted. Despite this appalling travesty of natural justice, the families and survivors remained resolute in their determination to challenge the Government, state institutions and an ambivalent media seemingly impervious to their resilient struggle. Unexpectedly, this came to a head on 15 April 2009 at Anfield. It was the 20th anniversary memorial service.

I arrived at the ground as dawn was breaking, invited to anchor the early-morning news show for BBC Radio 5 Live. For three hours national news was interspersed with pitch-side interviews, features and commentary. By mid morning I had given over 30 live interviews for national and international radio and television. The new edition of *Hillsborough: The Truth*, alongside several lengthy features I had written for various newspapers, contributed to a wider appreciation beyond Merseyside of the depth, detail and consequences of cumulative injustices that had come to blight so many people's lives.

As afternoon arrived so did the people. From Merseyside and across Britain, Ireland and Europe they came in unprecedented numbers for the mid-afternoon service held at the front of the Liverpool Kop, which seats approximately 12,000. The service is always attended by all staff and players – past and present – of Liverpool Football Club, which refuses to play a fixture on the 15 April. For the 20th anniversary the stadium opened its doors to over 30,000, exceeding all expectations. As the service began people were still taking their seats, quietly and solemnly, in time for the minute's silence at 3.06 p.m. – the moment the 1989 match was abandoned.

Over the years the format of the annual memorial service, broadcast live internationally on television, has changed little. Multi-denominational and accompanied by the Love and Joy Gospel Choir, it opens with the hymn 'Abide With Me', followed immediately by a reading of the names of the 96 who died from the Book of Remembrance. As each name echoes around the cavernous stadium a candle is lit in dedication. At precisely 3.06 p.m. the crowd stands, as one, in silence. Then a song of reflection and the First Reading. The poignant Irish hymn 'I Watch the Sunrise', the Second Reading, prayers, the Blessing and 'Amazing Grace' precede an address given by the chair of the Hillsborough Family Support Group. The service always ends with Liverpool's long-since adopted anthem 'You'll Never Walk Alone'. Following Hillsborough the words took on a new meaning. The address, given in 2009 by Margaret Aspinall, provides the Hillsborough Family Support Group with the opportunity to comment on the events of the previous year and review the campaign's progress.

While invited guests deliver the readings, other than the chair's address there are no speeches. In 2009, however, this changed.

Invited by the Hillsborough Family Support Group, Andy Burnham, MP for nearby Leigh and Secretary of State for Culture, Media and Sport, introduced himself as a representative of the Labour Government. As he began his address he was interrupted by a few angry voices. This triggered thousands to rise from their seats singing 'Justice for the 96'. The heckling subsided and a visibly moved but resolute Burnham stated that Hillsborough had been a 'man-made disaster' leaving 'deep wounds that will never be healed'. This was an important recognition of the myth of 'closure' imposed on the bereaved and survivors by those who have not experienced death, survival or both. On behalf of the Prime Minister, Gordon Brown, Burnham praised the 'dignity', 'resolve' and 'remarkable courage' of the bereaved families in coping with their loss while campaigning for justice. The city, he affirmed, had 'unified in a simple statement of defiance', demonstrating a 'spirit of community and solidarity never to be broken no matter how great the adversity'. He concluded: 'Those who died will forever leave their mark on this city and this country.' It was a fitting, heartfelt tribute to the dead and living.

Interviewed soon after his speech, Burnham confirmed 'there has been a major injustice'. Reluctant 'to hold out false hopes', he believed 'strongly that people should have access to the full facts and I am not yet certain that they do'. Together with other Liverpool MPs he called for 'full disclosure of any further documents that have not been put in the public domain and are held by any public body'. The politicians' objective was to negotiate the waiving of the 30-year limitation on access to public documents and Burnham welcomed the serving Chief Constable of South Yorkshire's previously stated commitment to 'review further whether there were any documents that could be put into the public domain'. All other public bodies, said Burnham, 'the ambulance service, the fire service and West Midlands Police

– who had a role in the aftermath' should follow suit, as 'the public interest lies very clearly in full disclosure of all such information, so that the families and others can make their judgement on all the facts'.

That evening the families received collectively the Freedom of the City of Liverpool. At the Town Hall ceremony Andy Burnham reiterated his intention to pursue full disclosure, accompanied by the Prime Minister's written endorsement of the families' campaign. In a letter received by each family, Gordon Brown praised their 'remarkable courage in working together, and with the wider community, to rebuild their lives', recognising they had 'fought for justice and to honour the memory of their loved ones'. He concluded: 'We will never forget those who died, but we continue to take inspiration from the strength shown by those left behind, and by all the people of Liverpool.'

Following this extraordinary turn of events, the Hillsborough Family Support Group met with the Home Secretary. With the support of Merseyside and other local MPs, I worked with the families on a proposal – 'Hillsborough, "Truth Recovery" and Acknowledgement' – which was duly submitted to the Home Office. Based on a comprehensive overview of the issues to be addressed, the proposal demanded full disclosure of all documents relating to: the causes and circumstances of the disaster; the immediate aftermath at the stadium, in the gymnasium (designated a temporary mortuary) and at the Medico–Legal Centre; the emergency services' responses at the stadium (the emergency plan, evacuation) and medical responses at the hospitals; the relationship between the official investigations and inquiries, including the central role played by the West Midlands Police in servicing all investigations and inquiries; the interventions, roles and responsibilities of South Yorkshire Police officers; the Coroner's inquiry; and the conduct and appropriateness of the Stuart-Smith Scrutiny.

The proposal also requested unedited and unredacted

disclosure of all minutes, briefings and contemporaneous records of meetings relevant to the conduct of the inquiries. In addition to meeting the needs of the bereaved and survivors, it proposed that disclosure would increase public awareness and understanding of the circumstances and immediate aftermath of the disaster, its findings published in a comprehensive report. It was a submission derived from the presumption that the 'right to truth' and the 'right to remedy' remain fundamental principles in meeting 'public interest' expectations and obligations. To achieve this end, the cooperation of all statutory and non-statutory agencies would need to be secured. Disclosed documents should be released to families without redaction and analysed by an independent research team. The proposal concluded: 'Prior to publication the report will be submitted to relevant bodies to consult solely on factual accuracy.'

The proposal was bold and radical, requesting a process unprecedented in the scrutiny of official documents or in the review of the legitimacy of previous investigations and inquiries. Behind the scenes the families' voices were having a resounding impact.

* * *

In late October 2009, and again in early December, aware of the negotiations between the Hillsborough Family Support Group and the Home Office, I was approached regarding my possible appointment to a panel that would oversee the disclosure of documents, make recommendations for a publicly available archive and report on its work, illustrating the relevance of disclosure to the wider public understanding of the disaster and its aftermath. After considering the proposed panel membership I raised concerns that, regardless of the professional competence of the then nominees, it did not have the expertise necessary to investigate and analyse a case with the complexity of Hillsborough. I recommended appointments of a lawyer with proven experience of high-profile inquests into deaths in contested circumstances and of an experienced researcher familiar with the details of the disaster. I also stated my reluctance to join a panel without knowing its terms of reference, requesting information on 'the detail of its role, scope, function and proposed operation'. I submitted that a 'thorough analysis of the documents' was essential, 'before, during, after and since the disaster' – throughout the period of the near disaster at Hillsborough in 1981 to the 2000 private prosecution of Duckenfield and Murray. My main concern was that, as with the Stuart-Smith scrutiny, the panel's work would be incorporated into a process that did not meet the families' demands and expectations.

The terms of reference were distributed internally in late December 2009. They noted that the 'disaster was a personal tragedy for hundreds of people and an event of major national and international significance in the subsequent minimisation of safety risks at football matches and similar sporting events'. They affirmed that the 'Government and local agencies in South Yorkshire' were now 'committed to maximum possible public disclosure of governmental and other agency documentation on events surrounding the disaster'. The panel would 'oversee this disclosure process, consulting with the Hillsborough families and statutory agencies where necessary'. Disclosure would be exceptional, giving the panel 'access to Hillsborough documentation held by Government and local agencies relevant to events surrounding the tragedy in advance of the normal 30-year point' for public access. The 'fundamental principles' would be 'full disclosure of documentation and no redaction of content, except in the limited legal and other circumstances outlined in a disclosure protocol'.

The panel's remit reflected the content of the HFSG's proposal, resolving concerns I had raised. It would: 'oversee full public disclosure of relevant government and local information within the limited constraints set out in the accompanying protocol'; 'consult with the Hillsborough families to ensure that the views of those

391

most affected by the tragedy are taken into account'; 'manage the process of public disclosure, ensuring that it takes place initially to the Hillsborough families and other involved parties, in an agreed manner and within a reasonable timescale, before information is made more widely available'; prepare 'options for establishing an archive of Hillsborough documentation, including a catalogue of all central governmental and local public agency information, and a commentary on any information withheld for the benefit of the families or on legal or other grounds'; 'produce a report explaining the work of the panel'. The essential responsibility given to the panel, without which I would have declined membership, committed its eventual report to illustrating '*how the information disclosed adds to public understanding* of the tragedy and its aftermath'. Consequently the work of the panel was not confined to information-gathering and archival dissemination but extended to research analysis and evaluation of the material. While the former objective would bring a mass of material into the public domain, the latter would produce findings based on rigorous inquiry into, and evaluation of, that material.

The 'scope of the disclosure process' was planned 'to cover all documentation held by central government, local government and other public agencies' relating 'directly to events surrounding the Hillsborough tragedy up to and including the Taylor Report, the Lord Stuart-Smith review of Hillsborough papers in 1998–99 [*sic*] and the private prosecution in 2000'. Key agencies listed were 'the police, ambulance service, fire service, coroner and Sheffield City Council'. It was noted that permission would be sought for disclosure of documents pre-1997, when the Labour Government was elected. Exceptions to disclosure included: 'information covered by legal professional privilege'; 'information which public bodies are legally prohibited from disclosing (including information provided in confidence by third parties)'; 'information indicating the views of ministers, where release would prejudice the convention of Cabinet collective responsibility'.

The decision to withhold information would be decided 'on a case-by-case basis by the holding agency' and where possible 'information that cannot be disclosed to the public' would 'be disclosed on a closed and confidential basis to the panel and a description of the information provided for public disclosure'. Rare issues of 'total confidentiality or non-disclosure to the panel' would be resolved by requesting a description of such material for publication from the agency concerned. Redaction of personal identities fell into several categories: 'members of the public who have provided written observations on events associated with the tragedy; civil servants who were not members of the Senior Civil Service at the time the document was produced; police officers who were constables or other ranks up to and including sergeant at the time the document was produced; other junior public employees who were not in a position to determine their agency's response to events prior to, during or in the aftermath of the tragedy'. The panel would prioritise and reflect the 'views of the Hillsborough families' through consultation 'when co-ordinating the publication of distressing or personal information regarding those who died'. Disclosure should not be made 'to any other involved party ahead of the families'.

The disclosure protocol also specified the Government's intentions regarding the content of the panel's report: 'the terms of reference and work of the panel'; 'the information reviewed by the panel and publicly disclosed'; 'the information provided to the independent panel on a closed basis, based on the summary description provided to the independent panel'; 'the withheld information', also based on the summary description; and 'how the information disclosed adds to public understanding of the tragedy and its aftermath'. Finally, the panel's work would be 'supported by a secretariat consisting of officials from the Home Office, Ministry of Justice and The National Archives' and would meet 'in London, Sheffield and Liverpool'.

In December 2009 the Anglican Bishop of Liverpool, the Right Reverend James Jones, was appointed by the Home Secretary as panel chair. In January 2010 I was formally appointed. The letter from the Home Secretary noted my potential contribution across all areas of the panel's work, recognising my 'long-term research in relation to Hillsborough' and my other 'relevant' research on 'disasters and their aftermath'. It focused on my established 'skill in relation to investigative research and documentation', specifically 'regarding the process of disclosure'. I would manage the research, taking the lead role in writing the final report.

The eventual panel membership reflected the professional expertise necessary to negotiate disclosure of documents, research their content and create a public archive: Raju Bhatt, a highly regarded lawyer specialising in inquests involving allegations of abuse of power or neglect of duty within the police service, the prison service and other associated law-enforcement agencies; Christine Gifford, a member of the Advisory Council on National Records and Archives who had advised the Government on the disclosure of highly sensitive material; Katy Jones, an investigative journalist and producer who researched and produced the award-winning drama-documentary *Hillsborough*; Bill Kirkup, a leading public-health specialist and Associate Chief Medical Officer in the Department of Health; Paul Leighton, former Deputy Chief Constable of the Police Service of Northern Ireland; Peter Sissons, well-known BBC and ITN media specialist; and Sarah Tyacke, former Chief Executive of the National Archives of England and Wales, responsible for the establishment of the National Archives.

Following months of negotiation, the Hillsborough Family Support Group (HFSG) welcomed these appointments. A panel secretariat, led by a Home Office senior civil servant, was established to meet regularly with families and other 'interested parties' and negotiate disclosure by contributing organisations including Sheffield-based agencies, public authorities, private companies and individuals. The HFSG Committee attended the panel's inaugural meeting in Liverpool on 4 February 2010, as did representatives of the Hillsborough Justice Campaign and Hope for Hillsborough. The panel met on 35 further occasions before the launch of the Report in September 2012.

During the early months of the panel's work the enormity of the task became apparent. In March 2010 I wrote a detailed timeline of the disaster, from the near tragedy at the 1981 Hillsborough semi-final through to the 2000 private prosecutions of David Duckenfield and Bernard Murray. This was based on an eight-phase framework for analysing disasters I had developed in previous research: historical context; immediate context; circumstances; the 'moment'; rescue and evacuation; immediate aftermath; short-term aftermath; long-term aftermath. This framework allows an analytical approach to all the key issues that contribute to a disaster over time, while also addressing the short-term responses and longer-term consequences. Clearly, people's lives are not conditioned by tightly defined, real-time phases. It was important, however, for the research and analysis of documents to establish a timeline that mapped the day of the disaster through to all that followed – the inquiries, police investigations, civil court cases, coroner's inquests and the private prosecutions – while also placing 'the moment' in its recent historical context.

Documents held and stored by contributing organisations and individuals were in hard copy and filed inconsistently. Accessing the stored material using any systematic method was a challenge, as there had been no coherent nor recognisable archival system used by the organisations and few clues about the documents in their possession. The main archive, primarily South Yorkshire Police material, was held at Sheffield City Archive, where a team was appointed to provide a working inventory of all documents held. This was a time-consuming and laborious process, especially as archivists could not be expected to assess the research significance of the documents they processed.

It was evident that in establishing the panel little thought had been given to developing the in-depth, documentary research necessary to meet the complex demands of analysis required to establish what disclosure would add to public understanding. Within six months the need to appoint an experienced research team became apparent. It was suggested that Home Office researchers could be seconded to support the panel but this was rejected given the involvement of Home Office staff in earlier controversies. Eventually a research team, based at Queen's University, was appointed to focus on the panel's agreed priority areas of inquiry: documentary analysis of all disclosed material relating to the context, circumstances and aftermath of the disaster focusing on crowd safety, policing, the emergency response and medical treatment; analysis of the documentary and case material relating to the inquiries, investigations, inquests and legal proceedings; content analysis of the available print and broadcast media coverage and CCTV recordings.

The researchers worked on hard copies of documents held in Sheffield and London until it was decided that all key documents would be digitised, enabling secure online access to them as they were released. Digitisation was essential to the development of the research and created the basis for the online archive that eventually would be publicly available. Early in 2011, based on research already in the public domain and the previous 12 months' groundwork, the priorities for investigation took shape. As stated above, beyond establishing what was 'known' or available in the public domain at the outset of the panel's work, the terms of reference obligated the panel to show how its research 'added to public understanding'. Twelve significant issues comprised the research framework: policies and practices relevant to safety and regulation at the stadium between 1981 and 1989; the 'moment' of the disaster; the emergency response, medical treatment and the handling of the bereaved and survivors; the pathology, blood-alcohol levels and taking and storage of tissue samples; the parallel civil, criminal and coronial investigations; the civil litigation cases; the conduct of the inquests, the verdicts and judicial reviews; the context and consequences of the 3.15 p.m. cut-off of evidence presented to the inquests; the review and alteration of statements by the police and ambulance service; Stuart-Smith's scrutiny of 'new' evidence; the private prosecutions; the role of the media.

Having established the key issues for the research, relevant documents were accessed, digitised and their content analysed to provide the foundation for the report, its findings, conclusions and recommendations. All disclosed documents were analysed in unredacted form. As established in the agreed protocol, redaction prior to publication or withholding documents from public access applied only in exceptional circumstances, restricted to sensitive personal data – particularly medical records. Documents and material already in the public domain were incorporated into the research. Cross-referencing of content was developed chronologically to construct a comprehensive sequence of events, reflecting the exchange of information and processes of decision-making between and within organisations before and after the disaster. Documents included organisations' internal reports and assessments, all forms of correspondence, transcripts of telephone call and radio transmissions, minutes of meetings, diaries and personal records.

* * *

The projected timescale for the panel's work anticipated publication of the report close to the 23rd anniversary, 15 April 2012. As the sheer volume and complexity of the disclosed material became apparent, and the technical demands of cataloguing, researching and analysing the data expanded, it was clear that the initial schedule could not be achieved. This drew criticism from some campaigners and placed the panel under considerable pressure to explain the delay. Without breaching confidentiality and placing the project at risk, it was not possible to reveal the range of factors underpinning the delay. Continuing negotiation of access to documents and material was complicated. Cataloguing documents from organisations and key individuals was time-consuming and then they had to be read, prioritised, cross-referenced and integrated into the report's eventual chapter structure. This was understood by many of the families and the Hillsborough Family Support Group publicly endorsed a new timeframe, stating that 'getting it right' was the main priority.

As the panel's work progressed it was essential that its focus and content remained confidential. There was constant pressure, particularly from the media, to reveal findings. The panel was aware that even the most apparently innocuous comment could generate and inflame speculation. Behind the scenes the panel faced considerable and immediate dilemmas as the documents were analysed. When the panel was appointed, a steering group representing the contributing agencies was established, funded by Government and chaired by the South Yorkshire Police. A panel representative, supported by the panel's secretariat, met regularly with the steering group to ensure the smooth running of the disclosure process. In the wake of a particularly difficult meeting prior to the research team's appointment it became apparent that a 'research brief' was necessary. This was drafted and negotiated.

The research brief confirmed to the steering group the panel's primary responsibilities within its terms of reference: the establishment of an archive of all available Hillsborough documentation and the production of a report that would add to public under-standing. To this end, therefore, the report would provide analytical overviews of 'all information reviewed by the panel and publicly disclosed' and 'all information provided to the panel on a closed basis and information withheld (based on the summary descriptions provided)'. The steering group was informed that the report would 'not seek to ascribe legal liability, either civil or criminal' and that disclosure would be with the agreement of 'the legal holders of the documentary material'. Documentary research would assist with the establishment of the archive and 'inform the substance of the report' through an evaluation of 'the information disclosed to the panel alongside that already known and in the public domain, to inform public understanding of the disaster and its aftermath'. The research focus would include: 'the context, circumstances and aftermath of the disaster, focusing particularly on crowd safety, policing, the emergency response and medical treatment'; 'the documentary and case material established by the inquiries, investigations, inquests and legal proceedings and their aftermath'; and 'the significance of media representation and CCTV recordings'. The research brief formed the basis of the procedural agreement between the panel and the steering group.

As the research progressed it emerged that the bodies of some of the deceased had tissue samples removed during pathological examination. At the time, this was regular practice in the course of establishing the precise cause of death. While this practice became unlawful following a series of cases, most notably the retention of organs and tissue at Alder Hey Children's Hospital, in 1989 relatives would not have been informed about the removal and the eventual disposal of tissue samples. Given growing public awareness and concern about organ retention, over time several Hillsborough families had requested information from the hospitals about retention of samples. While no organs were recorded as being retained, it transpired that in ten cases tissue had been taken and preserved.

Maintaining strict confidentiality, the panel contacted each family concerned, offering to provide immediately whatever information it held in accordance with the family's wishes. It was considered inappropriate to wait until the eventual publication of the report to reveal this information. As the panel concluded: 'While sharing this information with families presented them with a potential decision on what to do with remaining tissue material, not providing the opportunity for disclosure would amount to a failure in a duty of care.' Nine families were visited and given details on the post-mortem examinations. Their wishes regarding the retained tissue samples were met. The final set of tissue samples, not labelled, could not be identified despite attempts to match DNA. The panel was determined to respect privacy but information about this process was leaked to the media. It was decided to 'make no further comment concerning this issue' as it 'remains a confidential matter for the bereaved families directly involved'.

A further sensitive issue relating to medical evidence concerned post-mortem examination records on all who died. In response to the long-standing controversy discussed in earlier chapters regarding crush and traumatic asphyxia, the estimated time of each death, and the potential for recovery and survival, these records were revisited by panel member Dr Bill Kirkup, supported by a leading professor of forensic pathology. The details of each death, however, comprise personal medical records and the panel's responsibility was to maintain confidentiality. As will be discussed later, the findings regarding prolonged survival of a significant number of those who died raise serious generic concerns about the rescue and response at the time of the disaster.

* * *

One of the most controversial issues faced by the panel arose as a consequence of a Freedom of Information request submitted by the BBC to the Information Commissioner prior to the panel's appointment. Limited in scope, this requested access to Cabinet papers only for April 1989. In July 2011 the Information Commissioner, Christopher Graham, determined that 'the specific content of the information in question would add to public knowledge and understanding about the reaction of various parties to that event, including the government of the day, in the early aftermath'. His comments immediately raised public concern that significant information relating to the

Government's response to Hillsborough had been withheld. Because the BBC's request had been lodged before the panel's appointment, the Commissioner stated that it should be granted. His decision failed to address the potential negative impact on the panel's negotiation of access to a wider range of significant documents.

While realising its intentions might be misinterpreted, on the advice of the panel the Cabinet Office appealed the Commissioner's ruling. Its appeal stated that, in the circumstances, it was 'in the public interest for the process that is under way through the Hillsborough Independent Panel to be allowed to take its course', thus protecting the agreed principle of information disclosure 'to the Hillsborough families first'. Ironically, at that point the panel was in the process of securing disclosure of *all* Cabinet and government documents relating to Hillsborough, rather than solely Cabinet minutes for April 1989. It was the panel's objective, reiterated on numerous occasions to the campaign groups, not to drip-feed documents into the public domain but to secure the release of all documents in their appropriate context throughout the two decades following the disaster.

On 21 August 2011 the panel considered it necessary to 'affirm its independence of government in carrying out its research, publishing an analytical report and establishing a comprehensive public archive of documents and other materials'. It stated its commitment to the 'maximum public disclosure of all documents relating to the context, circumstances and aftermath of the disaster', noting that its 'guiding principle' was disclosure to Hillsborough families first, then to the public. All documents would be published through this process following 'detailed analysis by the panel's researchers under the direction of a panel sub-group and led by Professor Phil Scraton'. The panel noted that Cabinet Office documents were just 'one element of a highly complex range of material accessed from organisations and digitised for eventual release into the public domain as part of the comprehensive archive'. Within the panel's eventual report, analysis of the documents would be conducted 'in that context'.

Challenged publicly on the issue of withholding information, I stated unequivocally that the panel was not a 'gatekeeper', nor was it the panel's role 'to determine what is or is not published – our responsibility is full public disclosure'. I continued: 'Our role is not to filter information but to secure access to documents that otherwise would have been restricted for years to come. We are engaged in an unprecedented process and our priorities are the families, the survivors and the broader public interest'. Responding to a letter from Andy Burnham, then Shadow Health Secretary, the Prime Minister confirmed that the Hillsborough Independent Panel retained the full support of the Coalition Government. David Cameron commented, 'the Government is wholly committed to full disclosure of the Hillsborough information that it holds' and 'Cabinet papers, along with all other relevant Government papers, have been released to the Hillsborough Independent Panel'. He called for the 'upmost respect' for the panel and the bereaved families, reiterating the Government's commitment to 'full and public disclosure' first to the families 'prior to wider publication'. Unity, he maintained, was essential in assisting the panel to complete 'its important work'.

This very public debate had triggered doubts among some campaigners and at one point it was stated that the BBC was to be trusted more than the panel. When the research was at its most demanding, the controversy threatened to derail the very process campaigners were eager to protect. Although the panel had achieved a guarantee of full disclosure of all documents and materials held by Government, the UK's first ever e-petition was launched demanding: 'Full government disclosure and publi-cation of all documents, discussions and reports relating to the 1989 Hillsborough disaster'. It was successful, gaining well over the 100,000 signatures necessary to secure a Parliamentary debate. In the House of Commons on 17 October 2011 Steve

Rotheram, MP for Liverpool Walton, introduced the debate with an eloquent and sharply focused speech.

Replying for the Government, Home Secretary Theresa May affirmed that that 'the right way to release the papers is through the Hillsborough Independent Panel – to the families first and then to the public'. It was not for politicians, nor the media, to 'filter' the documents. She guaranteed 'full disclosure' to the panel, 'including Cabinet minutes'. Documents, she continued, 'should be uncensored and unredacted'. She confirmed that 'full unredacted Cabinet Office papers on Hillsborough have already been made available to the panel', including 'minutes of the meetings of the Cabinet immediately following the disaster'. The panel previously had not been able to reveal this information as it would have breached confidentiality. The Home Secretary emphasised the defining principle of 'full publication and minimal redaction . . . the panel seeing all of the papers, uncensored and unredacted as the families have rightly demanded: the whole loaf, not snippets. I stand ready to do anything I can to aid the independent panel in completing its task.'

Following an extensive and moving debate the motion was carried without opposition: 'That this House calls for the full disclosure of all government-related documents, including Cabinet minutes, relating to the 1989 Hillsborough disaster; requires that such documentation be uncensored and without redaction; and further calls for the families of the 96 and the Hillsborough Independent Panel to have unrestricted access to that information'. Already in possession of the disputed documents, the panel's research continued, fortified by the Coalition Government's very public commitment to full cooperation. While the negotiation of access to documents and their analysis continued, it was suggested by some that the delay in the report's projected release date raised questions about the panel's progress and competence.

In March 2012 the panel released further reassurances of its resolve and intention to secure 'maximum possible disclosure of all documents relating to the disaster and its aftermath, first to the Hillsborough families and then to the wider public'. It recognised that leaks relating to tissue samples, generated outside the panel, and criticisms of the panel's work had caused families and survivors 'understandable distress'. Yet it would not deny or confirm the validity of 'snippets of information' published in the media, nor would it present details of its research into disclosed documents 'piecemeal'. It stated, again, that in preparing a comprehensive, analytical and rigorous report all facts would be presented in context. Given doubts about confidentiality, the panel noted that while it consulted regularly with families to update them on the progress of its work, it did not disclose documents or information to them. Addressing the specific matter of tissue samples, it confirmed that the 'sole exception' to its rule had been the discovery of their retention following post-mortems, noting its ethical responsibility to share this information only with the bereaved families concerned as soon as the information was discovered. Additionally, the panel confirmed that the research team continued to receive new and significant documents, thus the report's completion and publication would be delayed until autumn 2012. This was accepted by the Hillsborough Family Support Group.

* * *

The final significant challenge negotiated by the panel related to the process of factual accuracy checking of the report's content by contributing agencies. It is established practice on completion of research into the operation and performance of organisations to provide them with a draft report, inviting comments on factual accuracy and interpretation. In the panel's process, because of its commitment to the 'families first' principle, submission of a full draft report to the contributing organisations would have breached its terms of reference. Yet the panel had also agreed that there would be 'no surprises' on matters of fact. In establishing the factual accuracy checking process the documentation provided to each organisation would remove all chapter headings and subheadings. Each of the main contributing organisations would be provided only with the text directly related to its operation, where the content relied specifically on the disclosure of documents from that organisation. They would not be given text that either contextualised or evaluated their disclosed material, as these were matters of interpretation. Thus factual accuracy checking was a process to establish accurate presentation of the disclosed material, not a process through which interpretation or evaluation of the material would be negotiated.

Following discussions with representatives of the lead organisations, who voiced concern about the perceived limitations of this process, meetings were held with each key organisation separately: the South Yorkshire Police; the South Yorkshire Coroner (West District); the Yorkshire Ambulance Service; and Sheffield City Council. Limited to reviewing the text derived directly from disclosed documents to ensure its representation was fair and factually accurate, hard-copy text extracts were provided and retrieved at the close of each meeting. Text was not distributed to representatives outside the meetings, nor did they have online access. Modifications to the text were restricted to matters of factual accuracy and objections concerning interpretation of the documents were rejected. Representatives of two organisations objected to the process, arguing that they could not establish whether or not the documents they had disclosed had been represented or interpreted fairly. After further protracted negotiations, changes suggested by the organisations were taken into account and the draft report modified where they concerned factual accuracy.

Just weeks before the report's publication, documents concerning the relationship in the aftermath of Hillsborough between the South Yorkshire Police, a local press agency and national newspapers were finally disclosed. These documents had taken many months to track down. They were central to understanding the prevalent popular discourse that dominated the immediate aftermath and popularised serious allegations regarding the fans' behaviour, ticketlessness and drunkenness. As will be discussed in the final chapter, these eleventh-hour disclosures to the panel not only established how myths originated and were transmitted, inevitably influencing subsequent investigations and inquiries, but also they shaped public opinion, turning sympathy into condemnation.

Chapter Fourteen

THE TRUTH WILL OUT

Wednesday, 12 September 2012 was the day the Hillsborough families and survivors had anticipated with hope. A day when their patient wait for the Hillsborough Independent Panel's report would confirm the 'truth' as they knew it, bringing official acknowledgement of the injustices they had endured and public recognition of their suffering. The launch of the panel's report, in closed session to the families first, was scheduled for 9 a.m. in the Nave – known as the 'Well' – of Liverpool's Anglican Cathedral, to be followed immediately by the Prime Minister's response beamed live from the House of Commons to the families.

I visited the cathedral the previous evening with Bill Kirkup to familiarise ourselves with the environment. A stage had been constructed, the width of the Well, accommodating a lectern and seats for the panel. Looking out from the lectern the location was impressive, the rows of chairs for the many bereaved family members nestling in the Well below, the cathedral's impressive Gothic-style pillars imposing solemnity appropriate to the occasion. I had harboured reservations about locating the launch in a cathedral associated with one denomination in a city historically divided by religion. I also had concerns for those with no religious beliefs. My reservations were not shared by the families and as we sound-checked the audio equipment they dissolved. It was a magnificent venue. I requested that the pink neon-lit phrase 'I felt you and I knew you loved me' above the doors be switched off. An installation by Tracey Emin, it seemed inappropriate in the circumstances.

I returned early next morning as dawn broke. The cathedral stands high on the city's south side: a view I know so well – across the Mersey to Birkenhead and Wallasey, to the Welsh hills beyond and out to the Irish Sea. I paused on the steps to take it all in, places of my past, and thought of the families and survivors leaving their homes or hotels to embark on their journeys. For 23 years and five months, almost to the day, they had waited to hear the words I now knew so well, to view the PowerPoint slides written and uploaded for the presentation, and to receive the 395-page report. I thought of those who would not be with us, whose lives had been taken prematurely by the grief of loss and pain of injustice.

Inside the cathedral the final preparations were under way. Panel members and the secretariat arrived; we shared a light breakfast. For the first time we held the hard copy of the report in our hands. It had been driven overnight to Liverpool ready for distribution to the families, survivors and, eventually, to the waiting journalists. What for months had been a virtual reality, restricted to the multiple edited versions on my computer, was now a weighty physical reality. It was an impressive feat of production, with every textual reference within the online version live-linked to the relevant document held in the digital archive. Scanning the pages, I realised the families were arriving in the reception area. I went to meet them, to share tea and a journey's end.

Soon we were together in the Well: the panel members on stage, the secretariat to the sides and the families seated below. No journalists were present and what followed was neither filmed nor recorded. We had remained resolutely committed to the 'families first' principle. I was aware that at that moment the Prime Minister was being briefed. Bishop James Jones, the panel's chair, welcomed the families and introduced the panel. During the next 90 minutes I delivered the research findings, pausing only for Bill Kirkup's meticulous presentation of the conclusions drawn from medical evidence. There was silence throughout, interspersed with occasional gasps in response to the revelations. As I finished there was a silent pause; time appeared to freeze. Then families rose, many in tears, to deliver a sustained standing ovation. The report was distributed to the families, the Prime Minister made his parliamentary address, we presented our findings to survivors from the Hillsborough Justice Campaign, followed by a press conference in the Lady Chapel where journalists had received the report an hour earlier.

* * *

As stated in the previous chapter, the panel's report provides an overview of 'what was known' prior to its work, reviewing previous official inquiries and reports into crowd safety at sports venues. It reflects how safety at soccer stadia had been compromised by the introduction of pens on standing terraces, inhibiting egress in emergencies, and by a crowd-control mindset driven by policing priorities viewed through the 'lens of hooliganism' discussed earlier. Such compromised safety was known, its risks foreseeable. Yet concerns raised in previous official reports were ignored, 'corralling' and 'penning' fans adopted as central elements of police crowd-control strategy throughout the 1970s and 1980s.

The report's overview of what was known notes the modifications made to Hillsborough's Leppings Lane terrace during the 1980s, describes the circumstances of the disaster, the rescue and evacuation, and the use of the gymnasium as a temporary mortuary. It reviews the Taylor Inquiry, the civil actions, the decision not to prosecute organisations or individuals, the inquests, the judicial review, the Stuart-Smith scrutiny and the private prosecutions of Duckenfield and Murray. It also considers the significance of the review and alteration of police statements established in 1999 by my research for the first edition of *Hillsborough: The Truth*.

The core of the report, however, reflects the comprehensive research into the disclosed documents – delivered in 12 detailed and fully referenced chapters. For the first time the period between 1981, when the near fatal disaster on the Leppings Lane terrace at an FA Cup semi-final was averted, and 1989 is comprehensively researched and analysed. Documents disclosed to the panel reveal the significance of decisions taken throughout this period by the stadium owners (Sheffield Wednesday Football Club), the club's safety consultants (Eastwood and Partners), the local authority (Sheffield City Council) and the South Yorkshire Police. These focus on terrace modifications and their consequences for the safe management of the crowd. Every decision taken, every modification made, all available correspondence, is published.

The report states: 'the safety of the crowd admitted to the terrace was compromised at every level: access to the turnstiles from the public highway; the condition and adequacy of the turnstiles; the management of the crowd by the SYP [South Yorkshire Police] and the SWFC [Sheffield Wednesday Football Club] stewards; alterations to the terrace, particularly the construction of pens; the condition and placement of crush barriers; access to the central pens via a tunnel descending at a 1 in 6 gradient; emergency egress from the pens via small gates in the perimeter fence; and lack of precise monitoring of crowd capacity within the pens'.

Analysis of the documents reveals that the terrace failed to meet the minimum standards established in the Green Guide (governing safety at sports grounds). The local Advisory Group for Safety at Sports Grounds conducted inadequate and poorly recorded inspections. Turnstile counters registered an overall figure for admission to the terrace but the construction of pens rendered the counters irrelevant as the distribution between pens was not monitored. Although the fire service considered emergency evacuation through the narrow gate at the front of each pen to be inadequate, its assessment was ignored.

Overcrowding at semi-finals in 1987 and 1988 demonstrated inherent dangers rooted in structural and organisational deficiencies. The report concludes that the 'risks were known and the fatal crush in 1989 was foreseeable'.

The report also focuses on the immediate context and circumstances in which the disaster occurred, scrutinising the South Yorkshire Police operational orders for previous semi-finals. It notes the documented briefings at which senior officers emphasised the potential for crowd disorder, drunkenness, ticketlessness and the behaviour of Liverpool fans. Research into the disclosed documents 'reveals that the flaws in responding to the emerging crisis on the day were rooted in institutional tension within and between organisations reflected in: a policing and stewarding mindset predominantly concerned with crowd disorder; the failure to realise the consequences of opening exit gates to relieve congestion at the turnstiles; the failure to manage the crowd's entry and allocation between the pens; the failure to anticipate the consequences within the central pens of not sealing the tunnel; the delay in realising that the crisis in the central pens was a consequence of overcrowding rather than crowd disorder'.

Custom and practice for crowd management and crowd safety at Hillsborough FA Cup semi-finals are identified as emerging from an uneasy relationship between the club and the police. The documents reveal complacency in the roles and responsibilities adopted by both organisations. While police operational orders concentrated on crowd control, police interventions were informal and unrecorded in the records of post-match debriefings. They included checking tickets and filtering fans as they arrived outside the stadium, redirecting fans to side pens to avoid overcrowding, and closing the tunnel at its mouth when the central pens appeared to be full. Despite their profound significance for crowd safety, these actions were not formally recorded, neither were they integrated into subsequent operational orders nor included in senior officers' pre-match briefings.

The findings show that, throughout the 1980s, 'considerable ambiguity' in the allocation and operation of crowd-management responsibilities between the police and the club remained unaddressed. Crowd management 'was viewed exclusively through a lens of potential crowd disorder'. As the 'ambiguity was not resolved despite problems at previous semi-finals', the club and the police 'were unprepared for the disaster that unfolded on the terraces on 15 April 1989'.

In the immediate aftermath the South Yorkshire Police initiated an internal inquiry, ahead of the appointment of Lord Justice Taylor as chair of the judicial inquiry. The report analyses the role and operation of the West Midlands Police in conducting the criminal investigation while serving the judicial inquiry and the coronial inquiry – distinct investigations operating in parallel. In its analysis of minutes of the initial meetings, it is clear that, 'from the outset' the South Yorkshire Police 'sought to establish a case emphasising exceptional levels of drunkenness and aggression among Liverpool fans, alleging that many arrived at the stadium late, without tickets and determined to force entry'. The day after the disaster, in Sheffield, senior officers presented this account to Prime Minister Margaret Thatcher and Home Secretary Douglas Hurd.

The research into the disclosed documents reveals details of investigations by the Health and Safety Executive (HSE) conducted after the disaster. Its role was to assess the 'technical aspects of the incident'. It concluded that the club's safety engineers had set 'the safe maximum capacity of the pens too high' – particularly for Pen 3 'where most of the deaths had occurred', which 'was substantially higher than the Green Guide maximum'. The panel's report states that not only were the capacities of the terrace and each pen 'significantly over-calculated but the structural alterations between 1981 and 1985 had been ignored'. The HSE investigation established that the safety barriers on the terraces were significantly lower than the recommended height.

While the assumed capacity for the central pens was 1,200 and 1,000, taking the alterations to the terrace and the positioning and height of the barriers into account, 'the allowable numbers . . . would drop to 389 and 540'. The crowd was estimated to be well in excess of 2,000 in each pen.

Consistent with the findings of my earlier research, the panel's report concludes that the 'restricted approach to the Leppings Lane end [of the stadium] and the comparatively low number of turnstiles resulted in inevitable congestion and delays in entering the stadium at capacity matches'. Forty-five per cent of the stadium's total capacity was expected to enter the stadium through 28 per cent of the available turnstiles at the Leppings Lane end of the stadium, where the crush outside led to the opening of Gate C – 24,447 fans had to pass through 23 adjacent turnstiles. Thus the number of fans processed through each of these turnstiles was between 2.9 and 3.5 times higher than turnstiles elsewhere in the stadium. The panel's report states, the HSE's 'calculated rate of admission shows that the crowd could not have completed entering the ground until approximately 40 minutes after the kick-off'.

In two post-disaster reports the HSE concluded that the Leppings Lane terrace was structurally deficient on every significant safety factor: restricted access outside the stadium; inadequate turnstile provision; steep tunnel entry to the central pens; failure to adapt capacity to accommodate the construction of pens; deficiencies in safety barriers – the collapsed barrier in Pen 3 where most deaths occurred was over 60 years old; inhibited escape via the perimeter fence at the front of each pen. These structural deficiencies were endorsed by the technical advisor to the judicial inquiry. Within weeks of the disaster the HSE report established the combination of known, potentially lethal factors that had rendered the central pens structurally unsafe. Based on technical evidence and its assessment prior to the disaster, the risk had been identified by the safety engineers and ignored by the club.

As stated previously, the emergency response to the unfolding disaster received minimal attention from the investigations, inquiries and inquests. It was assumed that it had been positive, efficient and effective in chaotic circumstances. Until the panel's research there had been no independent review or evaluation of operational performance or effectiveness, in part because it had been accepted that once bodies had been compressed, death was inevitable and relatively swift. The disclosed documents, however, show that rescue was inhibited by the emergency services' failure to put into operation the major incident plan, not least because there was a 'substantial delay in recognising that there were mass casualties'. Effective response was 'significantly hampered by lack of leadership, co-ordination, prioritisation of casualties and equipment'.

While senior police officers initially misinterpreted and misrepresented the severe crush as crowd disorder, thereby losing an important opportunity for rescue and recovery, Ambulance Service officers seated in the stadium as club guests 'were slower than police to identify and realise the severity of the crush despite being close to the central pens'. At this critical moment there was a failure to activate the major incident plan and radio communications were inadequate. There was no organisation of triage to identify, assess and prioritise those most in need of medical attention and basic rescue equipment was unavailable. Criticised by off-duty doctors and nurses who attended the match as spectators and participated in rescue and recovery, the South Yorkshire Metropolitan Ambulance Service (SYMAS) was defensive. The panel's report concludes that SYMAS 'responded vigorously to any criticism expressed publicly'. Further, 'its attempts to portray criticism as the views of ill-informed and impulsive doctors caught up in the emotions of the disaster' were 'factually incorrect. Although given wide credence, the SYMAS responses were misleading'.

The panel's research considers that medical evidence presented to the Taylor Inquiry and to the inquests suggesting that the deceased were 'irreversibly and fatally injured in the initial crush, and no response could have changed the outcome' was 'flawed and some, partially asphyxiated, survived for a significant period'. Having examined in detail the pathology reports, it confirms that those who suffered partial asphyxiation did not die minutes after being crushed and injured, concluding that 'a swifter, more appropriate, better focused and properly equipped response had the potential to save lives'. Thus, the medical evidence presented to the inquests asserting an 'unvarying pattern of death within minutes of the crushing' was flawed.

In the 1999 edition of this book I criticised the failure of the Taylor Inquiry to 'fully appreciate the level of care administered at the ground and at the hospitals', noting that using the gymnasium as a temporary mortuary and taking blood-alcohol levels should have been thoroughly evaluated. Taylor unquestioningly accepted the reliability of the medical evidence. This was an error of judgement, which extended to the inquests and the coroner's decision to restrict evidence of substance to 3.15 p.m. As stated earlier, this restriction implied 'that all who died did so inevitably, regardless of the treatment they received or deficiencies in planning which might have saved lives'. It rendered insufficient the coroner's inquiry and publicly promoted the erroneous view, presented as scientific fact, that all who died could not have been saved whatever the intervention.

Yet, as was proposed in my previously published research, there was a continuum of recovery. Some people regained consciousness relatively quickly, some after being left for dead and others at the hospitals. Two young men, including Tony Bland whose case is discussed in Chapter 12, were left in a persistent vegetative state – never regaining consciousness – starkly illustrating a continuum from survival through to death and the fundamental flaw in the coroner's interpretation of the medical evidence. As noted in earlier chapters, the judicial review of the inquest verdicts, despite expert opinion to the contrary, supported the coroner's position and considered his conduct of the inquests exemplary. Enduring doubt, however, informed the panel's decision to review the medical evidence, focusing particularly on conclusions drawn from the pathologists' reports.

On the panel's behalf, Dr Bill Kirkup accessed the medical records of all who died. His detailed analysis of the evidence dismisses the proposition 'of a single, unvarying and rapid pattern of death in all cases' as 'unsustainable'. Re-examination of the records establishes that some people died 'after a significant period of unconsciousness during which they might have been able to be resuscitated, or conversely may have succumbed to a new event such as inappropriate positioning' of their bodies. Dr Kirkup's precise reassessment of the medical evidence, in consultation with a senior pathologist, refuted the pathologists' initial assessment of consistent injury leading to immediate unconsciousness and swift death. As my previous research had suggested, the coroner conflated two distinct conditions – traumatic asphyxia and crush asphyxia. The findings are disturbing, providing 'clear evidence from the post-mortem reports that 28 of those who died did not have traumatic asphyxia with obstruction of the blood circulation, and asphyxia may have taken significantly longer to be fatal'. Further, separate evidence showed 'that in 31 the heart and lungs had continued to function after the crush, and in 16 of these this was for a prolonged period'.

The analysis is conclusive – many of those who suffered asphyxia and died might have been saved. Further, if they were placed in a position that restricted their airways, their recovery would have been compromised. The new analysis reveals that 'it cannot be concluded that life or death was inevitably determined by events prior to 3.15 p.m., or that no new fatal event could have occurred after that time'. This finding, based on a systematic review of the disclosed medical evidence, significantly undermines the coroner's decision to eliminate evidence relating to rescue and evacuation. As discussed in Chapter 8, it also affirms the judicial review's failure to accept the reliability of alternative expert medical opinions submitted by the families.

My previous research (see Chapter 7) strenuously criticised the coroner's decision to record and publish blood-alcohol levels of all who died, including children. The disclosed documents contain no justification for such an unprecedented decision, particularly as the figure of 80mg/100ml – known colloquially as the 'limit' for drivers – was used by the coroner, reinforced by media coverage, as a significant marker. At the inquests a statistical correlation was made between spectators' times of arrival and the amount of alcohol consumed. The inference, widely reported, was that those who arrived closer to kick-off had consumed considerable quantities of alcohol, thus contributing to the fatal crush. Following close analysis of the pathological evidence the panel's finding is emphatic: 'the attempt to draw statistical correlation between the time of arrival and alcohol level was fundamentally flawed in six respects, and no such link could be deduced'.

The panel's data analysis shows that alcohol consumption among those who died was 'unremarkable', concluding that the highly publicised correlation was 'inappropriate and misleading'. Further, criminal-record checks were conducted using the Police National Computer in an 'attempt to impugn the reputation of the deceased'. Some survivors who had been injured also had blood-alcohol levels taken, yet this was not recorded in hospital files. The report concludes: 'There was no evidence to support the proposition that alcohol played any part in the genesis of the disaster and it is regrettable that those in positions of responsibility created and promoted a portrayal of drunkenness as contributing to the occurrence of the disaster and the ensuing loss of life without substantiating evidence'.

As stated earlier, the coroner's decision to hold the inquests in two parts was, at the time, contentious. Chapter 7 recounts the unprecedented process adopted at the mini-inquests, through which the evidence presented on each of the deceased by West Midlands Police investigating officers was restricted to summarised statements. Although presented to the jury, it could not be examined. Analysis of the documents raises concerns about the context in which that decision was taken, the part played by West Midlands' investigating officers and the compliance of the families' lawyers. This extends to issues raised by bereaved families regarding restrictions on the examination of evidence relating directly to their loved ones. Further, it questions the appropriateness of the relationship between the police investigators and the coroner.

Between the preliminary and generic inquests the decision was taken not to proceed with criminal prosecutions. This placed intense pressure on the generic inquests. Families were led to believe that the generic stage would offer an opportunity to examine evidence under oath that could lead to a verdict of unlawful killing. In contrast, the South Yorkshire Police identified the generic stage as offering 'an opportunity to use the court to respond to criticisms levelled against the force and its senior officers by Lord Justice Taylor's Interim Report'. Consequently, the generic stage was adversarial in atmosphere, content and outcome. Although Taylor had concluded that drunkenness played no part in causing the disaster, the coroner was unconvinced. Consistent with his initial decision to record blood-alcohol levels, in selecting and sequencing of evidence at the generic stage he prioritised alcohol consumption, 'late' arrival of fans and alleged aggressive behaviour.

The documents disclosed to the panel by the coroner and other parties reveal the unreliability of the inquest process on several grounds: the limitations on evidence and its examination at the 'mini-inquests'; privileged police access to information gathered by the criminal investigation; imbalance in legal representation; and the imposition of the 3.15 p.m. cut-off. Based on its analysis of documents, the panel's findings support the bereaved families' concerns regarding sufficiency of inquiry. The generic hearing was a platform, as promised by the South Yorkshire Chief Constable, to revive and promote the spectres of drunkenness, ticketlessness and violent or abusive behaviour. At the inquests, senior police officers who had been discredited and severely criticised at the judicial inquiry repeated unsubstantiated allegations without challenge. Inevitably, these allegations were reported widely in the press.

In the final chapter of its report, the panel 'responds to bereaved families' and survivors' concerns to demonstrate how the documents disclosed to the panel' inform 'public understanding of the background to, and sources of, the initial media coverage'. Accordingly, the panel's research focused on the processes through which unsubstantiated allegations, strongly rejected by Taylor, resurfaced and were widely disseminated. Its findings are unequivocal. The initial allegations were made by South Yorkshire Police officers, the Police Federation Secretary and Irvine Patnick MP to a local Sheffield Press Agency, White's, and then disseminated to all national newspapers. The disclosed documents reveal the extent of an orchestrated campaign 'to develop and publicise a version of events that focused on several police officers' allegations of drunkenness, ticketlessness and violence among a large number of Liverpool fans'. This 'extended beyond the media to Parliament'. The panel's report notes that, 'from the mass of documents, television and CCTV coverage disclosed to the panel there is no evidence to support these allegations other than a few isolated examples of aggressive or verbally abusive behaviour clearly reflecting fans' frustration and desperation'.

The documents reveal how, on the morning *The Sun* published its notorious front page, the South Yorkshire Police Federation held a meeting in a Sheffield restaurant addressed by its secretary, whose priority in the days following the disaster had been to put 'our side of the story to the press and media'. He commented that the Chief Constable had stated while 'the truth could not come from him', the Police Federation had a 'free hand' in promoting police interests. As the meeting progressed, the Chief Constable arrived. Following discussion of evidence-gathering and responses to the media, he said the force had 'to catch it whilst it is hot . . . we must pull our case together and present our case to the inquiry team'. His senior team were 'preparing a defence . . . to prepare a rock-solid story'. The police 'would be exonerated' and 'if anybody should be blamed, it should be the drunken ticketless individuals'.

Taylor's interim report, however, heavily criticised senior police officers who gave evidence to the inquiry and rejected their claims that drunkenness and fans' aggressive behaviour had contributed to the disaster. Soon after its publication, the Police Federation held a meeting in Sheffield with its parliamentary representative, Michael Shersby MP. The report was criticised as 'unfair and unbalanced', and Shersby 'was invited to assist in the development of a counter attack to repudiate' its findings. Throughout the meeting, police officers 'repeated allegations of abuse, drunkenness and violence', dismissing the Taylor report as a 'whitewash'. This echoed the Chief Constable's public criticisms of Taylor, and he warned that a 'different picture would emerge at the inquests'.

Like Taylor, the panel's analysis 'found no evidence among the vast number of disclosed documents and many hours of video material to verify the serious allegations of exceptional levels of drunkenness, ticketlessness or violence among Liverpool fans'. It refutes allegations that 'fans had conspired to arrive late at the stadium and force entry', finding 'no evidence that they stole from the dead and dying'. The documents show that, while some fans 'became frustrated by the inadequate response to the unfolding tragedy', the 'vast majority of fans on the pitch assisted in rescuing and evacuating the injured and the dead'.

The report provides 153 key points illustrating how analysis of the disclosed documents 'adds to public understanding' of the disaster. Concluding my presentation in the cathedral, I read from the report's foreword:

> The disclosed documents show that multiple factors were responsible for the deaths of the 96 victims of the Hillsborough tragedy and that the fans were not the cause of the disaster . . . that the bereaved families met a series of obstacles in their search for justice . . . The panel produces this report without any presumption of where it will lead. But it does so in the profound hope that greater transparency will bring to the families and to the wider public a greater understanding of the tragedy and its aftermath. For it is only with this transparency that the families and survivors, who have behaved with such dignity, can with some sense of truth and justice cherish the memory of their 96 loved ones.

The bereaved families and survivors were overwhelmed by the unqualified exoneration of those who died and survived, combined with the clear attribution of responsibility for the disaster to profound and foreseeable institutional failings within the custom and practice of the public and private agencies involved. Their response was immediate:

> We have campaigned for 23 years for this but we never thought it would happen. It's unbelievable – not the findings but that it was all there and is now made public. All along we've been lied to, even our own lawyers let us down, but now it's there for all to see.

> Deep down I knew it. I was there [at the stadium] and saw what happened with my own eyes. However much I had faith in the panel, I never thought the truth would come out. But now the Government has to listen.

We've been in this situation so many times. Lawyers, politicians, journalists – they all told us they believed the system had failed, that there was no justice and they made their promises. Yet there was always a 'but'. Today it was all said, straight out, and there were no 'buts'.

After the presentation of the panel's findings, the families viewed a live feed to the cathedral from a packed House of Commons as the Prime Minister, David Cameron, delivered his response. In a detailed commentary he accepted without reservation the report's content and findings, stating:

Mr Speaker, with the weight of the new evidence in this report, it is right for me today as Prime Minister to make a proper apology to the families of the 96 for all they have suffered over the past 23 years. Indeed, the new evidence that we are presented with today makes clear that these families have suffered a double injustice. The injustice of the appalling events – the failure of the state to protect their loved ones and the indefensible wait to get to the truth. And the injustice of the denigration of the deceased – that they were somehow at fault for their own deaths. On behalf of the Government – and indeed our country – I am profoundly sorry for this double injustice that has been left uncorrected for so long.

* * *

The panel's press conference, held in the cathedral's Lady Chapel, was remarkable. Journalists had been given the report only an hour earlier. Full realisation of its significance and implications, flagged in the executive summary, was evident in the questions. Such an unequivocal, powerful critique, supported by chapter-and-verse analysis, had not been anticipated. They were aware that the Prime Minister already had uttered the Government's 'double apology' and now they focused on the reasons.

The following day, the panel's revelations dominated

newspaper front pages, comprehensively reversing the tone and content of reporting in the days following the disaster. *The Sun*, whose vitriolic allegations had deeply distressed the bereaved and survivors, was repentant: '23 YEARS AFTER HILLSBOROUGH . . . THE REAL TRUTH'. Four bullet points framed a photograph of a distraught fan sitting alone on the broken terrace: 'Cops smeared Liverpool fans to deflect blame'; '41 lives could have been saved says new probe'; 'Families of 96 victims call for prosecutions'; and, finally, '*The Sun*: We are profoundly sorry for false reports'. The newspaper sought forgiveness for its calumnies and restoration in its depleted sales. On Merseyside the apology cut no ice.

The *Daily Mirror* was unrelenting in parodying its rival. Above a 'JUSTICE 96' shirt its headline was unmistakable: 'THE TRUTH' accompanied by a masthead proclaiming, 'HILLSBOROUGH: AFTER 23 YEARS OF LIES AND SMEARS'. Its front-page bullet points read: '41 LIVES COULD HAVE BEEN SAVED'; 'TORY MP AND COPS LED COVER-UP'; '164 POLICE STATEMENTS DOCTORED'. It covered the panel's report over seven pages, including a detailed analysis from Brian Reade, who for two decades had consistently supported bereaved families. He wrote that families had

> pleaded with the Establishment's conscience to cease looking away and finally admit why 96 people, half of whom were 21 or younger, never came back from a football game. Yet they got nothing back but rants about whingeing and kicks in the teeth . . . Until yesterday, when the house of lies came tumbling down. When the sheer force of love and dedication and the refusal to be beaten forced out that truth.

The Guardian's headline read: 'HILLSBOROUGH: THE RECKONING' followed by three bullet points: 'Police cover-up exposed'; 'PM "profoundly sorry"'; 'New inquest expected'. David Conn, whose articles on Hillsborough had consistently reflected the best traditions of investigative journalism, wrote:

Throughout a momentous day at Liverpool's Anglican cathedral for the families of the 96 people who died at Sheffield Wednesday's football ground, one phrase dominated above all else: the truth. These were the words most infamously abused by the headline in *The Sun*, above stories we now know, in shocking detail, were fed by the South Yorkshire Police to deflect their own culpability for the disaster onto the innocent victims.

The *Guardian*'s four-page coverage included an apology from the *Sun*'s former editor, Kelvin MacKenzie, his credibility now in ruins.

The Murdoch-owned *Times* gave over its front page to the headline: 'VINDICATION FOR HILLSBOROUGH FAMILIES AFTER 23-YEAR STRUGGLE'. It also used bullet points: 'Police smeared victims of stadium tragedy in cover-up' alongside, 'Prime Minister offers unreserved apology'. Football editor, Tony Evans, wrote a deeply personal and sensitive account:

> It was the day Liverpool got its reputation back. For so long, the place had been sniggered at and derided, tagged 'self-pity city' and supposedly populated by whingeing conspiracy theorists. Yesterday it turned out that Liverpool was right all along . . . My eye-witness version – with its broken and twisted limbs and young people dying in the sunshine – was discounted as Scouse revisionism. After these conversations I would often wake from gruesome nightmares and howl with rage. I have been told to 'get over it' and 'move on'. British justice can today thank the families of the 96 who died and all those who fought for the truth for not moving on.

The Independent's coverage ran to six pages, its front page respectfully on a black background, its masthead in red: 'HILLSBOROUGH: AT LONG LAST, THE TRUTH'. Beneath a mid-page photograph of a rescued young fan was a second headline, 'NOW IT'S TIME FOR JUSTICE', followed by the paragraph:

Twenty-three years after 96 people died in the worst football tragedy in British history, an inquiry has exposed what many have long suspected: a vast cover-up by the emergency services. As the Prime Minister apologises to the people of Liverpool, calls are mounting for a new inquest – and for criminal charges against those responsible.

Above its front-page photograph of five fans carrying an injured young person on a makeshift stretcher the *i*'s headline read: 'HILLSBOROUGH – THE TRUTH AT LAST'. It used five bullet points: 'Report entirely exonerates Liverpool fans from blame'; 'PM "profoundly sorry" for failure to protect supporters'; '41 lives could have been saved with earlier treatment'; 'South Yorks Police doctored 116 statements'; 'Kelvin MacKenzie and current *Sun* editor apologise'.

On its front page the *Daily Mail* carried photographs of the 96 who died under the headline: 'FINALLY HILLSBOROUGH FAMILIES KNOW THE TRUTH: THE POLICE LIED AND LIED. NOW WILL THEY GET JUSTICE?' Beneath the photographs it wrote:

'The 96 victims of the 1989 Hillsborough disaster: New evidence revealed yesterday shows the police caused the tragedy and then covered it up'. The *Daily Star* front page read, 'HILLSBOROUGH Liverpool fans were NOT to blame' alongside a young child at the Anfield Memorial wearing a 'Justice 4 96' shirt. Its bullet points were: '96 died in 1989 FA Cup semi-final but 41 lives might have been saved'; 'Blood taken from kids in bid to prove fans were drunk'; 'Prime Minister apologises for cover-up shame'. Its lead article began, 'A shameful conspiracy to blame the Hillsborough disaster on innocent Liverpool fans was finally exposed yesterday.'

On Merseyside, 'VINDICATED' was the single word used by *The Post* over a photograph of the families at the previous afternoon's mass vigil outside Liverpool's St George's Hall. Above was the famous Kop banner dedicated 'TO THE VICTIMS OF

HILLSBOROUGH YOU'LL NEVER WALK ALONE'. Below, the key points were delivered: 'Panel says 41 deaths may have been prevented'; 'Cameron's "profound" apology for twin injustice'; 'Revealed: Full extent of police smear campaign'; 'Thousands salute fans and families at city vigil'. Its analysis covered ten pages. The *Liverpool Echo*'s headline 'REST IN TRUTH' was written above the names of the 96 that formed the backdrop to the vigil. Beneath was a photograph of the Hillsborough Family Support Group president, Trevor Hicks, and its chair, Margaret Aspinall, alongside the headline 'NOW FOR JUSTICE'. The lower page strapline pronounced, 'Fans cleared, police shamed, 41 fans could have lived . . . Britain's biggest cover-up'. Thirteen pages detailed the panel's findings.

Throughout the week Hillsborough dominated the national and international media as the full impact of the research underpinning the panel's report increasingly became apparent. Published online, it was easily accessible. Each reference was live-linked to the document of origin, enabling instant review. The browse facility allowed families, survivors, researchers and journalists to access all documents by name or location. Within hours, fans' websites, particularly redandwhitekop, developed new threads on key themes. Detailed interrogation of the documents began and has been sustained, not least through dogged persistence of Freedom of Information requests. Following the launch of the report, media interest, including a range of documentaries and features articles, ensured Hillsborough never again faded from public view.

* * *

Following the Prime Minister's 'double apology' the responses from state institutions were remarkable. On 10 October 2012, the Director of Public Prosecutions, Keir Starmer, announced that the Crown Prosecution Service (CPS) would 'consider' the material disclosed by the panel to 'identify what the focus of any further criminal investigation should be to determine whether there is now sufficient evidence to charge any individual or corporate body with any criminal offence. All potential offences that may have been committed and all potential defendants will be considered.'

Two days later the Independent Police Complaints Commission (IPCC) presented a 17-page review addressing its intention to investigate, alongside the CPS, potential police misconduct. According to its deputy chair, Deborah Glass, the panel's report had 'revealed extremely serious and troubling issues for the police'. She continued:

> We have learned details of the run-up to the disaster including the unheeded warnings from previous incidents, the disaster itself, and its aftermath, including what appear to be attempts to distort the truth. Justice demands that we do whatever is possible to investigate culpability for any offence that may have been committed, and to do so thoroughly and fairly.

Acknowledging that 'families have already waited for 23 years', she gave her 'assurance that we will do everything in our power to investigate these serious and disturbing allegations with the careful and robust scrutiny they deserve'.

Ten days later the panel's report was debated in the House of Commons. Opening the debate, the Home Secretary, Theresa May, stated:

> The report and the archive reveal the truth about the Hillsborough disaster and its aftermath. What the panel has uncovered is shocking and disturbing, and it was right for my Right Hon. friend the Prime Minister . . . to apologise to the families of the victims. In addition to that apology, however, there must be accountability. The bereaved families deserve a proper response to what is a comprehensive report.

She committed the Government, 'in the words of some of the families, to move from truth to justice'.

During the six-hour debate numerous MPs, many from the North-West, united in their condemnation of all that had been endured by the families and survivors. Concluding for the Opposition, Andy Burnham recognised the quality of the cross-party speeches, stating that 'the report has opened questions of the most profound kind for the institutions of our country, our Parliament and our society'. He stated it had shown the disaster 'was foreseeable', lives 'should have been saved' and the bereaved and survivors had been subjected to a 'campaign of vilification with no justification'. He praised the 'sheer comprehensiveness and quality of the painstaking research' underpinning the report.

Burnham said that the full 'scale of suffering and loss, the true human cost of the tragedy, and the devastating psychological impact on survivors' had not been recognised. Having experienced 'hell on earth' in the pens, survivors had been 'left to drift home' to 'make sense of what they had seen without counselling or support'. They had been 'lost souls' whose lives were forever changed. He proposed an 'integrated investigation' targeting all institutions whose deficiencies had been exposed by the panel's report: the football organisations, including Sheffield Wednesday Football Club and the Football Association; the media; the coronial service; the police; and, 'finally, this Parliament and this House of Commons'. Instructively, he asked: 'How did we let an injustice on this scale stand for so long? Hillsborough,' he concluded, 'is a story of an abuse of power, of class and of unequal justice.' Denouncing a society in which this could happen to 'ordinary people', he identified the 'moment' as a 'watershed'.

Concluding what he termed a 'powerful' debate, the Secretary of State for Health, Jeremy Hunt, stated that Hillsborough had 'caused us to look into the mirror and reflect on our own failings'.

He offered his 'condolences' and an 'unreserved apology' to 'families, friends and loved ones of those who died' for his previous negative comments on Hillsborough. Reiterating the Prime Minister's recognition that families and survivors had been the 'victims of a double injustice', he was 'deeply sorry for the part that the NHS played in their grief, both at the time and in any attempt to conceal those failings in the 23 years since'. Thus he had initiated a review of all professional procedures concerning emergency response to disasters, including ambulance services, hospital responses and medical pathology.

Beyond Parliament, the legal processes gathered pace. Given the panel's powerful critique of the original inquests, the Attorney-General, Dominic Grieve, applied to the High Court to quash the inquest verdicts thus allowing new inquests to be held. The application was made 'in the public interest' as a response to disclosures regarding medical evidence, the review and alteration of police and emergency services' evidence and stadium safety. Soon after, the Lord Chief Justice, Lord Judge, sitting with Lord Justice Burnett and Judge Peter Thornton, QC, concluded that the 'combination of circumstances . . . makes inevitable the order for a new inquest'. Stating that the 'interests of justice must be served', the 'facts must be investigated and reanalysed in a fresh inquest when, however distressing or unpalatable, the truth will be brought to light'. Thus 'the families of those who died in this disaster will be vindicated and the memory of each victim will be properly respected'. The outcome was unequivocal: 'All the inquisitions will be quashed. There will be new inquests in each and every case'.

* * *

The 'interests of justice' became a guiding principle yet its meaning was unclear. The Prime Minister noted the 'double injustice' that had remained 'uncorrected for so long' and agreed with the Leader of the Opposition that 'after truth must come justice'. The IPCC stated that 'Justice demands that we do whatever is possible to investigate culpability for any offence that may have been committed.' The question arising from such sincerely expressed and compassionate statements of intent centres on the meaning of 'justice'. When many thousands proclaim 'Justice for the 96', the meaning invested in their notion of 'justice' is not necessarily consistent. For some it is solely about disclosure, culpability, acknowledgement and apology. For others it is about liability, punishment and restitution. These are not extremes but parallels. For the state, however, 'justice' concerns the due process of the law, dependent on further investigations to establish possible cases for criminal prosecution and review police actions in the aftermath of the disaster – the very processes that previously failed the bereaved and survivors.

The IPCC established four priorities for its investigation. First, the reviewed and altered police statements: 'who ordered them, who knew about them, who was involved in the process, and was pressure put on officers to change them?' Second, 'allegations that misleading information was passed [by SYP officers] to the media, MPs, Parliament and inquiries'. Third, interventions by SYP officers in the immediate aftermath, 'questioning next of kin . . . checking blood-alcohol levels and . . . undertaking PNC checks on the dead and injured'. Finally, the role and function of the West Midlands Police investigation team would be scrutinised.

On 22 November 2012 the Home Secretary introduced the Police (Complaints and Conduct) Bill, giving necessary new powers to the IPCC to investigate Hillsborough. Fast-tracked through Parliament, the legislation enables the IPCC to compel police officers' attendance at interviews as witnesses. It also empowers the IPCC, in exceptional circumstances, to investigate any matters previously investigated by its predecessor, the Police Complaints Authority. The Home Affairs Committee welcomed the new legislation, considering it 'proportionate' and noting that while 'a number of agencies will have to work together closely and quickly to deliver justice' it was appropriate that the IPCC should take the investigative lead.

On 19 December the Home Secretary presented a ministerial statement to Parliament 'setting out the different pieces of work that will belatedly deliver justice for the [Hillsborough] victims and their families': 'investigation', 'inquest' and 'prosecution'. She stated that the 'integrated' investigations would progress the work of the panel, inquiring into 'all of the people and organisations involved – before, on and after 15th April 1989' under the joint responsibility of the IPCC and the criminal investigation team led by the recently retired Durham Chief Constable, Jon Stoddart. She considered that the seriousness and complexity of the investigation process, and the previous failures in police investigation, mitigated against the police having sole responsibility, stating: 'Investigation of the police in such a serious case is the job of the IPCC.' The coroner would have responsibility for conducting new inquests. Prosecutions would be the responsibility of the Director of Public Prosecutions and the Crown Prosecution Service (CPS). It was envisaged that the CPS should operate alongside the investigations, 'into the deaths at Hillsborough and . . . into the police actions in the aftermath'. Both investigations would be fully resourced and housed together in Warrington, close to Merseyside.

The Home Secretary also announced the establishment of a 'liaison board', supported by the Home Office, to 'integrate the three major pieces of work, ensuring effective planning, organisation and exchange of information'. Finally, the IPCC and the CPS would be responsible for the appointment of a 'challenge panel' (later altered to 'reference group') of three 'independent experts' to 'inform and advise the investigations and the work of the CPS'. She appointed the chair of the Hillsborough Independent Panel, Bishop James Jones, as her special advisor, supported by members of the panel's Home Office-based secretariat. On the day the Home Secretary made her announcement, as noted above, the High Court quashed the inquest verdicts and ordered new inquests in each case. On 13 February 2013 Lord Justice Goldring was appointed by the South Yorkshire (East) and the West Yorkshire (West) Coroners as their Assistant Deputy Coroner to conduct the new inquests.

Coincidentally, the Home Affairs Committee published a scathing report on the IPCC, stating it was 'not yet capable of delivering the kind of powerful, objective scrutiny that is needed to inspire [public] confidence'. It considered the IPCC was 'woefully underequipped and hamstrung in achieving its original objectives' without 'the resources it needs to get to the truth when the integrity of the police is in doubt'. The Committee reiterated a persistent criticism levelled against the IPCC, that of the police – 'who naturally favour their colleagues' – investigating the police.

The Committee's report drew sharp criticism of the IPCC from bereaved families and their lawyers. The Chair of the Hillsborough Family Support Group (HFSG), Margaret Aspinall, stated, 'At this moment in time I don't think they [IPCC] have the mindset to deliver . . . the letter from the IPCC chair, Anne Owers, offering reassurance about the Hillsborough probe, had the opposite effect. It has made us feel worse, it has done nothing to reassure us whatsoever.' Lord Charles Falconer, barrister for the HFSG, considered that the Committee's report 'confirms many of the doubts the families have had with the IPCC as a result of their experience with the organisation so far'. Responding, Dame Anne Owers accepted that 'we cannot do the job the public expects us to do'. Further, in correspondence she wrote that because of its 'past history' the IPCC needed 'to prove to you [the families] that we are both robust and independent'.

In its February 'newsletter' the IPCC repeated its intention to 'build on the panel's work to conduct investigations and the evidence taken will enable decisions to be taken about whether individuals should face criminal charges or misconduct hearings'.

Further, it stressed its commitment to reviewing the extensive documentary evidence disclosed by the panel and additional documents that had come into the public domain after the panel report's publication. The South Yorkshire Police had forwarded the names of 1,444 police officers on duty at Hillsborough or involved in the aftermath of the disaster. Four hundred police officers from 30 other police forces or police-related organisations were also under investigation, resulting 'in excess of 2,000 names to analyse'.

In late February, Jon Stoddart's team released its 'investigative strategy' affirming that its 'comprehensive' investigation would focus on 'events leading up to and including the disaster'. Listed within its investigative priorities were: 'planning and preparation for the match'; 'organisational decision making'; 'suitability of the stadium'; 'ground design'; 'stewarding and policing'; 'crowd monitoring and safety'; 'emergency responses and their effectiveness'; 'coronial processes'. It continued, the 'purpose being to secure all available evidential material . . . in pursuance of a criminal prosecution, in doing so bring to justice those persons who are considered to be culpable under the criminal law'.

The 'working hypothesis' it adopted was 'to prove or disprove that those who died at Hillsborough were unlawfully killed' and 'the time span for the investigation includes a phase after the disaster' through to the death of Tony Bland on 3 March 1993. The 'criminal offences under consideration' included 'individual manslaughter by gross negligence, the old common law elements of corporate manslaughter and misconduct in a public office'. Perverting the course of justice and perjury were also under review. The investigative strategy included plans to consult with the Health and Safety Executive to consider possible breaches of health and safety legislation. It committed to 'regular liaison between the police and the IPCC and the CPS', concluding: 'when all lines of enquiry have been exhausted the CPS will consider all of the evidential material, to determine whether it meets the prosecution threshold test within the code for the Crown Prosecution Service'.

* * *

The persistent reluctance of the South Yorkshire Police to apologise unreservedly for institutional failures that contributed to the disaster and their orchestration of the events that followed, not least the review and alteration of officers' statements, deeply troubled bereaved families and survivors. While partial apologies had been made, they were always tinged with ambiguity. Hours after being confronted with the panel's report findings the incumbent Chief Constable, David Crompton, had little choice but to deliver an unreserved apology. He stated that on 15 April 1989, 'South Yorkshire Police failed victims and families. The police lost control.' He accepted that immediately after the disaster 'senior officers sought to change the record of events'. These had been 'disgraceful lies . . . which blamed the Liverpool fans for the disaster'. The alterations 'sought to minimise police blame' and 'caused untold pain and distress for over 23 years'. On behalf of the South Yorkshire Police he was 'profoundly sorry for the way the force failed on 15th April 1989 and . . . doubly sorry for the injustice that followed, and I apologise to the families of the 96 and Liverpool fans'. He reassured the public that the force had changed significantly and would be 'fully open and transparent in helping to find answers to the questions posed by the panel today'.

Without prior access to the panel's report, Crompton was unprepared for the severity of its findings. It later transpired that five days before the report's launch he wrote an email to colleagues, including the South Yorkshire lead on the contributing agencies' steering group, Andy Holt. Addressed to 'Gents', he feared the force might be 'missing a trick' and proposed a 'public-facing website' that would 'amount to the case for the defence', challenging the families' 'version' of 'certain events' that had 'become the truth *even though it isn't*' (emphasis added).

Reminiscent of the mindset that had produced the actions for which he had just apologised so profusely, he wrote that the 'media machine now favours the families and not us'. Their response would need to be 'innovative' to 'have a fighting chance otherwise we will just be roadkill'. In content, language, presentation and style his comments reflected the defensive, disingenuous damage limitation that typified senior officers' responses following the disaster. Like his predecessors, his concern was geared exclusively to preserving what was left of his force's besmirched reputation.

Crompton's email surfaced as a result of a Freedom of Information request. On 22 February 2013 the South Yorkshire Police and Crime Commissioner, Shaun Wright, stated that Crompton's email had used 'language that could be construed as inappropriate and insensitive, especially for the families of those so tragically killed on that day'. As if in mitigation, Wright noted that the email had been written 'at a time when the force was under intense public scrutiny and pressure'. He affirmed the force's 'commitment to dealing with Hillsborough and its aftermath in an open, honest and transparent manner' and, consequently, had 'informed the Independent Police Complaints Commission and the Home Secretary of the existence of the particular email'. He had raised the issue with Crompton, who stated that it was not his intention to cause offence, commenting, 'I apologise if it has done so'. He continued: 'Nor was it intended to challenge the integrity and views of those who lost loved ones in the Hillsborough Disaster.'

Prior to the launch of the panel's report, however, Crompton's exchange with his senior officers was not an isolated event. The day before the launch, West Yorkshire Chief Constable, Sir Norman Bettison (whose involvement in the aftermath of Hillsborough and controversial appointment as Merseyside Chief Constable is discussed at length in Chapter 10), wrote to Andy Holt, copying in David Crompton. Bettison's email thanked Holt 'amidst all the turmoil of this week, for finding time to keep my personal position in mind'. Working 'on the assumption' that following the report's publication he would 'not be an immediate focus', Bettison was concerned that 'there is a legacy of unfair criticism of my role and, given I am almost the "last man standing" I could become a conducting rod for any ongoing criticism of SYP, and their handling of the aftermath of the disaster'.

In his correspondence, Holt stated that a key question anticipated by the SYP 'archive team' was Bettison's role 'in the disaster and its aftermath'. Bettison responded listing six key points. Off-duty, he had attended the match as a spectator. Realising the unfolding disaster he had 'put himself on duty, giving immediate assistance behind the South Stand'. He then set up the 'receiving centre' at Hammerton Road 'for supporters who had become separated from friends and family'. Four days later, as a non-operational Chief Inspector, he was appointed to a team under DCC Hayes to 'support him in piecing together what had taken place at the event'. This team ran in 'parallel' to the West Midlands Police investigation 'to inform senior South Yorkshire officers of the facts rather than rely on the speculation raging in the press at the time'. He stated he was not a member of the team involved in the review and alteration of statements. He had attended the entire Taylor Inquiry, briefing the South Yorkshire Chief Constable and his deputy 'on a regular basis'. Soon after the conclusion of the Taylor Inquiry he was posted to Rotherham 'and had nothing further to do with the subsequent Coroners [sic] Inquests and other proceedings'.

David Crompton, who had served under Bettison in West Yorkshire before being appointed Chief Constable of South Yorkshire, replied that he would 'bear' Bettison's 'points in mind should the accusation be raised yet again'. Instructively, Crompton commented that he was 'expecting a general "conspiracy" question rather than a direct focus on you' and should the panel find 'there was no conspiracy it rather takes the legs from under the whole argument and makes it easier to deal with'. He considered there had been 'nothing new' in the recent TV documentaries and he had 'chosen to maintain a dignified silence'.

In addition to what was known already, the panel's research confirmed Bettison's significant role in the aftermath of the disaster. The disclosed documents also revealed that he authored the preparation case for the Hillsborough Contribution hearings, monitored the inquests to brief the Chief Constable, and addressed a day-long meeting of the South Yorkshire Police Federation, where he had shown a compilation video. This was followed by a repeat presentation on behalf of the Chief Constable to an invited cross-party group of Westminster MPs. He informed the Chief Constable that the MP who represented Police Federation interests in Parliament, Michael Shersby, 'mentioned privately that he had taken the opportunity to discuss the Hillsborough disaster presentation with the Home Secretary, who had expressed interest in seeing the video tape'. As Chapter 10 records, Bettison consistently maintained that his role was 'peripheral', a term repeated by HM Inspectorate of Constabulary (HMIC). Prior to Bettison's appointment as Chief Constable of Merseyside, the HMIC appraisal of his suitability given to the Police Authority was written by Dan Crompton, David's father.

Following the publication of the panel's report, the Chief Executive of the West Yorkshire Police Authority, Fraser Sampson, and the Authority's Chair, Mark Burns-Williams, attempted to contact Bettison on 14 September. They failed. The following day Bettison informed Sampson that he had been in a Surrey hotel 'formulating a plan in response to the publicity'. He 'had been out of the signal area and therefore had not been able to respond to his messages'. Bettison's mobile phone records, however, show that on 14 September 2012 between 8.21 a.m. and 4.35 p.m. fifteen calls were made, between 10.08 a.m. and 4.16

p.m. fifteen texts were sent and eight calls were made to voice-mail. Also, 213kb of data was uploaded or downloaded during the twenty-four hours. The West Yorkshire Police confirmed that there was an expectation that its Chief Constable should be 'contactable'.

In his conversation with Fraser Sampson, Bettison proposed that 'the best way to proceed was for him [Bettison] to refer himself to the IPCC rather than the Authority make the referral'. Sampson advised him that 'this could not be done formally as the appropriate authority under the legislation was the Police Authority'. According to an IPCC Report, published in March 2013, on 3 October 2012 a West Yorkshire Police Authority committee determined that, following the panel report's publication, Bettison's 'conduct could be regarded as having the intention or effect of usurping the proper functions of the police authority and could undermine public confidence'. Six days later the issue was referred to the IPCC, where an independent investigation was conducted. Its terms of reference sought to 'determine whether there was any attempt by Sir Norman Bettison to improperly influence, intercept, delay and/or distort the deliberations of the Authority in deciding whether to refer complaints about him in connection with the Hillsborough disaster to the IPCC' and to identify whether he 'has a case to answer for misconduct or gross misconduct'.

On 24 October, five days before he was served formal notice of the investigation, Bettison resigned as Chief Constable of West Yorkshire. The IPCC investigation heard oral evidence from Fraser Sampson, Mark Burns-Williamson and Norman Bettison. Concluding its independent investigation the IPCC found, on the balance of probabilities, that Bettison had attempted 'to influence the decision-making of the Police Authority because he wanted the public to believe that he had referred himself to the IPCC to avoid any impression that he had done something wrong' thus 'put[ting] his own reputation as an individual above the need to ensure that a proper and transparent process was followed'. If proven, 'this would amount to breach of standards of professional behaviour, of discreditable conduct and abuse of authority'. The investigation considered that he had sought to 'manipulate the referral process'.

Setting the 'highest standards' of discipline was the Chief Constable's responsibility and the investigators noted that it was 'reasonable to expect him [Bettison] to have behaved with greater restraint and ensured that there was no room for any criticism of his conduct in relation to the referral'. They found he 'had a case to answer for discreditable conduct and abuse of position'. Consequently, 'his actions would so undermine the faith of those officers serving under him, and members of the public, that a panel considering this conduct would form the view that Sir Norman's position as head of the force was untenable and thus dismissal would be justified. This therefore amounts to gross misconduct'. The case did not progress to misconduct proceedings as Bettison was no longer a serving police officer. The Deputy Chair of the IPCC stated that the case served 'as a salutary reminder to chief officers everywhere of how much public confidence in policing is damaged when the conduct of leaders is called into question'. At the time of writing, a second set of complaints against Bettison alleging his 'involvement in disseminating misleading information' and regarding 'the statement he made following publication of the Hillsborough report' remain under IPCC investigation.

* * *

The impact of the research underpinning the panel's report is unparalleled in recent times. Its findings and revelations have continued to sustain intense media interest, with each new development returning coverage to newspaper front pages or the head of broadcast bulletins. Its reach has been international, with broadsheets throughout the world giving prominence to the story. At least five television documentaries have been broadcast.

Following the Prime Minister's lead, apologies for professional and institutional failings flowed from numerous organisations and individuals. Central to positive media coverage and acts of contrition was an acceptance that the bereaved and survivors had endured the loss of loved ones and/or the pains of survival exacerbated by the denial of justice in a climate of condemnation.

As the significance of the complex research findings was realised in the media and in official responses, it dawned that many of the documents researched and analysed had been available to previous inquiries and investigations. Yet their relevance had been overlooked. At the time of the panel's appointment numerous commentators questioned its relevance, reasoning that Hillsborough had been investigated by a judicial inquiry, a DPP investigation, the longest inquests in English legal history, a divisional court review, numerous compensation hearings, a judicial scrutiny, a private prosecution and several submissions to the Attorney-General. Two detailed independent research reports, the drama-documentary and early editions of *Hillsborough: The Truth* had provided alternative accounts to those generated by 'official discourse'. Over the years there had been several substantial House of Commons debates in which parliamentary privilege was used to make further revelations or allegations directed towards the authorities, not least concerning the role of the South Yorkshire Police in the immediate aftermath.

At each stage of the police investigation and inquiry, with the exception of elements of Taylor's interim report, revelatory and persuasive documentary evidence had been ignored, including much of the research and analysis in the earlier chapters of this book – first published in 1999. Despite the strength of evidence underpinning alternative accounts, there had been no comprehensive, integrated review of available material. The Stuart-Smith Scrutiny would have provided an appropriate opportunity had it not been confined to 'new evidence' and left to the discretion of a single judge working without an independent research team. Reluctance to conduct such a review reflects a well-established mindset of denial and protectionism. Jack Straw, as the Home Secretary who appointed Stuart-Smith, missed that opportunity – leaving the stones unturned for another decade.

At an early meeting with the panel, the then South Yorkshire Police Chief Constable confidently announced that the panel's research would find 'no smoking gun' in his force's archives. All primary contributing organisations, particularly the police, demonstrated an unswerving confidence in the previous investigations and inquiries. Yet it was clear from analysis of the documents that the South Yorkshire Police, particularly at a senior level, had operated from the outset to deflect responsibility while protecting its interests and reputation. The documents also reveal how this process affected the West Midlands Police investigation and the coronial process. The police forces, however, were not alone.

In conducting the judicial inquiry, Lord Justice Taylor was aware of the manipulation of evidence and called into question the integrity of senior officers. The initial phase of the inquiry, however, was too limited in scope and too soon after the disaster to examine fully its context, circumstances and aftermath. In fact, the judicial inquiry itself became embroiled in the manipulation of evidence. Following publication of Taylor's interim report, which held the South Yorkshire Police responsible for the mismanagement of the crowd leading to the fatal crush, the force embarked on a calculated mission to use the generic inquests to refute its findings. The full extent of that mission has been laid bare by the documents disclosed to the panel.

Since publication of the panel's report, further progress has been made in analysing the methodology adopted for constructing and presenting police statements to the investigations and inquiries. While the review and alteration of statements was identified in the first edition of this book and scrutinised by the panel, it is now evident that there was collusion in writing and/or editing statements. Close analysis of the statements reveals that there are passages copied verbatim. For example, in one serial of eight constables under the leadership of a sergeant, four statements have paragraphs copied word-for-word. Much of the sergeant's statement can be found in these constables' statements and the majority of one constable's text is taken directly from his sergeant's statement. As textual errors are duplicated in these 'official', processed statements, it is safe to assume that they were altered to correspond *after* they were initially written.

The copied text focuses on the perceived age of the fans (for example, using the phrase 'lower age bracket'), alcohol and drunkenness, fans' 'late arrival', violence, and aggressiveness towards the police. It is instructive that 'in preparation for the resumed inquest proceedings' the South Yorkshire Police team involved in reviewing and altering police statements sought to identify 'best evidence' from statements prioritising: 'unruly behaviour by Liverpool fans'; 'non-ticket holders gaining entry'; 'forged tickets'; 'drunkenness'; 'public houses in the area being crowded out'; and the 'volume of sales of intoxicants generally [by] off-licences & supermarkets'. This occurred in the period following Lord Justice Taylor's interim report, thus challenging his rejection of these issues raised by the police in submissions to the inquiry as contributory factors to the disaster.

The decision not to prosecute any individual on the grounds of insufficient evidence, the abandonment of disciplinary action against police officers due to ill-health and the accidental death inquest verdicts together contributed to the publicly held belief that those in authority had been rightly exonerated. Further, the persistent campaign of vilification directed towards those who died and survived, based on calculated and unsubstantiated allegations, cemented the scurrilous version of events that had dominated headlines in the immediate aftermath and became hard-wired into popular discourse. This was a discourse that ran deep. Those entrusted with the responsibility of approaching investigations and inquiries with value-neutrality often were inhibited by their prejudices and assumptions. Drawing on records and minutes of meetings, the panel's report provides numerous examples of this mindset.

The work of the Hillsborough Independent Panel, and the research process informing its extensive report, represents a new departure in truth recovery. While there are numerous independent panels of inquiry into controversial events, it was a unique Government-initiated process established outside statutory procedures. For future adoption in other contested cases, however, an inherent weakness lies in the lack of formal powers of investigation. In developing its research the panel had no *right* of access to unredacted documents and no authority to order their disclosure. All documents were 'donated' voluntarily to the panel and their digital publication on the panel's website was negotiated accordingly.

As a model for accessing, researching and analysing documents or other material held by public bodies, however, the process adopted by the panel has the potential to secure acknowledgement in contested cases when previously this has been denied. Accessing documents and relevant material in full, with redaction restricted to exceptional circumstances, is a significant end in itself. On this basis alone, there is considerable interest in adopting this form of 'truth recovery' – through independent scrutiny of all documents held by public agencies – as an adjunct to public inquiries.

Most significantly, the panel's findings provided the detailed and integrated analysis necessary to test the reliability and thoroughness of the investigations, inquiries and inquests required to secure 'justice' from 'truth'. The path had been cleared to initiate, legitimate and resource appropriate processes of investigation, including new inquests. Inevitably, given the passage of time, and the deaths of key people, these processes would be complex. Once again, the case broke new ground as the decision was taken to give priority to the new inquests.

Chapter Fifteen

THEIR VOICES HAVE
BEEN HEARD

For much of its history Warrington remained a relatively small market town in north-west England. Its population expanded significantly following the industrial revolution. A century later, heavy industries in decline, it was rebranded a 'new town'. From the late 1960s, families, mainly from Manchester, relocated close to newly built industrial estates. It is situated on Britain's earliest railway, linking Liverpool to Manchester, now on the main West Coast line. A northern motorway hub, it attracts light industry to high-tech business parks.

Birchwood was initially a strategic wartime base and home to the UK Atomic Energy Authority. It now projects itself as 'Warrington's leading business park', accommodating '165 organisations employing 6,000 people'. Located within a maze of avenues, roundabouts and heavily regulated car parks is Bridgewater Place, an award-winning commercial development. Identical modern, glass-fronted, three-storey office blocks are accessed via a pedestrian-only boulevard. Raised grass lawns, low shrubs and infant trees have been planted with geometrical precision, and a central water feature stretches the length of the boulevard.

Building 305 dominates Bridgewater Place, a large donut-shaped polished-steel sculpture at its front. In late September 2013 its ground floor was transformed into a coroner's court and a security check installed. Inside, beyond water fountains and bathrooms, a large area, akin to a bus station or hospital waiting room, offered four rows of metal seating anchored to the floor. A wide corridor led through two sets of double doors into an oblong hall. What was designed as an extensive open-plan office area had been transformed into a courtroom in the middle of a business park.

* * *

The journey from the panel's report to the new inquests was uncharted, pausing regularly for preparatory preliminary hearings. These established the parameters, determining who could be represented as 'interested parties' and resolving issues of procedure and evidence. The Hillsborough inquests were challenging, given the number of families, the quashed inquests, the rehearsal of evidence in previous forums, and the 'expert' witnesses required. Further complications were added by criminal and IPCC investigations running parallel to the inquests. As the previous chapter notes, the Home Secretary had committed to 'integrated investigations' with joint responsibility to establish culpability and grounds for prosecution. New inquests were additional to that work.

The coroner, Lord Justice Goldring, held the first preliminary hearing on 25 April 2013. He acknowledged that bereaved families had not 'ceased in their pursuit of a full understanding of the events of the day'. New inquests would 'seek to ensure' that 'the full facts are brought to light, that any culpable or discreditable conduct is exposed and brought to public notice'. His comments revealed the contradiction experienced by bereaved families who expect inquests to offer 'fact-finding' investigations into controversial deaths in contested circumstances – they establish culpability while not 'apportioning guilt'. The coroner stated that, in contrast to the first inquests, proceedings would not be 'scarred by degenerating into a kind of adversarial battle' between lawyers representing conflicting interests. Given what was at stake this was an unrealisable expectation.

Usually, inquests are held after all other investigations have been completed and prosecutions or disciplinary actions resolved. This, Lord Goldring stated, could delay the inquests by up to three years. Given the 'urgency attaching itself to the commencement of the inquest hearings' such a delay was unacceptable. The coroner's counsel noted that witnesses giving evidence to the inquests who anticipated prosecution 'may seek to rely on privilege against self-incrimination and decline to answer questions'. She was also concerned that, because of ongoing IPCC and police investigations, 'important material will emerge after the conclusion of the inquest process'. The DPP, however, had given unqualified support and the coroner committed to starting within a year. The ongoing investigations would service the inquests. This was unpopular with bereaved families, who questioned the independence of the investigation teams.

In a ruling on 2 May the coroner noted the IPCC and criminal investigations were 'still in their early stages'. The enormity of the investigations now became apparent. Several hundred full-time staff would take 'probably three years' to complete their work. The coroner conceded there were risks in proceeding with inquests ahead of the outcome of these investigations. Yet the inquests would 'be put into proper context and properly managed'. Acknowledging the Divisional Court's 'earnest wish' that 'new inquests shall not be delayed for a moment longer than necessary', and given the 'strong public interest' in progressing the proceedings, he envisaged a North-West location convenient for the bereaved and survivors.

A second hearing was held on 5 June 2013. The scope of the inquest was established: stadium safety; preparations for the 1989 semi-final; crowd management on the day; emergency response; the pathological causes of death; and the experiences of each deceased person immediately prior to death. Amendment of police statements and the recording of blood-alcohol levels would be explored. Returning to the families' concerns about the independence of the investigation teams, the coroner accepted that initial approaches made to the bereaved by 'family liaison teams' on his behalf had lacked sensitivity. Appropriate 'memoranda of understanding' could be agreed between the investigation teams and the coroner to meet requirements for accountability and independence while working to his priorities.

At the third preliminary hearing on 7 October 2013 the coroner stated that the 'scale' and 'complexity' of the available documents presented an 'unprecedented' challenge. A team of 20 junior counsel and paralegals were reviewing all material for relevance to the inquests. Concerns were raised about delays in accessing and evaluating existing documents and in processing recently commissioned pathologists' reports. Alongside generic and individual pathology reports, others would be commissioned on structural engineering, pre-hospital emergency care, and policing.

By the fourth preliminary hearing, held on 16 December 2013, the experts' reports on pathology, emergency response and stadium safety were complete. The key issues discussed included plans for jury selection, the order of evidence, 'expert' witnesses, pathology including toxicology, and witness interviews, particularly those of police officers. The IPCC revealed that 240 police officers' statements 'appeared' to have been altered. The coroner reminded legal teams that although the case was 'massive', the jury had 'lives that they want to go back to'. Thus 'time cannot be unlimited'. He expected lawyers' 'cooperation' to reduce repetition and conflict, reminding them, 'this is not an adversarial process; it is a fact-finding process'.

The final preliminary hearing, on 5 February 2014, discussed progress on pathology and the recruitment of intensive care and resuscitation experts. Further reports had been received on stadium safety and pre-hospital emergency care. The policing report criticised police planning, crowd management, the response of senior officers and the police emergency response. Previously, the coroner's counsel had emphasised that 'levels of blood alcohol in each of the deceased' were 'not relevant to either the cause of the disaster or the individual causes of death'. The Police Federation lawyer stated: 'We do not anticipate that the blood-alcohol levels of the deceased played any part in the disaster', but evidence alleging drunkenness and 'late arrivals' would be pursued.

Police lawyers were asked to indicate if they intended to propose 'that drunkenness among spectators contributed to the disaster'. Referring to the Lord Chief Justice's comments in quashing the original inquest verdicts, the coroner's counsel had stated previously: 'the facts must be investigated and re-analysed in a fresh inquest when, however distressing or unpalatable, the truth will be brought to light'. Counsel for the three senior officers confirmed that while blood-alcohol levels recorded in samples taken from some who died had no bearing on the cause of the disaster, this did not extend to other fans.

It was clear that fans' behaviour, particularly allegations of drunkenness, ticketlessness and so-called late arrival, was back on the agenda. Thus, before the inquests started, counsel representing the police and other authorities drew a distinction between the 'innocent' who died and others, referred to as a significant minority, who were 'guilty' survivors. A distinction aimed at attributing blame for the disaster, in part, to fans' behaviour had been made. It was a defining moment, with considerable repercussions.

* * *

On Monday, 31 March 2014, as Hillsborough's 25th anniversary approached, bereaved families, survivors and friends arrived in Birchwood Park. They travelled by coach, train and car. Throughout the North-West, 'Hillsborough Inquest' road signs demonstrated the extent of public interest. Walking the Bridgewater Place boulevard, families and survivors were greeted by a barrage of television crews and photographers. A long queue formed at the security check-in. They packed the courtroom, their nervous anticipation palpable.

At 11.43 a.m. the coroner opened the inquests, estimated to run for 12 months. Twenty-five potential jurors were invited into court, with selection completed during the afternoon. Next morning, counsel to the inquests read aloud the names of the 96 who died at Hillsborough. After the jury were sworn in, the coroner gave his opening address. He described how in the pens fans 'could not escape' and acknowledged that what followed was 'seared into the memories of the very many people affected by it', particularly the bereaved. The inquests would detail 'the experiences and the deaths of each one of the 96 individuals . . . something we must never lose sight of during the course of the hearing'. He explained that the previous verdicts had been 'set aside' by the High Court 'following a campaign by the bereaved families'. In pursuing new inquests the bereaved would be 'vindicated' and the 'memory of each victim properly respected'.

The inquest would bring the 'full facts to light', expose 'culpable and discreditable conduct', allay 'suspicion of wrongdoing', rectify 'dangerous practices and procedures' and give 'satisfaction' to the bereaved through 'knowing that lessons learned from his [sic] death may save the lives of others'. It would establish when, where and how each person died, recording the medical cause of death. The jury would 'consider the underlying circumstances which contributed to the cause of these deaths', whether any could have been 'saved' or their deaths 'prevented'. They would 'reach significant critical judgments about the circumstances in which the deaths occurred'.

Legal teams were introduced. First, counsel and solicitors to the inquests followed by lawyers representing 'interested persons' – individuals or organisations who 'have the right to take part in the hearing'. The families were represented by four distinct teams. Others represented were: the South Yorkshire Police Chief Constable; rank-and-file police officers through the Police Federation; three retired senior police officers (Duckenfield, Greenwood and Marshall); three senior officers (Jackson, Anderson and Hayes); two further senior investigating officers (Denton and Wain); Sheffield Wednesday Football Club; Sheffield City Council; the Yorkshire Ambulance Service; St John's Ambulance; South Yorkshire Fire and Rescue Service; Sheffield Teaching Hospitals Trust; the Football Association; West Midlands Police (the investigating force after the disaster); and the Independent Police Complaints Commission. Survivors of the disaster, some of whom had suffered near-death experiences or serious injury and, subsequently, deeply offensive media coverage, were not represented. This became contentious late in the inquests.

The coroner warned again that the examination of witnesses should not 'degenerate' into an 'adversarial battle'. His role was to direct the jury on 'the law'; their role was to decide on the facts, and their conclusions would rely solely on evidence heard in court. He told them to avoid all Hillsborough-related commentaries, published articles, television programmes, the Internet or social-networking sites. Anything they had read or heard previously about the disaster should be erased from their minds and they should refrain from discussing the case with family or friends. Noting the imminent 25th anniversary, he instructed the media to avoid prejudicing the verdict.

Since the disaster many witnesses had died, were ill or could not be traced. Their previous statements would be admitted as evidence but could not be examined. The coroner noted that key documents were missing. Expert witnesses would provide scientific, technical and professional opinion on 1989 standards and practices. He introduced the order of evidence: personal backgrounds of those who died; 'overview' of 'uncontroversial facts' including background structural information and a virtual reconstruction of the stadium in 1989; the stadium's safety, its history and modifications; preparation and planning for the semi-final; the day of the disaster; expert evidence on policing and pre-hospital emergency care; experiences of those who died illustrated by visual evidence and rescuers' accounts; revisiting the original pathological evidence to assess whether some might have been saved.

Illustrations and photographs were used to introduce the jury to Hillsborough as it was in 1989. The coroner described the transport arrangements for fans travelling to Sheffield, the stadium approach and access from Leppings Lane via the outer concourse. He detailed turnstile access, the inner concourse, tunnel, terraces, crush barriers, pens, perimeter fences and their gates. Focusing on stadium safety, he mentioned the 1981 near tragedy and the role of Eastwood and Partners, the stadium's safety engineers, in alterations to the terrace. He referred to the Hillsborough 1987 and 1988 semi-finals as background to the preparations, ticket allocations, club stewarding and policing in 1989.

The coroner's introductory statement, supported by photographs and maps, described the situation as fans arrived at Hillsborough and entered the central pens. He noted the well-known difficulties concerning access outside, restrictions on movement inside and difficulties leaving the pens. Crowd monitoring was deficient, with no accurate means of assessing when pens reached their safety limits. Entry to the north and west stands, and to the terrace via the narrow access point off Leppings Lane, 'meant that all 24,000 Liverpool supporters were expected to enter through 23 turnstiles'.

Commenting on policing, particularly Duckenfield's inexperience, the coroner outlined the chain of command in the control box, on the outer concourse and inside the stadium. Senior officers had delivered briefings on roles and duties before the match. The 'policy of the match commanders', he stated, 'was to let fans find their own level within the terraces', despite this not being possible due to radial fences. He described the events prior to Marshall's request to open the exit gates and the fatal crush in the central pens. He warned the jury they would 'hear very different accounts of the behaviour and mood of the supporters outside the turnstiles'.

The coroner described police officers' dawning realisation of the severe crush on the terraces as fans were trapped and dying. He noted that the match was stopped six minutes after kick-off. Fifteen minutes later a senior ambulance officer on duty at Hillsborough declared a 'major incident', triggering the emergency response. He informed the jury of Duckenfield's lie to the Football Association's Chief Executive, Graham Kelly, 'that gate C had been forced', causing 'an inrush of Liverpool supporters'. Yet there was 'no question of gate C having been forced', as it was Duckenfield who 'ordered that it be opened'. Duckenfield's misinformation 'resulted in some seriously inaccurate reporting of events' and the jury might want to 'consider why' he 'said what he did'.

The coroner described the arrival of ambulances, the transfer of injured fans to hospital, the use of the gymnasium as a temporary mortuary and the arrangements for relatives and friends who endured an 'obviously agonising' process. As a consequence, 'many of the bereaved remain distressed and angry to this day about the way in which they and the bodies of their loved ones were treated'. While the inquest would 'enquire into how the victims of the disaster came to die', evidence would also be heard regarding the 'procedures' faced by bereaved families and friends. New teams of pathologists and specialists in intensive care would review the original pathology findings. The coroner noted that it was 'not normal to test the victims of disaster for alcohol'.

The coroner explained the relationship between the initial investigations conducted internally by South Yorkshire Police officers and those subsequently carried out by West Midlands officers. They serviced the first inquests, gathered evidence for the Taylor Inquiry and for the original criminal investigation. Acknowledging police statements had been reviewed and altered, he concluded: 'it is not the task of these inquests to investigate every aspect of the process by which the amendments were made. That is for others.' While noting Taylor's report, no mention was made of the criticisms levelled against South Yorkshire Police senior officers. He outlined the process adopted by the South Yorkshire coroner at the mini-inquests and at the generic hearing. He made brief references to civil litigation, the Stuart-Smith scrutiny, the private prosecution and the report of the Hillsborough Independent Panel. The panel's 'views' were 'irrelevant as far as you [the jury] are concerned'.

Finally, the coroner listed six key topics, 'by no means exhaustive': the turnstiles and responsibility for recognising potential danger; overcrowding in the central pens and the expectation that fans would 'find their own level'; management of fans approaching turnstiles and the risk of crushing; implications of opening exit gates and the 'risk of a dangerous situation developing'; adequacy of the emergency response by the police, the ambulance service and other services; fans' behaviour.

Having delivered his opening statement, he moved to the first 'segment' of evidence – brief personal portraits of the 96, written by family members. For three weeks bereaved families presented moving tributes to their loved ones. Each was accompanied by a photograph shown prominently in court. Recent changes in inquest rules permit personal portraits subject to the agreement of all legal representatives. They provide juries and the media with powerful insights into lives and family histories, revealing the depth and pain of sudden personal loss. As relatives described their loved ones, the impact was profound. The jury was introduced to the 89 men and 7 women, the youngest aged 10, the oldest 67. Thirty-eight were under 20 years old, forty aged between 20 and 29, twelve aged 30 to 39 and six over 40. They included a father and son, three pairs of brothers and two sisters. United in mutual support, many families attended court throughout the personal statements. Respectful silence was interrupted only by fond reminiscences of happier days and occasional sobbing.

Many family members were told by their lawyers to remove any critical comments from personal statements to ensure approval from lawyers representing the police and other organisations. They resented reviewing and altering (a phrase not lost on them) statements: 'We had comments about previous failures in the system removed, although it was anything but controversial.' Yet Jan Spearritt considered it provided an opportunity 'to speak about our loved ones as real people rather than one of a collective number. I wanted to include a poem about my son but there was a line that was disputed so I left the poem out.' According to Doreen Jones, her daughter Stephanie, who survived, 'not only had the trauma of the day, but had to face the lies that followed, making her feel that somehow she played a part in Rick and Tracey's deaths'. Doreen wanted to raise this but was 'only allowed to talk about the trauma. I had to delete the rest.'

Sharing their collective grief, families spoke with immense dignity, memorialising their loved ones with warmth and affection. For the first time in 25 years they had the opportunity to have their loss and its impact acknowledged in a public forum. Their candid portrayals placed the 96 at the heart of the process. On these days at least, whatever limitations were placed on content, the voices of the bereaved were heard, their suffering and pride witnessed by the jury. Their accounts were reported in the media.

* * *

Having heard the personal statements, court was adjourned until 20 May 2014. Once they resumed, occasionally interrupted by complex legal submissions or juror illness, the volume of complex evidence became increasingly apparent. Completion within 12 months was a significant underestimation. Despite the coroner's regular reminders to lawyers about efficient time-management, the court sat for two years. Throughout complex inquests lawyers make detailed submissions. They are debated in court, the coroner gives rulings and the case progresses. These often combative exchanges take place without the jury and are not reported, leaving jurors to reach their conclusions solely on the evidence they hear. A formidable range of evidence about the events on the day was heard from several hundred witnesses. Technical 'expert' evidence focused on ground safety, policing, rescue and pathology. As was expected, the hotly contested issues of stadium safety and policing were central.

Safety consultant John Cutlack produced detailed reports and gave evidence based on in-depth analyses from his research: the height of crush barriers on the terraces; the distance between barriers; safe capacity of the pens and their monitoring; contingency planning for crowd congestion at the turnstiles; perimeter fences and adequacy of escape routes for emergency evacuation of pens; entrance and exit signposting. He also assessed organisations' specific legal and operational responsibilities for crowd safety, particularly the club as owners, Eastwood and Partners as engineers, and Sheffield City Council as the licensing authority.

Cutlack's evidence also focused on the stadium's development, modifications over time and, accordingly, whether ground capacity had been adjusted. This included the 1981 introduction of pens and their subsequent modification. Analysing the collapse of barrier 124A in pen 3, he focused on the removal of sections of safety barriers resulting in 'surge paths' leading to the overloading of barriers lower down the terrace. He concluded that the safety engineers failed to provide correct or sufficient advice to assist the club in complying with the safety certificate. There had been a comprehensive failure by all parties to identify deficient barriers and take remedial action. The safety engineers had wrongly assessed terrace capacity and the figure provided to the Football League had been 'far too high'.

Barrier 124A had collapsed due to three inter-related factors: excessive crowd density in pen 3, depth of crowd pressure and the ineffectiveness of crush barriers. His detailed analysis of crowd density in the central pens confirmed survivors' accounts of severe overcrowding. He established that the 'problem' of processing fans through the turnstiles was apparent an hour before kick-off. Regarding the significance of entry through gate C, he estimated approximately 2,000 fans had entered. Adding this figure to those recorded by the turnstile counters, the number of fans on the Leppings Lane terraces was *less* than the ticket allocation. Once and for all, allegations that a mass of ticketless fans had entered the stadium were laid to rest.

Cutlack's evidence was damning. Safe containment outside the stadium, safe passage through turnstiles and safe accommodation inside had been hopelessly compromised. Policing and stewarding were ineffective, mostly non-existent. Penning without appropriate distribution and monitoring, alongside multiple structural failures, had created a foreseeable danger. These fatal flaws were the backdrop to complacent and negligent policing. The safety engineers bore significant responsibility, as did the club and the city council.

While numerous police officers gave evidence over a long period, the week-long examination of the match commander, David Duckenfield, was crucial to establishing culpability for the disaster. It focused on senior officers' failure to make informed, appropriate decisions. Inevitably, given his highly publicised lie to the media and the hung jury at his manslaughter trial, Duckenfield's evidence was keenly anticipated. At the hub of the police operation in the control box, he cut an isolated figure on the witness stand. In court the atmosphere was that of subdued expectation. In public discourse, despised in print and song, he had become Hillsborough's *bête noire*.

Families and survivors hoped that Duckenfield's evidence would provide explanation for his failures on the day, both in deed and in honesty. Perhaps his arrogance would give way to contrition. Much was made of his lack of experience as a match commander, including the controversial circumstances of his appointment. He accepted he had 'limited knowledge' of commanding big games or of the stadium but had not 'paused for thought' in accepting his sudden appointment just three weeks before the match. He believed the 'team' he inherited, in the control box, inside and outside the stadium, would provide the 'necessary experience'.

He could not recall consulting the major incident manual, nor could he account for the missing minutes of the crucial preparatory meeting held two weeks before the match. Although contested by his assistant, he remained adamant that he had attended that meeting. He admitted unfamiliarity with relevant documentation, including contingency planning, stated he had never seen the safety certificate and had minimal knowledge of the stadium layout. Under examination, including particularly robust challenges from the Police Federation's barrister, who was representing rank-and-file police officers, the full extent of Duckenfield's ignorance regarding preparation, planning and operational decision-making was revealed.

On the day of the match, following the late-morning briefing, Duckenfield was absent from the police control box, returning at 2 p.m. His whereabouts were never explained. Having returned, he failed to act on verbal and visual concerns about the numbers accumulating at slow-moving turnstiles. He decided against delaying the kick-off, because he did not want to 'provoke a reaction' among fans. When Marshall radioed that injury and death might occur in the crush outside, Duckenfield said he had 'no option' but to open the exit gates to allow entry and relieve the crush. As the crisis unfolded he lied, claiming that the gates had 'burst open'. It remained, he said, 'one of the biggest regrets of my life that I did not foresee where fans would go when they came in'. He was 'so overcome that my mind, for a moment, went blank'. Why did he order the opening of gate C without sealing the tunnel when he could see that the central pens were already overcrowded? Had he 'been a knowledgeable, experienced match commander at Hillsborough,' he replied, he would have understood the inevitable consequences. 'But sadly I wasn't.'

In court Duckenfield stated that, as people were dying, he declared a 'major incident'. This was not true. His lie to Graham Kelly that fans had forced entry was a consequence of facing a 'very difficult moment, a tense situation'. It had been, he admitted, a 'dreadful mistake'. He continued: 'I was probably deeply ashamed, embarrassed, greatly distressed, and I probably didn't want to admit to myself, or anyone else, what the situation is [*sic*]'. It was 'something I deeply regret', a 'terrible lie in that everybody knew the truth'. In the immediate aftermath his behaviour amounted to 'a terrible fall from standards'. He could not explain why he called for dog handlers when those dying and injured required rescue.

When learning of the lie the Chief Constable's reaction had been 'disgust and despair'. Yet, as discussed previously, within days he advised his officers that 'if it is that drunken, marauding fans' were involved, 'let somebody else say that'. Whatever the embarrassment of Duckenfield's lie, it did not detract from an immediate, consolidating commitment within the force hierarchy to establish an agenda ensuring responsibility for the disaster would be laid at the fans' door.

Duckenfield stated he had not addressed his 'failings' until 2013, after publication of the Hillsborough Independent Panel report, 'because I didn't want to face them'. He accepted that failure to close the tunnel directly caused deaths on the terraces. On reflection he agreed he should have declined the role of match commander. He recognised that his lack of knowledge underpinned the sequence of serious omissions: not establishing cordons at the turnstiles to prevent crushing; not checking on the numbers entering the terrace prior to 2.30 p.m.; not considering existing crowd distribution in the pens before opening gate C; and not familiarising himself with the stadium and relevant documentation. He accepted he had not fulfilled his role as match commander properly and professionally before, during and after the match.

* * *

Despite Duckenfield's admissions, throughout the inquests lawyers for senior officers and for the Police Federation continued to walk the previously discredited path of fans' culpability. The police case was rooted in the previously discredited proposition that officers were confronted by an uncontrollable crowd, many arriving late, drunk and without tickets. This was the story promoted in the week after the disaster and played out at the first inquests. The coroner's commitment to objective fact-finding, and his determination that the inquests would not degenerate into adversarial disputes, had little discernible impact.

The most contentious evidence centred on fans' behaviour before the match. A sergeant, located some distance from the stadium, stated that within an hour of the kick-off fans outside a public house 'were beginning to get out of hand'. They were 'drunk, glasses and bottles were being broken, either deliberately or through sheer drunkenness'. He claimed they urinated in gardens, 'drink seemed to be taking over' and 'obscenities' increased. His comments were qualified – 'it is a football match for god's sake'. Another sergeant said that a number of fans were looking for tickets, some the worse for drink, but this was not unusual. His was not a view shared by other officers.

A police sergeant outside the stadium condemned the 'vast majority of fans' arriving in the half-hour before kick-off. They 'were the worse for drink', many carrying 'four packs of lager' and 'unsteady on their feet', an unprecedented number arriving late and ticketless. Another officer believed many fans without tickets were 'wild to get in'. A deceased officer's statement was read to the jury. He claimed that at the turnstiles women and children were being crushed but his appeal to stop pushing 'made no difference'. Defying instructions from mounted officers, they 'appeared fanatical to gain entrance' and 'were storming the turnstiles'. This was a claim echoed by an inspector who considered the situation to be 'frantic – mania, madness' with a 'huge volume of fanatical supporters arriving en masse, all intent and anxious to the point of desperation to get into the ground at any cost before kick-off'.

Another police inspector estimated 4,000 fans were at the Leppings Lane turnstiles as the teams took to the pitch. The crowd then pushed 'even more', and 'the smell of alcohol got worse the nearer they got'. A senior officer spoke of the fans' desperation to enter 'by hook or by crook', overwhelming the mounted and foot officers – 'brute force prevailed'. He concluded: 'a substantial number of people who arrived late at that [exit] gate had taken drink to such an extent that their standards of behaviour became unacceptable, loud, brash, aggressive; not aggressive, forceful'. It amounted to 'criminal behaviour endangering lives at the front of the queue at the turnstiles'. The 'fear' of an 'uncontrollable crowd' led to the demand to open the exit gates.

These allegations were repeated by police officers many times throughout the ever-extending inquests. Their initial accounts in court were often precise and compelling, in marked contrast to their responses under examination, when sharp memories appeared to fade as families' lawyers probed for detail. Further doubt was cast on officers' allegations by the many hours of CCTV, film and photographic evidence shown in court. This confirmed a distinct absence of aggressive conduct, drunkenness or fans searching for tickets. In fact, the visual evidence demonstrated the helplessness at the turnstiles and in the pens, and the abject failure of the police to respond appropriately. As advanced at the preliminary hearings by lawyers for the police, these allegations reflected a strategy to construct a case that groups of unidentifiable fans, but not the deceased, had contributed to the

461

disaster through their reckless and violent conduct. It was a difficult strategy to sustain, although not without consequences for the families.

For the Matthews family this was 'the most angering part of the inquest'. They criticised public funding for senior officers to 'peddle lies' with the intention of undermining a just outcome. Jan Spearritt's family was astonished that 'having said sorry to families following the panel's report, the South Yorkshire Police went on to try and defend themselves, continuing with their false allegations'. Doreen Jones saw this as clear evidence that the force 'had not learnt lessons'. According to Leo Fallon, former senior officers, particularly David Duckenfield, were 'permitted' to 'grandstand'. Paul Spearritt thought it 'nothing short of farcical' that the force was funded 'to present a case that it had accepted was discredited' by the panel's report. It 'caused more upset and anxiety that untruths were being put forward again'. How could they absolve 96 while 'blaming those who walked side by side with them?'

* * *

It is difficult to summarise over 300 days of intense evidence, thousands of pages of legal submissions and the complexity and diversity of positions taken by lawyers representing organisations and individuals determined to fight their corners come what may. Sometimes they worked together; occasionally they deflected responsibility to others. It became clear that the two core elements, briefly discussed above, were stadium safety and policing. Yet the significance of rejecting the previous inquest's 3.15 p.m. cut-off was that the ineffectiveness and disorganisation of rescue and evacuation attempts was revealed. Again, this relied on expert evidence together with a comprehensive examination of ambulance service evidence that had not been presented at the first inquests due to the imposition of the 3.15 p.m. cut-off. The jury were also told that both the South Yorkshire Police and the then South Yorkshire Metropolitan Ambulance Service had embarked on strategies to deflect claims of organisational failures and deny the culpability of their senior personnel. The jury heard evidence over several weeks about management meetings that were held for which no minutes existed, ambulance officers' statements had been systematically altered and those who resisted the party line felt their careers had been jeopardised.

On 11 May 2015, day 183, the inquests entered their final phase, hearing evidence specific to each of the deceased. The coroner noted that the jury had 'heard a large quantity of general evidence'. It would now focus on 'the experience of each individual', including 'arrival at the stadium, the movement of the individual into the pens, the experience of the individual in the pens and following retrieval from the pens and prior to death being confirmed'. This evidence took five months.

On 21 October, day 253, counsel to the inquests, Christina Lambert, recalled that it had been 'like putting in place the pieces of a jigsaw puzzle so as to allow as complete a picture as possible to emerge'. She concluded that: 'For some we have been able to obtain a full picture, for others, regrettably, it has not been so.' She recognised the stress experienced by family members, 'often very painful', in searching through AV footage to identify their loved ones. For many, expectations of a more complete picture had been raised, only to be dashed.

From this point through to January 2016 individual families returned to hear evidence from 'medical experts' concerning the cause of death of their loved ones, the 'mechanism' of death and, where possible, the time of death. Teams of neuropathologists, forensic pathologists and anaesthetists instructed by the coroner and by families had worked together to review each case, focusing on the original pathology finding, evidence heard from witnesses at the new inquests and available AV footage. In teams they were introduced to the jury as having 'particular understanding or expertise in resuscitation of casualties who have sustained life-threatening illnesses or injuries', particularly those 'which affect the circulation of blood and breathing systems'.

It became clear that the contents of the original post-mortem reports were unreliable, not least because they had been rushed, conducted by pathologists with different professional training, and inconsistent in methodology. Although the new teams had significantly more contextual evidence, especially AV footage, core issues relating to the cause of death, the precise time of death and the potential to survive were difficult to ascertain. With few exceptions, therefore, the generic cause of death was established as traumatic asphyxia and the time of death given as the time when death was pronounced. As the panel's report had established, many of those who died might have been saved had there been a quicker and more effective response to the crush in the pens. Yet it proved impossible to establish precise information.

While it was accepted that revisiting personal pathologies had given families some further evidence specific to the deaths of their loved ones, many felt it 'just seemed a process, sort of going through the motions'. Another family stated that to them 'it felt like damage limitation, supposition, minimising what the deceased went through, cold and clinical'. Others felt that 'new' witnesses 'added no weight' to the original pathology, providing no answers to their unresolved questions. There was 'a level of confusion and lack of detail, the original pathologies so poorly performed'. One family described 'resigning ourselves to the notion that he could have died through any one of four means offered to us over the years'. It was an 'enduring legacy of further torture created by such an orchestrated cover-up'. They 'have to focus on the fact that he was killed and try not to focus on the exact "how", as there have been no answers of any real meaning about the actual mechanics of death despite huge investment in time and resources'.

* * *

The medical evidence was completed on 5 January 2016, day 279. Court was adjourned for the coroner to complete preparations for his summing-up. It resumed three weeks later, on

25 January. Once again Building 305 was the focus of national attention. Designated car parks were full, the boulevard busier than usual, a long queue at security. Twenty-two months on from his opening statement, the coroner prepared to embark on his closing summary and jury direction. It would be the penultimate act before the jury retired to consider their verdict. Estimated to be completed in three weeks, it stretched over ten.

As bereaved families, survivors, journalists and curious visitors filed into court the atmosphere was reminiscent of so many previous moments of hopeful anticipation. All stood silent as the coroner entered, bowed and addressed the jury. Whatever re-assurances are given by judges and lawyers that courts and their processes belong to 'the people', the law's traditions and reveren-tial conduct are constant reminders to the contrary. In this setting no one is more revered than a high court judge summarising evi-dence and directing a jury. The coroner explained he would address the 'topics' as presented in court: stadium safety; match preparation and planning; the events on the day, including the emergency response; evidence-gathering by the South Yorkshire Police; details of the deceased, their experiences, injuries and treatment. 'The law,' he said, 'is for me. You have to accept what I say about the law. The facts, on the other hand, are for you.' The jury alone would 'decide on the facts', determining the signifi-cance and importance of the evidence. Occasionally he would interpret the facts but they should accept or reject his comments as they saw fit.

He instructed the jury on the 'determinations'. The inquest had to resolve four questions: the identity of the deceased, when they died, where they died and 'how' they died. The latter, being 'by what means and in what circumstances', was the 'most import-ant, difficult and controversial' question. At Hillsborough, he commented, there was no dispute about the physical cause of death, as all died because of the crush in the pens. As the evidence had shown, controversy centred on the circumstances leading to the deaths. Given the seriousness of the disputed circumstances, he emphasised that verdicts could not attribute criminal liability to a named individual, nor could they apportion civil liability. Although prohibited from finding 'any person guilty of a criminal offence' they could deliver 'important, robust and judgmental findings about how a person died'.

As stated earlier, in criminal trials 'guilty' or 'not guilty' verdicts are returned 'beyond reasonable doubt', the level of proof necessary to secure a conviction. In coming to their decisions at the inquest, however, all questions bar one were to be decided 'on the balance of probabilities', a lesser degree of certainty. The legal teams had agreed a questionnaire comprising 14 sections, each focusing on 'a separate and important issue'. Answers should reflect the jury's conclusions on the 'causes and circumstances of the disaster'. A second questionnaire related to each of the deceased, including the specific medical cause and time of death. These questionnaires were uncontested, in line with the conclusions of the medical experts. The jury's final duty was to present the 'record of inquest', recording personal information on the deceased agreed by the legal teams.

The coroner stated that in answering each question the jury's 'determinations', their 'decisions', should be unanimous. He noted that 'great care has been taken to prepare the questions'. The answers 'will resolve the key issues in the inquests, especially how the 96 came to die'. Each key question asked if a particular issue 'caused or contributed' more than minimally to the deaths. These were: police planning; policing on the day; police match commanders' decisions; the decision to open the exit gates; stadium safety; licensing and oversight of the stadium; the club's conduct prior to the match; its conduct on the day; the safety engineers' conduct; the police and emergency response; the ambulance service response. Two further questions stood out. Question 6 was a direct question to determine if the jury was 'satisfied' to the point of certainty 'that those who died were unlawfully killed'. Question 7 focused on fans' behaviour.

The coroner directed that because inquests do not directly attribute liability to individuals, those that could be held responsible should not be named. Yet, without naming him in their verdict, the jury 'would have to be sure that David Duckenfield, the match commander, was responsible for the manslaughter by gross negligence of those 96 people'. Even if they were sure beyond reasonable doubt they could not name him. To arrive at that verdict they had to be certain that Duckenfield owed a duty of care to those who died and that this duty was breached, causing the deaths and amounting to gross negligence. All legal representatives accepted he had a duty to ensure all fans 'could attend, watch and depart reasonably safely'. Such was the duty 'of a reasonable and competent match commander in 1989'.

The coroner stated that, to establish a breach of duty, the jury should focus on Duckenfield's reaction to the dangerous situation at the turnstiles and overcrowding in the pens prior to the opening of gate C. Should the jury decide that Duckenfield significantly breached his duty of care, it would be sufficient to establish gross negligence, regardless of other contributory factors. They had to be satisfied that his breach 'was so bad in all circumstances as to amount to a criminal act or omission', that as 'a reasonably competent match commander' he 'would have foreseen a serious and obvious risk of death to supporters in the central pens'.

On the balance of probabilities, Question 7 asked whether fans' behaviour 'caused or contributed' or 'may have caused or contributed' to 'the dangerous situation at the Leppings Lane turnstiles'. Outside the stadium, had fans been 'unusually forceful or resistant to police control?' Were there 'significant numbers' without tickets and, if so, was that a contributory factor? Was the volume of fans, their 'arrival pattern and/or their behaviour' that which 'could not be foreseen by experienced police officers'? This question was a direct consequence of repeated allegations against unidentified fans made in court over months.

In arriving at a conclusion on whether there was a 'realistic possibility that an error, omission or circumstance may have caused or contributed' to the deaths, the coroner stated that the jury should concentrate on 'defects in the systems and practices' as they applied in 1989. Their narrative verdict should exclude terms such as 'crime/criminal', 'illegal/unlawful', 'negligence/negligent', 'breach of duty', 'duty of care', 'careless', 'reckless', 'liability', 'guilt/guilty'. Alternatively, they could use 'non-technical' words such as 'failure', 'inappropriate', 'inadequate', 'unsuitable', 'unsatisfactory', 'insufficient', 'omit/omission', 'unacceptable', 'lacking'. These terms could be emboldened by adding 'serious' or 'important'.

Dating back to the 1870s, the FA Cup is a knockout competition organised and staged by the Football Association (FA). While earlier rounds are played at clubs' own stadia, semi-finals are played at 'neutral' venues. It was the FA's responsibility to negotiate venues. In 1989, despite criticisms from Liverpool Football Club and the Football Supporters' Association, Hillsborough was chosen for a repeat of the 1988 semi-final. As the organisation responsible for the competition, and the hirers of a stadium at which there had been previous crowd-safety issues, it appeared incongruous, particularly to bereaved families and survivors, that in reaching its narrative verdict the inquest jury had no question to answer on the role and responsibilities of the FA regarding its choice of venue. Had the FA made the appropriate checks on stadium safety – in particular was the safety certificate up to date? What knowledge did they have of previous incidents at the 'staging club'? What was their involvement in match planning and ticket allocation?

The coroner's summing-up stretched over two months. At the outset all legal teams were given a first draft of the full text. This led to multiple challenges and more than a week was lost to resolving the many objections and counter-objections raised. It was a difficult period, as families became frustrated by the process and its repeated delays. Considerable concern focused on the question regarding fans' behaviour. From the 1989 Taylor Report through to the 2013 panel report, fans had been exonerated. Yet previously discredited accounts, mainly from police officers, some of whom anticipated prosecution, raised the possibility that an unlawfully killed verdict could be supplemented by fans being held partly responsible. It was a difficult two months for bereaved families, but also for survivors who were now in the frame but without representation at the inquests. A group of fans submitted an eleventh-hour appeal for legal representation but it was rejected.

On 6 April 2016, day 308, the coroner completed his summing-up and jury direction. The jury failed to return from a lunch break. Something out of the ordinary had happened. So close to the end, many families and survivors who had made the journey to attend were left upset and angry, the process reigniting all too familiar emotions that had dominated legal proceedings throughout their quest for justice. Rumour abounded and doubts were raised concerning reconvening the next day. The following morning, however, the ten jurors returned to court. No doubt they were physically and emotionally exhausted by the previous two years of personal sacrifice and daunted by the enormity of the task they faced.

The coroner addressed the ten women and men: 'Juries are a random selection of members of the public of all backgrounds and ages. They have to work together in the interests of justice. We are conscious that you have devoted a very large part of your lives to these inquests. We have, of course, reached a very important stage of the inquests. You will shortly retire to consider your decisions. It is of the highest importance that all of you work together in the interests of justice. It requires you to be able to discuss the evidence together in a civilised manner. It requires you to work together as a team. It requires you to make your decisions together. It requires you to put to one side any personal issues which can sometimes arise. In the event that you are unable to deal with your very important decisions in the way I have indicated, you must immediately let me know.'

His final instructions were equally forthright. The case should be decided solely on the evidence heard or viewed in the courtroom. All else they had read, heard or discussed with others had to be erased from their minds. Deliberations should be dispassionate. 'Emotion' had to be 'put to one side', their 'critical findings' underpinned by factual justification. They had to take care in considering the accuracy of documents written in the aftermath, as these 'may have been produced with a particular recipient or audience in mind'. They should also 'consider the process by which accounts were made and statements taken'. In judging the actions and 'conduct' of those involved – before, during and after the disaster and its aftermath – the jury should 'apply the standards of the time, not the standards of today'.

The coroner thanked the jurors for their 'care' in listening attentively to his long summing-up. He warned them to discuss the case only with each other and only when together as a group, concluding: 'Please remember the warning which I have given you regularly throughout the case: don't talk about it; don't let anyone else talk to you about it; don't say anything about it on any social-networking site; don't seek out anything about it on the Internet or elsewhere.' At 3.10 p.m. the jury retired, supported by three newly sworn-in bailiffs.

As the jurors left the court their mood was difficult to gauge. For two years they had faced the families across a sterile space, the coroner to their left, lawyers to their right. It was a remarkable familiarity devoid of any relationship other than facial recognition and occasional eye contact. Families, survivors and lawyers came to identify and describe jurors by appearance, demeanour or their exchanges of notes and glances. Sitting behind their computer screens, they were under constant scrutiny, meanings attributed to the slightest change in behaviour. How were they managing their lives, handling the stress of hearing deeply upsetting evidence? How were they coping in their family relationships beyond the jury room, unable to discuss their innermost thoughts about the evidence? If there was tension between them it was never evident in court. Without question, their daily lives, jobs and relationships had been in limbo. Eventually they would return to their routines, changed for ever. On the first day of deliberation, a juror left. Her departure fed rumours, generating assumptions of dissent. In the public gallery, as ten became nine, the families feared that other jurors might leave.

Waiting for a verdict when so much is at stake is always difficult. While time passes quickly in jury-room debates, it drags outside in the waiting rooms. As time moved on, moments of occasional engagement arrived when the jury sought clarification on specific points, everyone returning to the court looking for clues regarding the direction of travel. But these moments were rare. Hours became days became weeks. Soon after midday on 20 April, as the families anticipated another week's deliberations, the jury submitted a note. They had reached a unanimous decision on all questions except unlawful killing and requested the coroner's guidance on how best to proceed. In the jury's absence the coroner invited submissions from legal teams. His counsel considered that a majority verdict would be appropriate. A direction would be given to the jury on Monday, 25 April. Having received direction, and following a further morning's deliberation, at 12.20 p.m. the jury forewoman stated that a majority verdict had been agreed. Court was adjourned until the following morning to enable families and survivors to travel to Birchwood for the verdict.

By then the world's media had laid siege to Building 305. Walking along the boulevard, families and survivors were greeted by a barrage of cameras. Outside the building, tickets for the court were distributed. Proceedings were beamed live to an adjacent overspill building and to a hall in Liverpool. Anticipating the drama of the long-awaited verdicts, unfamiliar yet often demanding journalists appeared insensitive to the subdued, contemplative emotions of those whose 27-year wait was about to end.

By mid morning history had been made. The coroner entered the court, routinely and politely acknowledging the rows of lawyers and those packing the public gallery. As the nine jurors settled into their seats he moved swiftly to the verdict. Given its length and complexity, the forewoman remained seated.

The tension was all-pervasive yet exchanges were calm and measured. The opening question put by the coroner to the jury was: 'Do you agree with the following statement, which is intended to summarise the basic facts of the disaster: "On 15 April 1989, 96 people died in the disaster at Hillsborough stadium as a result of crushing in the central pens of the Leppings Lane terrace, following the admission of a large number of supporters to the stadium through exit gates"?'

Her reply was simply 'Yes.'

The coroner moved to the first substantial question: 'Was there any error or omission in police planning and preparation . . . which caused or contributed to the dangerous situation that developed on the day of the match?'

Her reply was clear: 'Yes'. She continued, 'The jury feel that there were major omissions in the 1989 Operational Order, including: specific instructions for managing the crowds outside the Leppings Lane turnstiles; specific instructions as to how the pens were to be filled and monitored; specific instructions as to who would be responsible for the monitoring of pens.'

'Was there any error or omission in policing on the day of the match which caused or contributed to a dangerous situation developing at the Leppings Lane turnstiles?'

'Yes. Police response to the increasing crowds at Leppings Lane was slow and uncoordinated. The road closure and sweep of fans exacerbated the situation. No filter cordons were placed in

Leppings Lane. No contingency plans were made for the sudden arrival of a large number of fans. Attempts to close the perimeter gates were made too late.'

'Was there any error or omission by commanding officers which caused or contributed to the crush on the terrace?'

'Yes. Commanding officers should have ordered the closure of the central tunnel before the opening of gate C was requested, as pens 3 and 4 were full. Commanding officers should have requested the number of fans still to enter the stadium after 2.30 p.m. Commanding officers failed to recognise that pens 3 and 4 were at capacity before gate C was opened. Commanding officers failed to order the closure of the tunnel as gate C was opened.'

'When the order was given to open the exit gates at the Leppings Lane end of the stadium, was there any error or omission by the commanding officers in the control box which caused or contributed to the crush on the terrace?'

'Yes. Commanding officers did not inform officers in the inner concourse prior to the opening of gate C. Commanding officers failed to consider where the incoming fans would go. Commanding officers failed to order the closure of the central tunnel prior to the opening of gate C.'

Repetition of the words 'commanding officers' left no doubt as to where ultimate responsibility lay.

It is difficult to recreate the emotional crescendo enveloping the court as families held hands, eyes transfixed on the jury forewoman. All knew the significance of the next two questions. Slowly and deliberately the coroner asked the question that required a majority verdict beyond reasonable doubt. 'Are you satisfied, so that you are sure, that those who died in the disaster were unlawfully killed?'

She replied, 'Yes. By a majority of 7 to 2.'

Families could barely contain their relief. Yet they knew the next question was crucial.

'Was there any behaviour on the part of football supporters

which caused or contributed to the dangerous situation at the Leppings Lane turnstiles?'

Her response was a firm 'No.'

A wave of jubilation, of exoneration, swept through the court. Sitting with the Aspinall family at the front of the court I broke down, still attempting to write notes. Hugging arms came from all angles. In the overspill rooms at Birchwood and in Liverpool people were on their feet cheering, hugging and crying. In the courtroom families' lawyers were profoundly affected. Behind them other legal teams remained stone-faced. Silence resumed and the coroner continued.

Calm and composed, he asked, 'Were there any features of the design, construction and layout of the stadium which you consider were dangerous or defective and which caused or contributed to the disaster?'

'Yes. Design and layout of the crush barriers in pens 3 and 4 were not fully compliant with the Green Guide. The removal of barrier 144 and the partial removal of barrier 136 would have exacerbated the "waterfall effect" of pressure towards the front of the pens. The lack of dedicated turnstiles for individual pens meant that capacities could not be monitored. There were too few turnstiles for a capacity crowd. Signage to the side pens was inadequate.'

Sheffield City Council's responsibilities for ground safety followed. 'Was there any error or omission in the safety certification and oversight of Hillsborough Stadium that caused or contributed to the disaster?'

'Yes. The safety certificate was never amended to reflect the changes at the Leppings Lane end of the stadium, therefore capacity figures were never updated. The capacity figures for the Leppings Lane terraces were incorrectly calculated when the safety certificate was first issued. The safety certificate had not been reissued since 1986.'

Two questions were related to the stadium owners. First: 'Was there any error or omission by Sheffield Wednesday FC (and its staff) in the management of the stadium and/or preparation for the semi-final match on 15 April 1989 which caused or contributed to the dangerous situation that developed on the day of the match?'

'Yes. The club did not approve the plans for dedicated turnstiles for each pen. The club did not agree any contingency plans with the police. There was inadequate signage and inaccurate/ misleading information on the semi-final tickets.'

Second: 'Was there any error or omission by Sheffield Wednesday FC (and its staff) on 15 April 1989 which may have caused or contributed to the dangerous situation that developed at the Leppings Lane turnstiles and in the west terrace?'

'Yes. Club officials were aware of the huge numbers of fans still outside the Leppings Lane turnstiles at 2.40 p.m. They should have requested a delayed kick-off at this point.'

Then came the safety engineers. 'Should Eastwood and Partners have done more to detect and advise on any unsafe or unsatisfactory features of Hillsborough Stadium which caused or contributed to the disaster?'

'Yes. Eastwoods did not make their own calculations when they became consultants for SWFC, therefore the initial capacity figures and all subsequent calculations were incorrect. Eastwoods failed to recalculate capacity figures each time changes were made to the terraces. Eastwoods failed to update the safety certificate after 1986. Eastwoods failed to recognise that the removal of barrier 144 and the partial removal of barrier 136 could result in a dangerous situation in the pens.'

The coroner returned to the role of the police, concentrating on their lack of response to the unfolding crisis. 'After the crush in the west terrace had begun to develop, was there any error or omission by the police which caused or contributed to the loss of lives in the disaster?'

'Yes. The police delayed calling a major incident, so the appropriate emergency responses were delayed. There was a lack of coordination, communication, command and control which delayed or prevented appropriate responses.'

The Hillsborough Independent Panel findings had revealed the severity of the ambulance service's organisational failure. It was explored in depth at the inquests and included the revelation that its officers' statements also had been subjected to systematic review and alteration. The coroner asked, 'After the crush in the west terrace had begun to develop, was there any error or omission by the ambulance service (SYMAS) which caused or contributed to the loss of lives in the disaster?'

'Yes. SYMAS officers at the scene failed to ascertain the nature of the problem at Leppings Lane. The failure to recognise and call a major incident led to delays in responses to the emergency.'

Of the 25 critical findings against the institutions responsible for the safety and care of those attending the match, 15 were levelled against the South Yorkshire Police. The narrative verdict aligned closely with the panel's conclusions, including the complete exoneration of the fans. Inside and outside the courtroom the scenes were reminiscent of those at Liverpool's Anglican Cathedral in September 2012. A banner was unfurled. Above the illustration of a burning torch, the symbol of the Hillsborough campaigns, it read, 'WE CLIMBED THE HILL IN OUR OWN WAY'. Three and a half years on from the panel's analysis, its critique had been confirmed in a court. Throughout, the families and survivors conducted themselves with characteristic dignity. Despite the South Yorkshire Chief Constable's 2013 apology, they had suffered a rerun of the police case against the fans. Many families voiced their disappointment that lead counsel for the match commanders, the bullish John Beggs, QC, for whatever reason, was conspicuous by his absence.

As the enormity of the jury's verdict dawned, attention turned immediately to the South Yorkshire Police and its Chief Constable, David Crompton. It was he, just five months into his post, who in September 2012, while anticipating the panel's report, had written an infamous memo to his senior management team warning that should the families' 'version of events become "the truth" even though it isn't', his force needed 'to be a bit more innovative in our response to have a fighting chance otherwise we will just be roadkill'. Following the panel's report he backtracked, apologising 'unreservedly' for serious failings in policing Hillsborough. Yet police lawyers at the inquests made a concerted attempt to reverse the panel's findings.

The day after the verdict, in a House of Commons debate, Shadow Home Secretary Andy Burnham stated: 'Shamefully the cover-up continued in that Warrington courtroom' as 'millions of pounds of public money was spent retelling discredited lies'. Retired police officers' lawyers 'threw disgusting slurs around' while lawyers for the South Yorkshire Police 'tried to establish a case for the [fans'] opening of the gate'. Had the police 'chosen to maintain their apology' the inquests would have been considerably shorter. Their combative approach 'put the families through hell once again'. Burnham asked the Home Secretary whether the Chief Constable's position was 'now untenable'.

Within hours the South Yorkshire Police released a statement noting the coroner had 'ruled that to admit the previous 2012 apology into proceedings would be wrong and highly prejudicial'. It stated the coroner had also ruled that the 'conduct of SYP during the inquests was not inconsistent' with the earlier apology. The force had 'never sought to defend the failures of SYP or its officers' yet emphasised that 'these failures had to be put into the context of other contributory factors' within the 'overall picture'. Hours later the South Yorkshire Police Crime Commissioner announced he had 'no choice' but to suspend David Crompton, as 'trust and confidence' in the force had been eroded. The force's Deputy Chief Constable, Dawn Copley, was appointed as a temporary replacement, only to stand down as it emerged that she was under investigation regarding unresolved allegations when Deputy Chief Constable of her previous force. Finally, Dave

Jones, Chief Constable of neighbouring North Yorkshire Police, was appointed as a temporary arrangement.

The impact of the unlawful killing inquest verdict and the 25 institutional failures identified by the jury was reported internationally. Unsurprisingly, the Murdoch press was the exception. In the outpouring of relief mixed with vindication, bereaved families reflected on the personal toll taken by the inquests. Although content that the inquests should 'take whatever time needed as long as they were done properly and thoroughly', Paul Spearritt asked, 'How could the coroner be so far off in his estimation' of 12 months? He placed responsibility for creating families' 'continuous anxiety and worry' with the 'stance taken by police commanding officers and the ambulance service'. Maria Fallon said that the 'longer the inquests were dragged out, the more difficult everyday issues – house moves, job challenges and the like – became'. For her the 'logistics of trying to attend court alongside college and a full-time job became more and more difficult'.

Maria's father, Leo, felt that his 'life was totally on hold', a 'huge sag of the shoulders each day – and there were so many – when the jury did not sit'. It was like 'holding my breath. I don't know if I'll ever recover from that stress load'. Doreen Jones agreed that the ever-expanding inquests took a 'huge toll on everyday life, like a recurring nightmare for two years, and you pay the price for that health-wise'. The Matthews family described bearing the cost, financial and emotional, of hearing again 'the regurgitated lies that had been peddled for the first 25 years'. Jan Spearritt noted the 'friction caused for some family members with their employers when asking for time off to attend the inquests'. It was a profound 'strain' for families 'coming home exhausted having sat through evidence day after day'.

Linda Howard, whose husband, Thomas senior, and son, Thomas junior, died together, said, 'We were put through unbelievable pressure that could have been avoided if the senior officers had come clean in 1989.' Being compelled 27 years later to sit through 'harrowing evidence' had left her with 'flashbacks, sleepless nights and no appetite'. Her 'fear' was not knowing when and how it was 'all going to end'. It was 'like they had your mental health in their hands, you were on automatic pilot trying to cope with each day, counting down the months, desperate to end the torture pushing you to your limit'. Her son Alan was 'angry, given that after the panel report the South Yorkshire Chief Constable had apologised and now senior officers were back in court sticking to the allegations they made in 1989 – so his apology didn't mean anything'. After the verdict Linda felt a 'weight had been lifted off my shoulders' but she was left with 'a sense of numbness and shock'. She continued, 'I'm hoping we can now begin to grieve after all these years. We've never been allowed to before because our loved ones and us were vilified.'

Doreen Jones concluded, 'We have had to go through another inquest because of the failures of the first, fighting for access to material that should have been made available to us in the first place, and that's a bitter pill to swallow. Finally we have the right verdict but it should have been there at the first inquests. The price we've had to pay at times has been intolerable.' For the Matthews family, 'the ordeal has inevitably taken its toll' but the 'motivating factor for us has been the truth, and wanting the world to know what we as a family knew all along. We will not stop in our search for justice until the *whole truth* is known and accountability is placed on *every* person responsible for the past 27 years of hell.' Jan Spearritt felt 'immense relief that it is all over and we know we did our best as a family'.

All families shared the loss of the 96 and many faced the added pain of dealing with the premature deaths of loved ones during their long campaign. Reflecting on the death of her husband Eddie, Jan Spearritt felt a deep 'sadness' that he 'died not knowing that his efforts in this fight for truth and justice were not in vain'. Throughout the inquests their son Paul constantly worried about what would have been Eddie's responses – 'what questions he would be asking, whether he would have been happy with the way the legal team was handling things, if there was something he might have disagreed with. You have to deal with these emotions – that you've let them down or missed something crucial. Thankfully that was not the case.'

* * *

On Wednesday, 27 April Liverpool City Council held an early-evening memorial service in Liverpool's city centre. The square and streets around St George's Hall were closed to traffic as 30,000 people celebrated the lives of the 96 and an unambiguous verdict that, once and for all, set the record straight. Between the building's magnificent pillars white letters on a red background spelled out 'TRUTH' and 'JUSTICE'. Ninety-six lanterns stretched the length of the plinth, their flames burning brightly. At each lantern young players and staff from the Liverpool and Everton clubs placed a single red rose with the name of a loved one attached. Daniel Spearritt, on the staff of Liverpool, carried the rose for Adam, the brother he never knew.

It was a spring evening, reminiscent of 15 April 1989, the sun's warmth giving way to the lingering chill of winter. Standing with the families, alongside my partner Deena and my friend and co-researcher Kathryn, I looked across a sea of Liverpool's red and white interwoven with the blue and white of Everton's colours. The panorama has barely changed from my childhood – the Central Library, Walker Art Gallery, Wellington's Column, the Empire Theatre, Lime Street Station and its once-grand hotel, now a student hall of residence. As clergymen offered prayers, poems were read and defiant words were spoken, I thought back to the political context in which the disaster happened and my personal journey taken with the families and survivors.

I remembered speaking at rallies during the height of the coal dispute and the virtual occupation of pit villages by the South Yorkshire Police. In 1985 came Margaret Thatcher's fierce attack on the 'enemy within', a spectrum on which she placed trades unionists, 'football hooligans' and 'terrorists'. That year in Toxteth I witnessed the Merseyside Police's Operational Support Division laying siege to the Liverpool-born black community. This was the political climate in which Hillsborough occurred.

In 1989 I stood with my children in the mile of scarves across Stanley Park, linking Anfield with Everton's ground, Goodison Park – a collective act of defiance in the face of scurrilous allegations directed at those who had survived Hillsborough. I thought about the June 1989 phone call I made from an Edinburgh caravan park to Liverpool City Council requesting funding for vital research as an increasingly hostile media turned on the fans and the city. I thought about the 1990 local newspaper editorial stating that the 'usefulness' of the research should be questioned, given its cost to 'city ratepayers'. The pressures in my workplace to cease the research should it 'affect' my 'other college commitments' and from senior social workers who accused the research team of 'winding up' the families.

As the names of those who died were read by Andy Burnham, Steve Rotheram and Maria Eagle, the reverential stillness of the crowd was disturbed by a police helicopter hovering directly overhead – an inexplicable insensitivity. My mind drifted back to 1999 and being rung at home by Norman Bettison, then Chief Constable of Merseyside. The first edition of this book had been serialised in the *Sunday Mirror*. Coincidentally the newspaper carried a story about his appointment as Merseyside Chief Constable. In his application he had not disclosed his role as a South Yorkshire Police officer in the aftermath of the disaster. Had I written about his role in the book? I told him 'No'. However, this was not an assurance that extended to subsequent editions.

As the police helicopter left the area, I remembered a more sinister call to my ex-directory number. This was a quite different, well-spoken male voice, which calmly and accurately listed the projects I had researched, ending with the comment 'apologist for football hooligans'. Without pausing he named my children, their schools and what time they left home in the morning. Before putting down the phone he told me none of us were safe.

These reminiscences flashed through my mind quicker than they are recounted here. Reflecting difficult and threatening times, they do not bear comparison to the constant struggle of the bereaved and survivors who have lived under the heavy, often impenetrable cloud of Hillsborough and its cruel aftermath. The Mayor and campaign leaders spoke, thanking the people of Liverpool, the region and beyond for their support. The crowd responded with characteristic collective solidarity, singing 'You'll Never Walk Alone', the Liverpool anthem, with power, emotion and defiance.

I thought back to the 27th memorial just days earlier at Anfield. Over 22,000 people were in the stadium. Those present, many not born at the time of the disaster, had remained resilient and determined in the face of incalculable adversity, persistent in the quest for justice. I began by acknowledging the immense sacrifices made by the bereaved and survivors, the loss of those who had campaigned tirelessly yet had died prematurely. I paid tribute to Andy Burnham and the Merseyside MPs who had kept the issue alive in Parliament, and to my late great friend, Katy Jones, a woman of immense integrity and talent who had been integral to the panel's work.

I read the poem opposite, written soon after the panel's report was published, while I lived in the calm solitude of a forest near Amherst, Massachusetts. It recognises the unswerving commitment of those determined to honour the memory of their loved ones and the pain of survival.

Their Voices Will Be Heard

With early Spring sun came warmth and hope,
Spirits lifted through snow-capped hills
Streets alive with nervous laughter
Another adventure in another place
Vibrant voices breaking solitude's silence

Approaching Hillsborough calm and joyous,
Walking expectantly to a Wembley Final
Safe passage ended down that fateful tunnel
In pens, like cattle, between concrete and steel
Desperate voices so cruelly silenced

From callous indifference in a gymnasium's cold
To taking blood from the innocent, the young
Their deaths examined through a distorted lens
Rupturing further families' broken hearts
Bereaved voices cowed by contempt

Lies tripped easily from forked tongues,
Condemning, vilifying the rescuers, the brave
Relentlessly feeding pens filled with poison
Rewriting 'The Truth', spreading deceit
Survivors' voices denied, dismissed

Verdicts and judgments came and went,
Lawyers and politicians minced their words
A City portrayed as wracked by self-pity
Its people's isolation now complete
Determined voices now walking alone

Shattered by loss but unbroken in spirit
In the face of injustice you never backed down
You forced them to listen, you sacrificed your lives,
You bore witness with dignity on the day of reckoning
And their voices, your voices, have been heard

SOURCES AND REFERENCES

Belgian House of Representatives Report of the Parliamentary Commission of Inquiry [Heysel Disaster], 9 July 1985; Harrington, J.A., *Soccer Hooliganism: A Preliminary Report*, John Wright and Sons Ltd: Bristol, 1968; Home Affairs Committee, *Policing, Football Hooliganism Vols I and II* HAC, HMSO: London, 1991; McElhone, F., *Report of the Working Group on Football Crowd Behaviour*, Scottish Education Department, HMSO: London 1977; Moelwyn Hughes, R., *Enquiry into the Disaster at Bolton Wanderers Football Ground on 9th March 1946*, Home Office Cmnd 6846, HMSO: London, June 1946; Popplewell, Mr Justice, *Committee of Inquiry into Crowd Safety and Control at Sports Grounds: Interim Report*, Home Office Cmnd 9585, HMSO: London, July 1985; *Final Report*, Home Office Cmnd 9710, HMSO: London, January 1986; South Yorkshire Police, *FA Cup Semi-Final, Saturday 9 April 1988, Liverpool v Nottingham Forest: 'F' Division Operational Order 2/88*, South Yorkshire Police: Sheffield; South Yorkshire Police, *FA Cup Semi-Final, Saturday 15 April 1989, Liverpool v Nottingham Forest: 'F' Division Operational Order 1/89*, South Yorkshire Police: Sheffield; Taylor, Lord Justice, *Inquiry into the Hillsborough Stadium Disaster: Transcripts of Proceedings. May–June 1989*, Notes of: J.L. Harphan Ltd, Sheffield; Wheatley Rt Hon. Lord,

Report of the Inquiry into Crowd Safety at Sports Grounds, Home Office Cmnd 4952, HMSO: London, March 1972.

Chapter Two

Much of the primary material in this chapter is derived from personal interviews with survivors. The police accounts can be found in their 'recollections' and statements held in the House of Commons Library. Other material for this chapter was accessed through the Taylor Inquiry transcripts and the Inquest transcripts. Full copies of both are held at the Centre for Studies in Crime and Social Justice, Edge Hill University College. See also: Nicholson, H., 'Ticket to tragedy', *Nottingham Evening Post,* 14 November 1994; Ashton, J., 'Hillsborough, 15 April 1989', unpublished statement, 19 April 1989.

Chapter Three

Sources as Chapter Two. Additionally, interviews were conducted with Chief Superintendent Addis and the SYMAS Deputy Chief Ambulance Officer, Alan Hopkins, in Sheffield and Rotherham, March 1990.

Chapter Four

Sources as Chapters Two and Three. Additionally, interviews were conducted with Maire Butler of the Royal Hallamshire Hospital and John Adams of the Northern General Hospital, Sheffield, March 1990. See also: Home Office, *Dealing With Disaster* (2nd edn), HMSO: London 1994; Home Office, *Dealing With Fatalities During Disasters,* Report of the National Working Party, HMSO: London, 1994.

Chapter Five

All acounts in this chapter are taken from the transcriptions of interviews with bereaved families.

Chapter Six

For analysis of the media coverage after Hillsborough see: Coleman, S., Jemphrey, A., Scraton P. and Skidmore, P., *Hillsborough and After: The Liverpool Experience*, Hillsborough Project, First Report, Liverpool City Council, 1990; Scraton, P., Jemphrey, A. and Coleman, S., *No Last Rights: The Denial of Justice and the Promotion of Myth in the Aftermath of the Hillsborough Disaster*, Liverpool City Council/Alden Press: Liverpool, 1995. The discussion of the Hillsborough Solicitors' Group Steering Committee decisions is taken from their solicitors' and families' newsletters. Central to this chapter is: Taylor, Rt Hon. Lord Justice, *The Hillsborough Stadium Disaster: 15 April 1989. Interim Report*, Home Office Cmnd 765, HMSO: London, August 1989.

Chapter Seven

For a full discussion of the Inquests see: Scraton, P. et al., *No Last Rights* (op. cit.) Chapters 2–4. For a general critique of coroners, inquests and controversial deaths see: Scraton, P. and Chadwick, K., *In the Arms of the Law: Coroners' Inquests and Deaths in Custody*, Pluto Press: London, 1987. The discussion of the preparation for and conduct of the inquests is derived in documentary records of the meetings, the Steering Group newsletters, attendance and observation at the Inquests and the Inquest transcripts. A full set of transcripts is held at the Centre for Studies in Crime and Social Justice, Edge Hill University College. On the medical evidence see: Usher, A., 'Hillsborough – 15 April 1989: Pathological Aspects of the Disaster', Department of Forensic Psychology, University of Sheffield, Undated; Wardrope, J. et al., 'The Hillsborough Tragedy' in *British Medical Journal*, vol. 303, 30 November 1991; West I.E., 'Opinion on traumatic asphyxia relating to the deaths at Hillsborough' prepared for the Judicial Review, unpublished, 29 October 1993.

Chapter Eight

For a full discussion of both the Judicial Review and the Brian Clough controversy see: Scraton, P. et al., *No Last Rights* (op. cit). References to the death of Kevin Williams are: 'Kevin's Mum', *The Cook Report*, ITV, broadcast 2 June 1994; *Hansard*, 'Kevin Williams' Adjournment Debate Clmn 976–86, 26 October 1994. *Hillsborough* was written by Jimmy McGovern for Granada TV and broadcast 5 December 1996. The full media coverage of Jimmy McGovern's drama-documentary is held at the Centre for Studies in Crime and Social Justice, Edge Hill University. For the parliamentary debate referred to in this chapter see: *Hansard*, 17 December 1996, 'Hillsborough Tragedy' Clmn 855–62.

Chapter Nine

While the discussion of Lord Justice Stuart-Smith's meetings in Liverpool draws on personal observation the precise quotes from the meetings are derived in the transcripts held by the author, particularly: *The Hillsborough Scrutiny: Meetings Held at Merseyside Maritime Museum, Open Session*, 6 October 1997. Transcription by Harry Counsell & Co. See also: Stuart-Smith, Rt Hon. Lord Justice, *Scrutiny of Evidence Relating to the Hillsborough Football Stadium Disaster*, Home Office Cmmd 3878, HMSO: London, February 1998; *Hansard*, 'Hillsborough' Clmn 1085–97, 18 February 1998; written submissions on behalf of the Hillsborough Family Support Group to the Judicial Scrutiny into the Hillsborough Stadium Disaster, 1997 (held in House of Commons Library).

Chapter Ten

The documents relating to the former officer's case are held by the author. Examples given of the review and alteration of South Yorkshire Police recollections are taken from the 11 boxes of statements held in the House of Commons Library. Other material contained therein and referred to in this chapter include:

'Note of a meeting' between Lord Justice Stuart-Smith and South Yorkshire Chief Constable, Richard Wells, 25 November 1997; Transcript of a meeting between Lord Justice Stuart-Smith and former Chief Superintendent Denton, 1 December 1997. A letter from Peter Metcalf of Hammond Suddards to Lord Justice Stuart-Smith, dated 11 November 1997 and headed: *Preparation of Statements following the Hillsborough Disaster*, has been subsequently provided. Other sources include: *Hansard* 'Hillsborough' Adjournment Debate Clmn 942–1003, 8 May 1998; correspondence from Jack Straw, Home Secretary, 7 May 1998 and from Tony Banks, Sports Minister, 17 April 1998 and on behalf of the Prime Minister, 9 April 1998; statements from Norman Bettison, West Yorkshire Police, 14 October 1998 and 5 November 1998; statements issued by Merseyside Police Authority, 16 October 1998 and 3 November 1998; note of an informal meeting between Merseyside Police Authority and Norman Bettison, 2 November 1998; HMIC press release, 'Appointment of Norman Bettison', 23 October 1998; HMIC Inspector's Assessment, undated; South Yorkshire Police inquest distribution list, 28 November 1990; South Yorkshire Police memorandom from Sup. Bettison to Deputy Chief Constable headed 'Preparation of Case for Hillsborough Contribution Hearings', 12 July 1990; Walker, C., interview with Norman Bettison, 'First Day in the Hot Seat', *Liverpool Echo*, 16 November 1998.

Chapter Eleven

Quotes throughout this chapter are transcribed from contemporaneous verbatim notes taken in Leeds Crown Court, 6 June 2000 to 26 July 2000; ruling by Mr Justice Hooper, *Regina v David Duckenfield and Bernard Murray*, Case No: T19991569, Leeds Crown Court, 16 February 2000. Interview with Richard Wells, *Look North*, BBC, July 1998; Daines, I., 'Flawed Justice'; 'Great Expectations'; 'Hillsborough Legacy' in *Police Review*, 27 February 1998, 6 March 1998, 13 March 1998; Davis, H. and

Scraton, P., *Beyond Disaster: Identifying and Resolving Inter-Agency Conflict in the Aftermath of Disasters*, Research Report for the Home Office Emergency Planning Division, 1997; Davis, H. and Scraton, P., *Disaster, Trauma, Aftermath*, Lawrence and Wishart: London, forthcoming; Stuart, M., *Douglas Hurd: The Public Servant*, Mainstream: Edinburgh, 1998; Scraton, P. et al., *No Last Rights* (op. cit.).

Chapter Twelve

Chippendale, D., and Horrie, C. *Stick It Up Your Punter: The Rise and Fall of* The Sun, London: Mandarin, 1992; Clough, B. *Clough: The Autobiography*, London: Corgi, 1995; Cohen, D. *Aftershock: The Psychological and Political Consequences of Disasters*, London: Paladin, 1991; Dalglish, K., and Winter, H. *Dalglish: My Autobiography*, London: Hodder and Stoughton, 1996; Howe, J. 'The persistent vegetative state: treatment, withdrawal, and the Hillsborough disaster: Airedale NHS Trust v. Bland' *Practical Neurology* 6, 2006; Kerr, J.H. *Understanding Soccer Hooliganism*, Milton Keynes: Open University Press, 1994; Lewis, J.M. and Scarisbrick-Hauser, A-M. 'An analysis of football crowd safety reports using the McPhail categories' in R. Giulianotti, N. Bonney and M. Hepworth (eds) *Football, Violence and Social Identity*, London: Routledge, 1994; Walters, M. *Acid Row*, Sydney: Allen and Unwin, 2001; Williams, A., with Smith, S. *When You Walk Through the Storm*, Edinburgh: Mainstream Publishing; Young, K. 'Sport and Collective Violence', *Exercise and Sports Sciences Review*, 19, 1991. I am grateful to families for their contributions to this chapter made in January 2009. A full account of Brenda Fox's experiences can be found on the Hillsborough Family Support Group website.

Chapter Thirteen

The Hillsborough Family Support Group, *Hillsborough: Truth Recovery and Acknowledgement,* presented to the Home Office,

2009; Hillsborough Independent Panel, *Terms of Reference and Protocol on Disclosure of Information*, Home Office, December 2009; Letter of Appointment as Member of Hillsborough Independent Panel, Alan Johnson, Home Secretary to Professor Phil Scraton, 25 January 2010; House of Commons Parliamentary Debate, Backbench Business, 'Hillsborough Disaster', House of Commons Official Report, *Hansard*, vol.. 533, no. 207, pp. 662–724, 17 October 23011.

Chapter Fourteen

Primary material, including all quotes, regarding the findings of the Hillsborough Independent Panel, drawn from: *Hillsborough: The Report of the Hillsborough Independent Panel 2012*, London: The Stationery Office (available online with live links to all documents on the Hillsborough Independent Panel's website: http://hillsborough,independent.gov.uk/; Prime Minister's Response to the Hillsborough Independent Panel's Report, 'Hillsborough', *Hansard*, Clmns 283–306, 12 September 2012; All newspaper coverage of the Launch of the Report: 13 September 2012; Statement by Keir Sturmer, QC, Director of Public Prosecutions, *DPP decision in response to the Hillsborough report*, Crown Prosecution Service, 10 October 2013; Statement by Deborah Glass, Deputy Chair, Independent Police Complaints Commission, introducing the IPCC, 'Decision in response to the report of the Hillsborough Independent Panel', 12 October 2012; House of Commons Parliamentary Debate, 'Hillsborough', House of Commons Official Report, *Hansard*, vol. 551, pp. 720–804, 22 October 2012; Announcement, 'Attorney General applies for fresh inquests for victims of Hillsborough disaster', Attorney General's Office, 10 December 2012; Lord Chief Justice, Lord Judge, Judgment: HM Attorney General v. HM Coroner of South Yorkshire (West), HM Coroner of West Yorkshire (West) CO/13246/2012 High Court of justice Queen's Bench Division Administrative Court (19 December 2012), paras 28-30;

Secretary of State for the Home Department, Theresa May, *Hillsborough Investigation*, Written Minsiterial Statement, Clmns 111WS-112WS, 19 December 2012; Home Affairs Committee *Report on the Independent Police Complaints Commision* Eleventh Report, Session 2012-13, 1st February 2013; Independent Police Committee Newsletters; Independent Police Complaints Commision Hillsbsorough Newsletters and details of investigation at www.ipcc.gov.uk/ under Investigations; Independent Police Complaints Commission *IPPC statement following resignation of Norman Bettison* 24 October 2012; Media Statement from Shaun Wright, Police and Crime Commissioner for South Yorkshire re. disclosed internal emails, 22 February 2013; documentation re. Crompton/ Bettison email exchange via FoI; West Yorkshire Police reply to FoI regarding the use of mobile phone by Chief Constable, Norman Bettison, 16 August 2013; Independent Police Complaints Commission *Sir Norman Bettison: Alleged Attempt to Influence Improperly the Decision-Making Process of West Yorkshire Police Authority* Independent Investigation, Final Report, 25 March 2013. Following the publication of the panel's report, Freedom of Information requests by Jonathan Corke and Neil Shanahan have been made public and have informed this chapter.

Chapter Fifteen

Sources for this chapter include: Transcripts of the Preliminary Hearings (25 April 2013; 5 June 2013; 7 October 2013; 5 February 2014); Transcripts of the Inquests and Rulings accessed at: *https://hillsboroughinquests.independent.gov.uk/*

Further References

The Hillsborough Family Support Group and the Hillsborough Justice Campaign can both be contacted via the Internet. The HJC shop is close to Anfield at 178 Walton Breck Road, Liverpool, L69 4WR. The *Hillsborough Disaster Context and Consequences* and Phil Scraton's Hillsborough Archive can also be found on the web. Several other websites also carry discussion and debate about Hillsborough.